Kursk

- The Air Battle: July 1943

Kursk

- The Air Battle: July 1943

Christer Bergström

CLASSIC
PUBLICATIONS

KURSK - The Air Battle: July 1943
© 2007 Christer Bergström

ISBN (10) 1 857802 388 1
ISBN (13) 978 1 90322 388 8

Produced by Chevron Publishing Limited
Project Editors: Robert Forsyth, Chevron Publishing Limited
Cover and book design: Mark Nelson/Tim Brown
© Map and illustration: Tim Brown

Published by Ian Allan Publishing
Riverdene Business Park, Molesey Road,
Hersham, Surrey, KT12 4RG
E-mail: info@ianallanpublishing.co.uk
www.ianallanpublishing.com

Classic is an imprint of Ian Allan Publishing Ltd
Worldwide distribution (except North America):
Littlehampton Book Services, England
Telephone: 01903 828800   Fax: 01903 828802
E-mail: orders@lbsltd.co.uk

North American trade distribution:
Specialty Press Publishers & Wholesalers Inc.
39966 Grand Avenue, North Branch, MN 55056, USA
Tel: 651 277 1400   Fax: 651 277 1203
Toll free telephone: 800 895 4585
www.specialtypress.com

Printed in England by Ian Allan Printing Ltd
Riverdene Business Park, Molesey Road,
Hersham, Surrey, KT12 4RG

Visit the Ian Allan Publishing website at:
www.ianallanpublishing.com

CLASSIC
PUBLICATIONS

Contents

Acknowledgements

This book could not have been written without the help of *Luftwaffe* and VVS veterans and a large number of historians, aviation history enthusiasts and many others. I am deeply grateful for their interest, encouragement and kindness. These people have shown that history and historical facts belong to us all and that it is in our common interest to co-operate in uncovering every part of mankind's history.

First of all I would like to express my particular gratitude to my friend Andrey Mikhailov, my co-author in two previous books. Andrey's help has been most valuable. I also would like to express my particular gratitude to my friends and colleagues Vlad Antipov, Andrey Dikov, Nikita Egorov and Artem Drabkin. Their unselfish assistance and our exchange of material has been absolutely terrific.

In encouraging me to write this book and liaising with the publisher, Robert Forsyth has played a key role in this work. Without his input this book series would never have been written.

Matti Salonen has provided me with crucial help by allowing me to use his extensive work on *Luftwaffe* aircraft losses.

My friend and colleague Manfred Wägenbaur at Traditionsgemeinschaft JG 52 has been as crucially helpful as always.

And, of course, my dear family, Maria, Martin and Caroline, have showed a great patience, without which I could not have written this book.

I also wish to express my gratitude to Brigadier Captain Christian Allerman, Alfons Altmeier, Ferdinando D'Amico, Aleksey V. Andreev, Vladislav Arkhipov, Andrew Arthy, Michael Balss, Bernd Barbas, Csaba Becze, Holger Benecke, Dénes Bernád, Jan Bobek, Kent Bobits, Andreas Brekken, Pawel Burchard, Mikhail Bykov, Mikael Byström, Don Caldwell, Eddie Creek, Chris Dunning, Christian-Jacques Ehrengardt, Santiago A. Flores, Josef Fregosi, Carl-Fredrik Geust, Jürgen Grislawski, Pascal Guillerm, Håkan Gustavsson, Damian Hallor, Peter Hallor, Lutz Hannig, Tomislav Haramincic, Thomas Hasselberg, Carlos Herrera, Håkan Hillerström, Michael Holm, Ivanova Maya Ivanovna, Morten Jessen, Thomas Jönsson, *Polkovnik* Vsevolod Kanaev, Dmitriy Karlenko, Peter Kassak, Tony Kirk, Christian Kirsch, *General-Leytenant* Aleksandr Anatolevich Kudriavtsev, Viktor Kulikov, *Vitse-Admiral* Yuriy Kvyatkovskiy, Ola Laveson, Christopher A. Lawrence, Sean Leeman, *Brigadier General* Håkan Linde, Raimo Malkamäki, George Mellinger, Rolf Mewitz, Eric Mombeek, Martin Månsson, Donald Pearson, Martin Pegg, Jim Perry, Gennadiy Petrov, Dr. Jochen Prien, Rune Rautio, Günther Rosipal, Yuriy Rybin, Pär Salomonson, Carlo Sansilvestri, Reinhard Schröder, Hans Dieter Seidl, Hans E. Söder, Claes Sundin, Peter Taghon, Colonel Raymond F. Toliver, Dariusz Tyminski, Peter Vollmer, Walter Waiss, Bob Wartburg, Pierre Watteeuw, Carl-Johan Westring, *Brigadier General* Björn Widmark, *Director* Lyudmila P. Zapryagayeva, Vyacheslav M. Zaretsky, Jan Zdiarsky, *Admiral* Vasil'yevich Zelenin, and Niklas Zetterling.

WW II VVS airmen:
Starshina Petr Andreyevich Shvets, *General-Leytenant* Petr Vasilyevich Bazanov, *St.Lt.* Mikhail Petrovich Devyatayev, *Polkovnik* Nikolay Ivanovich Gapeyonok, *St.Lt.* Vasiliy Matveyevich Garanin, *General-Mayor* Semen Vasilyevich Grigorenko, *Kpt.* Viktor Alekseyevich Grubich, *St.Serzh.* Leonid Yakovlevich Klabukov, *General-Mayor* Vitaliy Ivanovich Klimenko, *General-Leytenant* Arkadiy Fyodorovich Kovachevich, *General-Mayor* Sergey Makarovich Kramarenko, *General-Mayor* Viktor Aleksandrovich Kumskov, *Starshina* Vasiliy Vasilyevich Kurayev, *General-Leytenant* Boris Dmitriyevich Melyokhin, *General-Leytenant* Stepan Anastasovich Mikoyan, *Polkovnik* Vladimir Vladimirovich Onishenko, *Polkovnik* Aleksandr Aleksandrovich Pavlichenko, *General-Mayor* Georgiy Vasilyevich Pavlov, *General-Leytenant* Vitaliy Viktorovich Rybalko, *St.Lt.* Aron Shavelich Shapiro, Petr Andreyevich Shvets, *Kpt.* Vera Tikhomirova, and *General-Mayor* Ivan Petrovich Vasenin.

WW II *Luftwaffe* airmen:
Oberst Gerhard Baeker, *Obstlt.* Hansgeorg Bätcher, *Lt.* Helmut Berendes, *Oblt.* Johannes Broschwitz, *Generalleutnant* Adolf Galland, *Major* Klaus Häberlen, *Oblt.* Hermann Heckes, *Ofw.* Karl-Heinz Höfer, *Lt.* Werner Hohenberg, *Ofw.* Hans Hormann, *Lt.* Udo Hünerfeld, *Hptm.* Erhard Jähnert, *Oblt.* Fritz Klees, *Ofw.* Hans Krohn, Felix Lademann, *Major* Friedrich Lang, *Major* Heinz Lange, *Oblt.* Erwin Leykauf, *Uffz.* Friedrich Lühring, *Generalleutnant* Günther Rall, *Lt.* Edmund Rossmann, *Uffz.* Heinrich Scheibe, *General* Johannes Steinhoff, *Generalleutnant* Hannes Trautloft, and *Ofw.* Dieter Woratz.

To any helpers whose names I may have missed, please accept my apologies and my implied gratitude.

Christer Bergström,
5 July 2007

Table of Equivalent Ranks

VVS	Luftwaffe	USAAF
Enlisted		
Krasnoarmeyets	Flieger	Private
Yefreytor	Gefreiter	Private 1st Class
	Obergefreiter	Corporal
	Hauptgefreiter	
NCOs		
Mladshiy Serzhant	Unteroffizier	
Serzhant	Unterfeldwebel	Sergeant
Starshiy Serzhant	Feldwebel	Technical Sergeant
Starshina	Oberfeldwebel	Master Sergeant
Warrant Officers		
	Oberfähnrich	Senior Officer Candidate
	Stabsfeldwebel	Warrant Officer
Commissioned Officers		
Mladshiy Leytenant		Flight Officer
Leytenant	Leutnant	Second Lieutenant
Starshiy Leytenant	Oberleutnant	First Lieutenant
Kapitan	Hauptmann	Captain
Mayor	Major	Major
Podpolkovnik	Oberstleutnant	Lieutenant Colonel
Polkovnik	Oberst	Colonel
General-Mayor	Generalmajor	Brigadier General
General-Leytenant	Generalleutnant	Major General
General-Polkovnik	General	Lieutenant General
General Armii	Generaloberst	General (4 Star)
Marshal Sovyetskogo Soyuza	Generalfeldmarschall	General (5 Star)
	Reichsmarschall	

Soviet political ranks and their equivalents

Rank of Political Instructor	Equivalent regular Army Rank
Mladshiy Politruk	Leytenant
Politruk	Starshiy Leytenant
Starshiy Politruk	Kapitan
Batalyonnyy Komissar	Mayor
Starshiy Batalyonnyy Komissar	Podpolkovnik
Polkovoy Komissar	Polkovnik
Divizionny Komissar	General-Mayor
Korpusnoy Komissar	General-Leytenant
Armeyskiy Komissar Vtorogo Ranga	General-Polkovnik
Armeyskiy Komissar Pervogo Ranga	General Armii

Glossaries and Abbreviations

AAA Anti-aircraft artillery.

Abwehr "Defence", Germany's intelligence service during World War II.

AD (*Aviatsionnaya Diviziya*), Aviation Division (Soviet).

ADD (*Aviatsiya Dal'nego Deystviya*) Long Range Aviation (Soviet); Independent branch of aviation, subordinated directly to the Stavka.

Adjutant Aviator Rumanian Air Force rank, equivalent to Technical Sergeant.

AE (*Aviatsionnaya Eskadrilya*), Aviation Squadron (Soviet).

Aerial victory, a confirmed shot-down enemy aircraft.

Airacobra U.S.-designed Bell single-engined single-seat fighter.

ANT (Andrey Nikolayevich Tupolev), Soviet aircraft designer.

Armeekorps Army Corps (German).

ARMIR (*Armata Italiana in Russia*) Italian Armed Forces in Russia.

Aufklärung Reconnaissance (German).

Aufklärungsgruppe, Reconnaissance (aviation) Wing (German).

AufklObdL (*Aufklärungsgruppe Oberbefehlshaber der Luftwaffe*), Reconnaissance (aviation) Wing, Commander of the Luftwaffe (German).

Aviaeskadrilya *or* **Aviatsionnaya Eskadrilya** Aviation Squadron (Soviet).

Aviadiviziya *or* **Aviatsionnaya Diviziya** Aviation Division (Soviet).

Aviakorpus *or* **Aviatsionnyy Korpus** Aviation Corps (Soviet).

Aviapolk *or* **Aviatsionnyy Polk** Aviation Regiment (Soviet).

Aviatsiya Voyenno-Morskogo Flota, Navy Air Force, VVS-VMF (Soviet).

Aviatsionnaya Shkola Pervonachal'nogo Obucheniya, Primary Flight Training School (Soviet).

Aviazveno Svyazi liaison flight (Soviet).

B-3 Soviet designation of U.S.-designed Douglas DB-7 (A-20 Havoc) - British designation DB-7B Boston III - twin-engined attack bomber.

BA (*Bombardirovochnaya Armiya*) Bomber aviation army (Soviet).

BABr (*Bombardirovochnaya Aviatsionnaya Brigada*), Bomber Aviation Brigade (Soviet); the equivalent of the Soviet Navy Aviation to the BAD of the Army Aviation.

BAD (*Bombardirovochnaya Aviatsionnaya Diviziya*), Bomber Aviation Division (Soviet).

BAK (*Bombardirovochnyy Aviatsionyy Korpus*), Bomber Aviation Corps (Soviet).

BAP (*Bombardirovochnyy Aviatsionyy Polk*), Bomber Aviation Regiment (Soviet).

Barbarossa code-name of the German attack on the Soviet Union in 1941.

BBAP (*Blizhnebombardirovochnyy Aviatsionnyy Polk*), Short-Range Bomber Aviation Regiment (Soviet).

Bell U.S. aircraft designer.

Beriyev Soviet aircraft designer.

Bf (Bayerische Flugzeugwerke), German aircraft designer; designation of Messerschmitt 109 and 110.

Bf 108 German single-engined Messerschmitt liasion and training aircraft.

Bf 109 German single-engined Messerschmitt single-seat fighter.

Bf 110 German twin-engined Messerschmitt two-place heavy fighter and fighter-bomber.

Boston British designation of U.S.-designed Douglas DB-7 twin-engine light attack bomber.

Capitan Aviator Rumanian Air Force rank, equivalent to Captain.

Capitano Pilota Italian Air Force rank, equivalent to captain.

Chayka 'Seagull', Soviet Polikarpov I-153 single-engined, single-seat biplane fighter.

Che-2 Soviet twin-engined Chetverikov amphibian reconnaissance aircraft.

Chetverikov Soviet aircraft designer.

ChF (*Chernomorskiy Flot*), Black Sea Fleet (Soviet).

Corpul Aerian Air Corps (Rumanian).

Curtiss U.S. aircraft designer.

"Curtiss" An incorrect German identification of the Soviet I-153 single-engined, single- seat biplane fighter.

DB (Daimler-Benz) German engine designer.

DB (*Dal'niy Bombardirovshchik*) Long-Range Bomber (Soviet).

DB-3 Soviet twin-engined bomber.

DBA (*Dal'ne-Bombardirovochnaya Aviatsiya*), Long-Range Bomber Aviation (Soviet), reorganised into the ADD in March 1942.

DBAP (*Dal'nebombardirovochnyy Aviatsionnyy Polk*), Long-Range Bomber Regiment (Soviet).

Deutsche Luftwaffenmission Rumänien, German Air Force Mission to Rumania.

Diviziya Aviation wing (Soviet); composed of four to six regiments.

Do (Dornier) German aircraft designer.

Do 17 German twin-engined bomber and reconnaissance aircraft.

Douglas U.S. aircraft designer.

Edelweiss "Edelweiss" (the name of KG 51).

Ergänzungsgruppe Replacement Aviation Wing (German).

ErgGr (*Ergänzungsgruppe*) Reserve Aviation Wing (German).

Escadrila Squadron (Rumanian).

Eskadrilya Squadron (Soviet).

Experten German designation for fighter aces.

F (*Fernaufklärung*) Long-Distance (strategic) Reconnaissance Aviation (German).

FAB (*Fugasnaya Aviatsionnaya Bomba*) High-explosive Aviation Bomb (Soviet).

Fernaufklärungsgruppe Long-Distance (strategic) Reconnaissance Aviation Group (German).

Fi (Fieseler) German aircraft designer.

Fi 156 Storch German single-engined liaison and reconnaissance aircraft.

Fiat (*Fabrica Italiana Automobili Torino*) Italian aircraft and car designer.

Fiat BR.20 Italian Fiat twin-engined reconnaissance bomber.

Flak (*Fliegerabwehrkanone*), anti-aircraft artillery (German).

Fliegerdivision Air Division (German).

Fliegerkorps Aviation Corps (German).

Flotiliya 'Flotilla'; Soviet small regional fleet.

Flugzeugführerschule Pilots' training school (German).

Folgore Italian Macchi C.202 single-engined fighter.

Front Soviet equivalent to Army Group.

Führerweisung "Leader's Instructions", Hitler's Orders.

Fw (Focke-Wulf) German aircraft designer.

Fw 189 Uhu German Focke-Wulf twin-engined, three-seat reconnaissance aircraft.

Fw 190 German Focke-Wulf single-engined, single-seat fighter.

Fw 200 German Focke-Wulf four-engined maritime reconnaissance bomber and transport aircraft.

G *or* **Gv** (*Gvardeyskiy*), Guards (Soviet).

GAL (*Gruparea Aeriană de Luptă*) Air Combat Group (Rumanian).

Gefechtsverband Combat unit (German).

General der Jagdflieger Fighter Aviation General; the German Inspector of Fighter Aviation.

Generaloberstabsarzt German military medical rank, equivalent to *Generalleutnant*.

General Wever the name of KG 4 (adopted after the first Chief-of-Staff of the Luftwaffe, *General* Walther Wever).

Geschwader Aviation Group (German); three or four *Gruppen*.

Geschwaderkommodore Aviation Wing Commander (German).

GKO (*Gosudarstvennyy Komitet Oborony*), State Committee for Defence (Soviet).

Gorbatyy 'Hunchback', Soviet nickname for the Il-2 ground-attack aircraft.

Greif 'Griffin'; the name of KG 55.

Grupul Bombardament Bomber Group (Rumanian).

Gruppe Aviation Wing (German); usually three *Staffeln*, see below.

Gruppenkommandeur Aviation Group Commander (German).

Gruppo Aviation Group (Italian).

Gruppo Autonomo Caccia Terrestre Independent Fighter Aviation Group (Italian).

Grupul Vânătoare Fighter Aviation Group (Rumanian).

Guards Honorary Soviet title to specially distinguished units.

Gv See 'G'.

GVF (*Grazhdanskiy Vozdushnyy Flot*) Civil Air Fleet (Soviet); civilian aviation.

H (*Heeresaufklärung*), Army (Tactical) Reconnaissance Aviation (German).

Hawker British aircraft designer.

He (Heinkel) German aircraft designer.

He 111 German twin-engined bomber.

He 177 German four-engined bomber.

Heeresaufklärungsgruppe Army (tactical) Reconnaissance Aviation Wing (German).

Heeresgruppe Army group (German).

Heeresgruppe Mitte Central Army Group (German).

Heeresgruppe Nord Northern Army Group (German).

Heeresgruppe Süd Southern Army Group (German).

Heinkel German aircraft designer.

Henschel German aircraft designer.

Hero of the Soviet Union (*Geroy Sovyetskogo Soyuza*); the highest Soviet 'appointment' for bravery in combat.

Hs (Henschel), German aircraft designer.

Hs 123 German single-engined Henschel single-seat ground-attack biplane.

Hs 126 German single-engined Henschel two-place Army co-operation and tactical reconnaissance aircraft.

Hs 129 German twin-engined Henschel single-seat ground-attack aircraft.

Hurricane British single-engined Hawker single-seat fighter.

I ('*Istrebitel*') Fighter (Soviet).

I-15 Soviet single-engined Polikarpov single-seat, fixed-gear biplane fighter.

I-15bis Soviet single-engined Polikarpov single-seat, fixed-gear biplane fighter.

I-16 Soviet single-engined Polikarpov single-seat fighter.

I-26 Alternate designation for Soviet Yak-1 single-engined, single-seat fighter.

I-61 An incorrect German name for MiG-1 and MiG-3.

I-152 Alternate designation for Polikarpov I-15bis.

I-153 Soviet single-engined Polikarpov single-seat fighter and ground-attack biplane.

I-301 An incorrect German designation for Soviet single-engined, single-seat LaGG-3 fighter.

IA (*Istrebitel'naya Armiya*) Fighter aviation army (Soviet).

IA PVO (*Istrebitel'naya Aviatsiya PVO*) Fighter aviation of the PVO (Soviet), a part of PVO established in January 1942. Previously, fighter units allocated for PVO duties were part of the VVS and were subordinated to PVO only operationally.

Il-4 designation of Soviet DB-3F twin-engined bomber from March 1942.

IAD (*Istrebitel'naya Aviatsionnaya Diviziya*), Fighter Aviation Division (Soviet).

IAK (*Istrebitel'nyy Aviatsionnyy Korpus*), Fighter Aviation Corps (Soviet).

IAP (*Istrebitel'nyy Aviatsionyy Polk*), Fighter Aviation Regiment (Soviet).

I.A.R. (Industria Aeronautica Română), Rumanian Aeronautical Industry (Rumanian aircraft designer).

I.A.R. 37 Rumanian single-engined, three-place light bomber, liaison and reconnaissance biplane.

I.A.R. 39 Rumanian single-engined, three-place light bomber, liaison and reconnaissance biplane.

I-A.R. 80 Rumanian single-engined fighter.

Il (Ilyushin) Soviet aircraft designer.

Il-2 Soviet single-engined Ilyushin single-seat (from late 1942 alternatively twin-seat) ground-attack aircraft.

Ilyusha Soviet nickname for the Il-2 ground-attack aircraft.

Immelmann The name of St.G. 2 (adopted after WWI ace Max Immelmann).

Ishak "Jackass", Soviet Polikarpov I-16 single-engined, single-seat fighter.

J (*Jagd*) Fighter (German).

Jagdflieger Fighter Pilots (German).

Jagdgeschwader Fighter Aviation Group (German).

Jagdstaffel Fighter Aviation Squadron (German).

Jagdwaffe Fighter Air Arm (German).

JG (*Jagdgeschwader*) Fighter Group (German).

Ju (Junkers) German aircraft designer.

Ju 52 German three-engined Junkers transport aircraft.

Ju 86 German twin-engined Junkers bomber and reconnaissance aircraft.

Ju 87 German single-engined Junkers dive-bomber.

Ju 88 German twin-engined Junkers bomber/dive-bomber and reconnaissance aircraft.

Ju 90 German four-engined Junkers transport plane.

KA (*Krasnaya Armiya*), Red Army.

Kaczmarek Wingman in German fighter pilots' slang.

Kampfflieger "Combat Aviators"; bomber aviators (German).

Kampfgeschwader German Bomber Aviation Group.

Katyusha "Little Katya", Soviet rocket-missile.

KBF (*Krasnoznamyonnyy Baltiyskiy Flot*), Red Banner Baltic Fleet (Soviet).

Kette 'Chain'; German tactical air formation (three aircraft).

KG (*Kampfgeschwader*), Bomber Group (German).

KGr (*Kampfgruppe*), Bomber Wing (German).

KGrzbV (*Kampfgruppe zu besonderen Verwendung*), Special Purpose (transport) Bomber Wing (German).

KGzbV (*Kampfgeschwader zu besonderen Verwendung*), Special Purpose (transport) Bomber Group (German).

Kittyhawk British designation of U.S.-designed Curtiss P-40E single-engined, single- seat fighter.

Knight's Cross One of the highest German military awards.

Kommandeur See *Gruppenkommandeur*.

Kommodore See *Geschwaderkommodore*.

Komsomol (*Kommunisticheskiy soyuz molodyozhi*), Communist Youth League (Soviet).

KOSOS (*Konstruktorskiy Otdel Opytnovo Samolyotostroeniya*), Experimental Aircraft Design Section (Soviet).

KOVO (*Kievskiy Osobyy Voyennyy Okrug*), Kiev Special Military District (Soviet).

Közelfelderitö-század Hungarian tactical reconnaissance squadron.

KüFlGr (*Küstenfliegergruppe*), Coastal Patrol Group (German).

KV (Kliment Voroshilov) Soviet heavy tank.

La (Lavochkin) Soviet aircraft designer.

La-5 Soviet single-engined Lavochkin single-seat fighter.

LaGG (Lavochkin, Gorbunov, Gudkov), Soviet aircraft designers.

LaGG-3 Soviet single-engined Lavochkin-Gorbunov-Gudkov single-seat fighter.

LBAP (*Legko-Bombarovochnyy Aviatsionny Polk*) Light bomber aviation regiment (Soviet).

Legion Condor Condor Legion; also the name of KG 53.

LG (*Lehrgeschwader*), Training Wing (German).

Li Lisunov, Soviet chief engineer of Factory No 84, where production of PS-84s took place.

Li-2 Designation of military transport and bomber variants of Soviet PS-84 twin-engine transport from 17 September 1942.

Locotenent Aviator Rumanian Air Force rank, equivalent to First Lieutenant.

Locotenent Comandor Aviator Rumanian Air Force rank, equivalent to Major.

Luftflotte Air Fleet (German).

Lufttransportführer Air Transport Commander (German).

Luftwaffe Air Force (German).

Luftwaffengruppe Kaukasus Air Force Groupment Caucasus (German).

Luftwaffenkommando "Air Force Command", command of the aviation within a defined geographical area (German).

Luftwaffenkommando Ost "Air Force Command East", the command of the Axis aviation which operated in support of *Heeresgruppe Mitte* from the spring of 1942.

M (*Motor*), engine (Soviet).

Macchi Italian aircraft designer.

Maggiore Pilota Italian Air Force rank equivalent to Major.

MAG NOR (*Morskaya Aviatsionnaya Gruppa Novorossiyskogo Oboronitel'nogo Rayona*) The Naval Aviation Group of the Novorossiysk Defence Zone (Soviet).

MAGON GVF (*Moskovskaya Aviatsionnaya Gruppa Osobogo Naznacheniya GVF*) Moscow Aviation Group of Special Purpose of the GVF (Soviet).

Magyar Királyi Honvéd Légierö Royal Hungarian Air Force.

MBR (*Morskoy Blizhniy Razvedchik*), Naval short-range Reconnaissance Aircraft (Soviet).

MBR-2 Soviet twin-engined Beriyev amphibian reconnaissance aircraft.

Mc. 200 Saetta Italian single-engined Macchi single-seat fighter.

Mc. 202 Folgore Italian single-engined Macchi single-seat fighter.

Me (Messerschmitt), German aircraft designer.

Me 108 Alternative designation of Bf 108.

Me 109 Alternative designation of Bf 109.

Me 110 Alternative designation of Bf 110.

MG (*Maschinengewehr*), machine gun (German).

MiG (Mikoyan, Gurevich), Soviet aircraft designers.

MiG-3 Soviet single-engined Mikoyan-Gurevich single-seat fighter.

MK (*Maschinenkanone*), automatic cannon (German).

MTAP (*Minno-Torpednyy Aviatsionyy Polk*) Mine-Torpedo Aviation Regiment (Soviet).

Nachtaufklärungsstaffel Night reconnaissance aviation squadron (German).

NAGr (*Nahaufklärungsgruppe*) Short-range (tactical) reconnaissance group (German).

NBAP (*Nochnoy Bombardirovochnyy Aviatsionnyy Polk*), Night Bomber Aviation Regiment (Soviet).

Neman Soviet aircraft designer.

NKVD (*Narodnyy Kommissariat Vnutrennikh Del*), People's Commissariat for Internal Affairs (Soviet).

NLBAP (*Nochnoy Legko-Bombardirovochnyy Aviatsionnyy Polk*), Night Light Bomber Aviation Regiment (Soviet).

O. A. (*Osservazione Aerea*) Aerial reconnaissance (Italian).

OAG (*Osobaya Aviatsionnaya Gruppa*), Special Aviation Group (Soviet).

Oboronitel'nyy krug Soviet defensive air combat circle.

OIAE (*Otdel'naya Istrebitel'naya Aviatsionnaya Eskadrilya*), Independent Fighter Aviation Squadron (Soviet).

OKH (*Oberkommando des Heeres*), Army High Command (German).

OKL (*Oberkommando der Luftwaffe*), Air Force High Command (German).

OKW (*Oberkommando der Wehrmacht*), Armed Forces High Command (German).

OMRAP (*Otdel'niy Morskoy Razvetyvatel'nyy Aviatsionyy Polk*), Independent Naval Reconnaissance Aviation Regiment (Soviet).

ORAE (*Otdel'naya Razvedyvatel'naya Aviatsionnaya Eskadrilya*), Independent Reconnaissance Aviation Squadron (Soviet).

OShAE (*Otdel'naya Shturmovaya Aviatsionnaya Eskadrilya*), Independent Ground-Attack Aviation Squadron (Soviet).

OSNAZ (*Osoboye Naznachenie*), Special Purpose (Soviet).

P-40 U.S.-designed single-engined, Curtiss single-seat fighter.

Panzer Armour (German).

Panzerarmee Armoured (Tank) Army (German).

Panzerdivision Armoured Division (German).

Panzerkorps Armoured Corps (German).

Para Soviet tactical air formation (two aircraft).

PBAP (*Pikiruyushchiy Bombardirovochnyy Aviatsionnyy Polk*) Dive-bomber aviation regiment (Soviet).

Pe (Petlyakov) Soviet aircraft designer.

Pe-2 Soviet twin-engined Petlyakov dive-bomber.

Pe-8 Soviet four-engined Tupolev/Petlyakov heavy bomber, designated TB-7 until 1942.

Pik As "Ace of Spades" (the name of JG 53).

Platzschutzstaffel Airfield protection (fighter) squadron (German).

Po (Polikarpov) Soviet aircraft designer.

Polikarpov Soviet aircraft designer.

Polk Regiment (Soviet).

These Bf 109 G-6s are believed to have belonged to I./JG 52 and were probably photographed at Anapa or Taman, both bases being used by the Gruppe at various times during 1943.

Apparently with great relief painted in their faces, the crew of a VVS bomber walks away from their Pe-2 to report yet another combat mission.

PS-84 Soviet licence-built US twin-engine Douglas DC-3 passenger and transport aircraft.

PVO (*Protivo-Vozdushnaya Oborona*), Home Air Defence (Soviet).

R (*Razvedchik*) Reconnaissance (Soviet).

R-5 Soviet single-engined Polikarpov light bomber and reconnaissance aircraft.

RAG (*Reservnaya Aviatsionnaya Gruppa*), Reserve Aviation Group (of the *Stavka*) (Soviet).

Rata "Rat", German and Spanish nickname for Soviet Polikarpov I-16 single-engined, single-seat fighter.

Red Falcons Soviet designation of Soviet fighter pilots.

Regia Aeronautica Royal Italian Air Force.

Reich "Empire" or "Realm" (German); *the Third Reich*, Hitler's designation for Nazi Germany.

Rotte German tactical air formation (two aircraft).

Rottenflieger wingman (German).

Rottenführer leader of a *Rotte* (German).

RS (*Reaktivnyy Snaryad*) aircraft-carried rocket-projectile (Soviet).

RS-82 Soviet rocket-projectile.

RS-132 Soviet rocket-projectile.

R/T Radio-telephone.

R-Z An upgrade version of Soviet single-engined Polikarpov light bomber and reconnaissance aircraft R-5.

Saetta Italian single-engined, single-seat M.C.-200 fighter.

SAD (*Smeshannaya Aviatsionnaya Diviziya*), Composite Aviation Division (Soviet).

SAK (*Smeshannyy Aviatsionnyy Korpus*), Composite Air Corps (Soviet).

SAP (*Smeshannyy Aviatsionnyy Polk*), Composite Aviation Regiment (Soviet).

SB (*Skorostnoy Bombardirovshchik*), High-speed Bomber (Soviet); a particular Tupolev twin-engined Soviet bomber.

SBAP (*Skorostnoy Bombardirovohchnyy Aviatsionnyy Polk*), High-speed Bomber Aviation Regiment (Soviet).

Saetta, Italian MC-200 single-seat, single-engined fighter.

SAGr (*Seeaufklärungsgruppe*) sea reconnaissance aviation group (German).

Savoia-Marchetti Italian aircraft designer.

SC (*Splitterbombe, cylindrisch*), cylindrical fragmentation bomb (German).

Sch or Schl (*Schlacht*) Ground-attack (German).

SchG or SchlG Assault Group; German Ground-Attack Aviation Group.

Schlachtflieger Ground-attack airman (German).

Schlachtgeschwader "Assault Group"'; German Ground-Attack Aviation Group.

Schwarm "Swarm" or "Flight"; German tactical air formation (four aircraft).

Schwarmführer *Schwarm* Leader (German).

Schwerpunkt see *Schwerpunktbildung* below.

Schwerpunktbildung "Creation of Main Focus", German military tactic of creating individual points of maximum strength at certain front sectors.

SD (*Splitterbombe Dickwand*), fragmentation bomb, hard-covered (German).

Sergente Italian military rank equivalent to sergeant.

ShAD (*Shturmovaya Aviatsionnaya Diviziya*), Ground-attack Aviation Division (Soviet).

ShAP (*Shturmovoy Aviatsionnyy Polk*), Ground-attack Aviation Regiment (Soviet).

ShKAS (*Shpital'nyy-Komaritskiy Aviatsionnyy Skorostrelnyy*), Rapid-Firing Aircraft machine gun; 7.62-mm, by designers Shpital'nyy and Komaritskiy (Soviet).

Shkola Voyennykh Pilotov Military Flight Training School (Soviet).

Shturmovik Soviet ground-attack aircraft.

ShVAK (*Shpital'nyy-Vladimirov Aviatsionnaya Krupnokalibernaya*), Large-calibre aircraft cannon; 20-mm, by designers Shpital'nyy and Vladimirov (Soviet).

SM (*Savoia-Marchetti*) Italian aircraft designer.

SM-79 Italian designed Savoia-Marchetti three-engined bomber and torpedo bomber.

SM-81 Italian designed Savoia-Marchetti twin-engined multi-role bomber, transport and utility aircraft.

Sonderstab Krim "Special Purpose Staff Crimea", the equivalent of an air corps commanding the Luftwaffe units in the Crimea in early 1942.

Sonderstaffel Special Purpose squadron (German).

SOR (*Sevastopol'skiy Oboronitel'nyy Rayon*) Sevastopol Defensive District (Soviet).

SPB (*Skorostnoy Pikiruyushchiy Bombardirovshchik*), High-Speed Dive-Bomber (Soviet).

Squadriglia, Squadron (Italian).

St (see *Stuka*).

Stab Staff (German).

Staffel Aviation Squadron (German); usually 12 aircraft.

Staffelkapitän Aviation Squadron Commander (German).

Stavka Headquarters of the Soviet Supreme High Command.

St.G (*Sturzkampfgeschwader*), Dive-Bomber Group (German).

Storch German Fi 156 single-engined liaison and reconnaissance aircraft.

Stuka (*Sturzkampfflugzeug*), Dive-Bomber (German).

Stukageschwader Dive-Bomber Aviation Group (German).

Su (Sukhoy) Soviet aircraft designer.

Su-2 Soviet single-engined Sukhoy two-place light bomber.

Sublocotenent Aviator Rumanian Air Force rank, equivalent to Second Lieutenant.

T-34 Soviet medium tank.

Taran air-ramming (Russian).

TB (*Tyazhyolyy Bombardirovshchik*) Heavy Bomber (Soviet).

TB-3 Soviet four-engined Tupolev heavy bomber.

TB-7 Soviet four-engined Tupolev/Petlyakov heavy bomber.

TBAP (*Tyazhyolyy Bombardirovochnyy Aviatsionnyy Polk*), Heavy Bomber Aviation Regiment (Soviet).

Tenente Pilota Italian military rank equivalent to lieutenant.

Tomahawk U.S.-designed Curtiss P-40B and P-40C single-engined, single-seat fighter.

Transportstaffel German Transport Aviation Squadron.

TShch (*tralshchik*) trawler (Soviet).

Tu (Tupolev), Soviet aircraft designer.

Tupolev Soviet aircraft designer.

U (*Uchebnyy*) (Basic) Training (Soviet).

UAG (*Udarnaya Aviatsionnaya Gruppa*) Strike Aviation Group, a groupment of aviation regiments (Soviet).

U-2 Soviet single-engined Polikarpov training and light bomber biplane.

UT (*Uchebno-Trenirovochnyy*), Basic Training (aircraft) (Soviet).

UTI (*Uchebno-Trenirovochnyy Istrebitel'*), Basic Fighter Trainer (Soviet).

VA (*Vozdushnaya Armiya*) Air Army (Soviet).

Victory see 'aerial victory'.

Vitse-Admiral Vice Admiral (Soviet).

VMF (*Voyenno-Morskoy Flot SSSR*), Naval Forces of the USSR.

VO (*Voyennyy Okrug*), Military District (Soviet).

VVS (*Voyenno-Vozdushnye Sily*), Military Air Force (Soviet).

Wehrmacht The Armed Forces (German).

Wehrmachtführungsstab Armed Forces Staff (German).

Westa See *Wetterkundungsstaffel* Weather.

Wetterkundungsstaffel Weather Reconnaissance aviation squadron (German).

Wiking "Viking" (the name of KGr 100).

W.Nr. (*Werknummer*) (aircraft) Construction Number (German).

Yak (Yakovlev) Soviet aircraft designer.

Yak-1 Soviet single-engined, single-seat fighter.

Yak-7 Soviet single-engined, single-seat fighter.

Yakovlev Soviet aircraft designer.

Yer (Yermolayev) Soviet aircraft designer.

Yer-2 Soviet twin-engined Yermolayev long-range bomber.

Yermolayev Soviet aircraft designer.

Z (*Zerstörer*) Heavy fighter (German).

ZAB (*Zazhigatel'naya Aviatsionnaya Bomba*), Incendiary Aviation Bomb (Soviet).

Zerstörer 'Destroyer'; German heavy fighter.

Zerstörerstaffel Heavy fighter aviation squadron (German).

Zerstörergeschwader Heavy Fighter Aviation Group (German).

ZG (*Zerstörergeschwader*) Heavy Fighter Aviation Group (German).

ZOVO (*Zapadnyy Osoyy Voyennyy Okrug*), Western Special Military District (Soviet).

Zveno Soviet tactical air formation (three aircraft).

Soviet Alternative Aircraft Designations

I-26 = Yak-1.

I-61 = (an incorrect German name for MiG-1 and 3. In reality, the MiG-1 prototype was I-200, while the serial MiG-3 had no other designation.)

I-152 = I-15bis.

I-301 = (an incorrect German designation for LaGG-3. In reality, I-301 was the designation of LaGG-1, the non-serial prototype of LaGG-3.)

Il-4 = Designation of DB-3F from 1942.

Pe-8 = Designation of TB-7 from 1942.

SB = ANT-40 (incorrectly described as SB-2 or SB2bis/SB-3).

SB-RK = ANT-40, dive-bomber version. The most common designation is Ar-2.

TB-3 = ANT-6.

TB-7 = ANT-42.

Po-2 = Designation of U-2 from 1944.

'Curtiss' = An incorrect German identification of the I-153 biplane fighter.

'Martin' = An incorrect German identification for the SB bomber.

V-11 'Vultee' = An incorrect German identification for the Il-2 *Shturmovik* or Su-2.

Note:

Soviet airmen frequently misidentified Bf 109 fighters as 'He 113s'. In reality, the Heinkel He 113 single-engined fighter was not mass-produced and never saw first-line service with the *Luftwaffe*.

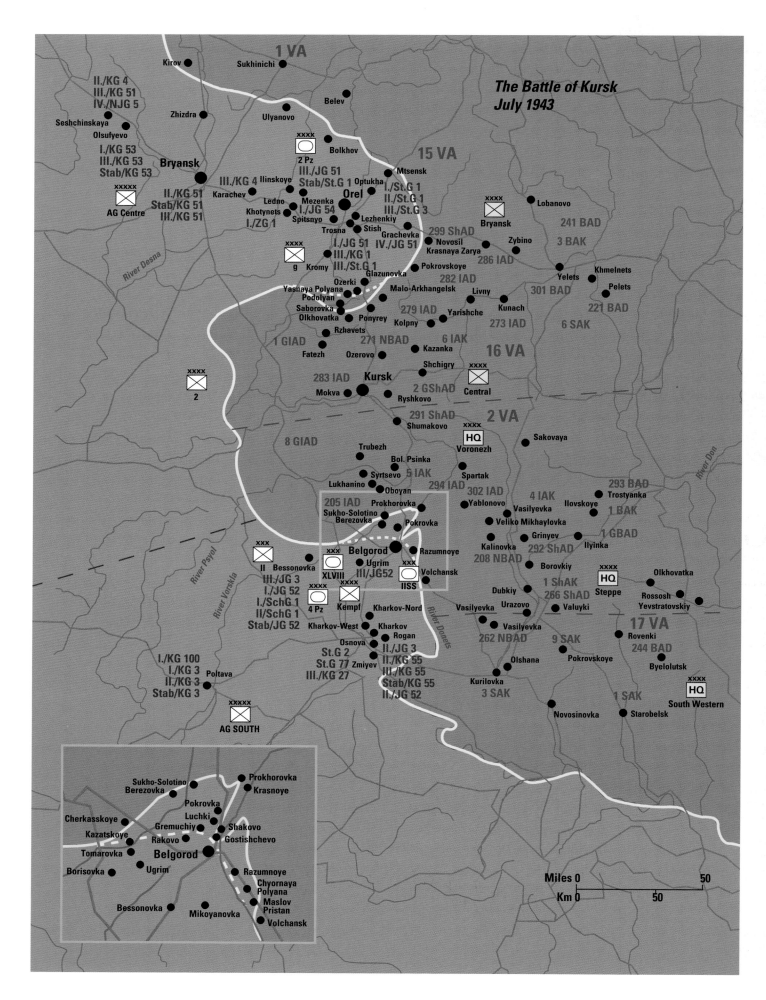

The Battle of Kursk
July 1943

1 VA

Kirov
Sukhinichi

II./KG 4
III./KG 51
IV./NJG 5

Belev

Zhizdra

Ulyanovo

15 VA

Seshchinskaya
Olsufyevo

2 Pz

Bolkhov

Mtsensk

I./KG 53
III./KG 53
Stab/KG 53

Bryansk

III./KG 4 Ilinskoye

III./JG 51
Stab/St.G 1 Optukha

I./St.G 1
II./St.G 1
III./St.G 3

Lobanovo

AG Centre

II./KG 51
Stab/KG 51
III./KG 51

Karachev

Ledno Mezenka
Khotynets
Spitsnyo
Trosna

Orel

I./JG 54

Lezhenkiy
Stish

Bryansk

241 BAD

3 BAK

I./ZG 1

Grachevka

299 ShAD

Zybino

I./JG 51
III./KG 1

g Kromy

IV./JG 51

Novosil
Krasnaya Zarya

286 IAD

Khmelnets

Yelets

Pelets

III./St.G 1

Glazunovka

Pokrovskoye

282 IAD

Ozerki

Yasnaya Polyana
Podolyan
Saborovka
Olkhovatka

Malo-Arkhangelsk

Livny

301 BAD

221 BAD

Ponyrey

279 IAD

Yarishche

273 IAD

6 SAK

Kunach

Rzhavets

1 GIAD

Fatezh Ozerovo

271 NBAD

Kazanka

6 IAK

Shchigry

16 VA

283 IAD

Kursk

Central

Mokva

Ryshkovo

291 ShAD

2 GShAD

2 VA

Shumakovo

8 GIAD

Trubezh

HQ
Voronezh

Sakovaya

Bol. Psinka

Syrtsevo

5 IAK

Spartak

294 IAD

293 BAD

Lukhanino

Oboyan

302 IAD

4 IAK

Yablonovo

Ilovskoye

Trostyanka

205 IAD

Prokhorovka

Vasilyevka

1 BAK

Sukho-Solotino
Berezovka

Pokrovka

Veliko Mikhaylovka

Grinyev

1 GBAD

Razumnoye

Kalinovka

292 ShAD

Ilyinka

II
Bessonovka

xxx
Belgorod

208 NBAD

Borovkiy

HQ
Steppe

Olkhovatka

XLVIII

Ugrim

III./JG 52

Rossosh

Yevstratovskiy

III./JG 3
I./JG 52
I./SchG 1
II/SchG 1
Stab/JG 52

Volchansk

1 ShAK

IISS

Dubkiy

266 ShAD

Vasilyevka Urazovo

Valuyki

4 Pz

Kempf

Kharkov-Nord

Vasilyevka

17 VA

Rovenki

Kharkov-West

Kharkov
Rogan

262 NBAD

9 SAK

Pokrovskoye

244 BAD

I./KG 100
I./KG 3
II./KG 3
Stab/KG 3

Poltava

Osnova

Olshana

Byelolutsk

St.G 2
St.G 77
III./KG 27

Zmiyev

II./JG 3
II./KG 55
III./KG 55
Stab/KG 55
II./JG 52

Kurilovka

3 SAK

1 SAK

HQ
South Western

AG SOUTH

Novosinovka

Starobelsk

(inset map)

Prokhorovka

Sukho-Solotino
Berezovka

Krasnoye

Pokrovka

Luchki

Cherkasskoye

Gremuchiy

Shakovo

Kazatskoye
Rakovo

Gostishchevo

Tomarovka

Belgorod

Borisovka

Ugrim

Razumnoye
Chyornaya
Polyana
Maslov
Pristan

Bessonovka

Mikoyanovka

Volchansk

Miles 0   50

Km 0   50

Chapter One

From Stalingrad to Kursk

On 31 January 1943, *Generalfeldmarschall* Friedrich von Paulus and the remnants of the German 6. *Armee* surrendered in the ruins of Stalingrad. In a single day, 90,000 German soldiers marched into Soviet captivity. It was the greatest defeat Germany had ever been dealt. To a great extent, the Battle of Stalingrad had been decided in the air. A strong attempt had been made to supply the besieged army from the air, just like the garrison at Demyansk had been supplied early in 1942. The Soviet victory was just as convincing in the air as on the ground. Organised by *General-Polkovnik* Aleksandr Novikov, the C-in-C of VVS KA, a Soviet air blockade had prevented German transport aircraft from bringing in an adequate amount of supplies. The consequences of the VVS's victory in the air over Stalingrad were of an importance similar to that of the RAF's victory during the Battle of Britain.

Merely three weeks after this stunning defeat, the *Luftwaffe* had pulled itself together and carried out an air operation which, alone, stopped the Red Army's broad offensive. In a breathtaking turn of events, the Soviet forces, which had swept successfully westward 644 kilometres from Stalingrad, were bombed relentlessly by massive German air attacks. With VVS fighters based too far away to be able to intervene effectively, the *Luftwaffe* continued for several days to strike at the Red Army forces on open snow fields with virtually no disturbance. Next, strong German reinforcements, which just had arrived by train – a whole SS *Panzer* Corps, equipped with factory-fresh tanks and SPGs – went into action. Led by *Generalfeldmarschall* Erich von Manstein, the new German *Heeresgruppe Süd* (Army Group South) – which had been created in mid-February 1943 by bringing together all German Army forces in the area extending from Taganrog in the south to the Kharkov sector – developed a counter-offensive.

On 14 March 1943, the SS troops took Kharkov, and four days later they re-captured the city of Belgorod, some 64 kilometres farther to the north. But by that time, the battle area was once again within reach of the Soviet air bases. Two whole Soviet air armies, 2 VA and 17 VA, were brought in, and the SS *Panzer* Corps became subject to intense aerial bombardment, while Soviet fighter pilots took control of the skies above.

This caught the Germans just as they were losing their main 'ace'– their own air support. In response to more critical situations farther south and in

the north, the bulk of *Fliegerkorps* IV's units were deployed elsewhere during the last ten days of March. By the end of the month, only three full *Kampfgruppen* (III./KG 27, II./KG 51, and I./KG 55), plus I./ZG 1, I./Sch.G 1, I./St.G 77, and elements of I./JG 52, remained for operations in the Kharkov-Belgorod sector. On 'the other side of the hill', the reinforced 2 VA alone was composed of 1 BAK, 1 ShAK, 4 IAK, 5 IAK, 217 IAD, and 291 IAD – a powerful force, particularly in terms of fighters. Meanwhile, 17 VA could muster over 700 combat aircraft.

The town of Kursk, which had been the next target for von Manstein's counter-offensive, remained in Soviet hands. With the beginning of the thaw period, which prevented any large-scale movements of heavy equipment along the roads, a new stalemate set in on the Eastern Front.

As a result of offensives and counter-offensives in February and March 1943, a complicated front situation had been created in this sector. Kharkov and Belgorod were in German hands, and 257 kilometres to the north of Belgorod, the Soviets had been unable to seize Orel. Almost exactly half way between Belgorod and Orel, the Soviets held Kursk and occupied positions 100 kilometres to the west of that city – the result of the Soviet offensive in early February 1943. Thus, one Soviet wedge into the German front line had been created around Kursk, and the Orel position had been turned into a German wedge into the Soviet front line. Since the Soviet counter-offensive in the winter of 1941/1942, Orel was an important cornerstone in the German defence system on the Eastern Front. With Belev, Sukhinichi and Kirov in Soviet hands since early 1942, the Orel position constituted a breakwater against any Soviet offensive directed at *Heeresgruppe Mitte* farther to the north.

Two other German wedges into the Soviet front line farther north – at Demyansk and at Rzhev – were evacuated in March 1943 in order to shorten the front. But Hitler decided to hold on to his two other wedges on the Eastern Front – at Orel and in the Kuban area in the north-western Caucasus. These were intended to be used as springboards for upcoming offensives. While *Generaloberst* Walter Model's 9. *Armee* was shifted from the old Rzhev Bulge in the north to the Orel Bulge, where it joined 2. *Panzerarmee*, the primary focus of the fighting on the Eastern Front was concentrated to the so-called 'Kuban Bridgehead' in the far south. By concentrating the whole 17. *Armee* to a bridgehead 100 kilometres deep

The film cassette is unloaded from an Fw 189 reconnaissance aircraft on the Eastern Front.

and 100 kilometres wide in the north-western Caucasus, Hitler maintained a deadly threat against the Soviet oil fields across the Caucasus. Intensified Soviet attempts to take control of this small sector were made, but failed – not least because the Germans withdrew the bulk of *Luftflotte* 4 from the Ukraine and concentrated it on *Fliegerkorps* I in support of the Kuban Bridgehead. During the spring of 1943, an air battle of a scale never previously seen on the Eastern Front was waged over the Bridgehead. In the end, the Germans held on to it.

Meanwhile, both sides drew up plans for operations after the thaw. The idea to mount a 'double envelopment' attack against the Soviet Central Front in the Kursk Bulge was originally an extension of von Manstein's counter-offensive plan in March 1943. On 14 March, the day when Kharkov was re-captured by *Waffen*-SS troops, von Manstein proposed that 2. *Panzerarmee* of *Generalfeldmarschall* Günther Kluge's *Heeresgruppe Mitte* would join the offensive by launching an attack toward the south from the Orel Bulge. But by this time, von Kluge was in no position to support von Manstein. The two armies on his army group's southern flank – 2. *Armee* to the west of Kursk and 2. *Panzerarmee* at Orel – had become split by elements of the Soviet Central Front's 2nd Tank Army and 65th Army which sliced through the seam between these two German armies. By the time von Manstein demanded offensive action, these Soviet troops stood in Novgorod Severskiy, 190 kilometres north-west of Kursk. To restore the situation in this sector was von Kluge's highest priority.

Instead of dispersing his forces by dispatching 2. *Panzerarmee* towards the south-east, von Kluge concentrated his forces and following a ten-day battle had managed to fight back the Central Front to Sevsk, some 80 kilometres east of Novgorod Severskiy and 120 kilometres north-west of Kursk. Meanwhile, von Manstein's offensive succumbed under a hailstorm of Soviet bombs.

But with the Kursk Bulge – 120 kilometres wide and 144 kilometres deep – established, von Manstein's plan for a double envelopment was never scrapped. The commander of *Heeresgruppe Süd* managed to convince Hitler

to go ahead with the offensive as soon as the thaw period – the infamous *rasputitsa* which turned the soil into quagmire – was over.

During the *rasputitsa* period, the *Führer's* thoughts on the upcoming summer operations matured. Just as one year previously, his forces had been so badly mauled that a general offensive was out of the question. In the spring of 1943, the availability of forces forced the Germans onto a largely defensive strategy. Hitler's hopes to be able to defeat the Soviet Union obviously had vanished at Stalingrad, and he now shifted to a strategy of containment in the East.

During the First World War, the Germans had shortened their lines on the Western Front in 1917 and withdrawn to the famous Hindenburg Line, which increased their defensive strength and probably saved Germany from defeat in that year. In Hitler's distorted view, the German army remained undefeated in the First World War, and succumbed only to the 'stab in the back' of political turmoil. He now planned to repeat the 'Hindenburg Line strategy' on the Eastern Front and ordered the construction of a series of massive defensive works known as the *Panther Stellung* (Panther Line), also known as the *Ostwall* (Eastern Wall), running from Leningrad in the north and along the Dnyepr River to Dnepropetrovsk, and southward on the Sea of Azov. The construction of this defence line was to be completed in late 1943, whereupon the German armies on the Eastern Front were about to be pulled back behind its fortifications – leaving the Red Army to bleed against it.

In order to achieve more favourable tactical preconditions, Hitler decided to launch two powerful offensives with the aim of weakening his enemy. In the north, he planned to mount what he hoped would be a decisive attack against Leningrad in order to once and for all capture the city. This would not only relieve the Germans from the need to hold a whole army locked at Leningrad, but above all it would probably encourage Finland to continue the war on Germany's side. Before the Leningrad attack was launched, Hitler intended to carry out von Manstein's proposed 'double envelopment' against the Kursk Bulge. The aim was to strike a devastating blow against the Soviet Central Front, repeating the great German success during the double envelopment operation against the South-Western Front, south of Kharkov in May 1942.

The plan was assigned the code-name *Unternehmen 'Zitadelle'* – Operation Citadel. On 15 April 1943, Hitler issued his Operations Order No. 6, according to which *Zitadelle* would be the first offensive of the year. He specified that a tremendous concentration of forces, including '…the best formations, the best weapons and the best commanders', were required.

Concentrated in the south were to be 4. *Panzerarmee*, under *Generaloberst* Hermann Hoth and *Armeeabteilung Kempf* under *Generaloberst* Werner Kempf. Hoth and Kempf belonged to the most able German army commanders and had played a vital role during the defensive battles from Stalingrad to Belgorod. One of three corps under Hoth's command was *SS-Obergruppenführer* Paul Hausser's II. SS *Panzerkorps*, which had gained a reputation for the near fanatical stamina with which many of its troops fought. Overall command of 4. *Panzerarmee* and *Armeeabteilung Kempf* was exerted by *Generalfeldmarschall* von Manstein.

In the north, the northern flank of the Orel Bulge was to be held defensively by 2. *Panzerarmee,* occupying deeply echeloned positions which had been constructed since late 1941. *Generaloberst* Walter Model's 9. *Armee* was tasked to deliver the southbound strike against Kursk. These troops were battle-hardened veterans who for a long time had resisted the Soviet attempts to compress the Rzhev Bulge to the west of Moscow – and Model was, without doubt, a military genius.

But the Soviets also had brilliant military commanders. One of those was *Marshal* Georgiy Zhukov, the Deputy Commander of the Red Army. On 16 March 1943, Josef Stalin sent Zhukov to the Kharkov-Belgorod sector, with the task of assisting the commanders to restore the situation in the face of von Manstein's counter-attack. Historians David M. Glantz and Jonathan M. House characterise Zhukov as 'the most famous and most effective of the *Stavka* representatives, the 'fixers' who went from crisis to crisis making decisions and stiffening resolve. Zhukov's style was to be brutally frank with everyone, from Stalin on down.'[1]

Having contributed in bringing the advancing German troops to a halt, Zhukov set about preparing for the forthcoming battles which would follow after the *rasputitsa*. On 26 March, *General-Mayor* Konstantin Smirnov was removed from his position as the commander of 2VA, tasked to support the Voronezh Front – which was lined up against Hoth's 4. *Panzerarmee* at Belgorod south of Kursk, while two days later, *General* Filipp Golikov was removed from the command of the Voronezh Front. Instead these two units got back two of their former commanders.

Hs 129s returning from a mission fly low over their airfield.

A Yak 9-D of the Red Air Force.

Hitler postponed Zitadelle until the arrival of sufficient numbers of the new the Tiger (seen here), the Panther and the super-heavy Ferdinand SPG.

Leading 17 VA, *General-Leytenant* Stepan Krasovskiy had cooperated effectively with the South-Western Front's commander, *General Armii* Nikolay Vatutin, during the winter battles of 1942/43. However, earlier in 1942, Vatutin and Krasovskiy had become the first commanders of the Voronezh Front and 2 VA when these two formations were formed; now they returned to their old assignments. Hence, Hoth's opponents on the ground and in the air would be led by two of the most formidable Soviet commanders, who had also developed mutual coordination since July 1942. *General-Leytenant* Vladimir Sudets, who previously had headed the bomber corps, 1 BAK, succeeded Krasovskiy as 17 VA's commander.

Much has been said about the *Rote Kapelle* ('Red Orchestra') spy network which provided the Soviets with information about Operation *Zitadelle*. However, it seems as though the value of this information has been exaggerated in some Western accounts. In fact, *Marshal* Zhukov was able to predict the German attack almost in great detail no later than early April 1943. On the 8th of that month, he summarised his strategic assessment in a message to Stalin, writing:

'*Having suffered serious losses in the winter campaign of 1942-43, evidently the enemy would not appear to be able to accumulate large reserves by the spring to resume the offensive against the Caucasus and to advance to the Volga to make a wide enveloping manoeuvre around Moscow.*

Owing to the inadequacy of large reserves, in the spring and first half of the summer of 1943, the enemy will be forced to launch offensive operations on a narrower front [...]

Having assembled as many of his forces as possible [...] and the greatest quantity of air support, evidently, during the first stage the enemy will deliver a blow with his Orel-Kromy grouping to envelop Kursk from the north-east and with his Belgorod-Kharkov grouping to envelop Kursk from the south-east.'

This led the Soviets to direct their intelligence finding missions – including partisan observation groups and an extensive aerial reconnaissance – to the right areas. Their findings confirmed Zhukov's predictions.

Stalin at first proposed a resumption of offensive operations as soon as the weather permitted, in order to forestall the German attack. But Zhukov managed to convince him that the most advantageous strategy would be to allow the Germans to strike first and let them bleed against well prepared Soviet defence positions, and only afterwards launch a whole series of successive Soviet offensives.

The Voronezh Front on the southern face of the Kursk Bulge and the Central Front (supported by 16 VA) on its northern face would play the main role in the defensive stage of the battle. The Steppe Front and 5 VA would be kept as a major strategic reserve in the rear.

During the next stage, the Western and Bryansk fronts would attack the Orel Bulge from the north in cooperation with the Central Front's counter-offensive from the south in a 'double envelopment' operation intended to annihilate 2. *Panzerarmee* and 9. *Armee*. Meanwhile, the Steppe Front would move forward to bolster the Voronezh Front for a frontal counter-attack against the German troops on the southern face of the Kursk Bulge, and farther south the South-Western and Southern fronts would launch diversionary offensives.

Throughout the spring of 1943, the Soviets laid vast resources on creating a powerful defensive system on both sides of Kursk. Around 4,800 kilometres of trenches were dug to a depth of 153 kilometres, tens of thousands of kilometres of barbed wire were laid, anti-tank obstacles were densely built, thousands of gun and mortar positions were constructed, dummy positions were built, and nearly one million land mines were laid. Meanwhile the heaviest artillery concentrations the world had ever seen were created.

Both sides undertook elaborate measures to conceal their build-up. German 9. *Armee's* headquarters, which on 30 March moved to Orel, was given an entirely defensive name – *Festungsstab* II ('Fortress Staff II'). The Army's commander, Model, recorded tank manoeuvres in Germany on tape and then played these tapes in powerful loudspeakers close to Soviet lines in forested areas, with the intention of giving the Soviets false impressions of the whereabouts of German tank forces. Forces that could be held back until the last minute were left remaining in other sectors. The vast reinforcements of the German air formations – 1. *Fliegerdivision* of *Luftwaffenkommando Ost* (re-numbered *Luftflotte* 6 in May 1943) in the north and *Fliegerkorps* VIII of *Luftflotte* 4 in the south – would not arrive until the eve of the attack.

The Soviet concealment was just as refined. Vast resources were spent on the construction of false trenches, dummy tanks, dummy aircraft on false airfields and deceptive radio signals. The Soviet Air Force also gave a good contribution to the concealment of the Soviet build-up. In early April 1943 *Luftwaffe* photo-reconnaissance units were tasked to initiate reconnaissance missions over the Kursk Bulge. However, on 17 April, Soviet aircraft attacked the aerodrome Orsha-South, destroying five Ju 88 reconnaissance aircraft from 1.(F)/100 and 4.(F)/121, plus three Do 17s or Do 217s of 2. *Nachtaufklärungsstaffel*.[2] The Soviet airmen repeated the attack three days later, destroying another ten Ju 88s or Do 17s of these two units.[3] As a result he only operational strategic reconnaissance *Staffel* available to *Luftwaffenkommando Ost* or *Heeresgruppe Mitte* was 4.(F)/14.[4]

Without doubt, the neutralisation of most of *Luftwaffenkommando Ost's* fleet of strategic reconnaissance aircraft contributed to the successful Soviet concealment. In fact, the Soviets were able to transfer the 27th and 53rd Armies from the North-Western Front near Demyansk to the Central Front, and the 46th and 47th Armies from the North Caucasus Front to the region east of Kharkov without any of these moves being detected by the Germans.

The construction of the Soviet defence positions also was greatly aided by Hitler and his commanders, who repeatedly postponed *Zitadelle* and thus provided the Soviets with more time to complete these works. Ironically, the few aerial photographs which *Luftwaffe* reconnaissance aircraft had been able to take of Soviet defence positions served as a deterrent which caused the Germans to postpone the operation further.

At first, Hitler set the attack for 3 May, but on 28 April, a concerned *Generaloberst* Model presented him with aerial photographs which showed an extensive Soviet work on defence positions in the area where Model's 9. *Armee* was intended to attack. In view of this, the *Generaloberst* tried to persuade Hitler to cancel the offensive and instead use the concentration of forces to meet an anticipated Soviet attack.

Uncertain, Hitler decided to postpone Operation *Zitadelle* at least past 3 May, and called the key commanders to a conference on 4 May. At that

conference, it was decided to go ahead with the offensive plan, but the information about the Soviet preparations caused Hitler to postpone it until a sufficient amount of the new modern tanks – the Tiger, the Panther and the super-heavy SPG *Ferdinand* – had been produced. This meant that the attack would be postponed until at least 10 June 1943. Then, when the German bridgehead in Tunisia fell on 13 May 1943, Hitler again postponed the offensive until the end of June in order to prepare the defence of Italy. In consequence of the Allied victory in Tunisia, *Generalfeldmarschall* Wolfram Freiherr von Richthofen was sent from the Eastern Front to Italy, where he assumed deputy command of German aviation. Von Richthofen was intimately associated with *Luftflotte* 4 and *Fliegerkorps* VIII – the German formations which were tasked to provide *Zitadelle's* southern thrust with air support – which he had commanded since the beginning of the war. *Generalfeldmarschall* von Manstein protested vigorously, asserting that von Richthofen's personal role was of utmost importance to successfully conduct German air operations. But this led him only into conflict with *Reichsmarschall* Göring, the *Luftwaffe's* C-in-C. *Luftflotte* 4 received a new commander in *General* Otto Dessloch, who formerly had led 1. *Flakdivision*.

On 16 June, *Generaloberst* Heinz Guderian – who had been appointed to oversee the rebuild of the *Panzer* forces in February 1943 – informed Hitler that further delays were necessary in order to complete the reconstruction of the armour units.

It was obvious that these delays would provide the Soviets with time not only to detect the build-up of the German attack force, but above all to reinforce their own defences in the assigned attack area. At this stage, the fortunes of war were turning decisively against Hitler. During the first eighteen months of the war against the Soviet Union, Germany had been able to hold the Western Allies at bay with fairly limited forces. But with the Axis defeat at El Alamein in Egypt in November 1942 and the subsequent Allied landings in Morocco and Algeria, that changed rapidly. In March 1943, RAF Bomber Command initiated its most effective operation to date, the 'Battle of the Ruhr' which involved concentrated air attacks at night against industrial cities in western Germany. Meanwhile, the four-engined bombers of US 8th Air Force began to raid Germany by day.

The month of May brought many ominous signs for Hitler's war efforts. The U-boat offensive against Allied shipping in the Atlantic had been the last area where Germany enjoyed unquestionable success. But when seven submarines were lost during an operation against the Atlantic convoy ON-55 on 5-6 May, it was obvious that the Allies had developed defensive equipment which would soon bring the German string of successes on the seas to an end. One week later, on 13 May, a quarter of a million German and Italian troops surrendered in Tunisia. The next day, over one hundred American heavy bombers attacked the German city of Kiel in broad daylight, killing 400 civilians. On the night of 16/17 May, the RAF succeeded in smashing the Eder dams in the Ruhr, resulting in a flood which killed more than 2,000 Germans. Another week later, *Admiral* Karl Dönitz came to an inevitable conclusion about the dramatically climbing U-boat losses – forty-one were lost in the month of May alone – and ordered the cancellation of the offensive against the Atlantic convoys. This in turn meant that the Allies would be able to ship the troops and equipment intended for the invasion, which everyone expected, across the Atlantic at will.

In the wake of these military setbacks, Germany's allies started to waver. In March 1943, contacts took place between the Finnish Government and the US State Department, with the Finns evidently seeking a way out of the war, which it had been fighting on Germany's side against the Soviet Union since June 1941. The Axis states of Rumania and Hungary conducted similar talks via neutral countries. The Italian dictator, Mussolini, was utterly demoralised and made repeated attempts to convince Hitler to seek peace with the Soviet Union.

Hitler was simply in desperate need of a victory in order to boost morale, which was on the decline both in Germany and among his allies. There was no turning back. Adhering to *Generaloberst* Guderian's opinion, the *Führer* decided to delay Operation *Zitadelle* until 3 July 1943, thus allowing the *Panzer* forces to be equipped with what undoubtedly were the best tanks in the world. On 1 July, he postponed it one last time – until four days later.

Armourers make final adjustments to an MK 103 cannon on an Hs 129.

Chapter Two

Preparatory Air Operations

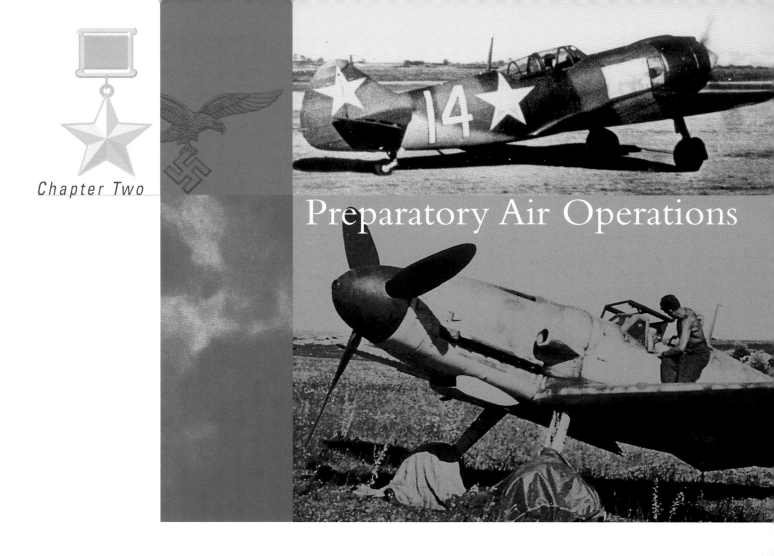

For several months prior to Operation *Zitadelle*, the air forces of both sides attacked their enemy's transport lines – particularly rail lines and rail installations – and airfields. However, this was not immediately linked with the forthcoming Battle of Kursk; the *Luftwaffe* and the Soviet air forces had carried out the same kind of attacks when the mud season had brought combat operations on the ground to a standstill during the spring of 1942.

The main difference between these semi-strategic operations in the springs of 1942 and 1943 was that the German attacks were weaker and the Soviet attacks were stronger in 1943 as compared with the previous year. While the Soviet aviation – both VVS KA and ADD, the long-range bomber force – had grown considerably in strength since 1942, the decline of the *Luftwaffe's* bomber operations against the Soviet rear area was more due to the fact that, by this time, the bulk of the *Luftwaffe* on the Eastern Front was concentrated on the Kuban Bridgehead, than any decisive weakening of the *Kampfgeschwader* on the Eastern Front. In fact, the *Luftwaffe* still mustered around 600 bombers on the Eastern Front in May 1943.

Throughout the spring of 1943, German air attacks against railways and rail installations in the Soviet rear area were performed mainly in small groups or by single bomber crews. In early 1943, the OKL formed three specialized *Eisenbahnstaffeln*, 'train-hunting' units: 9.(*Eis.*)/KG 1, 9.(*Eis.*)/KG 3, and 14.(*Eis.*)/KG 27. Crews were hand-picked for these units. The specialised long-range reconnaissance crews of *Aufklärungsgruppe ObdL* – redesigned into *Fernaufklärungsgruppe* 100 on 27 January 1943 – were tasked to locate targets for these train-hunting units. *Lt.* Udo Cordes of 9.(*Eis.*)/KG 3 developed a personal tactic for train attacks, and this led him to destroy forty-one railway engines and nineteen trains in only three weeks of action.[5] *Ofw.* Herbert Roewer of the same unit knocked out fifty-nine railway engines and fourteen military trains.[6] *Hptm.* Ernst Fach, 9.(*Eis.*)/KG 3's *Staffelkapitän*, achieved similar successes.

But the most effective air strikes against rail targets were delivered by the ADD. These were carried out with increasing intensity from early 1943. On the night of 16 March, no fewer than 300 ADD bombers were in action against rail installations at Gomel, Roslavl, Novozybkov and other places.[7] The following night, the ADD performed 279 combat sorties, 195 of which were directed against the railway junctions at Bryansk, Gomel, Novozybkov

and Bakhmach. All of these attacks were performed during the hours of darkness, with fairly primitive navigational devices but often with the guidance from bonfires lit by partisans. *Luftwaffe Generalleutnant* Walter Schwabedissen asserts that the Soviet bomber crews carried out these missions "…with remarkable courage and occasionally also with exemplary aggressiveness."[8]

According to Soviet intelligence reports, the ADD attack against the railway station at Zhukovka on the night of 21 March resulted in the destruction of five locomotives, with 70 Germans killed and 400 wounded. During a follow-up raid the next night, one armoured train and seventeen other railway wagons were reported destroyed.[9]

The War Diary of the German High Command noted that Orel's railway station was severely damaged during Soviet air attacks in late March and early April 1943.[10]

Although Hitler had originally decided to launch Operation *Zitadelle* on 3 May, and Marshal Zhukov had managed to guess the German plans early in April 1943, the month of April brought a decline in the air attacks against these targets. This was the month when the Battle of the Kuban Bridgehead reached its first climax, and both sides concentrated their primary efforts on this small area. The ADD was also ordered to perform a series of 'morale bombings' against Germany. Over two weeks, Il-4s and even some of the few four-engined Pe-8s flew against east German cities such as Königsberg, Tilsit and Danzig. But apart from the operation against Tilsit on the night of 20 April when 104 civilians were killed, these attacks failed to inflict any notable damage on the targets.

In May 1943, both sides resumed their air operations against rail targets. The night of 4 May saw very heavy ADD activity. The railway junction at Minsk was targeted by 1 GAD, 2 GAD and 4 GAD plus 36 AD of the ADD, dispatching a total of 109 bombers. Meanwhile 45 AD attacked the railway junction at Orsha with 109 bombers, including four-engined Pe-8 heavy bombers.[11] The War Diary of the German High Command noted the next day that 300 rail wagons, including three ammunition trains, were destroyed at Orsha.[12] "*Numerous enemy air attacks were made during the night,*" the same source noted on 5 May. "*Focus against the rear area of 2. Panzerarmee. In Gomel, Bryansk and Lokot heavy damage on buildings.*"[13]

These attacks were the result of the warning of an imminent German offensive which the Stavka had issued on 2 May. The repeated German postponements of Operation *Zitadelle* caused the Soviets to issue repeated 'false warnings'. Anticipating the German attack to be launched at any time between 10 and 12 May, the Soviets dispatched three days of coordinated air attacks against the airfields of *Luftwaffenkommando Ost* and *Luftflotte* 4, starting on 6 May 1943. The first wave of attacks involved 404 aircraft and took place between 04.30 and 06.00 in the morning. This caught the Germans by surprise and inflicted fairly heavy damage to the *Luftwaffe*. A total of 22 German aircraft were put out of commission on the ground, including eight from JG 51 and six each from KG 4 and 4.(F)/11. But when the Soviets returned with 372 aircraft between 15.00 and 20.00 hours that same day, the Germans were better prepared. In total, 21 Soviet aircraft were shot down on 6 May. The situation became even worse, from the Soviet perspective, during the two following days: a total of 346 Soviet sorties were made against German airfields, and all of these ran straight into an alerted German defence, which cost the Soviets 101 aircraft. The Soviet claims of 500 German aircraft destroyed is grossly inflated; between 6 and 8 May 1943, the *Luftwaffe* registered no more than 23 of its own aircraft as out of commission due to airfield attacks on the Eastern Front. [14]

The Soviets achieved greater success during the ADD's nocturnal operations. Between 3–11 May 1943, the ADD was in action against rail installations at Bryansk nine days in a row. According to German sources, 1,200 tons of ammunition was destroyed. [15]

Luftwaffe operations against similar targets still were relatively modest in comparison. On the night of 7/8 May, 31 He 111s were dispatched against the marshalling yards at Kursk. [16]

But larger German air operations were planned. In view of the obvious Soviet defensive preparations in the Kursk Bulge, and the decision to postpone *Zitadelle*, *Generaloberst* Robert *Ritter* von Greim, the commander of *Luftwaffenkommando Ost*, proposed to the OKL that a strategic bomber offensive against Soviet key industrial plants should be undertaken. Having examined the plan closely, OKL agreed. On 11 May 1943,

The crew of an ADD Ilyushin Il-4 bomber smile at the photographer. At night time, the Soviet aviation held an increasingly strong superiority in the air over the Eastern Front almost for the whole duration of the war.

Luftwaffenkommando Ost was redesigned *Luftflotte* 6, and almost the entire bomber force on the Eastern Front was temporarily brought under von Greim's command to carry out the offensive. This included elements of KG 1, KG 3, KG 4, KG 27, KG 51, KG 53, KG 55 and KG 100. Three main targets had been selected – the huge GAZ automobile plant at Gorkiy (today's Nizhniy Novgorod), the rubber plant at Yaroslavl and the oil refinery at Saratov.

The Germans also prepared massive air attacks against the important rail junction at Kursk with the aim of blocking the build-up of Soviet

A formation of Heinkel He 111 bombers. This sturdy aircraft remained the backbone of the Luftwaffe bomber arm throughout the war – from 1939, when it dropped some of the first bombs of the war against Polish airfields until 1944 when it carried V-1 flying bombs which were launched against the British Isles.

The Air Raids Against Gorkiy in June 1943

The vast, modern GAZ Automobile Plant – Gorkovskiy Avtomobilniy Zavod, which had been built between 1931-1932 – was the prime target of Generaloberst Robert Ritter von Greim's strategic bomber offensive in the early summer of 1943.

The first attack, on the night of 4/5 June, took the Soviets totally by surprise. The air raid sirens sounded at 23.40 hours. Shortly afterward, 128 He 111s and Ju 88s from III./KG 1, KG 3, II. and III./KG 4, KG 27, II. and III./KG 55 and I./KG 100 arrived to drop 179 tons of bombs against GAZ No. 1, Molotov. Many workshops were wooden conctructions, and these caught fire. With the water supply severed through bomb hits, the flames spread rapidly and soon a large parts of the plant were burning. The blacksmith workshop, the chassis workshop, the main conveyer and parts of the spring workshop were destroyed, as were several living compounds and the child nursery. The effect of this first attack can be described as nothing short of a disaster for GAZ No. 1.

The Luftwaffe returned to attack the repair works over two subsequent nights, causing even more widespread destruction. During repeated air attacks between 4 and 22 June 1943, all of the plant's 50 buildings, more than 9,000 metres of conveyers, 5,900 units of process equipment and 8,000 engines were destroyed or damaged. Russian authorities still have not officially disclosed how many people were killed in these air attacks, but the Germans estimated their number at 15,000.

However, owing to incorrect information, the Germans concentrated their attacks against GAZ No.1, the Molotov factory, where only the light tank T-70 was produced. Roughly more than half the Soviet Union's production of light tanks - 5,134 out of a total of 9,375 in 1942 – was made at GAZ No. 1. But the T-70 offered a considerably lesser threat to the Germans, when compared with the more powerful T-34 medium tank. These were manufactured at GAZ No. 112, the Krasnoye-Sormovo tank works, which were only lightly affected by the German raids.

The aerial bombings of GAZ No. 1 undoubtedly dealt a heavy blow against Soviet light tank production, mainly owing to the fact that the first attack caught the defenders unprepared. During subsequent attacks, the air defence became increasingly effective. Meanwhile other major industrial plants in Gorkiy were engaged in repair works and assisted in light tank production. After six weeks, production was resumed at GAZ No. 1, and by 18 August 1943 the plant was fully back in operations. During the fourth quarter of 1943, the Molotov factory superceded its production plan by 121 per cent, and the annual production plan was completed ahead of time, on 17 December 1943. GAZ No. 112 in Gorkiy actually increased T-43 production from 2,718 in 1942 to 2,851 in 1943 and 3,619 in 1944.

Ju 88 A-4s of 9./KG 76 on a mission over the Eastern Front.

The Germans also failed to inflict any damage to other important plants in Gorkiy such as Artillery Factory No. 92 or the Gorkiy Aircraft Construction Plant, where the La-5 and the brand new La-5FN fighter were produced.

In all, the Luftwaffe offensive against Gorkiy had no significant effect on the Red Army's armoured forces.

La-5 fighters on the production line. During the second half of 1942, a total of 1,129 La-5s were manufactured. These were produced at the Gorkiy Aircraft Construction Plant, which supplied 7,691 aircraft during the war – one fourth of all fighter manufactured in the Soviet Union between 1941 and 1945.

defensive forces. In order to strike such a target effectively, the operation had to be carried out in daylight. On 22 May, 64 Ju 87s, 29 Bf 110 fighter-bombers, ten Fw 190 *Schlacht* aircraft and eight He 111s were dispatched against Kursk, together with all available escort fighters from I./JG 26 and JG 51.[17] The aircraft were sent out in two waves. The first wave, consisting of 68 bombers and 60 escort fighters, managed to carry out a successful attack from 4,000 metres altitude avoiding interception by Soviet fighters. These had been alerted too late, and the result was devastating. The whole rail junction area was turned into an inferno. But the scrambling Soviet fighters – from 16 VA and 101 IAD/PVO – took a terrible revenge on the second attack wave. Led by *St.Lt.* Viktor Bashkirov, seven Yak-7B pilots of 519 IAP claimed six Ju 87s shot down in one fierce attack against I./St.G 1. In fact, eleven German aircraft, including nine Ju 87s from I./St.G 1 were shot down.[18]

It took the Soviets no more than between 10 and 12 hours to bring the rail junction back to work. This compelled the OKL to prepare a more elaborate attack against the same target.

Dubbed Operation *Carmen*, this air operation against Kursk was intended to be a so-called 'star attack' – meaning that various aircraft would attack simultaneously from all directions in order to confuse the defence. According to the instructions, the marshalling yards at Kursk were to be attacked relentlessly during the hours of daylight on 2 June and the following night. Both *Luftflotte* 6 and *Fliegerkorps* VIII of *Luftflotte* 4 would participate in the attack.

The first attack wave, consisting of around 100 bombers with 30 escort fighters, arrived at 04.00 hours. But this time the defenders were ready. Soviet fighters from 16 VA and 101 IAD/PVO intercepted the German formations, and managed to tear these apart and ward off the whole attack against Kursk. A total of around 100 bombers with 55 escort fighters participated in the second and third waves at 05.40 hours and 07.30 hours. These became involved in a bitter fight with 86 Soviet fighters and many aircraft were shot down on both sides. Fifty-five German aircraft managed to break through to the target area, but they arrived singly or in small groups and their bombs scattered, hardly inflicting any serious damage to the rail installations. The last German attempt to break through to the rail junction at Kursk was made shortly before 11.00 hours and involved another 100 bombers or so with fighter escort. These were met by 205 Soviet fighters which, once again, succeeded in fending off the bombing raid. Following this failure, all further daylight operations against Kursk were cancelled. In total, *Luftflotte* 6 had dispatched 95 bombers, 64 *Zerstörer* and 299 fighters, with a further 138 bombers from *Fliegerkorps* VIII to participate in these morning raids.[19] Seventeen of these aircraft were shot down and destroyed and another eight sustained severe battle damage.[20] A subsequent nocturnal raid with 202 bombers against the same target failed to inflict any major damage on the marshalling yards.

These two major setbacks over Kursk contributed to the OKL's decision to refrain from carrying out any air operations in daylight against the Soviet rear area during Operation *Zitadelle*. Undoubtedly, this would

---

Clash of Titans

At dawn on 5 July 1943, the world's two greatest military powers, Germany and the Soviet Union, had concentrated the cream of their forces for the Battle of the Kursk Bulge. The immense power concentration is evident in view of the fact that for Operation Barbarossa – the invasion of the Soviet Union along a 1,600 kilometre front line stretching from the Baltic Sea to the Black Sea in June 1941 – the Germans dispatched 3,000 tanks and 2,600 aircraft. For Operation Zitadelle, a larger armoured force and almost as many aircraft were dispatched against two small fronts which in total measured no more than around 240 kilometres.

On the northern flank, the German attack force constituted General Walter Model's 9. Armee of Generalfeldmarschall Günther von Kluge's Army Group Centre (Heeresgruppe Mitte) – posed to strike a blow towards the south from the German-held Orel Bulge. In this sector, air support for Operation Zitadelle was to be provided mainly by Generalmajor Paul Deichmann's 1. Fliegerdivision, supplemented by a number of units directly under the control of Generaloberst Robert Ritter von Greim's Luftflotte 6. Meanwhile, German 2. Panzerarmee was tasked to hold a defensive posture along the northern and eastern flanks of the Orel Bulge, where the Soviet Bryansk and Western fronts were lined up in relative passivity.

General Armii Konstantin Rokossovskiy's Central Front, with six armies, was assigned with the task of defending the northern two-thirds of the Kursk Bulge. However, two of these armies were positioned along the western face – opposed to German 2. Armee (not to be confused with 2. Panzerarmee) – and were not available to counter Model's strike. The Central Front would receive direct air support from 16 VA, commanded by General-Leytenant Sergey Rudenko.

On the southern flank, Generalfeldmarschall Erich von Manstein's Army Group South (Heeresgruppe Süd) marched up Generaloberst Hermann Hoth's 4. Panzerarmee to the west of Belgorod, ready to strike northwards, and Generaloberst Werner Kempf's Armeeabteilung Kempf between Belgorod and Kharkov, prepared to cross the Donets and advance towards the north-east. Air support would be provided mainly by Generalmajor Hans Seidemann's Fliegerkorps VIII of Luftflotte 4 – plus a number of units directly subordinated to Luftflotte 4, which since 13 June 1943 was commanded by General der Flak Otto Dessloch.

Von Manstein's forces were faced by General Armii Nikolay Vatutin's Voronezh Front, which was supported by General-Leytenant Stepan Krasovskiy 2 VA. In addition, the aviation of of General-Leytenant Vladimir Sudets's 17 VA – mainly assigned to support the Southwestern Front, which held defensive positions farther to the south – could be brought in to support the Voronezh Front's left flank.

In total, more than half a million German and 700,000 Soviet troops, with nearly 3,700 tanks and SPGs on the German side and 2,313 on the Soviet side, would be hurled against each other. In the skies above, the largest air battle in history – involving 2,300 German and around 3,000 Soviet aircraft - would commence.

These forces were grouped as follows:

Northern flank

	German	Soviet
Troops	335,000	331,000*
Tanks and SPGs	1,969	1,029*
Aircraft1,	100	1,151

Southern flank

	German	Soviet
Troops	224,033	368,000*
Tanks and SPGs	1,747	1,284*
Aircraft	1,200	1,641**

To the Soviet figures should be added the bulk of the ADD, with approximately 400 night bombers.

Also of great importance was the unparalleled Soviet concentration of artillery. At dawn on 5 July 1943, the Soviets had lined up no fewer than one million guns and mortars in the Kursk Bulge – with a slight overweight in the Central Front. These guns would constitute one of the major trump cards on the Soviet side, and thus also one of the Luftwaffe's primary attack targets.

* Included are only forces available to confront the immediate German attack. In addition, both Central and Voronezh fronts had considerable reserves. Including these reserves, the Central Front could muster 510,000 troops and 1,600 tanks and SPGs, and the Voronezh Front mustered 466,000 troops and 1,700 tanks and SPGs.
** 1,030 of 2 VA and 611 of 17 VA.

Generalmajor Hans Seidemann commanded Fliegerkorps VIII during Operation Zitadelle. Seidemann received his training as a fighter pilot in the Soviet Union – at Lipetsk, where Germany was allowed to establish a secret military training centre in the 1920s. Trained as a general staff officer, Seidemann was posted to the General Staff of the Luftwaffe from 1935. He was Wolfram Freiherr von Richthofen's Chief of Staff in the Condor Legion during the Spanish Civil War, and in Fliegerkorps VIII in 1940. When von Richthofen was sent to Italy in May 1943 to assume command of Luftflotte 2, Seidemann was brought in from his position as commander of the Luftwaffe forces in Tunisia to lead Fliegerkorps VIII. He would retain this position during the remainder of the war. Seidemann passed away on 21 December 1967, at the age of 65. (Photo: Martin Pegg.)

The Luftwaffe and the VVS in July 1943

From the second half of 1942 and onwards, the Soviet industry was out-producing Germany in military equipment. This photograph shows a row of Yak-7B fighters on the assembly line.

Although Soviet aviation enjoyed a slight superiority in quantity at Kursk on the eve of Operation Zitadelle, this was more than balanced by German advantages regarding quality. Having been the case since Germany invaded the USSR in 1941, this was the main reason for the appalling losses which the Soviet aviation had sustained in the past two years. Indeed, between the summer of 1941 and the summer of 1943, the Soviet Air Force went through a significant improvement. But so did the Luftwaffe, and the gap narrowed only slowly.

By mid-1943, Soviet aircraft output was generally about one year behind their German counterparts in terms of quality – mainly because of differing quality between the Russian manufacturers. The VVS air armies which were lined up for the Battle of Kursk had replaced all their their old Polikarpov fighters, and the LaGG-3s and MiG-3s of 1941. However, the most common Soviet fighters at Kursk in

the summer of 1942 – the Yak-1, Yak-7B and La-5 – can be regarded as more or less on pair with the German Messerschmitt Bf 109 E or Bf 109 F fighters of 1940-1942. By mid-1943, these types had been replaced in the Luftwaffe by the more modern Bf 109 G-4 and G-6 and Fw 190, equipped with stronger engines and more powerful armament.

Not even the new Yakovlev fighter which had entered service during the Battle of Stalingrad, the Yak-9, could be regarded as equal to the Bf 109 G or the Fw 190. There was just one Soviet fighter which could compete with the best of the Luftwaffe, and that was the La-5FN. Equipped with an ASh-82FN engine – rated at 1,470 horse power – the La-5FN actually was faster than both the Bf 109 G and the Fw 190 A and more manoeuvrable than the latter. But on the eve of the Battle of Kursk, the La-5FN had only recently been taken into service. Only a few La-5FNs saw action during the great battle in July 1943 – mainly with Polkovnik Valentin

The Messerschmitt Bf 109 remained in service with the Luftwaffe throughout the Second World War. The Bf 109 G-6 version, seen in this photograph, was the latest version and entered service shortly prior to Operation Zitadelle.

A Lavochkin La-5FN fighter. With improved aerodynamics, weight reduction and equipped with the new M-82FN fuel-injected engine – rated at 1,470 horse power – the La-5FN was not only a significantly improved version of the La-5; for the first time the Soviets had designed a fighter which was superior to any Luftwaffe fighter at that time. In the summer of 1943, a captured La-5FN was flown by German test pilot Hans-Werner Lerche. He found that the speed and acceleration of the La-5FN was about equal to the German Bf 109 G and Fw 190 A at low altitude. It possessed a higher rate of roll and a smaller radius of turn than the Bf 109 and a better climb rate than the Fw 190 A-8. Other tests showed the La-5FN to be faster than both German fighters.

Ukhov's 3 GIAD – and not even this aircraft's singular performance would save its pilots from sustaining heavy losses.

The latter was caused by several subjective factors, of which the most dominant was inadequate Soviet pilot training. A total of 14,700 Soviet aircraft were lost in 1942, along with thousands of pilots. In order to keep pace with these losses, it was necessary to maintain the reduced pilot training schemes which had been adopted as a consequence of the heavy losses in 1941. The 13,383 Soviet pilots who were trained in 1942 received an average of between 13 and 15 flight hours. Although the pilot training slowly improved, Soviet fighter and Shturmovik pilots were sent to front-line service after only 18 flight hours, and bomber pilots after just 15 flight hours.

Although the Luftwaffe had scaled back its pilot training scheme – to around 70 hours as compared to around 120 before the war – the gap was immense. Moreover, the rate of inexperienced pilots in Soviet air units was alarmingly high. In the Shturmovik units which took part in the Battle of Kursk, only 7 per cent of pilots had any combat experience at all prior to 5 July 1943. The situation was dramatically different on the German side, where a vast majority of the pilots were experienced. One Staffel which took part in Operation Zitadelle, 5./JG 3 Udet, may serve as an illuminating example: among eleven pilots on its roster on 4 July 1943, ten had attained personal victories in air combat: Kirschner (148), Grünberg (37), Schütte (35), Bringmann (20), Kloss (15), Dohse (11), Mohn (9), Bohatsch (3), Scheibe (3), and Lucks (1).

The gap in skills and experience was evident also at command level. In Rudenko, Krasovskiy and Sudets, the Soviets had highly seasoned aviation commanders at Kursk, and General-Polkovnik Aleksandr Novikov, the C-in-C of VVS KA, was personally responsible for much of the modernisation of the Soviet aviation in 1942. But at medium level, a lack of experience caused several mistakes to be made on the Soviet side, leading to significantly flawed air operations – of which we shall see many examples in the following.

Ahead of Operation Zitadelle, the Luftwaffe improved its anti-tank aviation. A number of Bf 110s and Ju 87s were equipped with 37 mm Flak 18 cannons, and the standard Panzerjäger, the Hs 129, received the new 30 mm MK 103 cannon, which had a higher rate of fire than the MK 101. Sch.G 1 also replaced its Bf 109 ground-attack aircraft with Fw 190s, which were able to sustain more ground fire. On the Soviet side, the new PTAB cumulative bomb was employed for the use against armour just on the eve of Operation Zitadelle. Also, an increasing number of Il-2s were equipped with a rear machine gun – a significant improvement as compared with the single-seat Shturmovik.

One special feature of the aerial warfare on the Eastern Front was the use of single-engined biplane trainers in the role of nocturnal harassment bombers with the main purpose of exhausting the enemy by carrying out relentless attacks at night. This had been adopted by the Soviets in 1941, and the operations by these aircraft soon proved to be quite effective in depriving the German troops of their badly needed sleep. In the autumn of 1942, the Luftwaffe copied the Soviet method, and the Luftwaffe formations earmarked for the support of Operation Zitadelle included nine such Staffeln – six with Störkampfgruppe Luftflotte 6 and three with

Störkampfgruppe Luftflotte 4. While the main component in the Soviet light night bomber regiments was the Polikarpov U-2, the Störkampfstaffeln used a variety of trainers – mainly the Ar 66, He 46, Go 145 and Fw 58, but also a few Junkers W 34 were used, together with Ju 87s and outdated Do 17 twin-engined bombers.

But otherwise, the air forces on both sides operated at Kursk in July 1943 with mostly the same aircraft types as during the Battle of Stalingrad. The Luftwaffe's main bombers were still the He 111 and the Ju 88 A-4, while the standard dive-bomber was the Ju 87. On the Soviet side, the Il-2 remained the single ground-attack aircraft, while most day bomber units operated the twin-engined Pe-2. Two bomber Diviziyas (221 BAD and 244 BAD) were equipped with the US designed Douglas A-20/Boston; a handful of Airacobras in two fighter regiments were the only other Lend Lease aircraft to see service with the VVS during Operation Zitadelle. The main component of the ADD remained the Il-4, which flew primarily at night time – just like in the past two years together with the U-2 biplane 'light night bombers' of the air armies.

One significant difference as compared with the previous year however was that the Luftwaffe's tactical reconnaissance units successively phased out their more vulnerable Hs 126s and even Fw 189s for Bf 109s and Bf 110s. Despite all lingering shortcomings, the VVS was in fact becoming an increasingly dangerous adversary to Hermann Göring's air force.

Ahead of Operation Zitadelle, the Luftwaffe improved its anti-tank aviation. A number of Bf 110s and Ju 87s were equipped with 37mm Flak 18 cannons. This photograph shows a Ju 87 G equipped with one of these cannons under each wing.

benefit the Soviets greatly, since the strong reinforcements which they eventually brought forward during the main battle in July was a key to their defensive victory.

Quite humiliating to von Greim, the War Diary of the German High Command for that day paid greater attention to the effect of a Soviet air attack against Orel than to Operation *Carmen*: "*The enemy Air Force attacked Orel with 115 aircraft. Heavy losses among the population. The electricity plant is severely damaged, probably out of action for a prolonged period. Bomb hits on the highway to Bolkhov, railway station buildings, water supply, telephone lines, Army Supply Store and Army Hospital.*" [21] A whole train loaded with one million rations and part of an Army ration dump were bombed out. [22] Meanwhile, Il-2s of 1 ShAK attacked German airfields in daylight, this time without sustaining any losses to *Luftwaffe* fighters. [23]

Owing to their healthy respect for Soviet fighters, the Germans decided to carry out *Generaloberst* von Greim's strategic bomber offensive exclusively during the hours of darkness. By this time the small Soviet night fighter force operated only with the guidance of searchlights on the ground, and with relatively simple ground radar station assistance. In consequence, only light *Luftwaffe* losses could be expected if the attacks were carried out under the cover of night.

The offensive commenced on the night of 4/5 June, when 128 bombers attacked the GAZ automobile plant at Gorkiy, where Soviet tanks were manufactured. The first attack caused vast destruction on the ground and claimed a large number of lives among the civilian population. Nevertheless, five bombers were shot down. [24] The following two nights, 300 bombers were dispatched against the same target, this time without losing more than

a single aircraft. When the German bombers returned on the night of 7/8 June, the night fighters of 142 IAD/PVO attacked with absolute desperation. *St.Lt.* Boris Tabarchuk of 722 IAP/142 IAD rammed II./KG 4's He 111, '5J+KN', which carried *Major* Cranz. But while Tabarchuk managed to bring down his fighter for an emergency landing, the pilot in *Major* Cranz's He 111, *Uffz.* Heinz Festner, succeeded in nursing his crippled aircraft back to the airfield at Orel-West.

In response to these devastating air attacks, three Soviet air armies – 1 VA, 2 VA and 15 VA – mounted another series of large-scale attacks against German air bases during the evening of 8 June. But this time the German defenders were just as prepared as the Soviet fighters had been at Kursk on 2 June. Near Orel, the whole of JG 51 fell down upon a formation of 70 Soviet aircraft – Il-2s and escort fighters – and claimed 19 *Shturmoviks* and 21 escort fighters shot down against only one loss of their own. According to a German report, "… *hardly any of [the Soviet aircraft] tried to fly in defensive curves.*" [25] This, and the result of the air combat, would indicate that the mission was flown largely by inadequately trained Soviet airmen. An attempt to repeat the attacks on 10 June resulted in further heavy losses to the Soviets.

In the meantime, 138 He 111s had attacked the rubber works at Yaroslavl on the night of 9/10 June, at a cost of three aircraft. [26] On the night of 10/11 June, 126 bombers of *Luftflotte* 6 were again sent against Gorkiy, and the following night the oil refinery at Saratov was targeted. This objective was struck again on the nights of 13th, 15th and 16th of June.

Finally, these strategic operations started to take a mounting toll of the attackers, since the Soviet night fighters could take advantage of the brighter summer nights. The raid against Gorkiy on the night of 13/14 June resulted in the loss of Knight's Cross holder *Hptm.* Helmut Putz, *Staffelkapitän* of 4./KG 27. On the night of 20/21 June, KG 1 lost two, KG 3 one and III./KG 27 three bombers, while a He 111 of KG 55 barely managed to evade an attack by a Soviet night fighter. [27] One of the He 111s was destroyed through another *taran,* performed by *St.Serzh.* Ivan Ushkalov of 959 IAP. The next night, when 101 bombers flew against Gorkiy, two He 111s were shot down by night fighters. [28] Thus ended the relatively short-lived German strategic bomber offensive on the Eastern Front. The attacks against Gorkiy could have been a great success from the German point of view, had it not been for faulty intelligence reports. As it was now, the production of the dangerous T-34 medium tank was hardly affected. In early July, *Generaloberst* von Greim's bombers were now prepared for daylight operations in support of Operation *Zitadelle*.

A Bf 109 G-6, apparently with overpainted spinner rings, believed to have belonged to the 13.(Slovak)/JG 52.

"We will make the enemy pay in blood!"

While the Soviets were aware of the German intentions, they were uncertain as to the attack date. However, on the southern flank, they managed to get a fairly good picture of the German build-up. In late June 1943, Soviet air reconnaissance detected the build-up of German motorised forces in the Belgorod-Kharkov area. Although the Germans made their movements mainly at night, the Soviet air crews were able to establish the concentration of strong armoured forces opposite Tomarovka, Zybino and Borisovka in the sector north-west of Belgorod on 1 July. The previous night, airmen flying U-2s of 17 VA's 262 NBAD had reported the spotting of 200 motor vehicles moving north along the roads leading northward from Belgorod. The following night, the same fliers reported approximately 700 motor vehicles on the same roads. The next night, the crew of a Boston from 244 BAD detected heavy road traffic between Kharkov and Belgorod.

The Soviets also noted the arrival of more than 300 German aircraft to the airfields in the Belgorod-Kharkov area in the afternoon of 4 July. This was Stab, I. and III./JG 52, St.G 2 and St.G 77 which arrived from Fliegerkorps I in the Kuban bridgehead in the last minute.

Resigned to the obvious fact that the Soviets had detected their build-up and were prepared to meet the onslaught, the Germans decided to launch a limited preparatory attack against the Voronezh Front's combat outposts on the day before the major attack. At 16.00 hours on 4 July, eighty Ju 87 Stukas struck down on the positions of Soviet 52nd Guards Rifle Division north-west of Belgorod. As these aircraft turned for home, advanced battalions from the 47. Panzerkorps on the 4. Panzerarmee's left (western) flank attacked. They ran straight into a determined and well-equipped defence. Bitter fighting raged for several hours before the Germans were able to secure their objectives.

Well aware of the difficulties that lay ahead, Hitler sent an order of the day intended to boost morale among his two army group commanders who would launch the fateful offensive the next day. It read:

'The armies scheduled to participate in the attack have been provided with all the weapons that German ingenuity and technology can produce. Personnel strengths have been raised to the highest levels possible. The supply of ammunition and fuel have been secured in sufficient quantities for this and future operations. The Luftwaffe has concentrated all of its strength to destroy the enemy's air capability, to bombard his firing positions, and support the infantrymen with continuous sorties.'

Indeed the Soviets were prepared to meet the onslaught. During the fighting on 4 July, they had seized a German soldier who revealed that the offensive would commence at dawn on 5 July.

Nikita Khrushchyov, the political advisor of General Armii Vatutin at the Voronezh Front, immediately called Moscow to forward the news. Shortly afterward, Stalin phoned back and asked Khrushchyov what his advice was.

"The commander [Vatutin] and I have been exchanging opinions, and we are very optimistic. We are just as glad that the Germans are opening an offensive tomorrow," Khrushchyov replied.

"Why?" asked Stalin.

"Because the defensive positions are solid, and we will make the enemy pay in blood when he tries to break through!"

Marshal Aleksandr Vasilyevskiy, the Stavka representative to the Voronezh Front, authorised the defenders to commence the counterpreparation. The great battle could begin.

Awaiting battle orders, these Il-2s are lined up at a Soviet first-line airfield.

Meanwhile, the Soviet aviation continued its offensive against rail targets in the German rear area. These attacks were supplemented by increased partisan activity. Owing to Hitler's repeated postponements of Operation *Zitadelle*, the Soviets were provided with an extended period to carry out these attacks – with consequences to the German transport system which far bypassed the effect of the *Luftwaffe* attacks against Kursk and other rail targets in the Soviet rear area. Between 1 April and 4 July 1943, the ADD performed 9,400 sorties against rail targets. [29]

Oberst Hermann Teske, the German officer in charge of rail transportation in *Heeresgruppe Mitte*'s sector, summarised the effect of the Soviet anti-rail operations in May and June 1943: "*The Soviets aimed their air and partisan attacks at the points of main effort, which in this case meant the important railroad stations at Gomel, Orsha and Minsk, as well as the critical short stretch of track between Zhlobin – Gomel. In May alone that section of railroad came under attack sixty-nine times, resulting in 156 hours of blockage on the single-track line and 222 hours along the double-track line. We also lost thirty-five locomotives and 106 cars.*

'In June, the last month of the strategic concentration, we saw another increase in troop movements for [German] attack units. Simultaneously, the number of interruptions in traffic and partisan raids increased to an average of twenty-four per day, culminating in a loss of 298 locomotives, 1,222 cars and forty-four bridges throughout Army Group Center's area." [30]

Teske registered 94 Soviet air attacks against rail targets in *Heeresgruppe Mitte*'s sector in April, 159 in May and 123 in June 1943. Through numerous counter-actions, such as re-routing and daytime-only traffic, the Germans

managed to limit the effect of these attacks against their supply system. But it was inevitable that the strikes against their rail installations put a severe constraint on the subsequent battle operations. *General der Flieger* Friedrich Kless, Chief of Staff of *Luftflotte* 6, later wrote: "*Towards the end of June, the total stocks of B 4 (89-Octane aviation fuel) dropped to 4,886 tons; daily consumption throughout June had Aaveraged 287 tons. Most of the B 4 stockpiles existed in the area affected by Operation Citadel. During June, against a total consumption of 8,634 tons of B 4, only 5,722 tons had been delivered. During the same month, the total consumption of C 3 (94-Octane aviation fuel) used by our Fw 190s had been 1,079 tons, as compared to 441 tons delivered. [...]*

"We had to introduce 'fuel tactics'. Any given main-effort operation found its strength influenced more by the quantity of fuel required than by the number of [aircraft] assigned. We consciously denied air support to ground units in many instances where the situation would normally have been characterised as tense. Only through such harsh measures could Luftflotte 6 *provide fully sufficient force whenever the situation became critical and the battle rose to a climax.*" [31]

Whereas the *Luftwaffe*'s raids against Kursk and Soviet industrial plants in June 1943 had only a limited impact on the Soviet war effort, the Soviet air and partisan attacks against the German rail network undoubtedly had a strongly negative effect on the German ability to build up forces ahead of the Battle of Kursk. Nevertheless, the forces which the *Wehrmacht* marched up on both sides of the Kursk Bulge at dawn on 5 July 1943 was still the most powerful concentration of German military forces ever assembled at one point. The same may be said regarding the Soviet side.

Chapter Three

5 July: North and South

5 July 1943: The Southern Flank

At 01.10 hours (German time) On the morning of 5 July, the Soviet artillery opened a massive barrage against German positions in the Belgorod sector. Shortly afterwards, the German artillery opened up with full force. While this artillery duel raged, the commanders of 2 VA and 17 VA received orders to launch the pre-emptive blow against Luftflotte 4's airfields which had been planned two months in advance. Thus the most famous air battle on the Eastern Front would commence.

At the airfield near Shumakovo, south-east of Kursk, eighteen Il-2s of 241 ShAP/291 ShAD took to the air and formed up for their flight towards the south. Their target was the airfield at Mikoyanovka, some 56 kilometres south-west of Belgorod.

Further to the south-east, and around 100 kilometres to the east of the front lines at Belgorod, other *Shturmoviks* took off and formed up. At Glinev aerodrome near Novyy Oskol, 292 ShAD's 820 ShAP sent thirty Il-2s into the sky. At an airfield near Dubkiy, north-west of Valuyki, the ground personnel watched with excitement as eighteen Il-2s from 266 ShAD's 66 ShAP and 735 ShAP left the runway. Even further to the south, the air at Pokrovskoye was filled with noise as 17 VA's 305 ShAD sent eighteen Il-2s of 237 ShAP into the air. All sixty-six *Shturmoviks* flew against German airfields in the Kharkov area. En route to their targets, the Il-2s were joined by their fighter escort.

The northern attack force, 241 ShAP, was assigned with an escort composed of 18 Yak-7B from 737 IAP of the same 291 ShAD.

The 48 Il-2s of 2 VA's 266 ShAD and 292 ShAD, which were tasked to attack the two airfields Pomerki and Sokolniki north of Kharkov, were escorted by 40 Yak-1s of 247 IAP and 270 IAP. At Olshana, 25 kilometres south-west of Pokrovskoye, ten La-5s of 17 VA's 31 IAP took off and joined the 18 Il-2s of 17 VA's 237 ShAP which flew against Rogan air base south-east of Kharkov. This was the second early take-off that morning. Sixteen La-5s of 164 IAP had already left Olshana and, by this time, were already in the vicinity of the front lines. Simultaneously, twelve La-5s of 40 GIAP had taken off from Oboyan.

Soviet aerial reconnaissance had detected the presence of 150 German aircraft at Kharkov-Rogan. It had been established that from first light, there was always an alert flight of fighters ready to scramble. 164 IAP's mission was

to circle above Rogan, thus preventing these fighters from taking off. 237 ShAP's Il-2s and their escort from 31 IAP meanwhile made their approach flight at only 400 metres altitude so that any German radar station in the area would not detect them. (In fact there was a German *Freya* radar station operating at Kharkov of which we shall learn more later.) Strict radio silence was ordered. When they crossed the front line, half the *Shturmoviks* climbed to 1,200 metres while four of 31 IAP's La-5s increased speed and left the other aircraft behind; their task was to join 164 IAP in the blockade mission.

237 ShAP was instructed to perform the attack divided into two groups. Led by *Kpt.* G. J. Tsygankov, the first group would attack from an altitude of 1,000-1,200 metres. The Soviets calculated that this would draw the attention of the flak gunners from the second group, which would perform its attack at treetop-level. The Il-2s were loaded with 500 kg fragmentation bombs and RS-132 rocket projectiles, which was intended to cause maximum damage among the rows of parked German aircraft.

A similar operation was planned against Mikoyanovka, which was to be blocked by veteran pilots of 40 GIAP, led by the ace *Mayor* Moisey Tokarev.

It was a well-prepared operation, and it had a good chance of dealing *Fliegerkorps* VIII a devastating blow. But circumstances would shred the whole plan, for the Soviet operation was ill-fated from the onset. The intended blockade of the German fighter airfields became a failure. Soviet aerial reconnaissance had detected large numbers of German fighters – in fact, most of JG 52 – at Mikoyanovka only two days previously, but on the eve of *Zitadelle*, the majority of these aircraft were shifted closer to the front line, to Ugrim. Kharkov-Rogan was indeed the main base of II./JG 3 *Udet*, but due to a lack in coordination, the sixteen La-5s of 164 IAP arrived over this airfield more than half an hour before the *Shturmoviks* attacked. In consequence, the La-5s were forced to return because they ran out of fuel before the Il-2s had arrived. Thus, the Soviet fighters proved no obstacle to the take-off of the German fighters, which took place from around 03.00 hours onwards – around a half hour before the *Shturmoviks* attacked.

The following air battle is well known, but misunderstood in most historical accounts. It is commonly held that the German *Freya* radar stations which had been established at Belgorod and Kharkov in the spring of 1943 provided the Germans with an early warning which settled the fate for the

Soviet airmen, and the figure of 120 aircraft shot down by *Fliegerkorps* VIII's fighter pilots in the subsequent battles frequently appears in accounts which are based on German figures. First of all, the latter is not true, even according to German documents.

Indeed, the *Freya* radar spotted some of the Soviet formations before the attack, and at Bessonovka and Ugrim south-west of Belgorod, JG 52 was scrambled. But the main Soviet mistake was to launch the *Shturmovik* attack at a time when *Fliegerkorps* VIII was sending its air units into the skies in order to deal the first strikes against the Soviet defence positions. Thus, at 03.10 hours, II./JG 3 took off from Kharkov-Rogan for a free-hunt mission.[32] Fifteen minutes later, II./KG 55's He 111s took off from the same airfield for a bombing mission with SD 2 fragmentation bombs against Soviet troops positions north of Belgorod.[33]

In fact, the Voronezh Front's artillery barrage also had the effect of reducing the effect of the Soviet air strike against the German airfields, since it compelled *Generalmajor* Seidemann to send his bomber units into the air earlier than planned. *Obstlt.* Walter Lehwess-Litzmann, the commander of KG 3 *Blitz*, recalled:

"In the morning of 5 July the troops who were prepared for the offensive experienced an unpleasant surprise: the Soviet forces opened the battle with an unexpected artillery barrage against the troop formations. I had just gathered my *Gruppenkommandeure* to assign them with their last instructions when I received an excited phone call which gave me revised orders. We were told to take off immediately, although it still was dark, and attack the Soviet artillery positions."[34]

En route to their target, 237 ShAP's formation met a large formation of German aircraft – bombers with fighter escort. We can only imagine how the Il-2 pilots – of which all but *Kpt.* Tsyankov and one other aviator was out on their very first combat mission with an Il-2! – must have felt when they saw these airborne *Luftwaffe* aircraft which they were supposed to strike by surprise on the ground. However, this will never be known since only a few of those *Shturmovik* fliers would survive the mission.

To the north, 241 ShAP with its Yak-7B escort from 737 IAP fared even worse: they were intercepted by a group of Bf 109s from III./JG 3 just as they crossed the front-line north-east of Belgorod. The German fighters

Soviet Il-2 fliers after an apparently successful mission.

struck down from above on the eighteen Il-2s, which flew at around 400 metres altitude, and shot down two of these. Just as the eighteen Yak-7Bs were about to intervene, another formation of Bf 109s – 2./JG 52 led by *Oblt.* Paul-Heinrich Dähne – dived down to perform a classic fighter attack. Dähne and one of his pilots destroyed two Il-2s and then attacked the Soviet fighters, claiming two of these shot down. The terrified Soviet pilots formed a defensive circle, and in that moment, a third group of Bf 109s – this time from 7./JG 52 – appeared on the scene. These had been scrambled from Ugrim only fifteen minutes earlier, and now hurled themselves against the Soviet aircraft.[35] *Lt.* Erich Hartmann opened up with all arms against an Il-2 and sent it towards the ground as a blazing torch. When the battle was over, the German fighter pilots had claimed six Il-2s and eight Soviet fighters shot down. 241 ShAP actually lost seven Il-2s.[36] At Mikoyanovka aerodrome, no one noticed any Soviet air attack.

Meanwhile, II./JG 3's Bf 109 pilots were vectored towards 237 ShAP's formation. Others attacked the four La-5s of 31 IAP which had rushed

Il-2s ready for battle.

A Lavochkin La-5 fighter. Developed in 1942 as a successor of the LaGG-3 in-line fighter, which had proven to be inferior to the German Bf 109 F fighters already operating by 1941, the La-5 was a disappointment. On 25 February 1943 famous Soviet aircraft designer Nikolay Polikarpov wrote to Joseph Stalin: "The engagements between the

Me109 G-2 and our Yak and La fighters at the Stalingrad front showed, according to numerous accounts, that the German fighter was far superior to our fighters. The forthcoming spring will bring us even more surprises and troubles if we fail to bring forward a really modern high-speed fighter."

ahead of the others. 237 ShAP was intercepted by ten Bf 109s from 4. and 5./JG 3 right above the Donets River. Four Il-2s – flown by *M.Lt.* Gorodnikov with the gunner *Serzh.* Novitskiy, *M.Lt.* Bykov, *M.Lt.* Truskov with the gunner *Serzh.* Zorin, and *M.Lt.* Rusayevich – were shot down in the first attack. Two of these ended up on the victory list of *Fw.* Hans Grünberg.

More Bf 109s joined in on the slaughter of 237 ShAP's inexperienced fliers. I./JG 52 struck down on them with terrible impact, and the *Gruppenkommandeur, Hptm.* Johannes Wiese claimed three shot down. When the remaining Il-2s approached Rogan, they also flew into the Hungarian fighter group 5/I. *Vadasz osztály*, the *Puma* fighter group commanded by *Örgy.* Aladár Heppes. Having been temporarily brought forward to Varvarovka airfield, the squadron 5/1. *Vadasz század* was held in readiness, while the Bf 109s of 2nd Squadron, 5/2. *Vadasz század*, were scrambled. *Föhadnagy* István Kálmán and *Hadnagy* Miklós Keyneres took off at 03.30 hours and became embroiled in combat with some of 31 IAP's La-5s, in the course of which the two Hungarians lost contact with each other. When the fighter combat was over, Keyneres joined another Hungarian Bf 109 – piloted by *Föhadnagy* Pál Kovacs – and went searching for the approaching Il-2s which had been reported. Keyneres later gave this account of the combat:

"To the east end of city we can see a large amount of *Flak* bursts. This is the best guide. The red-starred aircraft must be there. We spot four Russian ground-attack aircraft calmly approaching the city in close formation, in spite of murderous fire. We fly over burning debris. '*I shot that one down*,' said my wingman, '*and that one, a bit further away!*'

"Great! He has already attained two victories! I dive against the Russian formation. Without any regard, the Flak batteries continue their fire. In their great excitement, the Flak gunners don't pay any attention to the close proximity of our own aircraft. But we ignore their fire. We have our eyes only for the four red-starred aircraft. Then I see that I, myself, have miscalculated. Behind the four Russian aircraft another four were flying. I dived between the two formations but Lady Luck was smiling at --me again.

Hit by German fire, an Il-2 descends in flames..

Troops of the SS Division 'Leibstandarte Adolf Hitler' in action during the Battle of Kursk. German ground troops ran into an unexpectedly stiff Soviet resistance during Operation Zitadelle. This photograph illustrates that the days of the Blitzkrieg were long since gone. (Photo: Horst Mutterlose/Martin Månsson.)

Hadnagy (Leutnant) István Németh of Hungarian 3/1. Közelfelderítő század is showing the wing Shkas machinegun bullets of one of the 237 ShAP Il-2s which came down near Grobly during the dawn operation on 5 July 1943. (János Suttai Koppány's collection via Csaba Becze.)

"The machine on the left side peels off from the rest, with me in hot pursuit. The hunt begins. The Russian pushes close to the ground and escapes, hopping over trees. But we remain clung to his tail. On my right hand side, three Germans are pursuing it too. One of the Germans dives on it, but fails to bring it down. Now my turn has come. I pull up slightly and, from the side, I aim ahead of the engine but hold my fire for another moment. The distance still is too great. Then I squeeze both firing buttons. I pull up in an instant to avoid colliding. I skid out to the right. I get on its left side again and from above and behind I shoot at the cockpit. By now the Russian gunner does not return the fire. From a close distance I open up with the cannon. The machine shudders and hits the ground with its right wing tip. It slides along a creek, violently burning." [37]

By that time, 237 ShAP's route to Rogan was marked by a row of shot down Il-2s. Only six 237 ShAP pilots remained to conduct the attack when the target was reached, and this airfield escaped any harmful destruction. This can not be said for 237 ShAP, which lost thirteen Il-2s in the carnage. [38]

When the dispersed remnants of 237 ShAP withdrew, the airborne fighter pilots of II./JG 3 and I./JG 52 were ready to be vectored towards the Shturmoviks from 66 ShAP and 735 ShAP which tried to reach Pomerki. This group had not only lost contact with its fighter escort – due to accidents and engine trouble, but it force had been reduced to just

14 Il-2s during the approach flight. Eleven of these were shot down. In this clash, II./JG 3's *Oblt.* Joachim Kirschner took credit for four victories – two Il-2s and two Yak-1s. The few Il-2s that managed to attack Pomerki aerodrome – known to the Germans as Kharkov-North – failed to inflict any serious damage.

292 ShAD was lucky to sneak in between the attacks against Rogan and Pomerki. Only a few Bf 109s of II./JG 3 attempted to intercept these thirty Il-2s and their fighter escort. The latter – 270 IAP's Yak-1 pilots – shot down two Bf 109s. One of these ended up on the scoreboard of the ace *Kpt.* Sergey Luganskiy. [39] His victim may have been II./JG 3's *Ofw.* Josef Schütte, an ace with 40 victories, who baled out with severe injuries. Only two of 292 ShAD's Il-2s were shot down. Still the air attack against Sokolniki was also a failure, owing to the lacking experience of the Soviet airmen.

In total, the fighter pilots of *Fliegerkorps* VIII claimed to have shot down 38 Soviet aircraft during the air fighting when 2 VA and 17 VA attempted to attack the German airfields at dawn on 5 July.

As we have seen, the main reason why the attacks against the German airfields early on 5 July failed was because by the time the Soviet aircraft struck, most of *Fliegerkorps* VIII's aircraft were already airborne in order to support the ground offensive – an offensive which was three hours behind schedule. This was due to the Voronezh Front's massive pre-emptive artillery barrage against the German jump-off positions. Although most German troops were in shelters, saving them from sustaining severe losses to the artillery fire, the Soviet artillery barrage delayed the German attack until shortly before five in the morning.

Fliegerkorps VIII's aircraft commenced their attacks by focusing on the concentrations of artillery north-west of Belgorod from where this barrage was fired. Next, the air raids spread to include targeting Soviet infantry combat formations.

At dawn, 4. *Panzerarmee's* II. SS *Panzerkorps* and 48. *Panzerkorps* attacked the Soviet fortifications, with the aim of breaking through towards Oboyan and Kursk in the north. Against the heavily fortified and echeloned Soviet defence positions, air support was more vital than ever. And cooperation between ground and air units worked with perfection. Whenever a Soviet stronghold was identified, the German ground troops could call in air support via *Luftwaffe* liaison officers in the front line. *Generalmajor* Hans Seidemann, who commanded *Fliegerkorps* VIII, described how this worked:

'Providing quick and effective ground support necessitated smoothly functioning communications between the attacking armies, corps, and divisions and the headquarters at *Fliegerkorps* VIII. The *Luftwaffe* had maintained a corps of liaison officers since the beginning of the war, composed of men who had strong experience in ground support operations. As usual during an offensive, we attached these teams directly to Army Group South's corps and division headquarters, and they accompanied their units directly onto the field of battle. There the *Luftwaffe* officers also acted as dive-bomber and fighter guides, using their radios to direct approaching formations to the targets indicated by the ground commanders, correct their fire, and provide updates on the current tactical air situation in the local area. These liaison teams also reported the ground situation, air situation, and any unusual information directly to *Fliegerkorps* VIII every two hours. This procedure kept both the controlling headquarters and the flying formations constantly informed as to the progress of the attack. Two *Luftwaffe* signal communications regiments had installed *Fliegerkorps* VIII's signal network in a manner that permitted airfields to be contacted on two different telephone lines, as well as by telegraph and radio. Thus our available signal equipment was employed to facilitate the mass employment of our flying formations." [40]

This organisation was much more flexible than the organisation for air control on the Soviet side. Although the Soviet pre-planning for the battle had envisioned the dispatch of VVS liaison officers to the ground armies, 2 VA had failed to do so by the time the German attack was opened. "As a result, the control of aviation formations was accomplished from 2 VA's headquarters, that is, isolated from the ground forces. Consequently, air strikes were often late since data concerning the ground situation and air operation targets were transmitted through Front headquarters, which took considerable time." [41]

Radio guidance of fighter operations in the VVS had been pioneered during the Battle of Stalingrad. For command and control of Soviet fighter operations during the Battle of Kursk, radio stations, attached to larger fighter commands, had been located in the immediate vicinity of the front line along probable German offensive axes. However, the men who operated these radio stations were subordinates with no other task than to report the air situation to the higher headquarters of larger fighter commands in the rear. Before the main battle, when the air situation was relatively calm, this worked satisfactorily. But when the skies became filled with hundreds of German aircraft in wave after wave, in rapid succession, this organisation became too cumbersome. In addition, due to negligence in checking the technical condition of these radio stations, two of the stations which were located in the most critical combat zones were in disrepair in the morning of 5 July 1943.

The Soviet after-battle study concludes: '*Deficiencies in organising guidance, reporting, and control of fighter aviation by radio during the battle strongly affected the execution of aviation's most important mission – winning air superiority.*' [42]

Hence, VVS response to the German initial and massive onslaught was both slow and weak. *General-Mayor* Klimov's 5 IAK had been assigned with the task to provide the Soviet ground troops with air cover, but when the attack was initiated, the Soviets had no more than twelve La-5s of 41 GIAP airborne in the area. These were soon joined by eight Yak-7Bs from 508 IAP and thirteen La-5s from 88 GIAP, and they made a heavy impact on at least one *Luftwaffe* formation. 508 IAP struck down on He 111s of I./KG 100 which bombed the village of Dmitriyevka in support of II. SS *Panzerkorps.* *Hptm.* Hansgeorg Bätcher, who commanded 1./KG 100, recalled:

"We encountered a determined Russian fighter opposition right from the onset. During our first mission on 5 July, which was directed against the village of Dmitriyevka – take-off at 03.13 hours – we were attacked by twelve 'LaGGs'. These came from the astern, at an altitude of 3,000 metres, and attacked us like raging hornets, and each of them made two or three individual attacks. Our gunners met them with a concentrated defensive fire. *Uffz.* Saalfrank and *Uffz.* Troyer made an unconfirmed claim of a shot down Russian fighter. But in return, the gunner *Gefreiter* Richard Ebert was wounded when his He 111 was hit by fire from Russian fighters. The crew of *Fw.* Heinz Kaiser was shot down by Russian fighters, and Bollmann's He 111 was so badly damaged that it had to force-land near Varvarovka." [43]

But most other German airmen met no opposition from VVS fighters during their first mission against the Soviet defence positions in the early morning of 5 July 1943. During the first hour of the attack, the Soviets registered no fewer than 400 German aircraft operating over a sector only 32 kilometres wide. The 52nd Guards Rifle Division, which held positions opposed to II. SS *Panzerkorps's* left flank, reported atrocious losses to air

attacks which were conducted in formations of up to 80 aircraft at a time. Immediately to the west of 52nd Guards Rifle Division's positions, the 67th Guards Rifle Division fared even worse – being subject to five *Stukagruppen* which attacked in a massive formation to drop all their bombs in an area of the frontal defences only three kilometres in length and four and a half metres in depth. Following this hellish bombardment, what remained of this division's positions were stormed by *General* Otto von Knobelsdorff's [4] *Panzerkorps* with 3. *Panzer Division,* the *Panzergrenadier Division Grossdeutschland* and the 11. *Panzer Division,* mustering altogether 553 tanks and assault guns for the attack.

On the south-eastern flank, however, things looked different. *General* Werner Kempf's '*Armeeabteilung Kempf*' was assigned to march towards the north-east, across the Donets river at Belgorod. While five German divisions assaulted the 81st Guards Rifle Division of Soviet 7th Guards Army at the Mikhailovka bridgehead east of Belgorod, hardly any aircraft could be seen in the sky above. *Fliegerkorps* VIII concentrated most of its forces to support the 4. *Panzerarmee.* It also took several hours before 17 VA dispatched anything but a few reconnaissance missions to support the 7th Guards Army. The only air combat which is known to have taken place in this sector during the first seven hours of the German offensive occurred when *Uffz.* Rudolf Scheibe of II./JG 3 shot down Douglas A-20Bs from 244 BAD piloted by *Kpt.* Tarovoytov.

In the meantime, the 81st Guards Rifle Division inflicted bloody losses on the attacking German troops. This forced Kempf to cancel the attack in this sector and shift emphasis to a sector farther south. This gives a negative example of the decisive role played by the *Luftwaffe* for the German ground operations.

On the opposite flank, in spite of its huge numerical, technical superiority and the massive air support, 4. *Panzerarmee's* 48. *Panzerkorps* also ran into trouble from the onset. 'Grossdeutschland' mustered 350 tanks and assault guns, the bulk of the *Panzerkorps's* armour, concentrated on a front only three kilometres wide. But this tremendous force almost immediately became bogged down in minefields. Moreover, the entire area was ploughed up by hundreds of Stuka bombs, dropped in such a small area turning the grass fields into a muddy, cratered, moon-like landscape which complicated movements. "*General depression! My high spirits are gone*", wrote

With bandaged a eye - wounded few days earlier in a small accident – the Hungarian Bf 109 pilot János Suttai Koppány of 3/1. Közelfelderítő szazad is posing next to one of the Il-2s of 237 ShAP which were shot down at dawn on 5 July 1943. Suttai Koppány was a most exerienced pilot. By this time, he had served as a military pilot for eight years, with 1,500 flight hours recorded in his logbook. He conducted 136 combat missions during World War II and was awarded with the Iron Cross of the second and first classes. (János Suttai Koppány's collection via Csaba Becze.)

a *Leutnant* of '*Grossdeutschland*'. [44] Had it not been for the relentless attack from the air, which prevented the Soviets from launching an effective counter-attack, the stranded German tanks would have been in dire straits.

While the German bombers and close-support aircraft continued to deal heavy strikes, Bf 109s went out in *Rotte* or *Schwarm* groups over the Soviet rear area in order to intercept and ward off any attempt by enemy aircraft to reach the battle zone. South-west of Oboyan III./JG 52's *Lt.* Berthold Korts and *Uffz.* Karl-Heinz Meltzer took on a formation of Soviet fighters at 05.25 hours and shot down one each. Meanwhile, the *Rotte* of *Fw.* Hermann Wolf and *Uffz.* Hans-Otto Müller – also of III./JG 52 – took off from Ugrim for a free-hunt mission. [45] In the Syrtesvo area they pounced on a formation of La-5s and claimed one each shot down. Thus *Fw.* Wolf attained his 34th victory.

The Soviet battle analysis clearly pointed out that during the initial stage, the German fighters managed to prevent 2 VA's 5 IAK from its task to cover the Soviet ground troops from air attack. When he eventually learned of this situation, *General-Leytenant* Krasovskiy, 2 VA's commander, ordered most of his available fighters into combat. Only a few machines were held back in readiness in order to protect the airfields from air attack. These masses of Soviet aircraft, divided in formations of ten to fifteen, flying at altitudes up to around 3,000 metres, started to reach the combat zone shortly before 07.00 hours (German time).

2 VA's primary task was to achieve air superiority, which is why the *Shturmoviks* and bombers at this stage were kept at their airfields. Drawing on bitter lessons from the past, the Soviets had decided not to dispatch them when these could not be effectively covered by fighters.

Participating in this wave of fighters were twelve La-5s of 40 GIAP. This unit was commanded by *Mayor* Moisey Tokarev, an ace with 16 victories to his tally, and included several formidable fighter veterans. In the air over the blazing battlefield where the 67th Guards Rifle Division fought desperately to hold positions, the La-5 pilots spotted and attacked a single Bf 110 escorted by Bf 109s. [46] A comparison with German sources identifies the Bf 109s as belonging to III./JG 3. Two Bf 109s – piloted by 76-victory ace and Knight's Cross holder *Ofw.* Hans Schleef and *Hptm.* Leo Eggers – were shot down. One of these was chalked up on the tally of 40 GIAP's *Lt.* Zolotaryov. The Bf 110 was claimed by his unit mate, *Lt.* Olekhnovich. NAGr 6 recorded a Bf 110 G severely damaged by Soviet fighters. [47]

At around the same time, some 24 kilometres further to the east, a formation of He 111s from II./KG 55 was unloading its bombs over the positions between Gremuchiy and Gostishchevo which Soviet 51st Guards Rifle Division held against 3rd SS *Panzergrenadier Division 'Totenkopf'*. The SS troops managed to take the village of Gremuchiy, but in the air above, twelve Yak-1s from 27 IAP and ten La-5s from 41 GIAP fell down on II./KG 55 with great fury. In the subsequent combat, two of KG 55's He 111s were shot down and a third was damaged. [48] It is possible that KG 27 was also attacked by these Soviet fighters; when they returned to base, the Soviet fighter pilots reported no fewer than 14 German aircraft shot down. KG 27 recorded four He 111s damaged by Soviet fighters and a fifth shot down by anti-aircraft fire. [49]

516 IAP's *Lt.* Tokarenko and *Serzh.* Vysotskiy claimed two Fw 190s shot down near Tomarovka, where 67th Guards Rifle Division fought to ward off 11. *Panzerdivision's* attacks. [50]

Polkovnik Fyodor Dobysh, the commander of 1 GBAD, which was one of two Bomber Diviziyas which formed the Bomber Corps 1 BAK under command of Polkovnik Ivan Polbin. VVS General-Leytenant D.T. Nikishin described Dobysh as "...not only a master of preparing heavy blows against the enemy, but also a master in the training of subordinates." The latter was of particularly great significance at a time when the training of Soviet airmen at the flight schools left much to be desired. Under Dobysh's command, 1 GBAD sustained relatively limited losses during the Battle of Kursk. Born in 1907, Dobysh completed his pilot training at Borisoglebsk Military Air School in 1934. He served as a volunteer combat pilot in China's defensive war against Japan in the 1930s. When Germany invaded the Soviet Union in June 1941, Dobysh served as the commander of SB-equipped 31 SBAP. In July 1942, he was appointed commander of 263 BAD, which after the Battle of Stalingrad, was appointed the first Guards Bomber Diviziya.

When the encouraging reports from 2 VA's fighter pilots were submitted after these combats, Krasovskiy ordered the first bomber and *Shturmovik* operations to commence. These were all directed against the 4. *Panzerarmee's* immediate rear area. First out were the Pe-2 bombers from 1 BAK. Nikolay Gapeyonok flew a Pe-2 as a *Lt.* with 81 GBAP, which formed part of the first Guards Bomber *Diviziya* 1 GBAD of 1 BAK. Many years later he recalled this mission:

"We took off with two *Eskadrilyas* – altogether seventeen Pe-2s – early in the morning of 5 July. Our task was to attack enemy forces in the Pushkarnoye area, and our Polk commander, Guards *Podpolk.* Vladimir Gavrilov, led us towards the front lines. We ran into a heavy AAA barrage, which disrupted our bombing. Two Pe-2s exploded in mid-air as a result of direct hits, and a third bomber was damaged, but managed to reach our airfield where the pilot performed an emergency landing." [51]

Meanwhile, nine Pe-2s of 82 GBAP/1 BAK were intercepted by Bf 109s of JG 3 *Udet*. But without sustaining any losses other than a damaged bomber, the Soviet gunners managed to ward off the German attacks and even shot down one of the Messerschmitts. [52] Thus III./JG 3 lost *Fw.* Emil Zibler, another of its aces with 36 victories to his credit. Advancing German troops found his belly-landed Bf 109 G-4 the next day, but without a trace of the pilot. It may be assumed that Zibler died in Soviet captivity. [53]

After the Pe-2s followed *Shturmoviks*, which by that time had been reorganised after the disastrous losses early that morning. '*Grossdeutschland*' had been bogged down in the mud and minefields for two hours when the *Shturmoviks* fell down upon its tanks. Coming in at extremely low level, the Il-2s made a very sudden appearance, causing panic among the stranded German troops who dived for cover wherever such could be found. At 07.05 hours, 48. *Panzerkorps* reported: '*The entire corps sector is under heavy attack by Soviet Il-2 ground attack planes and bombers.*'

Twenty-five minutes later, the corps reported: '*The 11. Panzer and 167. Infantry Divisions attack. Both come under heavy air attack and ask for air support.*''

But by that time, Messerschmitt fighters intervened with great impact. JG 52's *Geschwaderkommodore*, *Obstlt.* Dietrich Hrabak, led an attack against the *Shturmoviks'* escort fighters – shooting down one Yak-1 for his 83rd victory, [54] while *Oblt.* Emil Bitsch led a group of JG 3 pilots against the Il-2s. In an astonishing scene above the heads of '*Grossdeutschland's*' soldiers, ten Il-2s were shot down. Bitsch personally was responsible for three of these. *Hptm.* Johannes Wiese, I./JG 52's *Gruppenkommandeur* who had knocked down three of 237 ShAP's Il-2s at dawn, destroyed two more.

But '*Grossdeutschland's*' troops were allowed only a temporary relief. At around 09.00 hours, Il-2s and Pe-2s took turns to attack the stranded force. II. SS *Panzerkorps* also became subject to air attacks, as its 2. SS *Panzergrenadier Division 'Das Reich'* reported at 09.00 hours: '*Strong enemy air activity.*' Once again the sky became the scene of diving and attacking Soviet and German aircraft, with fighters of boths sides mercilessly hunting their adversaries. The *Shturmoviks*, which flew in groups of six to eight aircraft at a time, became easy prey to the large numbers of Bf 109s which swarmed to the area upon calls from the *Luftwaffe* liaison officers with '*Grossdeutschland*'. One more Il-2 fell before the guns of *Hptm.* Wiese's Bf 109 G-6. All across the sky, burning Il-2s could be seen descending towards the ground, and more and more smoke piles rose, each marking the

point of impact of a shot down aircraft – most of which were *Shturmoviks*. But the Pe-2 gunners once again managed quite well. *Ofw.* Basilio Maddalena, an Italian pilot who served with I./JG 52, was shot down and killed when he attempted to attack a Pe-2. [55]

Meanwhile, 48. *Panzerkorps* issued a new report which gave echo to the grave situation: "*Soviet air forces repeatedly attack the large concentrations of tanks and infantry near the crossings at Berezovyy. There are heavy losses, especially among the officers. Grossdeutschland's Command Post received a direct hit, killing the adjutant of the grenadier regiment and two other officers.*" [56]

These attacks undoubtedly contributed to slow down 48. *Panzerkorps's* advance – albeit at a terribly high cost for the Soviet airmen. In a series of air combats which raged unremittingly between 07.30 and 10.30 hours, the German fighter pilots claimed to have shot down eighteen Il-2s. Added to the losses sustained in the early morning, this dealt a crippling blow against 2 VA's *Shturmovik* units. 1 ShAK, which had been in the forefront during both operations on 5 July, recorded 32 missing Il-2s before noon. Although it later trasnpired that nine of the Il-2s initially reported as missing by 1 ShAK had simply made emergency landings at other airfields, the losses were very heavy. To the missing aircraft should be added those who were in need of repair work. During the remainder of the day, 2 VA's *Shturmovik* units were basically knocked out.

Another fact which was quite worrying to the Soviet air commanders was that these losses had occurred in spite of the presence of fighter escort. This was the result of the close escort tactic where the fighters flew on the same altitude as the *Shturmoviks* and adopting their speed to the slow and bomb-laden Il-2s. Thus the Yakovlevs and Lavochkins were more or less sitting ducks when the Bf 109s performed their lightning strikes at high speed from above. With many more German fighters in the air, the Soviet fighter attacks against the *Luftwaffe* bombers and dive-bombers also became less effective; in any case far less effective than the German attacks against the *Shturmoviks*. *Ofw.* Hans Krohn, radio operator and rear gunner in the Ju 87 flown by I./St.G 2's *Oblt.* Heinz Jungclaussen, recalls:

"When we were intercepted by Russian fighters, our pilots usually formed a defensive circle which gave us rear gunners a possibility to cover the whole air space. Our twin machine-guns could be quite effective if a fighter came too close – particularly if it was an in-line aircraft which you could hit in the radiator." [57]

From 11.00 hours onwards, the reports from 48. *Panzerkorps* reflected the fact that the troops had been relieved from the pressure from the air: "*The 11. Panzer Division reports better progress… Division* Grossdeutschland *reports that two crossings are ready and ten tanks are across the ravine… The 3rd Panzer Division takes the western part of Berezovyy.*" [58]

Again 1 BAK's Pe-2s were dispatched, but once more they ran into Bf 109s from both JG 3 and JG 52. In a large air combat shortly after noon the German fighter pilots claimed to have shot down eleven Pe-2s and three Soviet fighters without loss. In total, 1 BAK conducted 115 sorties on 5 July, but eighteen of its Pe-2s were shot down, of which three made emergency landings in Soviet territory. [59]

The Soviet escort fighters continued to offer a meagre performance. Quite often, formations of Yakovlevs or Lavochkins which were dispatched to the battle zone were drawn into combat by free-hunting Bf 109s which roamed the skies over the Soviet rear area. *M.Lt.* Ivan Kozhedub of 240 IAP described this in his memoirs:

"As a rule the enemy hunters operated in pairs. Their dominant tactic was to carry out a surprise attack against our formations, shooting down the rearmost aircraft. These attacks were performed from out of the sun or from clouds, quite often from the air above the territories which had been liberated by our armies during the previous winter campaign." [60]

In the meantime, Soviet ground troops were subjected to continuous bombardment from the air. *Obstlt.* Walter Lehwess-Litzmann of KG 3 *Blitz* recounted:

"Throughout the whole day I remained in the *Geschwader* headquarters and coordinated flying missions. Each crew flew several missions – all the time there were take-offs and landings. The headquarters in Kharkov uninterruptedly sent us new demands. Everything which could carry bombs was brought into the air." [61]

An account from the Soviet side reads: "*Our aviation fought air battles primarily against enemy fighters along the approaches to the battlefield, while enemy bombers were operating almost continuously against our defending forces immediately over the battlefield along the main attack axis. […] Thus an area measuring 6 x 4 kilometres in the sector of the 52d Guards Rifle Division, which was defending along the Germans' main attack axis, was subjected to 15 hours of uninterrupted air attacks while, during this time as many as 20 bombers were continuously in the air. Such intense enemy air operations against our forces made it considerably easier for German tanks and infantry to penetrate our defence and advance 6-8 kilometres into the depth of our positions.*" [62]

Considering the fact that more than 30 per cent of 52nd Guards Rifle Division's 8,000 men, were killed or injured, it is little wonder that II. SS *Panzerkorps* managed to break through the first Soviet line of defence.

General-Leytenant Krasovskiy had no choice but to order out 2 VA's battered *Shturmovik* units again. At 13.53 hours, SS *Division Das Reich* reported: "*The enemy renews his air activity.*" But only small and weak formations could be employed by this time, and the *Luftwaffe* fighters were waiting for them. Flying his third mission that day, *Lt.* Erich Hartmann of

II./JG 52 shot down an Il-2 for his 20th victory. Another *Shturmovik* fell before the guns of II./JG 3's *Fw.* Hans Grünberg – his fifth victory that day.

Soviet 7th Guards Army, defending the south-eastern flank east of Belgorod, also was encountering mounting difficulties against *Armeeabteilung Kempf*'s new attacks across the Donets south of Belgorod. German 7. *Panzer Division* managed to split the defences in the centre of Soviet 78th Guards Rifle Division. In this situation, *General* Sudets dispatched the *Shturmovik* units of his 17 VA to attack the German pontoon bridges and ferries across the Donets in an effort to isolate the German bridgehead. Shortly after 15.00 hours, the *Luftwaffe* liaison officers with 7. *Panzer Division* radioed an urgent call for fighter protection against attacking Soviet aircraft. *Ofw.* Hans Schleef, who was back in the air after surviving getting shot down nine hours earlier, was first on the scene. In four minutes he was credited with the shooting down of three Il-2s. During the remainder of the day, the bulk of the air fighting took place over the Donets crossings on the south-eastern flank.

During four hours, 17 VA's *Shturmoviks* arrived in groups of six to eight Il-2s, which suffered grievously at the hands of large numbers of Bf 109s which were called in to ward off their attacks. What had initially been scattered skirmishes in the sky above the river grew to become a huge air battle as Sudets dispatched all available Il-2s at around 18.00 hours.

"My *Schwarm* was scrambled at 18.20 hours and directed towards Belgorod, where the Russians attacked with Il-7s [sic] and Il-2s in several waves,' wrote *Hptm.* Josef Haiböck of 1./JG 52 (the 'Il-7' was an erroneous German designation for the Il-2 twin-seater). 'Flying 'White 11', I attacked an Il-7 but was only able to fire briefly because I had too much speed. I positioned myself behind a second Il-7 and opened fire from short distance. It caught fire in the engine and the right wing, descended vertically and exploded on impact. When I attempted to attack another Il-7, I was drawn into combat by the fighter escort, three LaGG-3s. Shortly afterward, I spotted a formation of three Il-2s which I immediately attacked. I hit the rearmost Il-2 with such effect that its pilot went down for an emergency landing close to our lines. The Il-2 nevertheless turned over in a grenade crater and exploded, killing the pilot. I failed to shoot down the next Il-2 because both I and the Il-2 were subjected to fire from our own anti-aircraft artillery, although without hitting either of us." [63]

Meanwhile, *Lt.* Johann-Hermann Meier and *Lt.* Herbert Fränzel of Haiböck's *Schwarm* shot down three and two Il-2s respectively. *Oblt.* Joachim Kirschner of II./JG 3 contributed by shooting down another four Il-2s – thus bringing his total for the day to eight victories. Also participating in that combat was I./JG 52's *Hptm.* Johannes Wiese, who claimed six Il-2s. Wiese wrote the following combat report:

"At 18.25 hours on 5 July 1943 I took off as a *Rottenführer*. Enemy aircraft had been spotted. Because I flew low in order to get close to the Il-7 formation, my wingman lost sight of me. During repeated attacks against Il-2 and Il-7 formations, I opened fire against an Il-2 from astern from close range, with the effect that bright flames immediately erupted from the engine. The aircraft descended vertically and exploded on impact.

I immediately attacked another Il-7, which had been unsuccessfully attacked by another Bf 109. The pilot of this Bf 109 witnessed how I set this Il-7 burning. The Bf 109 pilot confirmed my victory through a radio call.

Pursuing the Il-7 formations to the east of the Donets, I made another attack against a lone-flying Il-7. I opened fire and parts were torn off the fuselage and fin. The Il-7 descended vertically and exploded on impact. This victory too was confirmed through a radio call.

Since I had lost contact with my flying mate during the bitter air fighting, I continued the patrol mission over the front area alone and again I came across enemy aircraft. This time it was four Il-2s which were flying towards Belgorod on a southerly course. I attacked one of the Il-2s from above and behind and opened fire from a short distance. The Russian aircraft dived steeply but did not recover and it hit the ground. Shortly afterward I managed to score hits on another Il-2.

During the subsequent pursuit I again managed to position myself behind a lone-flying Il-2. I opened fire from 30 metres distance and kept shooting as I closed in with a heavy impact. Parts of the right wing were torn away and the enemy aircraft went down vertically and crashed into the ground.

Having shot down five enemy aircraft, I opened fire against a lone Il-7 which tried to escape, but obviously without having noticed my presence. Leaving a trail of black smoke, the aircraft put its nose down and performed a belly-landing. As it skidded along the ground, one of the wings of the Il-7 touched the steep bank of a creek, and this caused the aircraft to overturn. I was not able to observe the further fate of the aircraft because of the heavy dust cloud which was produced by the crash. I opened fire into the dust cloud and then a lack of fuel in my own aircraft compelled me to turn back for home. The next morning I flew back to the point of impact and was able to establish that the aircraft lay totally destroyed in our own territory. I never learned anything about the fate of the crew." [64]

The air battle continued to rage without any pause for over an hour. Both sides kept sending in new aircraft. When Haiböck, Kirschner, Wiese and other pilots were returning to base, others took off to keep up the defensive fight against the Il-2s. I./JG 52's *Ofw.* Walter Jahnke, who had shot down three Il-2s during two other air combats that day, would shoot down the last Il-2 of the day at 19.10 hours. He wrote:

"On 5 July 1943 I scrambled on the observation of enemy aircraft in the Belgorod area. My position was that of a *Rottenflieger.* My *Rottenführer* went down to the deck, and I lost sight of him, so I continued by myself. After a while I spotted several Il-7s heading back towards the Soviet lines. I selected the Il-7 which was positioned on the extreme right in the formation and attacked from below. Parts flew

A Bf 109 G-6, 'White 10', of I./JG 52 at Kharkov-Rogan in July 1943. This particular aircraft was flown by Lt. Herbert Fränzel, who claimed two Il-2s during the evening air battle over the Donets on 5 July 1943.

General-Leytenant Sergey Rudenko, the commander of 16 VA during the Battle of Kursk. Born in 1904, Rudenko had been a trained combat pilot since 1927. In January 1941, Rudenko was assigned to command 31 SAD in the Far East. This Diviziya was subordinated to VVS Western Front in July 1941 and played a vital role in the defence of Moscow during the subsequent winter. In the first half of 1942, Rudenko served as the assistant commander of the air forces of the Kalinin, the Volkhov and the Southwestern fronts. When the new 16 VA was formed in September 1942, Rudenko at first served as its assistant commander, but eas soon elevated to lead the air army. He would command 16 VA until the end of the war.

away from the rudder and wings. Fiercely burning, the Il-7 descended in a shallow angle and was totally destroyed as it hit the ground. My own aircraft had received bullet hits in the left wing and the undercarriage, and this forced me to make a belly-landing at the airfield." [65]

The Soviets had tasked several fighters to block the German airfields, but this failed. Nevertheless, in one case it led to at least a partial success. 7./JG 52's *Oblt.* Walter Krupinski and *Lt.* Erich Hartmann tangled with a group of La-5s above their own airfield at Ugrim, shooting down one of the Soviet aircraft each. But Krupinski's Bf 109 also was hit in the combat, and Krupinski described the following event:

"During a wild turning combat over our own airfield, my Me 109 was badly hit in the rudder and near the radiator. With the rudder functioning badly, I immediately decided to land because I knew that I was in a dangerous position. Just as I put my aircraft down for a force-landing, the alert *Schwarm* scrambled on my right-hand side. By that time, my aircraft was so low that there was no turning back, and I realised that I would either collide with the scrambling aircraft of the alert *Schwarm* or crash onto the runway. I desperately tried to avoid a collision, with the result that my aircraft flipped over and crashed onto its back. I hit my head against the gunsight and briefly passed out. When I came back to my senses, I found myself hanging in my straps upside down. I was soaking wet and at first I thought that it was me, bleeding profusely, and that gave me a quite nasty shock. But I soon established that most of the moisture was leaking fuel.

The emergency team rescued me from the wreckage and took me to the medical clinic. My injuries left me unable to fly for six weeks." [66]

According to Erich Hartmann, "...the departure of Krupinski was a severe strike against the *Staffel*, and particularly against me." [67]

At a cost of six Bf 109s shot down, the German fighter pilots claimed to have destroyed 44 Il-2s over the Donets in the evening of 5 July. Another twelve had been claimed earlier in the afternoon, bringing the total to 56 Il-2s claimed shot down over the Donets, of which 45 were confirmed. Thus, in terms of German victory reports, the scope of this air battle surpassed the famous air fighting during the morning of 5 July.

Actual Soviet losses in 17 VA's attacks against the Donets river crossings and ferries in the afternoon and evening of 5 July were horrendous: 200 sorties were made, and 55 Il-2s were shot down! 305 ShAD, which had lost 13 Il-2s in the dawn operation, lost eleven (nine from 175 ShAP and two from 955 ShAP), 290 ShAD lost 16 out of 32 dispatched, and 306 ShAD recorded 28 aircraft and 19 crews lost.

The scope of air fighting on 5 July 1943 has few, if any, parallels in the history of aerial warfare. On the southern flank alone, the Soviets lost around 150 aircraft. 2 VA recorded own losses of 78 aircraft – 36 fighters, 27 *Shturmoviks* and 15 bombers – on 5 July. To those figures should be added 17 VA's losses of at least 70 Il-2s plus an undisclosed number of fighters. Fighting large formations of Il-2s, piloted mainly by inexperienced and often inadequately trained airmen and escorted by similarly inexperienced fighter pilots in inferior fighter aircraft, the German Bf 109 G pilots reaped a grim harvest. *Hptm.* Johannes Wiese claimed no less than 12 Soviet aircraft shot down on this day. *Oblt.* Joachim Kirschner, the *Staffelkapitän* of 5./JG 3 was credited with eight victories. *Fw.* Hans Grünberg of Kirschner's *Staffel* followed closely behind with seven victories on this day, and *Oblt.* Emil Bitsch, the *Staffelkapitän* of 8./JG 3, attained six victories. (The frequently repeated assertion that *Oblt.* Krupinski of 7./JG 52 achieved 11 victories on 5 July 1943 however, appears to be a misconception, since he in fact recorded only two victories on that day.)

In addition to these *Luftwaffe* records, the Hungarian *Puma* fighter unit claimed five victories – two of which were due to *Törzs.* Pál Kovacs. [68]

Most accounts of this air battle quote the German wartime figures according to which *Luftflotte* 4 lost 19 aircraft on 5 July 1943. In fact, the loss returns to the *Generalquartiermeister der Luftwaffe* show that *Luftflotte* 4 on 5 July 1943 lost 27 aircraft to hostile action or unknown reasons on operations, while another 18 sustained severe or medium damage.

In any case, the Soviet reports of shot down German aircraft are, most probably, wildly exaggerated. 2 VA alone claimed the destruction of 154 German aircraft. However, some of the claims for individual achievements by Soviet pilots may be correct. Four of 2 VA's fighter pilots were credited with four victories each on 5 July 1943 – *St.Lt.* Nikolay Gulayev and *M.Lt.* Ivan Shpak of 27 IAP, *St.Lt.* M. S. Vanin of 41 GIAP, and *St.Lt.* O.V Belikov of 88 GIAP.

The situation on the ground was less assuring to the Germans. At a cost of more than 6,000 casualties, only a few regional breakthroughs had been achieved – nowhere even close to anything of strategic nature. A whole day's bitter fighting, where hundreds of tanks had been hurled against a single Soviet division – the 67th Guards Rifle Division – had brought 48. *Panzerkorps* no more than 6-7 kilometres from its jump-off positions. On 48. *Panzerkorps's* right (eastern) flank, II. SS *Panzerkorps* had managed to work itself less than 16 kilometres through defence positions held by Soviet 52nd Guards Rifle Division. It was even worse farther to the east, where *Armeeabteilung Kempf* barely had made it across the Donets river to capture a bridgehead 13 kilometres wide and between three and six kilometres deep.

The Soviets had sustained almost 8,500 casualties, but it should be considered that a large amount of these were due to the very heavy German air attacks.

5 July 1943: Northern Flank

Contrary to the situation on the southern flank, the Germans succeeded in concealing their build-up on the northern flank. While Soviet aerial reconnaissance detected the arrival of strong reinforcements to *Fliegerkorps* VIII in the south on 4 July, German radio signals led the Soviets to draw the conclusion that KG 27, KG 51 and KG 55 were withdrawn from *Luftflotte* 6's air bases at Bryansk and Orel on 2 July 1943. This is interesting it true that KG 27 and KG 55 were shifted from *Luftflotte* 6 – but only in order to return to *Luftflotte* 4 when the short-lived strategic bomber offensive was over. Meanwhile, KG 51 remained with *Luftflotte* 6 at Bryansk.

General-Leytenant Sergey Rudenko's 16 VA was assigned with the task of

Yak-9. On the first day of Operation Zitadelle, flawed tactics resulted in excessive fighter losses on the Soviet side. 6 IAK was particularly badly hit, recording 51 fighter aircraft lost by the end of the day. However, in spite of all their hardships the Soviet airmen continued to challenge the Luftwaffe for the supremacy in the air.

supporting the defensive fight of *General Armii* Konstantin Rokossovskiy's Central Front in this sector. These two formations were the victors of the Stalingrad battle, and 16 VA's operational coordination with Rokossovskiy's troops was much better organised than 2 VA's flawed structure for cooperation with the Voronezh Front's ground forces. An air force command and control post, headed by 16 VA's deputy commanding officer, was stationed at the 13th Army's command post. In coordination with the 13th Army's headquarters and its reports on the ground situation at the front, 16 VA's deputy commanding officer was authorised to employ aircraft direct to the battlefield from this post.

Just as was the case with 2 VA and 17 VA in the south, a detailed combat plan had been made for 16 VA's operations to counter the expected German offensive. First of all, 6 IAK was tasked to establish Soviet control of the air by defeating the *Luftwaffe* in aerial combat. Comprised of 273 IAD and 279 IAD with six regiments equipped with some of the best Soviet fighter aircraft, including Yak-9s, 6 IAK had been formed in February 1943, and served under 16 VA since May of that year. (Note that this formation should not be confused with the famous home defence air unit 6 IAK PVO –

which on 9 June 1943 was transformed into the 1st Air Fighter Army of the PVO, 1 VIA, *Vozdushnaya Istrebitelnaya Armiya PVO*.)

The remainder of 16 VA's aviation was tasked to act in tactical support of the ground forces. The major air operation was intended to start with a massive air offensive against the German launching areas during two or three days prior to the German attack. To this end, detailed plans had been made.

'The overall plan for the combat employment of air formations envisioned the same operational stages, common ground forces missions and air missions in the event of [a German] offensive along this or that particular axis in each army's belt. The number of possible [German] offensive axes (variants) for each army varied but, as a rule, did not exceed four. [...] The plan assigned aviation formations not only missions but also the areas, number of aircraft, and times for delivering the air strikes. Air strike delivery times were designated as 'H' + x hrs, x mins (where 'H' represented the time when the enemy assumed the offensive).

'The Front command approved the plan for the combat employment of aviation formations, after which excerpts from it were distributed to aviation formations. On the basis of these excerpts, aviation corps commanders compiled their own plans for the combat use of aviation formations, while division commanders established timetables for combat flights, which indicated the composition of each aircraft group, the numeration of air units, the names of group leaders, areas where [German] fighters were expected to be encountered, the time for take-off, and the attack objectives. Planning documents developed by the air army and the aviation corps commanders were approved by the air army commander.' [69]

But all of this fell apart because the Soviets failed to establish the exact date of the German attack. The heavy costs to the VVS for the airbase offensives in May and June had the effect of making 16 VA's commanders cautious. Thus, when intelligence reports indicated that large elements of 1. *Fliegerdivision* were withdrawing from Bryansk and Orel on 2 July, the signs of an impending German attack were not interpreted as the build-up for the actual major offensive.

Meanwhile, the last among 1. *Fliegerdivision's* air units arrived at their respective operational airfields in the evening of 4 July. The logbook of I./KG 53's *Oblt*. Martin Vollmer shows that he took off for the transfer flight from Shatalovo at 17.15 hours. [70] His personal diary reads: '*We are excited and feel that something 'big' is going to happen. We assume that there will be heavy fighting between Orel and Kharkov and that we are going to support the army. At 9 o'clock in the evening we arrive* [at Olsufyevo near Bryansk]. *At 10.10 hours the air raid alarm sounds. One aircraft after another fly past without attacking our airfield. We get to bed only at midnight, and at 01.30 we are woken up…*' [71]

1. *Fliegerdivision* - the plan for operations on 5 July

General der Flieger Friedrich Kless, the chief of staff of Luftflotte 6, outlined the operations plan for 5 July 1943:

The 1. Fliegerdivision will launch its initial sortie as early as possible on 5 July, attacking the heavy concentrations of Russian aircraft on airfields in the Kursk area. Elements of the division will attack strong enemy artillery groups around Malo-Arkhangelsk in coordination with 9. Armee's artillery fire plan.

Thereafter, the division, making a continuous and supreme effort, will concentrate its formations and support the swift breakthrough of the XLVII Panzerkorps through the enemy defenses and its subsequent swift thrust toward Kursk. The most important priority is to drive the points of the attacking force forward relentlessly with the help of ever-present ground attack formations and to maintain the momentum of the attack force after the breakthrough.

Elements of the division must support and ensure the advance of XLVI Panzerkorps, preventing the danger of enemy flanking thrusts from the west against XLVII Panzerkorps.

In a similar manner it may become important to neutralise enemy forces along the flank in the Malo-Arkhangelsk area (specifically, Soviet artillery groups) and at a later date to combat enemy reserves advancing west from the Kolpna-Shchigry area. The XLVI Panzerkorps must be in a position to shift its main effort quickly.

Any missions in 2. Panzerarmee area require the approval of Luftflotte headquarters.

Reconnaissance sorties are to be flown continuously and with complete coverage. Aerial reconnaissance will pay particular attention to identifying, in the earliest possible stage, enemy assembly positions and the concentration of reserves (especially tanks) on the flanks and all advances toward our attack wedge.

In addition, it is of vital importance that the enemy main effort opposite the northern sector of 2. Panzerarmee be observed constantly in a manner that will permit the discovery of major enemy attack preparations in time.

The 12. Flakdivision will reliably protect the Orel supply areas (main priority) and Bryansk, as well as airfields in use but will employ the minimum forces to accomplish these missions. The primary mission of the division is to protect the advancing attack wedges and the most important supply roads of the attack divisions from enemy air raids. The main strength of the division will be concentrated in the sector of XLVII Panzerkorps.

Strong Flak elements are to be committed directly behind the most advanced Panzer elements. Flak will be committed against enemy tanks only temporarily and whenever such action is unavoidable. Individual Flak Kampfgruppen must not be used for antitank action; the minimum flak force committed in action will be of battalion strength.

Certain Flak elements will, by way of exception to the foregoing, be moved up to participate in the preparatory artillery fire within the scope of 9. Armee's artillery fire plan for the first attack on the morning of 5 July. These Flak elements will destroy particularly strong enemy centers of resistance and in this manner facilitate the initial penetration.

The 10. Flak Brigade will for the moment continue to protect the important objectives already assigned, concentrating its forces at Konotop. The brigade will move up all motorized flak elements in time before the attack elements of 2. Armee jump off and furnish the troops with Flak protection at the two points of main effort.

Stukas towards the front! These aircraft are Ju 87 D-3s of 4./St.G 3 'Immelmann'. This particular Staffel was one of the most fortunate dive-bomber Staffeln during the course of Operation Zitadelle, and recorded only a single aircraft loss throughout July 1943.

A Ju 87 D-1 of III./St.G 3. Formerly (until January 1942) numbered II./St.G 2, this Stukagruppe was transferred from the Mediterranean area to the Eastern Front in May 1943. Following a long period of rest, III./St.G 3 first saw action on the Eastern Front on the first day of Operation Zitadelle, 5 July 1943. During the next eighteen days, the Gruppe performed 69 dive-bomber missions and had ten of its aircraft shot down.

The original plan for 1. *Fliegerdivision's* operations called for an opening major strike against the Soviet airfields in the Kursk area. [72] However, this was not what the airmen who were gathered in operations rooms on *Luftwaffe* bases around Bryansk and Orel late on 4 July heard. Instead, *Generalmajor* Paul Deichmann's 1. *Fliegerdivision* was to act as flying artillery. The prime targets were the powerful concentrations of Soviet artillery, and defence strongholds at the points where the German ground troops would launch their attacks.

It was clear that the intended strikes against the Soviet airfields simply could not be carried out with any success. First of all, *General-Leytenant* Rudenko had dispersed his aviation among a large number of airfields which were well camouflaged, and several dummy airfields had been created. Secondly, the Soviet air defence at these airfields had proved to be too strong to permit the kind of massive air attack which the German plan envisaged. The German commanders expected heavy own aircraft losses during the first days of tactical support of the new offensive, and their forces could not afford, on top of that, losses during operations against more remote targets as during the two air attacks against Kursk in May and June 1943. Gerhard Baeker, who with the rank of *Hauptmann* was *Gruppen* Technical Officer in III./KG 1, recalled:

"When the crews received the instructions, it was obvious that this would be quite an unorthodox operation. For the first time since Operation *Barbarossa* two years previously, the *Wehrmacht* would launch a major offensive without any preceding aerial onslaught against supply routes, rail installations, headquarters, airfields etc in the Russian rear area. That there would be no attacks against Russian airfields was particularly unusual. That meant that we would have to encounter the whole Russian aviation in the air instead of wiping out large elements on the ground, as we had done previously." [73]

The fact that both 1. *Fliegerdivision* and *Fliegerkorps* VIII were tasked to act mainly as a flying artillery was not only a result of the heavy losses the *Luftwaffe* had suffered during its two attacks against Kursk in May and June 1943; it also reflects the healthy respect which the German commanders had developed for the echeloned Soviet defence to the north and south of Kursk in general, and the Central Front's eleven thousand guns and mortars – the most powerful artillery concentration ever to be assembled in such a limited territory – in particular.

The Soviet defenders remained unaware of the massive firestorm which would be unleashed against them the next day. On the southern flank, their commanders had a better picture of what was going on. While the Voronezh Front opened a pre-emptive artillery barrage in the south at 00.10 hours (German time), and 2 VA's and 17 VA's airmen were made ready to deliver their air strikes against *Fliegerkorps* VIII's airfields, the Soviets were uncertain as to whether the Germans would launch their main attack on the northern flank simultaneously with the attack in the south.

Slightly less than an hour later, a Soviet patrol captured a German soldier from 47. *Panzerkorps's* 6. *Division*, and he revealed that the offensive would commence at 03.00 hours on 5 July. This was immediately reported to Marshal Georgiy Zhukov, the Stavka representative to the Central Front, and Zhukov authorised Rokossovskiy to order an artillery barrage against the German positions. Central Front's mighty artillery opened up at 01.20 hours (German time). This was sufficiently effective to cause the Germans to postpone the attack by two and a half hours.

Meanwhile, the German-occupied airfields came alive. *Lt.* Erhard Jähnert of III./St.G 3 took off from Konevka with his bomb-loaded Ju 87 D-3 at 02.50 hours (German time). [74] *Oblt.* Martin Vollmer of I./KG 53 took off from Olsufyevo at 02.53 hours. [75]

Fw 190 fighters flew into the Soviet rear area, in vain searching for enemy aircraft to attack, while reconnaissance aircraft took the Soviet artillery positions and defence stronghold on the ground under surveillance. The first bombers attacked the Soviet artillery positions at Malo-Arkhangelsk.

At 03.25 hours, 1. *Fliegerdivision* launched its first major attack in the operation. A tight formation of sixty He 111s of II./KG 4, I./KG 53 and II./KG 53 roamed in above the artillery positions north-west of Malo-Arkhangelsk. [76] Immediately afterward, twenty Ju 88s of II./KG 51 dived down and dropped their deadly cargo against the same target, which disappeared in explosions and huge smoke clouds. Only minutes later, Ju 87s of St.G 1 and III./St.G 3 appeared to perform an attack in three waves against the artillery. These German air attacks were supplemented by a simultaneous 80-minute artillery barrage against the same targets.

The first air combat during Operation *Zitadelle* took place as a Yak-1 of 54 GIAP *Stalingradskiy* shot down Ju 87 D-3, 'J9+DH' of 7./St.G 1. The pilot, *Uffz.* Heinz Heil, baled out into captivity. Although his colleagues

An Fw 190 A of 1. Fliegerdivision covers a formation of Ju 87 Stukas from Soviet fighter attacks. Due to the Fw 190s of JG 51 and JG 54, the bombers and dive-bombers of 1. Fliegerdivision were able to carry out their operations with only very limited losses to Soviet fighter interception during Operation Zitadelle.

reported the cause of the loss as "*Flak* fire", [77] the Soviet report asserts that he indeed was shot down by a fighter. [78]

Similarly to *Fliegerkorps* VIII's Bf 109 fighters in the south, *Generalmajor* Deichmann instructed 1. *Fliegerdivision's* Fw 190 fighters to operate in fighter sweeps into the Soviet rear area – with the intention of tying down the Soviet aviation before it was able to reach the battle zone – rather than providing the bombers and close-support aircraft with escort. The Fw 190s of JG 51 *Mölders* and JG 54 *Grünherz* gained air supremacy from the very beginning, owing much to mistakes on the Soviet side.

General-Leytenant Rudenko still was unsure whether this was actually the major German attack, so instead of employing his fighter aviation *en masse* as the combat plan envisaged, he issued a fateful order to 16 VA early on 5 July: only one third of the fighters was to be employed against the *Luftwaffe*! The remainder of the fighter aviation was kept "in readiness". Moreover, only one third of the *Shturmovik* and bomber aviation was even alerted for action at 06.00 hours.

In effect, this meant that 16 VA's air units were dispatched piecemeal against a 1. *Fliegerdivision* which made an all-out effort. Small formations of Soviet fighters were hurled against masses of *Luftwaffe* aircraft, and found themselves attacked from various directions by several groups of Fw 190s.

At around 03.45 hours, eighteen Yak-1s and Yak-7Bs of 157 IAP flew towards the sky above Malo-Arkhangelsk, which was filled with German aircraft of several types. In the distance the Soviet pilots could see huge black smoke clouds rising from the ground. These airmen were no beginners. The unit commander, *Mayor* Viktor Volkov, was a veteran who had been fighting since the first day of the war. He divided the aircraft into two groups. *Kpt.* Vladimir Zalevskiy took charge of eight Yaks which were instructed to attack a large formation of Ju 88s and Fw 190s. Zalevskiy was a Hero of the Soviet Union who had amassed a total of 40 victories, including 17 shared, since 1941. The remaining ten fighters, led by Volkov himself, would act as top cover.

But the Soviet fighter pilots were unable to do much against the vast German numerical superiority. Operating independently in *Schwarm* formations, Fw 190s from *Stab*/JG 51, 7./JG 51, 8./JG 51, 9./JG 51, 12./JG

51, 1./JG 54 and 2./JG 54 fell down upon the Soviet fighters. The two first Yak-7Bs fell before the guns of 8./JG 51's *Fw.* Hubert Strassl.

Kpt. Zalevskiy was seen to bale out of his stricken Yak-7B, Serial No. 41-44, but he was dead when he reached the ground. Four of 157 IAP's Yak-7Bs were lost. The returning pilots reported three Ju 88s shot down, but this is difficult to verify with German records. It is possible that the Ju 88 'V4+AS' went down as a result of this engagement. The whole crew was killed or missing. Thus 8./KG 1 *Hindenburg* lost one of its most experienced pilots, the *Staffelkapitän*, *Oblt.* Hermann Michael, who was killed on his 282nd combat mission. [79] Michael was awarded with the Knight's Cross posthumously.

But the Fw 190s definitely held the upper hand. Other Yakovlevs – possibly Yak-9Ds of 163 IAP – intervened and also sustained severe losses. *Mayor* K. D. Pelipets led eighteen La-5s of his 486 IAP into the same mêlée. Although Pelipets was another highly experienced pilot – with 1,489 flight hours recorded in his logbook by late January 1943 – he could not prevent the disaster. Attacked by elements of both JG 51 and JG 54, six of his unit's La-5s fell burning to the ground. *Mayor* Pelipets was shot down in single combat with twelve Fw 190s and baled out but drifted into German-controlled territory and was taken prisoner. *Kpt.* Ovsiyenko and *Mladshiy Leytenants* Mamayev, Krivtsev and Ovchinnikov were killed or reported as missing. Only one of 486 IAP's shot down pilots managed to return to his unit – *M.Lt.* Rybchenko, reporting that he had mistakenly been shot down by a Yak-1! In addition to those losses, *M.Lt.* Limonov was wounded when he crashed his La-5 after it ran out of fuel, and *M.Lt.* Grachyov performed an emergency landing with his badly shot up La-5.

In total, 1. *Fliegerdivision's* fighters reported sixteen Soviet fighters shot down in the Malo-Arkhangelsk area between 03.45 and 04.20 hours on 5 July – nine of which can be identified as Yak fighters (although the Germans reported them as other in-line engine fighters, 'MiG-3' and 'LaGG-3' types, neither of which were active in the area) and seven La-5s. It seems as though the price for this accomplishment was limited to the loss of a single Fw 190.

Meanwhile, the bombers and Stukas were in relentless action. The Soviet after-battle analysis reads:

'*Active air combat operations commenced at 04.25 hours* [Soviet time] *on 5 July and at this time the first enemy raids were conducted against our artillery firing positions, centres of resistance, and infantry and tank combat formations in the Malo-Arkhangelsk Station region. More than 150 bombers took part in the raid under the protective cover of 50-60 fighters. At the beginning of the attack a large number of these aircraft, having broken up into groups of 4-6, flew forward 10-15 kilometres and created a screen to intercept our aircraft, which were approaching the battlefield.*' [80]

Lt. Erhard Jähnert, a Stuka pilot of III./St.G 3, describes the special tactic which was employed by the *Luftwaffe* formations:

"In order to hold down the Russian artillery fire, we were sent in against their positions in rolling attacks. When we arrived over the assigned target area, we succeeded another formation. Then we circled over the artillery positions for up to 20 minutes, with each aircraft dropping down to attack singly, one at a time. Thus a maximum pressure was exerted on the Russian artillery crews, who were relentlessly exposed to air attacks.

"After we had completed our mission, another *Stukagruppe* arrived to hold down the Russian artillery for up to 20 minutes, and so it went on. We landed at our base and our aircraft were refuelled and loaded with new bombs, and then we took off for the same mission again.

"All of this, of course, also exposed ouselves to the Russian defences, but during the opening stage of the great offensive, our own fighters held the Russian fighters at bay, and miraculously enough our unit was saved from sustaining any losses to *Flak* on the first day. This is quite remarkable in view of the very heavy *Flak* concentrations which the Russians had brought to the area. I guess we were simply lucky. Another *Stukagruppe* lost several aircraft to the Russian *Flak* on the first day." [81]

Jähnert's logbook shows that he landed at 04.00 hours at Konyevka after his first mission, and at 05.40 hours he took off for his next dive-bombing operation. [82]

"Every 10-15 minutes after the enemy bombers left the battlefield a new group of aircraft arrived and subjected our first-line defensive forces to attack," established the Soviet after-battle report. [83]

At 04.30 hours (German time), *Generaloberst* Walter Model launched the first attack on the ground, ordering *General* Johannes Freissner's 23. *Armeekorps* on the eastern flank of his 9. *Armee* against the seam between Soviet 13th Army and its eastern neighbour, the 48th Army. The main goal for this attack was Malo-Arkhangelsk, eight kilometres from the German point of departure. Previously, this target would have been seized in a matter of hours, but the troops of the 9. *Armee* ran into the strongest defence they had ever encountered. Despite massive support by the *Luftwaffe*, which launched relentless air strikes against the Soviet positions at the will of the ground commanders, 23. *Armeekorps* became bogged down in fierce and very costly fighting. But this was only the preliminary attack.

The German main attack was delivered at 06.30 hours, with 41. and 47. *Panzerkorps* – in total three *Panzer* and four infantry divisions – pouncing on Soviet 15th and 81st Rifle divisions north-west of Ponyrey. Although hopelessly outnumbered and suffering a hellish bombardment from the air, the two Soviet divisions withstood four attacks before they were finally pushed backwards.

The Fw 190s of 1. *Fliegerdivision* effectively held most Soviet aircraft away from the skies above the battlefield, shooting down scores of Soviet fighters. To the east of Malo-Arkhangelsk, six Yak-9D and two Yak-7B of 163 IAP were intercepted by 8./JG 51, 9./JG 51 and 1./JG 54 and lost five of their number while only one Fw 190 was shot down. Flying his second mission that day, *Fw.* Hubert Strassl was in the forefront again, this time knocking down three more Soviet fighters.

While this took place, *Mayor* V. L. Plotnikov led 347 IAP against the masses of Ju 87s and He 111s which tormented the troops of 15th and 81st Rifle divisions north-west of Ponyrey. But Plotnikov and his pilots only found themselves attacked by IV./JG 51 and lost four Yak-9s while the Soviet airmen were able to record only one He 111 shot down. [84]

When 16 VA's fighters at last were fully employed at 08.30 hours, five hours after 1. *Fliegerdivision* had started its major operations, it was too late to alter the situation. Moreover, the way in which the fighters were sent out was according to the previously drawn up plans, and did not subscribe to the actual air situation, which was characterised by the presence over the battlefield of *Luftwaffe* forces on a scale not anticipated by the Soviet planners. The instruction was to maintain 30 fighters continuously on patrol over the front lines. This clearly was inadequate, particularly since these were divided into groups of ten to twelve fighters. Each such group was provided with a reserve of 16 fighters in standby alert at the airfield, but when such a group of sixteen was alerted, it often only became subject to renewed German fighter attacks en route to the battle zone.

All of this rapidly wore down 6 IAK's fighter units. According to the Soviet plan, the *Shturmoviks* and bombers would be launched only after the fighters had established control of the air; hence these units were slow and hesitant to go into action against the German troops – the close cooperation between the 13th Army and 16 VA made it absolutely clear to the Soviet air commanders that the enemy was in total command of the air.

When the first *Shturmoviks* finally were dispatched, they arrived in small groups of only eight aircraft at a time, producing further disasters to the VVS. Performing his second mission on that day – and 401st in total – *Oblt.* Joachim Brendel of 1./JG 51 encountered the first formation of *Shturmoviks*,

eight Il-2s escorted by two "MiG-3s" (actually Yak fighters) shortly before 09.00 hours. [85] Brendel shot down two of the Il-2s, and his wingman, *Uffz.* Oskar Romm, sent a third towards destruction.

Constantly roaming the skies over the Soviet rear area, German fighter pilots found rich hunting grounds in the Malo-Arkhangelsk – Livny region. At 08.57 hours, *Oblt.* Franz Eisenach of 3./JG 54 took off from Orel for his second mission that day to lead his *Schwarm* on a fighter sweep. [86] Forty-five minutes later, flying at 2,300 metres east of Malo-Arkhangelsk, Eisenach spotted a formation of La-5s positioned at a higher altitude. Undetected, the four Germans made an attack from below and shot down two La-5s. *M.Lt.* Nestertsev saved his life by baling out, but *M.Lt.* Galayev was less successful. While Galayev fell towards his death, *Oblt.* Eisenach and *Uffz.* Alexander Söder returned home to report their victories.

Still practically without any support from their own air force, the troops of Soviet 15th Rifle Division had been forced to abandon the three small villages Yasnaya Polyana, Ozerki and Nikolskaya, about 1.6 kilometres from their initial positions, by 09.30 hours. This led to a shift in Rokossovskiy's tactics. He now ordered the two bomber divisions 221 BAD and 241 BAD to dispatch 150 bombers against the German breakthrough area. He also instructed the fighter units to send 200 fighters to the same area.

But the Soviet air operation came underway in an unorganised manner. *'The Soviet countersorties were at first unimpressive, which indicated that at least tactical surprise had been achieved in the timing of the attack…'* wrote *General der Flieger* Kless. [87]

Again led by *Mayor* Plotnikov, the ill-fated 347 IAP was ordered out on a new combat mission over the battlefield at Ponyrey, where it ran into 2./JG 54 at around 10.00 hours. The Soviet combat formation was dispersed into pairs or single aircraft and in the subsequent combat three of 347 IAP's Yak-9s were shot down – including the Serial No 01-65, which was flown by *Mayor* Plotnikov. [88] A fourth pilot was wounded and performed a force-landing, while another Yak-9 limped back to base with severe battle damage. The *Jagdflieger* of 2./JG 54 claimed to have shot down six Soviet fighters without loss in this engagement, but they appear to have had some difficulties in identifying the Yak-9s – which they reported as "LaGG-3s", "Airacobras" and even "P-40s".

By 10.00 hours, 16 VA had performed 520 combat sorties – the majority of which were flown by fighters – but meanwhile, Soviet air observation posts had logged at least 1,000 *Luftwaffe* sorties, of which around 800 were by bombers. By that time, the fighters of 1. *Fliegerdivision* had already reported nearly 50 Soviet aircraft shot down against only limited own losses.

Only slowly did the Soviet counter-action in the air become better organised. Between 10.00-11.00 hours, 1. *Fliegerdivision* had to fight hard against an increasing number of Soviet aircraft – including more Il-2s and large numbers of bombers. During his third mission of the day, *Fw.* Hubert Strassl reported the feat of shooting down six Soviet aircraft – four La-5s, an

A Yak-9 takes off for a combat mission.

Il-2 and a Boston. Also, *Oblt.* Hermann Lücke (9./JG 51) and *Oblt.* Horst-Günther von Fassong (10./JG 51) were credited with two La-5s each.

It is difficult to establish at which extent these claims match actual Soviet losses. La-5-equipped 192 IAP lost *M.Lt.*s Sazonov and Sivayev, and probably also further La-5s, while escorting Pe-2s. Additional La-5 losses were sustained by 92 IAP.

However, at a high cost to themselves, the Soviet fighter pilots actually managed to accomplish their mission of providing the bombers with an effective fighter cover. The dive-bombing which was performed by 241 BAD's Pe-2s had a particularly heavy impact on the troops of 41. and 47. *Panzerkorps.* German reports indicate that losses due to these Soviet air attacks were not insignificant.

Nevertheless, the Soviet ground troops had to endure much more intense attacks from the air. 1. *Fliegerdivision's* aviators were in engaged in relentless and exhaustive activity. At 11.20 hours, *Lt.* Erhard Jähnert of III./St.G 3 took off for his fourth dive-bombing mission of the day.[89] Only few of 1. *Fliegerkorps's* bombers and Stukas were intercepted by Soviet fighters on 5 July 1943. St.G 1 and III./St.G 3 performed a total of 647 sorties, losing four Ju 87s (all from St.G 1) to hostile action – none of which was due to fighter interception.

Testifying both to the strength of the Soviet ground defence positions and the stamina with which the Red Army troops fought against the attacking German *Panzer* forces, not even such a vast onslaught from the air sufficed to break the resistance on the ground. And the troubles would increase for the *Panzer* troops.

Shortly after noon, more Il-2s appeared. Many of these were flown by Stalingrad veterans of 2 GShAD who dropped new PTAB anti-tank bombs against the German armour. Led by Hero of the Soviet Union, *Mayor* Viktor Golubev, a group of six Il-2s of 58 GShAP alone reported that they knocked out ten German tanks during their first attack with PTAB bombs. A Soviet eyewitness on the ground recorded: "Our *Shturmovik* and fighter aviation appeared over the battlefield. Lunging forward, the penetrating enemy tanks began blowing up in the minefields."[90]

Savagely cutting an Il-2 formation and its fighter escort into pieces, I./JG 54's *Major* Reinhard Seiler and *Ofw.* Otto Kittel reportedly brought down three Soviet aircraft south of the Soviet lines at Ponyrey. But the Soviet airmen kept arriving to strike back. One hour later, 221 BAD was dispatched again. Intercepting fighter pilots from III. and IV./JG 51 claimed to have shot down five Bostons.

By this time, the German offensive had completely stalled. Both sides continued to strike hammer blows from the air during the remainder of the day. The diary of one of the participants on the German side, He 111 pilot, *Oblt.* Martin Vollmer of KG 53, reads:

'Shortly before 3 o'clock [in the morning] *we took off for our first mission, which for the first time brought us against ground troops. On this day I flew three missions during the forenoon and one in the afternoon, which makes four in total. This meant altogether eight hours of formation flight. In the evening, when adverse weather grounded us, we were completely exhausted. But we are happy to fly when we know that we are able to support our lads on the ground, who are involved in a bitter fight. Oh boy, what a sight the battlefield offers from above, and how interesting was it to watch the coming and going of our flying formations, fighters and bombers, and a relentless air battle raging throughout the whole day!'* [91]

The fiercest air fighting on Operation *Zitadelle's* northern flank on 5 July took place in the evening, when 2 GShAD and 299 ShAD sent in large numbers of Il-2s. The latter unit was largely composed of rookies, and suffered badly at the hands of the German fighters which also appeared on a large scale. 217 ShAP lost six Il-2s in a single mission.[92] During a full hour's relentless air fighting, 1. *Fliegerdivision's* fighters recorded 42 Soviet aircraft shot down. On his fourth mission that day, *Fw.* Hubert Strassl chalked up another four kills – bringing his total for the day to an almost unsurpassed fifteen victories! Meanwhile, *Lt.* Günther Scheel of 2./JG 54 was recorded to have shot down four Il-2s for a total of eight victories on 5 July 1943.

Otto Kittel served as a pilot trainer when World War II broke out. In February 1941 he received his first front line assignment when he was posted to I./JG 54, a unit he would remain with. Kittel attained his first victory on 23 June 1941 and earned fame for bringing home the Grünherzgeschwader's 4,000th victory in February 1943. When Operation Zitadelle commenced, Kittel had amassed a tally of more than 50 victories. He was awarded with the Knight's Cross for 94 victories on 26 October 1943. Kittel's greatest successes as a fighter pilot were achieved during the final period of the war. When he was shot down and killed by an Il-2 in February 1945, he had a score of 267 victories.

But the *Shturmoviks* continued to exert a heavy pressure on the German armoured forces. 2 GShAD reported no fewer than 31 German tanks destroyed during this day when for the first time, it deployed its PTAB anti-tank bombs.

Thus ended one of the bloodiest days of the Second World War. Having failed to achieve a penetration of no more than 8 kilometres deep and 16 kilometres wide at most, *Generaloberst* Walter Model's 9. *Armee* had sustained over 7,000 casualties. [93] Even worse, about two-thirds of 300 tanks and SPGs that Model had sent into battle had been put out of commission. Even if many of these could be repaired, at least 20 per cent of Model's armour was irrevocably lost on this first day of the battle.

The picture in the air was more complex. Without doubt, even the small German gains on the ground would not have been possible without the tremendous effort by 1. *Fliegerdivision.* Throughout 5 July, 1. *Fliegerdivision* carried out 2,088 combat sorties – 647 by Stukas, 582 by bombers, 522 by fighters, 168 by *Zerstörer,* 141 by reconnaissance aircraft and 28 by transport aircraft. [94]

An important key to 1. *Fliegerdivision's* tactical success was a series of mistakes at Soviet command level, which also resulted in very heavy Soviet losses in the air. This obviously was not admitted by 16 VA's commander, *General-Leytenant* Sergey Rudenko, who describes the apparently embarrassing scene at *General Armii* Rokossovskiy's headquarters that evening:

"When darkness fell, I reported the results of the day to the Front commander. I specified how many enemy aircraft that had been shot down and emphasised that the fight had been severe. Suddenly a phone call was made. I. V. Stalin called K. K. Rokossovskiy. They used to hold telephone conversations each day, but previously I had not been present. This time, however, I heard everything.

"Rokossovskiy began by reporting the results of the day, but he was interrupted by Stalin: *'Have we gained control of the air or not?'*

That proved to be his main interest! Rokossovskiy replied: *'Comrade Stalin, it is impossible to tell. There have been very hard combats in the air and both sides have suffered heavy losses.'* But Stalin just retorted: *'Tell me precisely, have we won in the air or not? Yes or no?'* Rokossovskiy spoke again: *'It is impossible to give a definite answer to that question, but tomorrow we shall solve this positively.'* – *'And Rudenko – will he cope with this matter?'* Rokossovskiy looked at me, and after a short pause he answered: *'I will consult him.'* […]

"A short while later, Zhukov arrived and turned to me and said: *'Stalin just phoned and his first question was regarding the domination in the air. What do you think?'*

"I explained and showed that our plan for the use of fighters was correct. But since the enemy possessed such large forces, it was impossible to destroy them all at once. The operations of the enemy aviation during the battle had immediately been met by counter-action from our side. Powerful groups of fighters had risen to the air. The commanders had led the operations with great vigour and in due time increased the forces. It had been necessary to employ bombers and *Shturmoviks* to attack strong enemy forces." [95]

In reality, Rudenko's fighter force had suffered a disastrous bloodletting. 6 IAK alone recorded 51 fighters lost. [96] Indeed, the Soviet fighters had managed to prevent the Fw 190s from inflicting similar losses on 16 VA's bomber units. In 221 BAD, losses were restricted to one Boston B-3 shot down and five A-20Bs which made emergency landings. 241 BAD escaped with only two force-landed Pe-2s. While 299 ShAD had lost 14 Il-2s, 2 GShAD had got away with only two losses.

But many of 6 IAK's units had been bled white. As a result of this single day's fighting, the strength in 92 IAP went down from 27 to 19 La-5s, and in 192 IAP and 486 IAP from 24 to 13 La-5s. Moreover, many *Shturmovik* units had been dealt grievous losses. In total, 16 VA recorded exactly 100 aircraft lost in combat on 5 July 1943 – 83 fighters, 16 *Shturmoviks* and one Boston. [97]

On the German side, 1. *Fliegerdivision* filed heavy overclaims as it recorded 165 Soviet aircraft shot down, all but two in air combat. Against this total,

The Soviet PTAB anti-tank bomb

The PTAB (Protivotankovyye Aviabombyy, which simply means Anti-tank bomb) was constructed to penetrate the armour of a tank through a directed cumulative explosion which eventually set the tank burning. The blast wave reached a speed of 11,000 metres per second.

The PTAB bomb weighed only 2.5 kg, with a warhead of 1.5 kg. These bombs were employed mainly by Il-2 Shturmoviks. Each Il-2 could be loaded with up to 192 PTABs in four cartridges or up to 220 PTABs in four bomb racks. When released in level flight at a speed of between 337 and 354 kilometres per hour from an altitude of 200 metres under normal wind conditions, the PTAB bombs would land with a density of one bomb per 15 square metres. The PTAB load from a single Il-2 thus would cover an area of 3,000 square metres.

The Germans were greatly alarmed by the employment of the PTAB bombs, and their immediate counter-action was to stop operating their tanks in close formations. This dispersed their attack forces and made the task less difficult to the Soviet defenders on the ground.

After the battle at Kursk, the Soviet Commissariat of the Defence made a meticulous study of the effects of the PTAB at Kursk, and published the results in January-February 1944 in the 10th Edition of the report Sbornik materialov po izucheniyu opyta voynyy (The Collection of Materials in Studying the Experiences of War, the Military Publishing House of the National Commissariat of the Defence in Moscow).

This report arrived at the conclusion that among all of the air force's weapons against enemy tanks – guns and various bombs and rocket projectiles – the PTAB bombs were the by far most effective. Close examination of abandoned German tanks on the battlefield showed that the PTAB bomb had a capacity to penetrate armour of 60 mm thickness if it impacted vertically. On the battlefield near Ponyrey, the Soviets examined one of the huge 65-ton Ferdinand self-propelled guns which had been destroyed by a PTAB bomb. It was found that the bomb had penetrated the 20 mm thick armoured cover of the left fuel tank, causing the fuel to explode, which in turn set the whole SPG on fire, igniting its ammunition.

Near Khotynets on the Bryansk-Orel highway, one of the new 43-ton Panther V tanks, which had been destroyed by a PTAB bomb, was examined. It was established that the PTAB had penetrated the 45 mm armour on the chassis next to the gun tower and set the whole tank on fire.

On the outskirts of the village of Dragunskaya, 10 kilometres north-west of Tomarovka, six of 'Grossdeutschland's' Panthers were found to be the victims of PTAB bombs. All of them had been set alight by the bombs, and in the case of four of them, the fire had caused the ammunition to blow up.

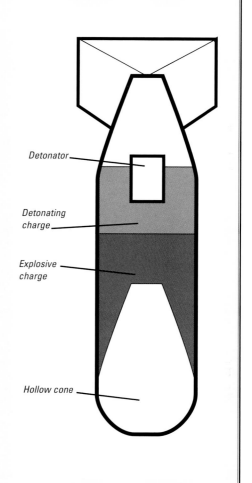

Detonator

Detonating charge

Explosive charge

Hollow cone

German tanks set ablaze during Operation Zitadelle. The Soviet PTAB anti-tank bomb was constructed so that when it hit a tank, it did not bounce aside, but penetrated the armour through a directed cumulative explosion which eventually set the tank burning.

A shot down Il-2 on the battlefield.

reported initially seven own losses. [98] The latter figure however is too low, as the records from the daily loss returns to the *Generalquartiermeister der Luftwaffe* show. These files reveal that *Luftflotte* 6 in fact sustained 29 aircraft put out of commission due to either unknown reasons or hostile action on 5 July 1943, and of those, 18 were total losses. [99]

In any case, the figure of 100 lost Soviet aircraft against only seven shot down and destroyed 1. *Fliegerdivision* fighters reflects a considerable German superiority in the air. This impression is further reinforced in view of the fact that out of 16 VA's 1,720 combat sorties on 5 July, 817 were by fighters – as compared with 522 fighter sorties from the German airfields.

Including both flanks, the first day of Operation *Zitadelle* cost the air forces on both sides heavy losses. 2 VA, 16 VA and 17 VA lost altogether around 250 aircraft, and *Luftflotten* 4 and 6 had 74 aircraft put out of commission due to hostile action or unknown reasons on operations – of which 45 were total losses. (See Appendix 3.)

Chapter Four

Northern Flank 6–8 July: Head Against the Wall

6 July 1943: Northern Flank

As soon as the Soviets had established the commencement of the expected German major attack, they began preparations to seize the initiative in the battle, for which they had detailed plans. At noon on 5 July, *General Armii* Rokossovskiy instructed his armies "…to begin operations according to Variant No. 2 at dawn on 6 July." According to this plan, five corps – the 13th Army's 17th and 18th Guards Rifle Corps, the 19th Independent Tank Corps and the 2nd Tank Army's 3rd and 16th Tank Corps – would launch an attack in the Ponyrey sector in coordination with strikes by the 70th and 48th Armies on the 13th Army's left and right flanks.

Air support was to be provided by 16 VA and the ADD, which also had detailed plans for this operation. During the night of 5/6 July, the ADD flew 169 sorties to attack German troop and vehicle concentrations in the Olkhovatka and Ponyrey area.[100] These attacks were supplemented by 387 sorties by the U-2s of 271 NBAD.

Meanwhile, *General-Leytenant* Rudenko prepared the air operation which would commence at first light in the morning of 6 July. He planned to deal a most powerful first strike against the German troops, as later described in his memoirs:

"*I decided to change the tactics of the strike aircraft. I concluded that it would be more expedient to deal one devastating strike against a large force of enemy troops, so for this end I decided to dispatch our aircraft in massive strength. The idea also was that this massing of our aircraft would suppress the enemy's air defence and thus reduce our own losses. Moreover, we would not only cause great material damage on the enemy, but also render a major moral impact on his ground troops. Rokossovskiy was convinced by my reasons.*"[101]

The strong emphasis which was laid on the fighter escort clearly reflects the respect for the German fighters which the Soviets had been taught; the lessons from previous operations indeed had been well learned. In order to facilitate the fighters' escort task, the bombers and the *Shturmoviks* were instructed to operate at the same flight altitude – 2,000 metres for the bombers and between 100 and 1,000 metres for the *Shturmoviks*. Also, each *Shturmovik* or bomber unit, as a rule, was escorted by one and the same particular fighter escort unit.[102] Thus, for example, 57 BAP was 'connected' to 517 IAP, 745 BAP to 774 IAP; and 8 GBAP to 127 IAP.[103]

But again the detailed Soviet planning would be faced with many unexpected obstacles. First of all, throughout 5 July, the 17th Guards Rifle Corps was subjected to repeated and heavy German air attacks which considerably delayed the Corps' march to its intended jumping-off position. Next, at 22.00 hours (Russian time) on 5 July, the troops which were preparing to launch the attack received new orders from Rokossovskiy: Since the German main assault was being delivered slightly more to the west than the Soviets had first anticipated, the Soviet attack force had to again regroup. The positions held by 47. *Panzerkorps* were the main target.

At 02.50 hours (German time) a new, massive, artillery barrage fell down upon the troops of German 9. *Armee*. German artillery responded only weakly. By that time, the first among 16 VA's bombers started to taxi out on the runway in order to take off for the first combat mission.

The Soviet air attack would be performed in four successive waves, the first of which consisted of 25 Bostons of 221 BAD. En route to the front line, the bombers passed by in the air above the airfield at Kunach where their fighter escort unit, 282 IAD, was stationed. With the pilots waiting at cockpit alert, the Yak-1s could take off rapidly when the *Shturmovik* appeared, and then climbed to assume their assigned positions.

With German troop positions and vehicle columns in the immediate vicinity of the front as target for the Boston bombers, the undertaking would be most unorthodox by VVS standards. During the first two years of the war the Soviet aviation had operated mainly in small formations. Moreover, contrary to the general VVS practice, the targets were located directly at the front line. Until then, most Soviet air attacks had avoided the front line and instead been directed against targets located at least a three kilometres into the German rear area; this out of fear that they might hit their own troops.

One fighter formation, the *Stalingradskiy Diviziya* 1 GIAD, had set off in advance for a fighter sweep in the target area. However, its fighters arrived too early over the battlefield; apart from a few Bf 109 reconnaissance machines, there were almost no *Luftwaffe* aircraft in the air. *Generalmajor* Paul Deichmann had decided to allow his exhausted airmen to rest that morning. But the advanced Soviet force had the effect of alerting the Germans, and 1. *Fliegerdivision* ordered fighters to scramble. At the large airfield at Orel

A Douglas DB-7 Boston – known to the Soviets as B-3 – in VVS service. During the Battle of Kursk, the Douglas attack bomber operated with great success – and only relatively limited losses – with 16 VA's 221 BAD and 17 VA's 244 BAD.

West, the recently awoken pilots of *Hptm.* Fritz Losigkeit's III./JG 51 and *Hptm.* Rudolf Resch's IV./JG 51 ran towards their Fw 190s.

Meanwhile 221 BAD's Bostons reached their target area. A pair of Bf 109 reconnaissance aircraft made a futile attempt to intercept, but they were easily taken care of by the Soviet fighters. 1./NAGr 4 had two of its Bf 109s badly shot up. Piloting one of them, the *Staffelkapitän*, *Hptm.* Herbert Findeisen, performed an emergency landing at the airfield at Panikovo. The Bostons released their bombs over a large congestion of tanks and motorised infantry of 47. *Panzerkorps's* 2. *Panzer Division* between the villages of Podolyan and Sonorovka – and with considerable impact, as testified by *General der Flieger* Kless:

"*On 6 July the Soviets began committing bombers in large numbers, including a major formation of Bristol bombers* [sic] *that – considering all that we had seen of previous VVS operations – exhibited particularly good flying discipline and exceptional aggressiveness.*" [104]

As the Bostons turned back for home the Soviet ground offensive commenced. The sky was dominated by the VVS at that moment, but the Soviet attack plan could not be fully implemented. Due to the regrouping which had been ordered at the last minute, only the 16th Tank Corps and elements of the 17th Guards Rifle Corps were available for the assault. Owing to the repeated air attacks which the latter had endured during the previous day, these formations had great difficulties in coordinating the operations between the armour and the infantry.

Stunned by the previous attack, the troops of 2. *Panzer Division* were unable to hold out for long and had to retreat. At around 04.00 hours, the 17th Guards Rifle Corps had advanced to a line west of Druzhovetskiy-Step-Saborovka. But the Soviet success would prove to be short-lived.

More aircraft were approaching from both sides of the front line – German fighters, and Soviet bombers and *Shturmoviks* with their respective escort. The Fw 190 pilots of *Jagdgeschwader Mölders* were guided by the huge black smoke clouds which rose from the targets attacked by 221 BAD's first Bostons. The *Jagdflieger* arrived on the scene just as a large formation of Il-

Hptm. Herbert Findeisen is congratulated after a mission with his Bf 109, 'Black 3'. Findeisen served as a Luftwaffe reconnaissance pilot in North Africa and over the British Isles from 1942. In the spring of 1943, he was posted to NAGr 4, which flew Bf 109s on the Eastern Front. Findeisen soon displayed talents as a fighter pilot and attained over 40 victories as a reconnaissance pilot. In February 1944, he was awarded the Knight's Cross. In late 1944, he was transferred to JG 54, where he became the Gruppenkommandeur of II. Gruppe. Findeisen finished the war with a score of 67 victories. He was killed in a car accident in 1963.

The of Staffelkapitän 1./NAGr 4, Hptm. Herbert Findeisen takes off in his Bf 109 G-6, "Black 3".

A formation of Il-2s heading for the battle zone. By bringing the Il-2s together in larger formations, General-Leytenant Sergey Rudenko, the commander of 16 VA, managed to reduce Shturmovik losses and increase the impact of the attacks against the targets on the ground.

2s came in at 1,000 metres altitude, surrounded by Yak-1s and Yak-7Bs. This was 2 GShAD, escorted by 283 IAP. The German pilots hurled themselves down on their enemy from a position high above. This time the roles were reversed. There was nothing the Soviet fighter pilots could do against the Fw 190s which, at high speed, dived down and shot the Il-2s to pieces, and then by using the accumulated energy from their dives, made rapid climbs to a position for a new high-side attack. The instruction to fly slowly at the side of the heavy Il-2s deprived the Soviet fighter pilots of a fighter's greatest advantage – speed. In a matter of minutes, 2 GShAD lost fifteen Il-2s. [105]

By the time the third wave of Soviet aircraft arrived – shortly after 05.00 hours – the whole of JG 51 was airborne. A huge air battle developed from 3,66 metres down to treetop level. The German fighters managed to score some successes during their initial attacks. *Fw.* Josef Mader from 1./NAGr 4 attacked the Bostons with his reconnaissance Bf 109 and destroyed one of the bombers. *Oblt.* Joachim Brendel led his 1./JG 51 against a formation of fifteen 221 BAD Bostons escorted by fifteen 282 IAD Yak fighters (Brendel misidentified the latter as "MiG-3s") and blew one of the Bostons out of the sky. [106] III./JG 51's *Oblt.* Hermann Lücke and his wingman, *Fw.* Wilhelm Küken, brought down two other Bostons. However, the Soviet escort fighters soon managed to lock the Focke-Wulfs and Messerschmitts into rugged dogfights, which allowed the bombers to carry out the attack against their intended targets.

But here the Soviet planning went wrong again. Although cooperation between air and ground units was better organised on the northern flank than on the Kursk battle's southern flank, the Soviets were hampered by a lack of air liaison officers in the front line, as the Germans had. In consequence, by the time the Bostons arrived over the battlefield, the locations which they had been assigned to attack had been captured by the Red Army. The bombs fell over Soviet troops! Next, 107th Tank Brigade of Soviet 16th Tank Brigade fell into an ambush set up by the German 505. *Schwere Panzerabteilung*, equipped with Tiger tanks. When the battle was over, 46 of 16th Tank Brigade's tanks had been destroyed.

At 06.00 hours, Rudenko received an urgent telephone call from Rokossovskiy. The commander of the Central Front demanded to know when the next air attack was planned. "In two hours time," Rudenko replied. Apparently unsatisfied with that answer, Rokossovskiy asked if there

were any reserves available. When he was told that there was one *Shturmovik Diviziya*, 299 ShAD, in reserve, he demanded: "Use it to repeat the attack immediately!"

Shortly after 07.00 hours, 299 ShAD delivered 16 VA's next attack. This time the Soviet airmen arrived over the battlefield at a time when most of 1. *Fliegerdivision's* fighters had returned to base to refuel and rearm. The *Shturmoviks* hit the German troops with devastating effect. *General-Leytenant* Rudenko wrote:

'*The impact of their attack was powerful and obviously unexpected by the enemy. Smoke piles rose from his positions – One, two, three, five, ten, fifteen: It emerged from burning Tigers and Panthers. Despite the danger, our soldiers jumped out of the entrenchments, threw their helmets into the air and shouted "Hurrah!" Meanwhile one* Shturmovik *after another dived from their circle in the air above. The air was filled by an unceasing rumble of exploding bombs.*' [107]

General-Leytenant Aleksey Rodin, the commander of Soviet 2nd Tank Army, received information that the *Shturmovik* attacks had set fire to 14 German tanks and put another 40 out of commission. But in spite of this success, and the fact that only one Il-2 was lost on this mission, the Soviet counter-offensive had irrevocably been grounded to a halt.

Amassing nearly 300 tanks, 47. *Panzerkorps* attacked the 17th Guards Rifle Corps and 16th Tank Corps. The bombers, Stukas and *Zerstörer* of 1. *Fliegerdivision* now appeared over the battlefield again and paid back the previous VVS attacks. The Soviet fighters hurled themselves against them. Four Yak-7Bs from 519 IAP attacked a formation of Bf 110s and *St.Lt.* Stepan Kolesnichenko claimed the destruction of two of the German aircraft. I./ZG 1 recorded one Bf 110 shot down and a second which performed an emergency landing due to "engine damage." [108] I./St.G 1, III./KG 1, and possibly also III./KG 51, lost one aircraft each to Soviet fighter interception. A He 111 of I./KG 100 was badly damaged in combat with 54 GIAP. This Guards fighter unit had recently been equipped with the new Yak-9T, armed with 37 mm cannon. *Lt.* Antokhin blasted away ten of these heavy shells at the Heinkel.

Led by *Kpt.* Nikolay Tregubov, a group of 721 IAP La-5 pilots claimed to have shot down six German aircraft during a single engagement. [109] This nevertheless appears to be an exaggeration of the actual result. With the exception of JG 51's successful interception of 2 GShAD at dawn, the

'CIRCLE OF DEATH'
Il-2 Shturmoviks against the Panzers
KURSK, JULY 1943

Ilyushin Il-2 Shturmovik
One/two-seat assault aircraft, powered by Mikulin liquid-cooled 12 cylinder engined carrying offensive load of ShVAK and/or ShKAS wing-mounted and rear-firing machine guns and VYa cannon supplemented by 1000 kg RS-82 82 mm rocket and bomb-load.

1. Panzers break cover and enter open ground in daylight.

2. The German armour is spotted by an two-man Il-2 crew and its position is radioed back to the parent unit.

4. The Sturmoviks form a circle over the Panzers.

3. The Il-2s arrive in squadron strength of eight aircraft.

6. Target area is the vulnerable rear where armour is thinnest.

5. Taking turns, the Il-2s select targets and begin their attack in a shallow dive against the tanks using bombs, rockets and cannon.

7. Aircraft return to re-arm and refuel.

Repeat attacks were often conducted as low as six metres.

The attack is maintained for up to seven hours.

The attacks are devastating to even the most modern and well-armoured of the new German tanks, destroying as many as twenty in one strike.

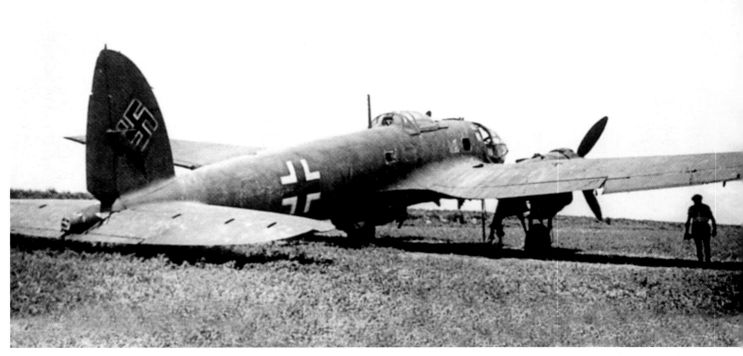

An He 111 at an airfield on the Eastern Front. The vast open spaces in the southern parts of Russia and Ukraine offered good opportunities to establish airfields.

A Yak-7B fighter. The inscription reads "Novosibirskiy Pioneer".

een probably after a day filled with severe air fighting - in front of his Yak-9, Mayor
iktor Volkov, the Commanding Officer of 157 IAP, shows a visibly tired face. 16 VA's
ghter units sustained very heavy losses during the first days of Operation Zitadelle.
olkov's 157 IAP recorded a loss of four Yak-7Bs in a single engagement on 5 July, and
even Yak-1s, Yak-7Bs or Yak-9s on the following day.

Major Reinhard Seiler, who commanded I./JG 54 Grünherz at the onset of Operation
Zitadelle, was one of the most experienced airmen in the Battle of Kursk. Trained a
fighter pilot in the mid-1930s, Seiler flew with the Condor Legion during the Spanish Civil
War, where he was credited with nine aerial victories. Prior to Operation Zitadelle,
Seiler had amassed 97 kills during World War II. However, he was shot down and badly
injured on the second day of Operation Zitadelle – thus becoming one of the first among
several veterans which the Battle of Kursk would cost the Luftwaffe.

ghters of both sides tied each other into relentless air combats – ninety-
wo in total during 6 July, according to Soviet records – which prevented
nem from interfering effectively against each other's bombers. In most
ases, the different tactics applied by the opposing sides provided the
German fighter pilots with an advantage in both altitude and speed, which
esulted in most unequal results during these dogfights.

While on patrol over the battlefield, seventeen La-5s of of *Mayor* Boris
olomatin's 92 IAP spotted forty Ju 88s. 92 IAP's formation was broken up
n the thick clouds which had gathered in the region, and before the Soviet
ilots had been able to reach the Junkers bombers, they were bounced by
everal groups of Fw 190s. *Major* Reinhard Seiler, I./JG 54's
Gruppenkommandeur, led some of his pilots to attack 92 IAP, and so did
0./JG 51's *Oblt.* Horst-Günther von Fassong and 11./JG 51's *Hptm.* Adolf
Borchers. While *Major* Seiler blew one of the La-5s out of the sky for his
8th victory, 10./JG 51's *Fw.* Rudolf Wagner was credited with no fewer
han five Lavochkins shot down.

Without sustaining any losses, the participating German fighters inflicted
errible losses on 92 IAP. The Soviet unit's records show that eight
a-5s were shot down. Among the killed pilots was *Kpt.* Ivan Sidorov, who
vas the unit's top ace. The German aircraft which he was reported
o have shot down in this combat – unsubstantiated, according to German
ources – was filed as his 23rd victory (a figure which included seven
hared kills).

15 VA, responsible for Soviet air cover along the north-eastern – by this
me quite tranquil – flank of the Orel Bulge, dispatched some fighters to
upport 16 VA and divert the *Luftwaffe's* attention. This nevertheless cost one
f the participating units, 32 GIAP, dearly. *Mayor* Boris Lyubimov, the

regimental commander, and his deputy, *Mayor* Nikolay Tarasov, were shot
down over German-held territory and posted as missing.[110] German sources
indicate that they fell prey to *Hptm.* Diethelm von Eichel-Streiber and
Hptm. Herbert Wehnelt of JG 51.

When 16 VA's Bostons and Il-2s returned for 16 VA's fourth strike at nine
in the morning, III./JG 51 intercepted and claimed to have shot down seven
La-5s, two Il-2s and a Boston for no loss.

If not immediately reassuming their air supremacy, the Germans gradually
established at least a balance in the air over the 47. *Panzerkorps. Generalmajor*
Deichmann concentrated most of 1. *Fliegerdivision's* air units to this critical
sector. Soviet 17th Guards Rifle Corps reported: '*Appearing in formations of
20-30 or even 60-100 aircraft at a time, the enemy air force played a vital role in
the battle.*' As a consequence, the Soviet troops had to pull back to their point
of departure.

Meanwhile, the German 41. *Panzerkorps* renewed its effort to split the
Soviet 13th and 48th Armies apart on the German left flank. But with most
of 1. *Fliegerdivision's* bombers and Stukas tied to the right flank, this attack
failed. Nevertheless, German fighters were at hand, and at noon 8./JG 51's
Hubert Strassl, who had scored such huge successes on the previous day,
took part when III./JG 51 clashed with a large formation of La-5s in this
region. Strassl had just been promoted to *Oberfeldwebel*, and now he followed
up his previous successes by contributing with three of the eight Soviet
fighters reported shot down by III./JG 51 in that combat. At least two of

With serious faces, these two Soviet Il-2 fliers reflect on a narrow escape from German fighters.

these can be identified as La-5s of 192 IAP, with the pilots *Mladshiy Leytenants* Kornyukhin and Volkov getting shot down.

157 IAP also fared badly on this day. Early in the morning, *Lt.* Stepanov had to take to his parachute after his Yak-7B had been shot down in flames by IV./JG 51's *Gruppenkommandeur, Major* Rudolf Resch. The unit's next mission saw the loss of *Kpt.* Morozov; he was shot down and killed by one of *Major* Resch's pilots. At around 13.00 hours, *Oblt.* Karl-Heinz Weber led a *Schwarm* of Fw 190s from III./JG 51 into a diving attack against another formation of 157 IAP Yak-7Bs, shooting down three in rapid succession. Finally, *St.Lt.* Savchenkov and *M.Lt.* Arkhiyereyev failed to return from an engagement with Fw 190s during an the afternoon mission in the Malo-Arkhangelsk area. One of them ended up on the scoreboard of 2./JG 54's ace, *Oblt.* Hans Götz.

But the fighter combats were not entirely one-sided. *Fw.* Lothar Mai – who had shot down one of 157 IAP's Yak-7Bs – was rammed by a Yak-1 of 55 GIAP. The Soviet pilot, *M.Lt.* Rostislav Polyanskiy, saved his life by baling out.[111] *Fw.* Mai barely managed to nurse his crippled aircraft back to Orel-West.

At 13.50 hours, *Major* Reinhard Seiler led I./JG 54 into the air for an escort mission for Stukas of II./St.G 1.[112] En route to the target, the Germans ran into several formations of Soviet aircraft – including La-5s, Yak-9s and Il-2s which were escorted by the Airacobras of 30 GIAP. In the ensuing series of combats, *Oblt.* Franz Eisenach and *Ofw.* Rudolf Rademacher were credited with the destruction of two Lavochkins each, and *Major* Seiler reportedly shot down a "LaGG-3" for his 99th victory. Eager to achieve his 100th, Seiler pursued one of 30 GIAP's Airacobras. He managed to hit it, but in the next moment another Soviet pilot attacked Seiler's Fw 190 and set it ablaze. Bleeding from bullet wounds, Seiler took to his parachute.

When the Germans returned to their airfield, another pilot was missing, *Uffz.* Alexander Söder. It is possible that his Fw 190, 'Yellow 2', was rammed by the Airacobra flown by 30 GIAP's *Lt.* Lev Koptev, who was able to perform a belly-landing in friendly territory. Reinhard Seiler was rescued by German troops. The severity of his wounds made it necessary to fly him to Germany for medical treatment. He would never return to first-line service. Thus 1. *Fliegerdivision* had lost one of its most experienced unit commanders. Seiler was replaced by *Hptm.* Gerhard Homuth.

Later that afternoon, a group of pilots from 8./JG 51 intercepted six Il-2 and ten Yak-1s but lost two of their own Fw 190s without being able t shoot down any of the Soviet aircraft.

On the ground the German situation continued to deteriorate. Their a reconnaissance brought home worrying reports of a strong concentration (Soviet armour to the west of Olkhovatka, on 47. *Panzerkorps'* right flan This was the 19th Independent Tank Corps, which just reached its jump-o position and prepared to launch its attack. *Generalmajor* Deichman immediately called in his aviation for a major strike against this new threa He 111s attacked in a large formation, dropping clusters of armour-piercin bombs over the Soviet tanks. I./KG 53's *Oblt.* Martin Vollmer recalle "The mission was performed in close formation flying. We climbed abov the overcast and detected a hole in the clouds straight abov the target."[113] Meanwhile Stukas carried out pin-point attacks. Sovi fighters tried to intervene, but only managed to damage a He 111 fro I./KG 53.

The Soviet 19th Independent Tank Corps commenced its attack at 17.3 hours, but it was rapidly torn to pieces by the concentrated aerial onslaugh The Soviet after-battle report noted: '*The enemy met our attacking tanks wi fire from artillery and heavy tanks located in shelters as well as with an air attack which up to 100 aircraft took part. The tank brigades' motorised rifle battalions, whi were following behind the tanks, were cut off from the tanks. Consequently, and owir also to the losses they suffered, the brigades were withdrawn from combat and t Corps received orders to occupy a defence along the Teploye and Krasavka line.*' [114]

Thus ended a day of bloody fighting which had resulted in almost r territorial gains to either side. The situation at *Generaloberst* Model's 9. *Arm* looked increasingly dismal. The accumulated losses after just two days (fighting surpassed 10,000 casualties, and no decisive breakthrough was i sight. But it was a crisis for both friend and foe. Rokossovskiy had no reaso to be satisfied; his offensive against 47. *Panzerkorps* had been badly savaged

16 VA had restored its honour after the failures on the previous day – th 840 sorties which had been performed by its *Shturmoviks* and bombers (38 of which were at night) had been a decisive factor during the day's groun battle. But the price for this was high. 2 GShAD had lost 15 Il-2s, all in o disastrous German fighter attack in the morning. Nevertheless, the oth *Shturmovik Diviziya*, 299 ShAD, had escaped with fairly moderate losses seven Il-2s, and 221 BAD recorded nine Bostons missing. All in all, 16 V recorded the loss of 91 aircraft on 6 July. Sixty of these losses were fighte – which equals a fearsome 15 percent loss rate!

The hardest hit formation was 6 IAK, which had 25 fighters – 11 La-5 10 Yak-9s and 4 Yak-7Bs destroyed. [115] There were several reasons for thes high fighter losses – the mistake of dispatching the Soviet fighters either i close escort for slow flying *Shturmoviks* or bombers at low altitude, or th predominantly defensive use of VVS fighters.

With their aggressive posture, the Fw 190 fighter pilots of JG 51 *Mölde* and JG 54 *Grünherz* could strike at will against slower Soviet formatior from tactically advantageous positions. This enabled them to submit n fewer than 121 victory claims against only two own fighters lost and tw more damaged – an exceptional ratio of sixty to one – on 6 July 194. In total, 1. *Fliegerdivision's* combat losses on this day were limited to 1 aircraft destroyed and seven damaged. This is a very low figure in view of th fact that 1,023 sorties were flown on that day.

A Yak-9 at a Soviet frontal airfield. Although an improvement when compared with the Yak-1 or the Yak-7B, the Yak-9 proved to be inferior to the Luftwaffe's Messerschmitt Bf 109 G and Fw 190 A.

With clear signs of battle wear, this Il-2 of a Guards Shturmovik regiment revs its engine ahead of a new combat mission.
The slogan on the fuselage side – Za chest' Gvardii! – reads 'For the Honour of the Guards!'

The inequality in the air combats called for both an overhaul of Soviet tactics, and reinforcements. All that remained of 6 IAK after two days of fighting was 48 aircraft. In 1 GIAD, the proud Guards Fighter Division which carried the name of honour *Stalingradskiy,* the three Yak-1-equipped regiments – 53 GIAP, 54 GIAP and 55 GIAP – had no more than 26 fighters between them.

Although displeased with Rudenko's request for reinforcements, Zhukov decided to recommend the Stavka to bolster 16 VA's fighter strength by shifting 234 IAD from 15 VA.

But *Generalmajor* Deichmann also had reason to feel concerned. The intensity of the air battles had taken a heavy toll on his shrinking fuel reserves. Even if 6 July had seen very critical developments on the ground, the number of bomber sorties flown by 1. *Fliegerdivision's* units had dropped radically from 582 to just 164, and the operations by the Stuka units had been cut in half as compared with the previous day – from 647 sorties on 5 July to 289 on the 6th. [116] The fact that fighters flew more sorties than any other aircraft type in 1. *Fliegerdivision* – 317 on 6 July – bears testimony to the heavy pressure exerted by the Soviet aviation. Despite impressive results by JG 51 and JG 54, this showed no tendency to decline.

7 July 1943: Northern Flank

During the night of 6/7 July, Soviet aircraft continued to hammer 9. *Armee*. The ADD was active throughout the night, dispatching 238 crews in 495 sorties against Model's tormented troops. [117] Meanwhile, the light night-bomber crews of 271 NBAD performed 469 sorties. The Germans stood no chance in competing in terms of nocturnal aerial activity. The *Störkampfgruppe* of *Luftflotte* 6 managed to carry out 44 sorties, losing a He 46 biplane of 1. *Staffel* in the process. Meanwhile thirty-five He 111s of KG 4 *General Wever* attacked the railway station at Yelets.

The next day, 16 VA brought its radio combat guidance and control service into better order. Moreover, Rudenko had implemented a tactical change. The method of sending fighters to patrol missions in one large formation at a uniform altitude had proven to be a major reason to 16 VA's excessive losses. Instead the Soviet fighter units were instructed to launch patrols with several cooperating smaller formations – each consisting of four to six aircraft – which were echeloned with respect to altitude. Also, more fighters were placed in alert at their airfield, ready to be called in by the airborne fighters when larger German formations appeared in the air. This change in tactics would markedly influence the air combat situation on 7 July – although not to the extent as has been assumed in Soviet and Russian history writing.

On the Central Front's combat zone, Wednesday 7 July began with a renewed frantic effort by German 9. *Armee* to achieve a breakthrough. Contrary to the previous day, 1. *Fliegerdivision* bombers and Stukas were in action already before 05.00 hours.

The German attack was met with a hellish fire both from the ground and in the air. But the sky was also filled with Fw 190s from JG 51 and JG 54, and a fierce air battle commenced. Since 2 GShAD had sustained such heavy losses the previous day, 299 ShAD's *Shturmoviks* were in the forefront. 874 ShAP was unfortunate to run straight into Fw 190s from I./JG 54 on their first mission with ten Il-2s north-east of Malo-Arkhangelsk at around 05.00 hours (German time). *Lt.* A. S. Baranov's single-seat Il-2 was immediately shot down by the Focke-Wulf fighter pilot *Lt.* Gerhard Loos. According to Soviet eye-witnesses, Baranov's crippled *Shturmovik* crashed into a group of German tanks. Two other Il-2s were badly damaged but managed to escape. *Lt.* K.S. Protsenko put down his twin-seat Il-2 (with the gunner Pervunin) in an emergency landing near Malo-Arkhangelsk, and *Lt.* V.G. Bengua crashed his single-seater at the airfield. [118] In addition to *Lt.* Loos, I./JG 54's

The ground crew and a Luftwaffe pilot around a Fw 190 A-4 of JG 51 at Orel in July 1943.

Il-2 twin-seat ground-attack aircraft lined on a Soviet airfield. Any German soldier who survived the Battle of Kursk can testify to the relentless pressure from the air which was exerted by the VVS Shturmoviks. The Soviet evaluation of the battle testifies to the efficiency of the air attacks against 9. Armee on 7 July 1943: "Our ground forces highly valued the work of the aviation on the battlefield. Several enemy attacks were thwarted thanks to our air operations. Thus on 7 July enemy tank attacks were disrupted in the Kashara region. Here our Shturmovik aircraft delivered three powerful attacks in groups of 20-30 aircraft, which resulted in the destruction or disabling of 34 tanks. The enemy was forced to halt further attacks and to withdraw the remnants of his force north of Kashara."

Ofw. Otto Kittel and *Uffz.* Gerhard Görlach submitted one victory claim each in that engagement – filed as "Curtiss P-40s". No such aircraft operated in this area, so it is possible that these were either misidentified Il-2s or perhaps even La-5s of 165 IAP, which recorded *M.Lt.* Kutukov and *M.Lt.* Bedeneyev shot down in the same area. '*One huge air combat rages in the sky over the battlefield…*' wrote *Oblt.* Martin Vollmer of I./KG 53, one of the units which performed the day's first mission between 04.56 and 06.37 hours. [119]

Meanwhile, 2 GShAD sent in a few *Shturmoviks* from the south, and it cost this battered unit two Il-2s missing with another three performing belly-landings due to battle damage. German fighters claimed three Il-2s in the Ponyrey area in the early morning hours. One of those ended up on the tally of the by now well-known *Ofw.* Hubert Strassl of III./JG 51, who also claimed one of the Soviet escort fighters – the latter possibly the Yak-1 piloted by 127 IAP's *Serzh.* Yudin, who baled out after getting shot down by a German fighter.

The *Shturmovik* attacks were supplemented by strikes by 3 BAK's Pe-2s – which now for the first time entered the battle – and 221 BAD's Bostons. These were sent in against the German ground forces in heavily escorted waves, which had the effect of dividing the German fighters in the area. Shortly after 08.00 hours (German time; 09.00 Russian time), I./JG 51's *Oblt.* Joachim Brendel encountered a formation of eight Bostons escorted by six Yak-1s, of which he shot down one of the former. Meanwhile, the 2./JG 54 *Schwarm* led by *Lt.* Günther Scheel intercepted seven Il-2s of 874 ShAP on this unit's second mission of the day. Scheel was credited with the destruction of four Il-2s and another pilot claimed a fifth. Soviet records nevertheless show only one Il-2 lost – the aircraft piloted by *Lt.* A.V. Trubetskov, who managed to belly-land.

In spite of their losses, the Soviet airmen contributed greatly to stalling all German attacks on the ground. In five hours, five German attacks were thrown back with severe losses. The last of these occurred at around 09.00 hours (German time), when Soviet 307th Rifle Division, supported by 299 ShAD's Il-2s and 3 BAK's Pe-2s, counter-attacked and took back the parts of Ponyrey which the Germans had managed to seize in the morning hours. This time, 16 VA's fighters succeeded in providing their bombers with almost 100 per cent cover against German fighter attacks. The Soviet bomber units which supported the counter-attack at Ponyrey lost no more than two aircraft.

1. *Fliegerdivision* was called in to employ all its forces in a desperate effort to achieve a decision. KG 51 was dispatched en masse, while Fw 190 fighters were sent out in advance to clear the sky from Soviet fighters. *Ofw.* Hubert Strassl was in action again and claimed to have shot down three La-5s, possibly from 486 IAP. But the new tactics adopted by the Soviet fighters enabled the Lavochkins and Yakovlevs to break through the German fighter shield and attack the German bombers. The Soviet after-battle report concludes:

"*On 7 July our fighters had already reached the battlefield and commenced their successful fight, not against the fighter screens but more directly against enemy bombers, which forced enemy aviation to increase its altitude to 4,000 meters and to bomb our forces while in flight with [only] one pass.*" [120]

General der Flieger Kless admits that "*…almost every Luftwaffe air attack met with considerable enemy air defences.*" [121]

KG 51's morning mission was intercepted by fighters of 6 IAK which claimed to have shot down three, dispersing the German formation in the process and forcing the Junkers crews to jettison their bombs – with many bombs falling over the German lines. [122] III./KG 51 recorded two Ju 88s shot down – although attributed to anti-aircraft fire. [123]

The bombers of KG 51 were followed by St.G 1 with 55 Ju 87s, escorted by 30 Fw 190s. These were, in turn, intercepted by Yak-1s and Yak-9s of 1 GIAD, which claimed two Stukas shot down. *Hptm.* Kurt-Albert Pape, the *Staffelkapitän* of 3./St.G 1, died when his Ju 87 D-3, 'L1+AL', exploded in mid-air; the bomb underneath his aircraft had been hit and went off. Pape was a Knight's Cross holder who had logged around 350 dive-bomber missions since 1941. [124] He was another veteran who would be hard to replace.

It was only the third German bomber formation in close succession which managed to perform its attack without being hit by Soviet fighters. Under the impact of these concentrated aerial bombardments, the Soviet troops were unable to hold the small village of 1-e Maya, and the Germans reached the northern outskirts of Ponyrey.

Model now had brought in fresh troops – the whole 18. *Panzer Division* – and at 11.00 hours he launched a strong armoured attack against Soviet 6th Guards Rifle Division, slightly to the west of Ponyrey. The attack was given powerful support from the air. Formations of fifty to seventy Stukas and twin-engine bombers systematically pounced on the Soviet positions. Efforts by 1 GIAD to ward off these *Luftwaffe* operations were met by fighter attacks by I./JG 54. In the subsequent dogfights, both sides however made gross exaggerations of the number of enemy aircraft that they managed to shoot down. *Lt.* Heinz Prill and *Ofw.* Otto Kittel of 2./JG 54 claimed two victories each in a clash with 30 GIAP, but this unit was actually saved from any losses on 7 July. [125]

Meanwhile, Soviet aerial reconnaissance detected a large new group of around 150 German tanks and self-propelled guns north of Ponyrey, and Rudenko sent in a concentrated force of 120 bombers and *Shturmovik* against this force. As if it was pursued by bad luck, 874 ShAP drew the attention of no fewer than eighteen German fighters, according to the Soviet report. In less than three minutes, five of the seven *Shturmoviks* from 874 ShAP were shot down. [126] The pilot casualties included the formation leader, *Lt.* Ivan Udovenko. The German fighter pilots – from I./JG 51 – reported seven Il-2s shot down out of a formation of nine. [127] *Fw.* Bernhard Hessel and *Uffz.* Klaus Dietrich each were credited with "double kills."

But 874 ShAP's misfortune was an exception. Most of the Il-2s, Pe-2s and Bostons carried out their attacks while provided with a splendid cover by their own escort fighters. Havoc was wrought among the German armoured forces on the ground. Employing the new PTAB anti-tank bombs, the *Shturmoviks* of 16 VA attacked in three waves – each consisting of between 20 and 30 Il-2s – and claimed to have destroyed 34 tanks or armoured vehicles. Additional destruction was caused by the Boston bombers and Pe-2s. 57 BAP/221 BAD was reported to have destroyed 26 tanks and 3 motor vehicles without sustaining any losses on 7 July.

Other Soviet twin-engined bombers flew in large formations into the German rear area to attack supply columns and stores and airfields around Orel. Pilots of II./KG 4 became casualties of Soviet bombing attacks. [1] By flying 235 sorties in daytime on 7 July, 16 VA's bomber units nearly doubled their participation in the battle as compared with the previous day.

This increasing pressure from the Soviet aviation was apparently difficult to absorb for many on the German side. Neglecting the fact that 1. *Fliegerdivision* carried out more sorties than 16 VA on 7 July – 1,687 against 1,185 (plus 185 by 15 VA in the north) – *General der Flieger* Friedrich Kless, the Chief of Staff of *Luftflotte* 6, attempted to explain the advances made by 16 VA:

"*By 7-8 July the Soviets were able to keep strong formations in the air around the clock. […] Unremitting air actions of extended duration necessarily caused the*

The German airfields at Orel were meticulously prepared from the autumn of 1941, and were far better equipped than the average improvised first-line airfield on the Eastern Front. The runway included areas laid with steel mesh to provide a firm surface if the ground was softened by rain. However, there was no guarantee against the human factor – particularly not in a situation when severe combat strained the men's nerves. This pilot obviously missed the mesh area when taxiing with the result that his aircraft nosed over. In the Luftwaffe, this kind of accident was known as a Fliegerdenkmal, an 'airman's memorial'. This particular aircraft possibly was 'Yellow 2' of 3./JG 54, usually flown by Fw. Helmut Meis. This pilot was credited with the shooting down of a La-5 in the forenoon of 7 July 1943. Four weeks later, on 4 August 1943, Meis and the Staffelkapitän of 2./JG 54, Knight's Cross holder Hptm. Hans Götz, both were shot down and killed in combat with Il-2s near Karachev. On that date, JG 54 lost five pilots.

Fw 190 A-4s of I./JG 54 Grünherz.

technical serviceability of our formations to decrease, therefore making it unavoidable that the quantitative Soviet superiority should temporarily be in a position to act directly against German troops during temporal and spatial gaps in the Luftwaffe fighter coverage. Since Ninth Army's ground troops remained engaged in an extremely important offensive, the unavoidable Soviet tactical breakthroughs were at all times very unpleasant.

Russian air attacks began to hit the important supply roads of our spearhead divisions to an increasing extent, with raids striking points as far as twenty-five kilometres behind German lines. Fortunately, as yet the VVS had little experience or skill in such operations, and these attacks never constituted a serious threat to our supply lifelines. In isolated areas Soviet aircraft attacked heavily occupied German airfields, particularly the complex around Orel. Here again, the results achieved by the enemy were consistently poor. A large measure of the credit could be ascribed to the superior accomplishments of the German radio intercept service. Our operators frequently picked up the take-off messages of Russian formations, allowing those formations to be intercepted as they approached and defeated with heavy losses." [129]

Apparently, Kless's memory fails on a number of items. It is true that the Soviet air attacks still left much to desire regarding bombing accuracy – this was particularly the case when the densely occupied German airfields were targeted – but the fact remains that the Soviet air attacks were "very unpleasant" to the German ground troops, and contributed to prevent the Germans from achieving a decisive breakthrough on 7 July. Also, in spite of Kless's statement, 16 VA lost no more than four bombers – three Bostons of 221 BAD and a Pe-2 of 3 BAK - on 7 July 1943. [130] The fighter pilots of 1. *Fliegerdivision* did not even claim more than four Bostons and two Pe-2s shot down on that day.

Even though the Soviet air attacks greatly impressed the ground troops on both sides, who had rarely seen such massed shows of Soviet air power, undoubtedly 1. *Fliegerdivision* continued to hold the upper hand in the air on 7 July. This is particularly remarkable in view of the fact that 16 VA on this day overpowered 1. *Fliegerdivision* in one field, namely the number of fighters employed over the battlefield. While JG 51 and JG 54 were able to bring 307 fighters into the air on that day, 16 VA's fighter units performed more than twice that number of sorties – 731.

Each side's accounts of the battle give a somewhat distorted picture of the actual events, but regarding the air battle over the Orel Bulge on 7 July 1943, the conclusions in most Soviet accounts are definitely incorrect. *General-Leytenant* Rudenko wrote in his memoirs:

"On 7 July, fewer enemy aircraft appeared above the battlefield than before. The [German] *pilots also displayed a significant uncertainty. Probably our opponent was unable to restore his losses in aircraft and aviators. Because of this I decided to release my aviation reserve. From 7 July and onward, our aircraft dominated the air above the Central Front.'* [131]

General der Flieger Kless had a more realistic view when he stated that the German fighters '...*rarely had difficulty attaining air superiority, even in cases of extreme numerical inferiority [although] everyone recognized that this could not continue indefinitely."* [132]

The figures for 1. *Fliegerdivision* on 7 July 1943 speak for themselves. The reconnaissance units carried out 195 flights without losing a single aeroplane, and in the bomber and Stuka units, the loss ratio was below 1 per cent. Ground fire and not fighter interception proved to be the most effective Soviet counter-measure against German air attacks. *"During the last two missions we faced considerable Flak fire, particularly during mission No. 3, when we flew at 1,400 metres altitude and were subject to an intense fire from light Flak guns..."* wrote *Oblt.* Martin Vollmer of I./KG 53 in his diary. [133]

The air fighting on 7 July was characterised by bitter dogfights between the fighters on both sides. These cost 16 VA a loss of 30 aircraft, while only six of 1. *Fliegerdivision's* Fw 190s were shot down (of which three managed to return to friendly territory for emergency landings). This reflects an unquestionable German supremacy, which is attributable primarily to two factors. First of all, the Germans had many more experienced pilots. Secondly, the prevalent defensive character of the Soviet fighter operations tied the Soviet fighter pilots either to close escort missions, or to fighter patrols where they were restricted to certain regions and thus unable to pursue damaged enemy aircraft beyond the boundaries of such a region.

A large share of 1. *Fliegerdivision's* victories on 7 July were attained during aggressive fighter sweeps into the Soviet hinterland. This was the case when the so-called 'Nowotny Schwarm' of 1./JG 54 stormed a group of Yak-7s in the morning. Although the famous commander of this *Schwarm*, *Oblt.* Walter Nowotny, was on home leave (following his 124th victory in June 1943), its four pilots – *Oberfeldwebels* Rudolf Rademacher and Anton Döbele and *Feldwebels* Peter Bremer and Anton Held – returned from that engagement with one victory each.

The last air combat involving 1. *Fliegerdivision* on 7 July took place when III./JG 51's *Ofw.* Hubert Strassl brought his *Schwarm* all the way to 486 IAP's airfield, where Strassl attacked and shot down the La-5 piloted by *Kpt.* Melnikov. With one of the wings of his aircraft torn off by 20 mm shells from Strassl's cannons, Melnikov was barely able to bale out. He was badly injured when he hit the ground on his parachute. His La-5, Serial No. 0135, was 486 IAP's sixth combat loss that day. Thus 486 IAP was, next to 874 ShAP, the hardest hit among 16 VA's units on 7 July. When Strassl landed at Orel half an hour later, he could chalk up his seventh victory that day – and his 62nd in total.

Thus, 24-year old Hubert Strassl was able to look back on an amazing string of victories over the past few days. He had served with JG 51 since 1941, and had accumulated a total of 19 victories until March 1943, when he was posted to France to serve as a fighter instructor under the famous *Major* Hermann Graf at *Ergänzungsjagdgruppe Ost*. When Strassl returned to first-line service in late May 1943, it was obvious that he had learned much. Between 30 May and 4 July, he increased his tally from 19 to 42. On the first day of Operation *Zitadelle*, he was credited with another eleven kills, followed by three on 6 July and six on the seventh. (These figures are based on the RLM victory register at the *Bundesarchiv/Militärarchiv*; other figures in other printed sources appear to be based on second-hand sources.)

Another 1. *Fliegerdivision* pilot who earned great fame for his 'serial kills' during these first days of *Zitadelle* was *Lt.* Günther Scheel of 2./JG 54. On 7 July, Scheel attained seven victories in only two missions. The 21-year old Scheel was, without doubt, an unusually talented fighter pilot. He had been posted from training school to I./JG 54 as late as in January 1943. Having achieved thirty victories on his first fifty combat missions, Scheel would never return from a combat mission without submitting at least one victory – often two, three or four victories – during Operation *Zitadelle*.

It is difficult to establish to what extent the undoubtedly spectacular victory claims of Strassl and Scheel can be verified with Soviet loss records; the magnitude of the air fighting – which in itself is a major explanation of the inflated victory claims which both sides made – makes it impossible to link each loss to a claimant on the opposite side. Both sides greatly exaggerated the enemy's losses in the air on 7 July. The 81 Soviet aircraft reported shot down by 1. *Fliegerdivision* – 74 by fighters and 7 by Flak – should be compared with 16 VA's actual losses of 43 aircraft. [134]

But the main battle, of course, was fought on the ground, and intervention by the aviation of both sides on the battlefield was more equal. According to German estimations, the air attacks performed by 1. *Fliegerdivision* on 7 July resulted in the destruction of 14 Soviet tanks, around 60 other motorised vehicles, 22 artillery pieces and eight ammunition stores. Additionally, 22 tanks were reported damaged and 25 artillery pieces 'silenced'. [135] After relentless German air attacks, the exhausted troops of 41. *Panzerkorps* were finally able to take hold of most parts of Ponyrey, while the 41. *Panzerkorps* managed to occupy Teploye farther to the west.

But these were only limited tactical gains, and they cost the attackers heavily. The day's fighting imposed another 3,000 casualties on *General* Model. [136] Although he had employed fresh forces, 18. *Panzer Division*, the efforts to achieve a strategic breakthrough failed. Subject to impatient demands from the OKH, Model decided to throw in even more of his reserves, 4. *Panzer Division*, the next day.

4. *Panzer Division* conducted the march to its new area of deployment, at Teploye, in heavy rainfall during the night of 7/8 July. But the adverse weather did not deter the Soviet airmen, who carried out unremitting attacks against 9. *Armee's* rear area throughout the night – repeatedly hitting columns of 4. *Panzer Division* vehicles. Eighty-three ADD bombers were in action against German vehicle columns in the area. Another eighty-four ADD sorties were made against the railway station at Glazunovka. Meanwhile, 16 VA's 271 NBAD made 422 harassment sorties with U-2 biplanes.

When Thursday 8 July dawned, the German troops were tired and faced a soaking wet battlefield under dark skies which would not allow any substantial air support.

8 July 1943: Northern Flank

Owing to its excellent radio intercept service, 1. *Fliegerdivision* was able to assume the initiative just before sunrise on 8 July. The radio interceptors picked up an order to 299 ShAD to dispatch a large formation of Il-2s at dawn. At Orel, *Major* Erich Leie, the *Gruppenkommandeur* of I./JG 51, was instructed to send out a group of Fw 190s to intercept the Soviets. Led by *Oblt.* Brendel, the German fighters caught up with the Soviet aircraft –

A German infantryman carrying anti-tank mines moves along a trench.

"*With the little sleep we get,*' wrote I./KG 53's *Oblt.* Vollmer, '*we become quickly exhausted by this idiotic flying in bad weather. You are completely finished after each such mission which involves difficult formation flight in and out of the clouds.*' [139] - These missions were even more ardous to the Soviet airmen, who often were less trained than their German counterparts, and who also ran a far greater risk of being subject to very dangerous fighter interception. At 08.00 hours, 221 BAD's Bostons, escorted by Yak-1s of 282 IAD, ran into Fw 190s of IV./JG 51 and I./JG 54. The Germans succeeded in shooting down three Bostons – one of those by *Lt.* Günther Scheel – but 3./JG 54's *Oblt.* Franz Eisenach was injured by return fire from the Bostons after securing his 21st victory. [140] Eisenach was able to bring his Fw 190, 'Yellow 6', back to base, but the wounds he had sustained rendered him unfit for combat service for two months. [141] About an hour later, a group of Fw 190 pilots from *Major* Leie's I./JG 51 achieved another major success against a formation of Il-2s. *Uffz.* Dietrich Hessel again was able to chalk up a 'double', this time against an Il-2 and one of its escorting La-5s, and *Lt.* Höfemeier and *Uffz.* Romm added one more Il-2 each to their successes earlier that morning. In total, I./JG 51 reported six Il-2s and one La-5 shot down for the loss of one Fw 190 which came down in friendly territory. [142] A *Rotte* from 7./JG 51 also intervened, with *Fw.* Lothar Mai claiming a seventh Il-2 shot down. This time the suffering Soviet unit was 2 GShAD, which registered eight Il-2s missing in action on 7 July, plus two more which performed emergency landings in friendly territory after getting shot up by German fighters. [143] Meanwhile, the *Stabsstaffel* of JG 51 teamed up with Bf 110s of I./ZG 1 to intercept another formation of 221 BAD Boston bombers. There were only four Bostons, escorted by eight Yak-1s, and the fact that the Soviets flew in such a small formation would cost them dearly. Three bombers were shot down in quick succession – the Germans claimed four, including three by I./ZG 1.

The weather continued to deteriorate. When *Oblt.* Vollmer took off for the day's third mission at 13.15 hours he flew straight into a wall of dark clouds: "When I returned two hours late after today's third mission, I had already been added to the MIA list. Having lost contact with the formation in clouds and a raging storm, and having been subject to anti-aircraft fire north of Orel, I finally received a wrong heading from ground control and drifted alone into enemy air space. When we were subject to heavy ground fire, I gave up and dropped my bomb against the AA position. Then I flew towards the west, not knowing where we were, but received excellent heading from the radio beacon from Smolensk. Reaching the air above Smolensk, I followed the highway to our airfield where I landed in very adverse weather. By that time, my nerves were quite upset and I made a really hard touchdown. When our aircraft finally stopped, Gobert – what a great guy he is! – came forward and showed a merrily smiling face. He was so glad that we were back!" [144]

With the *Luftwaffe* severely hampered by the weather, all German attacks on the ground were forced back with apalling losses. A report from the 20. *Panzer Division* illustrates the scope of the fighting: "*Within an hour all the officers of 5th Company, 112th Panzergrenadier Regiment, had been killed or wounded. [...] The battalions melted away. Companies became mere platoons... The famous battle of matériel of El Alamein, where Montgomery employed 1,000 guns to bring about the turning point in the war in Africa was a modest operation by comparison. Even Stalingrad, in spite of its more apocapyltic and tragic aura, does not stand comparison in terms of forces employed with the gigantic, open-field battle of Kursk.*" [145]

The battered German troops were further tormented by bombs dropped from a formation of Pe-2s from 3 BAK which attacked late in the afternoon. The escorting La-5 pilots from 92 IAP were able to ward off the attempt by numerous Fw 190s from III./JG 51 and I./JG 54 to break through to attack the Petlyakov bombers, but it cost them a loss of three of their own. *Lt.* Grakhov and *Mladshiy Leytenants* Vedin and Stupinskiy all failed to return from that engagement. Other Soviet fighter units also were in action

30 Il-2s, escorted by 15 fighters – in the Fatezh area, some 40 kilometres south-west of Ponyrey. [137] By performing a series of diving attacks, they managed to shoot down four Il-2s – two by Brendel and one each by *Lt.* Heinrich Höfemeier and *Uffz.* Oskar Romm – and then made a quick escape into the clouds, leaving the Soviet formation in disarray.

This strike seriously interfered with 16 VA's planned action in support of a counter-attack at Ponyrey. But it was an exception in more than one sense. When the 307th Rifle Division, in cooperation with 51st and 103rd Tank Brigades, launched the counter-attack at Ponyrey one hour later, the weather was too bad to allow either side to receive any air support. Following a three-hour battle in mud, rain and fog, the Soviet troops were able to re-take the village of 1-e Maya.

By that time, General Model had launched between 300 and 400 tanks of 47. *Panzerkorps* against Olkhovatka and Samodurovka, 19 kilometres further to the west. Regardless of bad weather, the aviation commanders on both sides sent their units into the sky. Of 1. *Fliegerdivision's* 274 bomber sorties and 378 Stuka sorties on 8 July, the majority were performed to support the attacks by 47. *Panzerkorps* in the morning. But bad visibility hampered bombing accuracy, and no more than five tanks were claimed destroyed. [138]

Pzpkfw IV medium tanks with extra armour plating protection attached to the sides advance on Russian motorised units.

in that area by that time, and the Germans claimed 14 Soviet fighters shot down – eleven La-5s and a Yak-7, a LaGG-3 and an Airacobra. (The latter was either a misidentification or an erroneous claim, since no Airacobras were lost by 16 VA on that day, and the "LaGG-3" probably was a misidentified Yak fighter.) While 2./JG 54's *Lt.* Günther Scheel was credited with two victories, bringing his total for the day to three, III./JG 51's *Ofw.* Hubert Strassl and *Unteroffiziere* Lothar Mai and Fritz Reitinger each claimed three on this mission.

Strassl, who performed his 221st combat sortie, claimed a LaGG-3 at 17.38 hours, followed by two La-5s at 17.50 and 17.51 hours – recorded as his 65th through 67th victories. Immediately after he had dispatched the last fighter, a "LaGG-3" (according to the German report but obviously a misidentification, since there were no LaGG-3s operational in this area) came up below Strassl's Fw 190 and opened fire. Strassl attempted to evade by putting his Fw 190, 'Black 4', into a dive. But it was in vain – large flames erupted from the aircraft. The German pilot baled out, but by that time he was too low. There was no time for the parachute to envelop, and the pilot fell to his death. Thus one of the most remarkable fighter ace careers in JG 51 ended abruptly. Hubert Strassl was posthumously awarded with the Knight's Cross on 12 November 1943.

It is possible that Strassl fell prey to the Soviet ace, *Lt.* Stepan Kolesnichenko, of 519 IAP. According to the Soviet report, Kolesnichenko participated in a fighter sweep in the Olkhovatka area when he suddenly discovered two Fw 190s which were performing an attack against a Soviet fighter. While the Soviet machine was shot down, Kolesnichenko opened full throttle on his Yak-7B and roamed up to a position beneath one of the Fw 190s, where he pulled up and opened fire. Apparently caught unaware, the German pilot followed his steeply descending aircraft as it plunged earthward in its last dive.

Kolesnichenko was 519 IAP's most successful ace by that time. By mid-July 1943, he had amassed a total of 16 individual and four shared victories on 114 combat missions.

An evaluation of the reports filed by both sides in the air war over the northern flank of the *Zitadelle* battle on 8 July 1943 shows most conspicuously an incredible Soviet overclaiming. 16 VA reported 88 German aircraft shot down. [146] *Luftflotte* 6 recorded only nine aircraft damaged (all but two due to hostile action) and two shot down and destroyed on 8 July. [147] Although there is a possibility for errors in these records, a comparison with casualty lists shows that the Soviet claims for 88 shot down German aircraft must be dismissed as vastly exaggerated.

Indeed, the number of enemy aircraft shot down which 1. *Fliegerdivision* reported on 8 July is also higher than actual Soviet loss records. *Luftflotte* 6 reported 73 Soviet aircraft shot down – 67 in aerial combat and 6 by *Flak* – on 8 July. Meanwhile, 16 VA filed 49 own aircraft shot down and destroyed and 11 which made emergency landings due to battle damage. [148]

The low pressure which dominated the area on this day provided the German fighters with the opportunity to launch surprise attacks from the clouds against VVS formations. 1. *Fliegerdivision* still maintained a numerical superiority in the air over the battlefield – flying 1,173 daylight sorties on 8 July, against 913 by 16 VA and 157 by 15 VA.

Indeed, 16 VA was resurging strongly in the air after the first disastrous day of Operation *Zitadelle*. The number of *Shturmovik* and bomber sorties declined between 7 and 8 July – from 219 and 235 respectively to 130 and 170 – but this was primarily due to the worsened weather. The impact of these air operations was so strong that even *General der Flieger* Kless felt that the VVS maintained a powerful and unremitting presence in the air throughout 8 July too. [149]

However, Rudenko had all reason to be concerned about how long his badly mauled units could maintain this activity. The very heavy losses in fighters forced 16 VA to reduce its fighter operations day by day – from 817 on 5 July to 779, 731 and 613 respectively on the following days.

In any case, their contribution to the battle had been absolutely vital. The Central Front had been able to hold back their enemy, and as historians David M. Glantz and Jonathan M. House point out: '…by 8 July any hope of German success at Kursk rested squarely on the shoulders of Hoth's armada struggling tens of kilometres to the south.' [150]

Chapter Five

Southern Flank 6–9 July: The Battle Intensifies

6 July 1943: Southern Flank

Just as on the northern flank, the Soviets made a strong effort on 6 July to wrestle the initiative from the Germans on the southern flank, where *General Armii* Nikolay Vatutin, the Voronezh Front's commander, prepared a massive counter-offensive. To this end, he moved the 1st Tank Army and the independent 2nd Guards Tank Corps and 5th Guards Tank Corps forward. While the former was tasked to strike against the 48. *Panzerkorps*, the latter two were tasked to attack the II. SS *Panzerkorps* from the east and from the north respectively. In the headquarters of 2 VA, plans were made for the air support of this operation.

During the preceding night, the ADD went into action to bomb German armour and motorised infantry at Tomarovka, Borisovka and Pushkarnogo. At the former site, the bomber crews reported three large explosions as a result of their attacks.

The day started well for the Soviets. At dawn, 5 IAK's fighters were dispatched en masse over the front lines north-west of Belgorod. They only met few German aircraft, and hardly any air combats were fought. Shortly afterward, the fighters of 4 IAK joined in. These were released from their escort tasks and instead were assigned to patrol above the battlefield north-west of Belgorod. When the first Soviet airmen landed at their airfields following these early morning missions, they optimistically drew the conclusion that the *Luftwaffe* had been beaten off from the skies following the previous day's bitter air fighting.

However, *Fliegerkorps* VIII's absence from the air early on 6 July was due to a far less dramatic reason – a cold front which brought low clouds compelled *Generalmajor* Seidemann to allow his airmen to rest. [151] This lasted until shortly after 09.00 hours when 4. *Panzerarmee* resumed its attack. Then the German aircraft suddenly appeared over the battlefield again. Around 200 close air support sorties were launched against the badly mauled remnants of Soviet 52nd and 67th Guards Rifle divisions.

Next, the *Luftwaffe* attacks shifted towards the west, against positions held by Soviet 6th Tank Corps. But most of these attacks were conducted by close-support aircraft. Adhering to desperate calls from *Armeeabteilung Kempf*, Seidemann diverted most of *Fliegerkorps* VIII's fighters towards the east. This left the air over the 4. *Panzerarmee* at the mercy of Soviet fighters – which had not been anticipated by the Germans. Thus,

Soviet fighter attacks blocked many of *Fliegerkorps* VIII's close support operations for 4. *Panzerarmee*. A large formation of St.G 77 Stukas was badly mauled by seventeen La-5s at around 09.00 hours. The Soviet fighter unit 88 GIAP, claimed to have shot down five Ju 87s, three Bf 109s and an Hs 126 for the loss of a single La-5, piloted by *Lt.* Aleksandr Gorovets, who was killed. The widespread version that Gorovets single-handedly shot down nine Ju 87s in his last combat, rests on a misinterpretation, and obviously finds no support Russian archives. [152]

In any case, the various missions on 6 July cost St.G 77 dearly. In total, ten of this *Stukageschwader's* Ju 87s were shot down or severely damaged, and SchG 1 lost another four ground-attack aircraft – including three Fw 190s. [153] In its daily report on the evening of 6 July, 3. *Panzer Division* of 48. *Panzerkorps* complained: '*Fewer German fighters than yesterday.*' [154]

The Soviet battle analysis concluded: "*Before the end of the day the Germans attacked the 6th Tank Corps' defensive lines four times, each time with air support which bombed our combat formations with 60-70 aircraft. However, all enemy attacks were driven back.*" [155]

From his perspective on the other side of the hill, *General* Friedrich von Mellenthin, Chief of Staff of 48. *Panzerkorps*, noted that the German air attacks failed to decrease the Soviet artillery which opened up against the *Panzer* troops. [156] With their fighters more or less in control of the air, 2 VA sent in 291 ShAD's *Shturmoviks*. Operating in groups of six to eight aircraft, they attacked German vehicle columns, and with quite some success – as *General* von Mellenthin recorded: "Russian aircraft operated with remarkable dash … many tanks fell victim to the Red Air Force." [157]

"*Strong enemy air activity over the entire combat area, especially at the bridge east of Berezovyy,*' reported the '*Grossdeutschland*' Division of 48. *Panzerkorps*." [158]

However, while 2 VA accomplished what could be expected from its airmen, the planned counter-attack on the ground for which all of this air support was conducted never materialised. Faced with large numbers of Tiger and Panther tanks, *General-Leytenant* Mikhail Katukov, the commander of the 1st Tank Army, chose to order his troops into defensive positions rather than wage an uncertain attack against a superior enemy. This was probably a sound decision. Faced with attacks from the air, faltering friendly air support, and a significantly reinforced Soviet defence on the ground, 48. *Panzerkorps* was unable to achieve another breakthrough and alted after taking severe losses. By the end of the day, 'Grossdeutschland' had no more than 80 of its 350 tanks still operational.

On 48. Panzerkorps' right (eastern) flank, SS-Obergruppenführer Paul Hausser's II. SS Panzerkorps was more successful, and managed to push forward about thirteen kilometres. In the evening, the SS Leibstandarte Division was beset by the counter-strike from Soviet 2nd Guards Tank Corps. Carrying the the name of honour 'Tatsinskaya' for its famous raid against the German transporter base on Christmas Eve 1942, the Soviet corps mustered about 200 tanks. In a situation which was close to altering the whole situation on the SS Panzerkorps's eastern flank, Major Alfred Druschel's Sch.G 1 scrambled against the Soviet armoured columns. The Hs 129s of .(Pz)/Sch.G 1 and JG 51's Panzerjägerstaffel dived down on the Soviet tanks. Meanwhile, I./Sch.G 1's Fw 190s, many of which were of the new ground-attack version the Fw 190 F, attacked the Soviet troops with 500 kg AB bomb containers. Each of these containers released a hailstorm of small SD-2 anti-personnel bombs which covered an area 18-30 metres wide and 30-55 metres long. The effect on unprotected soldiers was devastating.

These air attacks completely disrupted the intended counter-attack and inflicted heavy losses on the 2nd Guards Tank Corps. "After a two-hour contest in cooperation with the army's Flak, the aircraft succeeded in beating off the Russian attack and when the last pilot left the battlefield for home, dusk was falling." [159]

Undoubtedly, this was the Luftwaffe's greatest achievement on that day. Hptm. Bruno Meyer, the Staffelkapitän of 4.(Pz)/Sch.G 1, described what the scene looked like after the battle:

"The countryside presented a weird sight with its smouldering and fiercely burning tanks. From time to time a tank exploded and a heavy pall of smoke curled upwards into the air. There had been virtually no losses on our side, though some machines had been slightly damaged on their undersides by debris hurled up by exploding tanks. Emergency repairs were hurriedly carried out during the night so that our aircraft were fully serviceable again in the morning and ready for operations. It was impossible for us to count exactly how many tanks we had knocked out since the whole success was shared with army units." [160]

The result of the devastating air attacks against the 2nd Guards Tank Corps was that the 5th Guards Tank Corps alone launched a counter-attack against the powerful II. SS Panzerkorps, and consequently failed bitterly.

Further south, Armeeabteilung Kempf's troops made a major effort to break out of their little bridgehead on the eastern side of the Donets, south of Belgorod. The Il-2s of 2 VA's 1 ShAK and 17 VA's 3 SAK and 9 SAK, which since the first day of the German offensive had been fully engaged against the pontoon bridges and ferries across the Donets, were met by large numbers of Bf 109s as the prime emphasis of Fliegerkorps VIII's fighters was placed on providing Kempf's troops with air cover.

Just like the previous day, the Il-2s arrived in several waves in small groups. The first Shturmovik attacks were carried out at 06.00 hours, but from around 10.30 hours, the frequeny of these attacks was intensified. Over and over again, groups of four to eight Bf 109s were hurled against the Il-2s, shooting down large numbers in a repetition of the events of 5 July. The Germans claimed over 30 Il-2s shot down. The Hungarian Puma fighter unit contributed with one more, through the unit commander Örgy. Aladar Heppes. His colleague Obstlt. Dietrich Hrabak, Geschwaderkommodore of JG 52, increased his victory tally by three, of which two were against Il-2s. [161]

In reality, these attacks cost 17 VA a loss of 37 Il-2s on 6 July. Among the 22 Shturmoviks lost by 2 VA on 6 July, the majority were lost over the Donets. The worst hit unit was 306 ShAD, which lost 19 Il-2s on this day, with only 34 Il-2s remaining in the evening of 6 July. [162]

Owing to this excellent support in the air, Armeeabteilung Kempf was able to bring a sufficient troop force across the river to launch a successful offensive. Soviet 7th Guards Army was unable to withstand the powerful attack, and by the end of the day Kempf's three Panzer divisions had managed to occupy the strategic heights at Myasoyedovo, thirteen kilometres to the east of Belgorod.

When the sun set over the blood-stained battlefields on the southern flank of the Kursk Bulge, it was clear to the Germans that their enemy had been far better prepared than they had expected. Indeed, the SS Panzerkorps and Armeeabteilung Kempf had been able to make fairly good advances, and whole Soviet tank corps had been beaten back by Luftwaffe attacks. But the trouble which 48. Panzerkorps had run into was ill-boding – both on the ground and in the air. Already on the second day, it was obvious that not even the massive concentration of German aviation to such a small sector was sufficient.

Alfred Druschel, the commander of Schlachtgeschwader 1 during Operation Zitadelle. Druschel was one of the Luftwaffe's most experienced ground-attack aviation veterans and had flown a Hs 123 in close-support operations during the invasions of Poland and France in 1939-1940. He commanded 4.(S)/LG 2 during the invasion of the Soviet Union in 1941. The next year, when the Luftwaffe's first Schlachtgeschwader, SchG 1, was formed, Druschel was appointed Gruppenkommandeur of its first Gruppe. Shortly afterward he was made the unit's Geschwaderkommodore. Awarded with the Knight's Cross in August 1941 and the Oak Leaves in September 1942, Druschel became the first among Germany's Stuka or ground-attack pilots to be awarded with the Swords to the Oak leaves on 19 February 1943. At the age of only 27, and with the rank of an Oberst, Alfred Druschel was killed in action on the Western Front on 1 January 1945.

Bruno Meyer was one of the Luftwaffe's most experienced ground-attack pilots and unit commanders. By the time he led the Hs 129-equipped Panzerjagdkommando of Sch.G 1 during the Battle of Kursk, he could look back on a long and successful career as a ground-attack flier. He had served with Fliegergruppe 20 – the nucleus of the Luftwaffe's first ground-attack unit, II.(S)/LG 2 – since the summer of 1938. During the Blitzkrieg years, he flew a Hs 123 biplane and Bf 109 fighter-bombers on hundreds of missions over Poland, in the West, over the English Channel, in the Balkans and on the Eastern Front. In the winter of 1942/1943 he led Hs 129-equipped 4./Sch.G 2 against Allied tanks in Tunisia. Just ahead of Operation Zitadelle, the Panzerjagdkommando of Sch.G 1 was formed under Meyer's command. Later redesignated IV.(Pz)/SG 9, this unit would achieve great success against Soviet armour during the remainder of the war. Meyer himself was posted to the OKL staff in July 1944. (Photo: Martin Pegg.)

The silhouette of a Henschel Hs 129 anti-tank aircraft often was enough to make the crew of a Soviet tank abandon their vehicle and seek cover – particularly when caught on open ground with little possibility of escape. (Photo: Martin Pegg.)

Bf 109 G-6s of I./JG 52 at Bessonovka aerodrome in July 1943. 'Black 10' was flown by Gefreiter Friedrich Göpfer, the wingman of Oblt. Paul-Heinrich Dähne, the commander of the unit's 2. Staffel. At around 10.20 hours on 5 July 1943, Dähne and Göpfert intercepted a group of Il-2s that attempted to attack the II .SS Panzerkorps and reported one Il-2 each shot down. Göpfer would follow up this success by claiming a Pe-2 and a Yak-1 on 16 July. In the evening of 25 July 1943, Göpfer participated when a group of I./JG 52 Bf 109s engaged a formation of Yak-1s. In the ensuing combat, Göpfer claimed a Yak-1 shot down – the only German success in that engagement – but was shortly afterward himself shot down by another Soviet fighter. Göpfer was posted as missing.

Il-2 Shturmoviks at a Soviet airfield. During the Battle of Kursk, the Shturmovik units operated a mixture of single-seat and twin-seat Il-2s. The former sustained particularly atrocious losses at the hands of German fighter pilots. One of 17 VA's Il-2-equipped units, 306 ShAD, recorded 47 aircraft losses on 5 and 6 July 1943 alone.

In qualitative terms, the *Luftwaffe* still held a convincing superiority. Although St.G 77 had been dealt harsh losses, overall, *Fliegerkorps* VIII's combat losses on 6 July were quite modest – eleven aircraft were destroyed and eleven damaged. Soviet aviation had paid a considerably higher price for its gains on 6 July: 2 VA recorded 45 aircraft losses (23 fighters and 22 *Shturmoviks*). The statistics for 17 VA for this period are not available, but as we have seen, its *Shturmovik* units alone lost 37 aircraft on 6 July. Thus it may be concluded that the VVS air forces operating against *Fliegerkorps* VIII lost approximately 90 aircraft on the second day of *Zitadelle* – a severe bloodletting. However, the Soviets had also showed that they would not be discouraged by such losses.

During the following night, the ADD dispatched 163 bomber crews to attack the German rear area north-west and north of Belgorod. Four-engined Pe-8s of 45 AD also participated in these attacks. Each of these heavy bombers carried a payload of no less than four metric tons. Additionally, the U-2 equipped night bomber regiments of 2 VA and 17 VA performed 269 harassment sorties against the same targets. The Germans were in no position to compete with this significant nocturnal activity. During that same night, *Fliegerkorps* VIII sent a total of six bombers 'train-hunting' between Kursk and Kastornoye, while forty-six crews of *Störkampfgruppe/Luftflotte* 4 dropped their small bombs against targets of opportunity in the Soviet rear area.

Meanwhile, in the VVS headquarters, the air operations were carefully analysed, leading to an important conclusion: one of the dominant reasons for the grievous *Shturmovik* losses during the first two days was the tactic of dispatching the Il-2s piecemeal, in small formations which could easily be hacked to pieces by the German fighters – which operated in groups of four to eight aircraft. Drawing on the lessons of 16 VA's tactic to bring together its *Shturmoviks* into larger formations, *General-Leytenant* Krasovskiy, 2 VA's commander, instructed his *Shturmovik*

A formation of Ju 87 Stukas of I./St.G 2. During Operation Zitadelle the Luftwaffe Stukas and bombers operated in larger formations than usual on the Eastern Front. On the two first days of the offensive, the Stukas of Fliegerkorps VIII carried out a total of 1,864 sorties in support of the German offensive. Bearing in mind that most of these dive-bomber attacks were carried out against an area measuring only around 200 square miles, it is easy to understand the amount of pressure which the Stukas exerted on the defending Soviet ground troops.

Podpolkovnik Vladimir Abramov, the commander of 746 AP, poses in front of one of his unit's huge four-engined Pe-8 heavy bombers. 45 AD was the ADD's heavy bomber Diviziya, equipped with Pe-8s. It was active during the Battle of Kursk, when it consisted of two regiments – Abramov's 746 AP and 890 AP.

units to form such large groups in the air during the operations the next day.

7 July 1943: Southern Flank

Fliegerkorps VIII was already turning into a 'fire brigade' as late in the evening of 6 July, it promised 4. *Panzerarmee* that this force would receive the bulk of air support the next day – primarily through reinforced fighter cover and air attacks against Dubrova, and against the hill north of Lukhanino and Gremuchiy. [163]

Early on 7 July, *Armeeabteilung Kempf*'s request for air support received the reply that no more than a single *Stukagruppe* could be diverted from the *Schwerpunkt* in 4. *Panzerarmee*'s area. [164] When 4. *Panzerarmee* resumed its attack at dawn on 7 July, *Fliegerkorps* VIII was present in full force in the sky above the armoured columns. Again Soviet fortifications, tank and other vehicle columns, anti-tank gun positions and artillery concentrations were the main targets. The Soviet battle analysis reads: "*The tank attacks were supported by aviation which bombed our troop dispositions every 5-10 minutes in groups of 60-80 aircraft each. As a result of the repeated attacks, the enemy penetrated the 1st Brigade's front and forced it to withdraw in the direction of Syrtsevo.*" [165]

While *Fliegerkorps* VIII's Stukas and ground-attack aircraft dived down on the Soviet positions, 2 VA's *Shturmoviks* attacked the *Panzer* troops. This time, the *Shturmoviks* applied Krasovskiy's instructions of attacking in large formations. *Lt.* Erich Hartmann and three other Bf 109 pilots from 7./JG 52 had taken off from Ugrim at 03.06 hours for a fighter sweep over II. SS *Panzerkorps*'s forward positions; a half hour later they were stunned to see forty-six Il-2s with strong fighter escort emerge from the haze in the north. The *Shturmoviks* came from 1 ShAK, and from an altitude of about 460 metres they went straight against the positions of the '*Leibstandarte*' division of II. SS *Panzerkorps* at Yakovlevo. Without hesitating, the German fighters hurled themselves against the mass of Soviet aircraft. They managed to shoot down five Il-2s and a La-5 – Hartmann and *Ofw.* Günter Toll bagged two each, but lost one of their own – *Ofw.* Toll's Bf 109 (the pilot survived with injuries). Of course, the massive attack against the German troops could not be warded off.

During this mission, the Il-2 piloted by *Kpt.* Stepan Poshivalnikov, an *Eskadrilya* commander in 800 ShAP, was damaged by an AAA shell which exploded close to the aircraft and killed the rear gunner. One of the German fighters attempted to finish off the crippled *Shturmovik*, but thanks to the intervention of *Lt.* Gridinsky, who actually attacked the Bf 109 with his Il-2, Poshivalnikov was saved. The German fighter disengaged, but

Il-2 ground-attack aircraft en route to the battle zone. During the first five days of the battle, the troops of Heeresgruppe Süd were subjected to attacks involving around two thousand Shturmovik sorties.

II./K.G. 76 operated from Kursk-East to support the opening phase of the German summer offensive against the Soviet Union. This Ju 88 A-5, coded F1+AM of 4./K.G. 76, is typical of the unit's aircraft at the time.

Poshivalnikov's aircraft could not be saved. Poshivalnikov performed a belly-landing in enemy-controlled territory, but before any German troops had arrived on the scene, Gridinskiy had landed next to the crashed *Shturmovik*, picked up his *Eskadrilya* commander and flew him back to safety at the base.

Two hours later, 1 ShAK attacked the '*Leibstandarte*' with another concentrated formation, this time 33 Il-2s with strong fighter escort. According to Soviet estimations, these two concentrated attacks by 1 ShAK resulted in the destruction of over 200 German tanks. [166]

Undoubtedly, several German vehicles were knocked out by these Soviet air attacks, but German sources show that very few tanks actually were destroyed.

Further to the west, 291 ShAD dispatched 82 Il-2s, escorted by 122 fighters, in several attacks against 'Grossdeutschland' and 3. *Panzer Division*. Not only did these concentrated *Shturmovik* attacks overwhelm the German fighter shield, but they also produced a far better result against the ground targets. 'Grossdeutschland's' advance was severely disrupted, as the unit's chronicle noted: "*Very heavy attacks by enemy close-support aircraft disrupted these movements considerably; in some places the fighting in the system of positions entailed very heavy losses*" [167]

During these missions, 291 ShAD alone dropped more than 10,000 PTAB anti-tank bombs. One of 291 ShAD's attacks against a large vehicle column of 'Grossdeutschland' and 3. *Panzer Division* on the road from Tomarovka to Cherkassk on 7 July 1943 has become renowned in war literature. The attack was opened by eight Il-2s, led by *Lt.* Baranov, which dropped 1,600 PTAB anti-tank bombs from 200-300 metres altitude. Next followed another eight Il-2s, led by *Lt.* Golubev. When the *Shturmovik* fliers left the scene, they reported that twenty tanks were burning on the road.

As with the previous day, 2 VA's fighters again challenged the *Luftwaffe* for control of the air. This resulted in repeated fighter-to-fighter combat. On one such occasion, a quite extraordinary feat was ascribed to a Soviet fighter pilot of Georgian descendance. It started when 183 IAP's Yak-1s attacked a formation of Ju 88s, and *Kpt.* Shalva Kiriya shot down a Ju 88. Next, a group of Bf 109s intervened. Kiriya reportedly shot down one of these too, but in the next moment his own Yak-1 was set on fire. The Soviet account asserts that in spite of the damage to his own aircraft, Kiriya managed to shoot down two more German fighters – and nurse his own aircraft back to base where he performed an emergency landing!

Another engagement on 7 July, shortly after 07.00 hours, saw a group of La-5s from 40 GIAP intercepting a formation of Ju 87s and claiming five Ju

87s shot down. When a group of Bf 109s intervened to protect the Stukas, the La-5 pilots claimed three of the German fighters shot down against two own losses. [168] *Kapitans* Nikolay Kitayev and Dmitriy Nazarenko were credited with three and two victories respectively. On the German side *Uffz.* Karl-Heinz Meltzer and *Uffz.* Werner Hohenberg, both of 8./JG 52, claimed the destruction of one La-5 each.

Shortly afterward, 203 IAD's Yak-1s attacked various groups of German aircraft in the same sector, with 516 IAP claiming the destruction of three Ju 88s and three Ju 87s against the loss of two Yak-1s (from 247 IAP). [169]

According to *Luftwaffe* documents, the German losses in all of these engagements were confined to a damaged Ju 87 from 9./St.G 2, while the "Ju 88s" claimed by 183 IAP and 516 IAP could be identical with some of the three He 111s which I./KG 27 and I./KG 100 lost. [170]

Although the Soviet claims for destroyed German tanks and aircraft were exaggerated, the massed *Shturmovik* attacks doubtlessly met with great success. Throughout 7 July, 2 VA lost no more than 13 Il-2s – a significant decrease compared with the two previous days.

This was in stark contrast with 17 VA's operations further to the south-east that morning. Indeed, the bulk of *Fliegerkorps* VIII was dispatched to support 4. *Panzerarmee*. However, because of the vulnerability to air attacks of the supply lines across the Donets river, *Generalmajor* Seidemann assigned JG 3 *Udet* to cover the Donets crossings early on 7 July. At dawn – at the same time as *Lt.* Erich Hartmann and three other Bf 109 pilots of 7./JG 52 encountered a mass of over sixty Soviet aircraft in the north – *Major* Wolfgang Ewald and at least twelve Bf 109 pilots of *Jagdgeschwader Udet's* II. and III. *Gruppen* met small formations of Il-2s from 17 VA's 306 ShAD which, in traditional manner, attempted to attack the pontoon bridges. JG 3 *Udet* had earned a reputation among its Soviet adversaries during the Battle of Stalingrad, and now it would prove that it was a no less dangerous an opponent than it had been one year previously. In running battles which lasted thirty minutes – from 03.45 to 04.14 hours in the morning – JG 3's fighter pilots claimed twelve Il-2s shot down. These losses compelled 17 VA to discontinue its attacks against the pontoon bridges.

But later in the day, when the *Udet* fighters had disappeared from the air over *Armeeabteilung Kempf*, the *Shturmoviks* returned. This time it was in order to support the 7th Guards Army's counter-attacks against the flanks of the bulge which had been created by *Armeeabteilung Kempf's* advance towards the north on the eastern side of the Donets. These counter-attacks "*...inflicted severe casualties on the German 320th Infantry Division and prevented*

Already after the first day of the commencement of Operation Zitadelle, the Luftwaffe was turned into a fire brigade, with its operations rushed from one sector of the battlefield to another. On 7 July, the hard-pressed Armeeabteilung Kempf received the reply from Fliegerkorps VIII that it could not receive air support from more than a single Stukagruppe. Seen in this photograph, Ju 87 Stukas of II./St.G 77 are approaching the Donets river. This Stukagruppe had suffered badly during Operation Carmen, the aerial assault against Kursk on 2 June 1943, when six of its Ju 87s were shot down.

the 106th Infantry from relieving 7. Panzer Division *forces so that they could shift their full strength to the critical drive to the north.'* [171] The role which the *Shturmoviks* played to this Soviet defensive success is evident from the report which 17 VA received in the evening of 7 July: '*The commander of the 7th Guards Army and the commanders of the 81st and 73rd Guards Rifle Divisions wish to express their gratitude to the air crews who attacked and destroyed enemy tanks in the Melekhov and Chyornaya Polyana areas from 15.00 and 16.00 hours, and also to the Shturmovik fliers for their actions in the Maslov Pristan area between 13.25 and 14.13 hours.'* [172]

In the afternoon of 7 July, 17 VA made a new attempt to neutralise elements of *Fliegerkorps* VIII by launching a surprise attack against the aerodrome of Rogan. Due to a navigational error, the Il-2s of 237 ShAP and 775 ShAP attacked Varvarovka instead. They were able to destroy only a single Fw 190 (of Sch.G 1), but managed to escape without any losses. The latter owed much to the fighter escort of 5 GIAP, which tied the intercepting Bf 109s of II./JG 3 into a whirling dogfight. This cost 5 GIAP a loss of four La-5s. [173] Two of these ended up on the victory account of 6./JG 3's *Uffz.* Gerhard Thyben, bringing his total for the day to three.

That *Fliegerkorps* VIII had not been weakened by the intended strike against Rogan was testified by 814 IAP of 17 VA a little later, as two of its Yak-1s were shot down by a lone German fighter pilot, 6./JG 3's *Hptm.* Paul Stolte. Meanwhile, and over 4. *Panzerkorps's* combat sector, 7./JG 52's *Lt.* Erich Hartmann claimed to have knocked down three La-5s – which gave him a result for the day of five victories.

In total, *Fliegerkorps* VIII reported 96 Soviet aircraft shot down on 7 July. Its bombers and close-support aircraft meanwhile claimed to have destroyed one armoured train, 44 tanks, 20 artillery pieces and 50 other motor

Törzsőrmester (Oberfeldwebel) Dezső Szentgyörgyi and Szakaszvezető (Unteroffizier) István Fábián, two pilots of the Hungarian 1/1. Vadászszázad in front of Szentgyörgyi's Bf 109 G-2/R-6. Szentgyörgyi was credited with the shooting down of a La-5 near Belgorod on 5 July 1943. Fábián also claimed a Soviet aircraft shot down on the same day, but this was not confirmed. Szentgyörgyi and Fábián both survived the war - with a credit of 29 and 14 victories respectively. (Photo: Becze.)

vehicles. Even though these figures also appear to be inflated, the impact on the ground operations by the massive German air operations on 7 July was considerable. '*Excellent* Luftwaffe *support …*' it was recorded in the history of *Leibstandarte,* which in spite of the Soviet air attacks, managed to slice into a weak spot in the Soviet defence lines. This led the II. SS *Panzerkorps* onto the road towards Prokhorovka, ten kilometres farther to the north-east. Further to the west, 48. *Panzerkorps* also was able to continue forward: "More than 300 German tanks, including up to 40 Panthers, supported by waves of dive-bombers, ground through the 1st and 3rd Mechanised Brigades' defensive front in an agonising slow, costly, but inexorable drive." [174] At Lukhanino, 3. *Panzer Division* managed to cross the Pena river and establish a bridgehead on the other side. However, this was only ten kilometres from 48. *Panzerkorps's* point of departure two days previously. The deepest German penetration had been achieved by II. SS *Panzerkorps* on the eastern flank, but its forward columns south-west of Prokhorovka had advanced no more than 20 kilometres since the morning of 5 July. These meagre territorial gains had cost 4. *Panzerarmee* and *Armeeabteilung Kempf* more than 10,000 casualties.

The situation was very much different in the air, where *Fliegerkorps* VIII had secured a convincing supremacy on 7 July. Against the *Korps'* 1,829 combat sorties on 7 July, the Soviets only managed to perform slightly more than 1,500 – 847 by 2 VA and 689 by 17 VA. [175]

While the *Shturmoviks* attained some remarkable success on 7 July, the Soviet fighters proved unable to challenge the *Luftwaffe* to air superiority. The VVS fighter units recorded quite impressive victory scores: 2 VA's fighters scored 74 victories against 24 own losses. 203 IAD reported a particularly great success by chalking up 24 of these victories for only two losses. [176]

A Bf 109 G-4 of 9./JG 52, sporting the Gruppe crest, the Mihail cross, a reminder of the unit's time in Rumania in 1940 – 1942, and the Karayastaffel's famous red heart.

But on each mission, the air situation revealed that their enemy had not been weakened. According to German statistics, *Fliegerkorps* VIII lost no more than eleven aircraft to hostile activity, with another eleven sustaining damage, on 7 July. [177] Apart from these losses, there was only one Hungarian Bf 109 F, piloted by *Hdgy.* György Debrödy, which performed a forced landing at Varvarovka following damage through ground fire. (Meanwhile, the Hungarians reported four unconfirmed and one confirmed victory.)

In return, 2 VA lost 37 aircraft. 17 VA's total losses are not known, but amounted to at least 26 aircraft: Ten fighters – five La-5s from 5 GIAP, three La-5s from 116 IAP and two Yak-1s from 814 IAP [178] – and 16 Il-2s from 306 ShAD. [179] It may be assumed that about two-thirds of the Soviet aircraft which were reported as shot down by *Fliegerkorps* VIII can be substantiated with actual Soviet losses, which means that *Fliegerkorps* VIII still brought down an average of six enemy aeroplanes for each own loss.

During the following night, while the exhausted ground troops on both sides rested, the two Soviet air armies performed 275 combat sorties mainly by light biplane bombers which deprived the German soldiers of their sleep. Meanwhile, the ADD sent 66 bombers to attack German ferries across the Donets and the pontoon bridge which the Germans were building across the Pena river to the 3. *Panzer Division's* bridgehead on the northern side of this river. Despite the lack of devices for any precision bombing at night – and probably through a lucky strike – the Soviets actually managed to destroy the pontoon bridge across the Pena. This was a great tactical setback to the 48. *Panzerkorps* as it prepared to reopen its attack towards Oboyan the next day.

8 July 1943: Southern Flank

On 8 July, *Generalmajor* Seidemann continued to concentrate the bulk of *Fliegerkorps* VIII to the support of 4. *Panzerarmee*, which now launched all available forces to widen the previous breakthrough. On the western flank, 48. *Panzerkorps* massed its armoured forces in an attempt to reach Oboyan in the north. The first strategic goal on the road to Oboyan was the heavily fortified village of Syrtsevo. Supported by air attacks in groups of up to fifty aircraft at a time, 'Grossdeutschland' was hurled against the Soviet defence lines.

What could be achieved when the Soviet fighters were used in a tactically aggressive and sound way was demonstrated when nine La-5s of 240 IAP bounced a group of Ju 87s. In total, St.G 77 lost five Ju 87s, with a sixth sustaining severe damage by Soviet fighters. 240 IAP reported five Ju 87s shot down, plus a Bf 109. It is possible that III./JG 52's *Oblt.* Gerhard Lüty, who was posted as missing, fell prey to 240 IAP. This success was the result of the able command of *Kpt.* Sergey Podoroznyy and the accomplishment of a single pilot, *M.Lt.* Kirill Yevstigneyev. Twenty-six year old Yevstigneyev had served as a flight instructor for two years when he was posted to 240 IAP in March 1943, and thus was a skillful pilot. Afterward he described the engagement with the Stukas – called 'Clogs' by the Soviets - on 8 July 1943:

"Our *Polk* commander, [*Mayor* Sergey] Podoroznyy led a large group of fighters, consisting of two *Eskadrilyas*, to the Belgorod area. We were divided into several groups. The attack group, eight fighters, was commanded by *Starshiy Leytenant* Aleksandr Gomolko and flew at 2,500 metres altitude. These were provided with top cover by four fighters. Another group was

A Henschel Hs 129. This aircraft became the backbone of the Panzerjäger units of the Luftwaffe in 1943.

The Focke-Wulf Fw 190 displayed its abilities as a ground-attack aircraft during Operation Zitadelle. At the same time, the Battle of Kursk showed that the Ju 87 Stukas were no longer able to survive against the improved Soviet fighter aviation. Thus, in the autumn of 1943 the Stukageschwader were reorganised into Schlachtgeschwader, and most Ju 87s were exchanged for Fw 190s.

eld in reserve above and behind both these groups, keeping the entire air pace under surveillance. This group was led by *Eskadrilya* commander Fyodor] Semyonov. Fyodor had not yet recovered from the wounds which e had sustained; he had to use a stick to walk, and did this only with great ifficulty, but nevertheless he had decided to participate in this flight.

"In order to keep the whole formation under control, Podorozhnyy had lecided to lead the covering group which flew at the rear. *Mladshiy Leytenant* Shabanov flew as his wingman. His second *Para* was commanded by Grishin, our deputy *Eskadrilya* commander.

"We soon spotted the Fascists: Three formations of dive-bombers, and bove them twelve fighters. The visibility was quite bad. This was a common eature of these July days – thick smoke which rose from numerous burning ehicles on the ground characterised the battle of Kursk until the end.

We heard our *Polk* commander's voice in the ether:

"Climb to gain altitude! "

"Then Podorozhnyy radioed: 'Prepare to attack! Yevstigneyev – attack the eader of the first nine-plane formation! Gomolko – attack the second roup! Semyonov – engage the 'Schmitts' at the top!'

"We cut across the enemy aircraft's flying path. My four fighters were in he lead, rapidly closing in on the 'Clogs', and I could hear Podorozhnyy's outhfully fervent voice in my headphones:

"Attack! Whip the Fascists!"

"Our two *Paras* dived straight towards the leading aircraft of the German bomber formation. The Messerschmitts were turning towards us, but they eacted too late. Hit by my guns, the leading Ju 87 was enveloped in flames, olled over its wings and tumbled down earthwards. Meanwhile, another pilot among us four shot down a second Fascist.

"As I turned away from my first attack, I managed to avoid a pair of Messerschmitts. I came up on the other side of the enemy formation, and in diving turn I closed in on another Junkers. I was so close that I could see ll the details on the Junkers when I opened fire, still turning. As the Junkers lescended towards the ground, I could hear Podorozhnyy's pleased voice:

"That's great, Kirill! Give them what they deserve!"

"By now, the commander led his four planes to attack. The enemy lost one more Junkers, and his formation became dispersed – some of their aircraft dived, others turned in panic to avoid the fire from our fighters. The second of the Fascist nine-plane formations jettisoned its bombs and turned away and abandoned the first formation. They quickly vanished from our sight in the distance. Our commander cried excitedly:

"Fritz is trying to escape! Continue your attacks!"

"By this time, the combat had descended to low altitude. Occasionally, a Messerschmitt dived down to assist the 'Clogs', but most of the time they were tied down by our other fighters. I attacked another Junkers from the left hand side, and the pilot of this aircraft dived in the direction of Tomarovka. I noticed that the rear machine gun pointed straight upwards, which was an indication that the gunner probably was dead or severely wounded. Suddenly I heard Podoroznyy's warning:

"Yevstigneyev, don't be so eager! Break off!"

"I turned my head and looked all around, but nowhere was there any enemy fighter to be seen, so I called my commander:

"Only one attack – I will finish this reptile!"

"I opened fire almost at ramming distance, but the enemy aircraft held its course. I adjusted my speed to that of the Junkers and gave it one more burst of fire, then a second and a third... *Bang*! Suddenly the Fascist aircraft slammed into the ground. I had been so occupied pursuing him that I had failed to notice how low we were. It was mere luck that allowed me to pull up my aircraft just a few inches above the ground.

"By this time, the only enemy aircraft which remained in the combat were his fighters, and these did not fight with the same fury any more. They displayed great caution and it was obvious that they were looking for the first opportunity to disengage and escape homewards. Since we were starting to run low on fuel and ammunition, we decided to disengage.

"When we returned to our base, we discovered that one was missing – Mikhail Shabanov. No one had seen him go down." [180]

Günther Rall commanded III./JG 52 during the Battle of Kursk. By this time, Rall was among the Luftwaffe's most successful fighter aces, a position he would retain for the remainder of the war. Rall's logbook shows that he flew his first combat mission during the Battle of Kursk on 7 July 1943 – a free-hunting mission which resulted in two victories. On 8 July he flew three more combat missions, resulting in another four victories. These were Rall's 482nd-484th combat missions and his victories Nos. 148-151. Serving with JG 52 from early 1940, Rall flew more than 700 combat missions, was shot down several times and severely wounded on two occasions, but survived the war with a total tally of 275 victories.

The muzzle of a 30mm MK 103 anti-tank cannon under the fuselage of a Hs 129. The MK 103 was a development of the earlier MK 101, and through the use of a gas-operated piston and electrically-fired ammunition, it had a higher rate of fire than its predecessor. The rate of fire was increased from the MK 101's 250 rounds per minute to 420 with the MK 103. On this photo, a member of the ground crew locks the collars which are used to prevent the long barrel from fluttering while the aircraft was in flight (Photo: Martin Pegg.)

Among the airmen lost by St.G 77 on 8 July 1943 was Knight's Cross holder *Hptm.* Karl Fitzner. He and his radio operator, *Fw.* Ernst Meyer, were killed when his Ju 87 D-3 exploded in the air near Syrtsevo. Having conducted way over 600 dive-bomber missions, Fitzner belonged to the most experienced Stuka pilots. Also on 8 July, III./St.G 2 lost Knight's Cross holder *Hptm.* Bernhard Wutka, another Stuka veteran who had performed around 600 dive-bombings. In 27 IAP, the ace *St.Lt.* Nikolay Gulayev was credited with the shooting down of two Ju 87s and a Bf 109 on this day.

Meanwhile, the fighting in the air cost the Soviets the loss of one of their most successful fighter pilots, 40 GIAP's *Mayor* Moisey Tokarev, credited with 22 victories. At 09.55 hours (Russian time), *Polk* commander Tokarev led a group of 40 IAP La-5s into the air for a patrol mission over the front lines. [181] By then, a group of Bf 109s from III./JG 52 were already airborne on a fighter sweep. The two formations clashed at 2,500 metres altitude in the area south of Prokhorovka. When the combat was over, *Lt.* Erich Hartmann had claimed two "LaGGs" shot down. Soviet records show that at least one La-5 was lost – the aircraft piloted by *Mayor* Tokarev, who was killed in action.

88 GIAP, another La-5 equipped unit in 8 GIAD – of which 40 GIAP was a part – also lost its regimental commander, *Mayor* Stefan Rymsha, in combat on that day.

As with the previous day, *Fliegerkorps* VIII managed to overpower it opponents in the air even in sheer numbers on 8 July. Although 2 VA increased its activity to 957 combat sorties on 8 July, the losses sustained by 17 VA on the previous day allowed this air army to perform only 228 sortie – one third of the sorties on the 7th. Thus, while four days of intense ai activity inevitably brought down the capacity of the air forces on both sides the number of sorties carried out by *Fliegerkorps* VIII dropped only from 1,829 on 7 July to 1,686 on 8 July, while the combined effort of 2 VA and 17 VA declined from 1,536 to 1,185.

The bulk of *Fliegerkorps* VIII's missions on 8 July were carried out by the two *Stukageschwader*, which dispatched 701 combat sorties, mainly in support of 4. *Panzerarmee*. In every sense, this was badly needed. The Soviet defended every metre of land with an almost unparalleled tenacity. Often i took very heavy German air attacks to achieve even the slightest progress on the ground. Soviet 200th Tank Brigade withstood twelve attacks by 'Grossdeutschland' – while it was relentlessly subjected to fierce air attacks The Tank Brigade was forced to pull back behind the Pena river only afte it had sustained grievous losses from German air strikes. 'Grossdeutschland' own chronicle admits that it was able to '...*claw its way into the town o Verkopenye*' only after intensive Stuka attacks.

But the most decisive German air attacks took place farther east, in suppor of the II. SS *Panzerkorps*. On this day, Vatutin prepared another counter-attack to defeat the *Waffen*-SS units which had made the deepest penetration since

A Pz IVs with anti-tank armour plating protection attached to the sides advance on Russian motorised units.

A destroyed Soviet tank and other wrecked military equipment amidst totally destroyed defence positions during the Battle of Kursk – possibly the result of a German air attack.
(Photo: Horst Mutterlose/Martin Månsson.)

Ivan Kozhedub was the top-scoring fighter pilot on the Allied side during Wold War II. Born in 1920, Kozhedub served as a pilot trainer during the first years of the war. In March 1943, he received his first front assignment when he was posted to 240 IAP, which was equipped with La-5 fighters. Kozhedub was a hair's breadth from getting shot down by a Bf 109 during his first combat, but he quickly learned from his mistakes. He achieved his first two victories on 6 and 7 July 1943. On 9 July, he attained his first 'double' against two Bf 109s on two sorties. In October 1943, Kozhedub added 16 victories to his rapidly growing tally. In 1944, he flew free-hunting sorties over the German rear area, returning from almost all air combats with new victories. Kozhedub was appointed a Hero of the Soviet Union three times – on 4 February 1944, on 19 August 1944, and on 18 August 1945. This honour was bestowed upon only two other Soviet citizens during the war. His total score was 62 victories.

the German offensive started. However, he no longer had the sufficient resources at disposal. The 2nd Guards Tank Corps was sent in to launch another strike against the SS *Panzerkorps's* eastern flank. This unit had been severely mauled by Sch.G 1's anti-tank aircraft two days previously, and most of its tanks were of obsolescent models. Shortly before noon, *Hptm.* Bruno Meyer, the commander of the Hs 129-equipped *Panzerjagdkommando* of Sch.G 1, detected the marching troops of 2nd Guards Tank Corps before these had even made contact with the German troops, and immediately alerted his *Staffeln*. The Hs 129s had their 30 mm MK 103s loaded with armour piercing shells and scrambled to attack the Soviet tanks. Just like on the previous day, the Fw 190s of I./Sch.G 1 joined in en masse to attack the soldiers which covered the tanks.

"When we arrived in the area we saw marching infantry well concealed in the woods," recalled *Oblt.* Georg Dornemann, one of the *Schlachtflieger* who took part in that mission. [182] *Hptm.* Bruno Meyer described the following event:

"Then followed the tanks. Totally obsolete light tanks rolled out of the woods behind the infantry. Medium and heavy tanks followed, using the road from the villages behind the woods. After our *Schlachtgruppe Kommandeur* had personally satisfied himself of the enemy's incredible behaviour, the Fw 190 hurtled down from above to drop their SD 2 bomb containers into the masses, each direct hit knocking down a whole block of infantry." [183]

Not a single Soviet fighter appeared to relieve the Soviet troops from the merciless assault from the air. This was the result of effective German fighter sweeps over the whole Soviet rear area.

Several German aces were in the air, fending off any attempt by Soviet fighters to reach the sector where Sch.G 1 butchered the 2nd Guards Tank Corps. *Hptm.* Wilhelm Lemke of 9./JG 3 claimed a LaGG-3 for his 117th victory at 12.03 hours north of Belgorod. Half an hour later, fighters of 9./JG 52 – the famous *Karayastaffel* – fought other Soviet fighters near Prokhorovka farther to the north. At around 13.00 hours, Bf 109s of III./JG 3 engaged both La-5s and Yakovlevs in the Shakovo area – just north of the scene of the carnage on the ground – with the result that *Oblt.* Emil Bitsch shot down two for his 87th and 88th victories. *Hptm.* Günther Rall – who took off from Ugrim at 13.30 hours for a fighter sweep north of Belgorod in companion with a number of other Bf 109s from his III./JG 52 – blew two Soviet fighters out of the sky. [184] These were recorded as his 149th and 150th victories. A third "LaGG" was shot down by III./JG 52's *Lt.* Berthold Korts. However limited in scope these fighter clashes may appear, they were absolutely sufficient to hold the Soviet fighters at bay.

The desperate troops of the 2nd Guards Tank Corps had to rely only on what they could afford in terms of anti-aircraft guns for defence against the *Schlachtflieger*. The German ground-attack aircraft indeed were faced with a hellish fire from the ground – the whole tank corps turning all its firepower against the attacking aircraft. Few of Sch.G 1's aircraft escaped being hit, and there were two total losses, with one pilot killed and one injured. [185] But this was a quite limited cost compared with what the German airmen achieved. "*Staffel* after *Staffel* attacked, returned to base (about 20 minutes away by air), reloaded and refuelled, and then went back to the attack. This uninterrupted aerial assault lasted about an hour, and not only delayed, but, some places completely stopped the Russian advance. It also compelled Soviet armoured units to face about and hasten back to their jump-off positions in the forest. The Russians lost a large number of tanks and motor vehicles, and suffered heavy casualties. Most of the enemy tanks and vehicles were left burning on the battlefield." [186]

One of *Hptm.* Mayer's pilots, *Oblt.* Dornemann, recounted: "My *Staffeln* together with other *Staffeln,* attacked in relays and the enemy suffered heavy losses. Our pilots could see the panic-stricken response of the Russian tank crews and the retreating armour presented splendid targets for us. Each pilot made his run-in at low level and fired his armour-piercing shell at just the right instant, just like on a firing range. When we went in for the kill, a steady approach and a well-aimed shot were vital to knock out a tank – I would say that it was a real art.

"When the tanks were knocked out, they belched fire and smoke. Others did not get clear of those which had been knocked out and collided with them. Later, interrogated prisoners confirmed just how successful our attack had been and that they had been forced to withdraw." [187]

Altogether, fifty Soviet tanks were destroyed by the Hs 129s. [188] This completely routed the 2nd Guards Tank Corps and also settled the fate for Vatutin's planned counter-attack. In what became more or less a repetition of Vatutin's failed counter-attack two days previously, *General Major* Burkov's 10th Tank Corps – which had been tasked to launch a counter-attack "on the nose" of the SS corps – was left alone against

A lone Il-2 single-seater in the air.

A Ju 87 Stuka, shot down in July 1943. The Battle of Kursk signalled the beginning of the end of the Luftwaffe's Stukageschwader.

Obergruppenführer Hausser's armoured thrust, with its Tiger tanks in the lead. *Burkov's brigades launched piecemeal attacks, which the Germans repelled with heavy losses.*[189]

In total, *Fliegerkorps* VIII reportedly destroyed 84 Soviet tanks, five artillery pieces, two rocket projectile launchers, two AAA guns and around forty other vehicles on 8 July, and in addition to the damaged 21 tanks. However, in spite of the German fighters' successful screening off of the battle area where Sch.G 1 operated at around noon, the air fighting on 8 July showed a tendency of improved Soviet ability in air combat. On the previous day, *Fliegerkorps* VIII had claimed 96 Soviet aircraft shot down against eleven own combat losses. On 8 July, the gap narrowed to 43 victory claims against nine combat losses, with another twelve aircraft sustaining battle damage.[190] As we shall see, this was no isolated case but marked a tendency which would deepen during the next days. 17 VA's losses on 8 July are not known, but must have been fairly limited in view of the fact that only 228 combat sorties were performed (*Fliegerkorps* VIII claimed only four Soviet aircraft shot down in 17 VA's area of operations). 2 VA's combat losses on 8 July amounted to 24 fighters, 16 *Shturmoviks* and one bomber.

Nevertheless, in general the *Luftwaffe* still held a qualitative advantage, and the numerous rookies in the Soviet air units would continue to suffer dearly at the hands of German pilot veterans. One of the last fighter combats on 8 July took part when III./JG 52's *Hptm.* Günther Rall performed a fighter sweep in company with *Lt.* Erich Hartmann, forming an deadly duo. When the two German aces landed at Ugrim at 18.45 hours, Hartmann reported two shot down Soviet fighters, while Rall contributed a third. Although the Germans filed these Soviet aircraft vaguely as "LaGGs", it is probable that Rall's and Hartmann's successful mission is identical with this critical assessment which can be found in the Soviet after-battle analysis:

"Eight Yak-1s in the Provorot' region observed two Me 109s off their flight path. Paying no attention to the enemy aircraft, our fighters continued their own flight. Seizing a convenient moment, the German fighters attacked our aircraft and shot down three Yak-1s."[191]

But in the intense air fighting, the VVS was indeed learning by the day. Just like 16 VA's *Shturmoviks* had set a new tactical outline on 6 July by starting to operate in large formations, the VVS fighters drew many important conclusions from the error which had cost three Yak-1s in the evening of 8 July, as well as from 240 IAP's successful fight against St.G 77 earlier that day. At the Soviet airfields and headquarters, tactical discussions were held continously, and each day's combat missions were carefully analysed in the evening. In this situation, all previous conservative thinking was banned, and the Soviets strove to refine their fighting methods. First of all, the large groups of fighter aircraft – 18 to 30 in a single mass – were dissolved into small groups (generally four to six aircraft) echeloned by altitude. Of equal importance was the new instruction that eased the

previously strictly defensive mode of the Soviet fighter operations; fighter pilots began to be tasked to move their patrols forward, to airspace above German-controlled territory, which was one step closer to free-hunting missions similar to the German style. This gave the Soviet fighter pilots a possibility to operate with more flexibility and with greater aggression.

Fliegerkorps VIII's airmen would wake up to find an improved resistance in the air as early as the next day, 9 July.

Meanwhile, the Soviets made important preparations for a reinforced resistance also on the ground. On 8 July, the Stavka ordered *General-Leytenant* Rotmistrov's 5th Guards Tank Army to be deployed from the Steppe Front – which still was held in reserve in the rear – to the Voronezh Front and to take up positions at Prokhorovka. The transfer of the tank army commenced in the evening of 8 July, and took place only at night to reduce the risk of German air attacks. The Stavka also ordered the 5th Guards Army, with 80,000 men, to move under similar conditions from the Steppe Front to the Voronezh Front.

9 July 1943: Southern Flank

9 July was the day when *Generaloberst* Hermann Hoth hoped he would achieve the final breakthrough to Oboyan and Kursk. For this purpose, his 4. *Panzerarmee* again received full air support from *Fliegerkorps* VIII.

But the day, which would mark a turning point in the air war and which preceded the turning point on the ground, started bad for the Germans. At 03.00 hours, *Hptm.* Günther Rall dispatched a *Schwarm* from his III./JG 52 on a weather reconnaissance mission.[192] The whole *Schwarm* was lost over Soviet-controlled territory. What actually happened to all four Bf 109 pilots remains unclear, but it is possible that the German fighters were subjected to well-organised Soviet fighter interception among the clouds. *Ofw.* Edmund Rossmann, a veteran with 93 victories who commanded the *Schwarm*, told the author:

"Our task was to perform weather reconnaissance in the Oboyan area. It was very cloudy, and *Feldwebel* Lohberg, who led the second *Rotte*, lost track of his wingman, *Leutnant* Puls. I turned around to try and locate Puls. When my wingman, *Leutnant* Seidel, tried to follow me, he disappeared into the overcast. I heard nothing more from him. Then I suddenly discovered a parachute enveloping about 100 metres above the ground.

"Lohberg and I dived down towards the parachute. We saw how the parachutist hit the ground, and when we came closer, we could distinguish a group of Russian soldiers approaching him. We held them at bay through several low-level attacks with our machine guns.

"Suddenly I saw Lohberg's aircraft pouring smoke, and it left towards the west. After a short while it belly-landed in a field about 20 kilometres to the west of Oboyan. When I saw Lohberg climb out of his aircraft and wave at me, I turned around and landed next to his belly-landed Messesrschmitt

Large numbers of mobile Soviet Flak units were successfully employed against low flying Luftwaffe aircraft attacking Russian armour.

with the intention of picking him up. He raced towards my aircraft, but just as he climbed onto the wing, he bent forward and fell to the ground. I unstrapped myself and jumped out to help him. In the next moment I received a terrible blow from a Russian soldier's rifle butt. . ." [193]

The loss of a whole *Schwarm* was, of course, a severe blow for III./JG 52, which thus had lost sixteen Bf 109s – destroyed or put out of commission – and eleven pilots since 5 July. But the *Gruppenkommandeur Hptm.* Rall soon had other concerns.

The 4. *Panzerarmee's* attack was renewed at 06.00 hours, "… *preceded by Stuka attacks on what appeared to be enemy armoured spearheads and troop concentrations further to the north,*" according to 'Grossdeutschland's" history: "*Waves of dive-bombers dropped their loads with precision on the Russian tanks.*" [194]

On this day, Hoth really got all the air support he requested – "*outstanding air support*" according to 'Grossdeutschland's' history. The first goal for 48. *Panzerkorps* was the town of Verkhopenye. Further to the east, the SS *Panzerkorps* shifted the axis of its advance towards the north-east, towards Prokhorovka.

Stukas, Ju 88s and He 111s came roaming in the hundreds to break up the Soviet defence positions. At Ugrim, *Hptm.* Rall took off with elements of his III./JG 52 to escort bombers which were tasked to attack targets in the Petrovka sector. [195] The frantic air attacks enabled the Germans to break through in both sectors. Following a massed Stuka attack, Verkhopenye fell into German hands.

But the VVS was also in the air, and this day with greater effectiveness than before. Bitter air combats raged above the battlefield. Flying against Soviet troop positions opposed to II. SS *Panzerkorps*, a group of He 111s of II./KG 55 was subject to both anti-aircraft fire and heavy fighter attacks. '*Confronted by Flak and fighters. Left engine hit and set on fire,*'

wrote *Uffz.* Rolf Engelke, a crew member in 'G1+FN flown by *Lt.* Ernst Croner. [196] Another II./KG 55 He 11 went down and crashed in Soviet-controlled territor [197] Croner's bomber crew was in action twice more that da On the second mission, between 11.20 and 13.00 hour strong anti-aircraft fire was recorded. Later in th afternoon, the third mission was reported in Engelke logbook in the following words: '*Attacked by 10 Russi fighters. Heavy Flak.*' [198] *Fliegerkorps* VIII's Stuka units lost s aircraft on 9 July, including five from St.G 2 *Immelma* alone.

Interfering against a formation of La-5s over Germar controlled territory north of Belgorod, 6./JG 3 claimed t have shot down three, but at a cost of one of their ow Bf 109s which belly-landed. Meanwhile, a group of Bf 10 from 9./JG 3 led by *Hptm.* Wilhelm Lemke intercepted formation of Il-2s with fighter escort which attempted t attack the German airfield at Varvarovka. They managed shoot down two Il-2s, while one of their own Bf 109s w badly shot up and had to force-land.

Among the Soviet fighter pilots who were in the air ov the battlefield on the morning of 9 July was *M.Lt.* Iva Kozhedub, who had achieved his first two victories on and 7 July. On this day, Kozhedub had been assigned to le his La-5-equipped *Eskadrilya* of 240 IAP – the ordinar *Eskadrilya* commander, *St.Lt.* Fyodor Semyonov, havin been wounded in air combat the previous day. Kozhedu later recalled:

"Early in the morning I received the task: take off wit four aircraft to cover our armies in the Oboyan sector. reported this to Semyonov. He warned me that I shoul look out for free hunting enemy fighters. As a rule, the operated in pairs and performed sudden snap attacks again our formations, shooting down one of the last planes. M commander had good reason to warn me. …

"I discussed the mission carefully with my commande We paid special attention to different variants of comb tactics in the event of fighter attacks. …

"When we arrived in the air above the front line, w found the same scene as yesterday – a raging tank battle o the ground. Usually your attention is drawn to the sector the air where enemy bombers might appear. But aware the tactics used by the 'hunters', I scanned the airspace abo our heads.

"Almost immediately I discovered two aircraft high abov I recognised the sleek silhouttes of Messerschmitt 109s. They approached from our own territory. Clearly these were a pair of hunters! The opponen started to turn towards us, obviously with the intention of attacking us fro the front.

"By this time, we were right above our own ground troops. Mukhi was behind me, and so was Kolesnikov's pair, although they wer positioned higher.

"The two hunters closed in, now with the obvious purpose to attack m plane. But I also got the leader in my gunsight when they were at an altitud of 4,000 metres. I waited for the distance to reduce before I opened fir I knew that I could not afford to miss. Then when I opened fire, I was th first to shoot. I held the firing button squeezed and blasted away a lor burst, and it was sufficient! The leader turned over from his steep dive and saw him hit the ground. It was my third victory. I was able to bring dow the enemy expert because I had seen him from afar, and I was able to fores his intentions and made the correct manoeuvre to counter his attack I also was confident that I was covered by my wingman and the Kolesnikov pair. …

"I made two more sorties that day to cover our armies, and I managed t shoot down one more enemy aircraft." [199]

The Bf 109 claimed by Kozhedub came down in the Novoselovka are just sixteen kilometres from Pokrovka. [200] It is possible that the pilot of thi aircraft was none other than *Hptm.* Günther Rall. Although Rall's shot dow aircraft is one probably not reported to the *Generalquartiermeister d Luftwaffe,* [201] an entry in Rall's own logbook clearly shows that he was sho down at 07.30 hours on 9 July. However, he was lucky to survive unhur and although he came down in no-man's land – which was in th Novoselovka area – a German *Panzer* commander brought him back t

This Bf 109 G-2/R6 was flown by Helmut Bennemann, the Kommandeur I./JG 52 and carried the Gruppe's badge on the nose and the Geschwader's winged sword and shield badge under the windscreen. The pilot's life jacket and flare pistol cartridges are hanging from the pitot tube.

afety. [202] Just before Rall got shot down, he had claimed a "LaGG" (possibly La-5) downed at 3,000 metres altitude. It is possible that III./JG 52 also lost a second Bf 109 on that mission.

In stiff air battles which continued to be fought throughout the morning, it was evident that the Soviet airmen operated with considerably higher effectiveness than previously. I./JG 52 clashed with Il-2s with fighter escort and claimed three *Shturmoviks* shot down but lost two own pilots in the air combat. 4./JG 3 claimed two Soviet fighters but at a cost of one own Bf 109 shot down.

Many Soviet airmen who returned from their missions on this day reported a tendency among the German airmen to show an increased caution. While small groups of German fighters had previously attacked larger groups of Soviet fighters with boldness, they now often engaged in combat only when they enjoyed a tactical or numerical superiority. The German fighters also scaled down their free-hunting missions and began to provide their bombers and close-support aircraft with stronger fighter escort.

However, there was one exception during the day's air fighting, and that took place in the afternoon. By that time, *Hptm*. Rall had returned to his base at Ugrim. Thirsting for revenge, he took off in a new Bf 109 G-6 together with his wingman *Uffz*. Karl-Heinz Meltzer, and set off for a free-hunting sortie. 27 IAP, escorting a formation of Il-2s, was unfortunate to come across them. In a running fight, the two German pilots shot down two Soviet aircraft each. Although Meltzer reported one of his victims as an Il-2, 27 IAP actually lost four Yak-1s and four pilots – *Eskadrilya* commander *Mayor* Aleksandr Volkov, the ace *M.Lt*. Ivan Shpak, *M.Lt*. Nikolay Shapkin and *Lt*. Khopan Zabrodskiy. [203]

All in all, the air fighting on 9 July was anything but satisfactory to the Germans. *Fliegerkorps* VIII reportedly shot down 38 Soviet aircraft but had 28 own aircraft put out of commission – of which 19 were destroyed. The five Ju 87s lost by St.G 2 *Immelmann* was a harsh warning signal of mounting difficulties to use these slow aircraft in operations in daylight. The setback

suffered by *Stukageschwader Immelmann* on 9 July was merely the next in a line of a row of severe losses inflicted on *Fliegerkorps* VIII's Stuka units: St.G 77 had lost ten Stukas on 6 July and six Stukas on 8 July, and the operations on 5 July had cost St.G 2 six Stukas. In consequence, *Fliegerkorps* VIII started to use its Stukas with increasing caution: The number of Stuka sorties were over one thousand on 5 July and between 700 and 800 each day during the next four days, but after 9 July the figure dropped to only half that level.

Meanwhile the VVS was on the advance. While *Fliegerkorps* VIII's losses reached the highest level since after 5 July, 2 VA's own losses dropped to its lowest level since the battle opened: On 9 July, only 16 fighters, 15 *Shturmoviks* and a single bomber were lost.

Provided with an increasingly effective cover by their own fighters, and operating with better tactics, the *Shturmoviks* were able to intervene with greater effectivity on the battlefield. Indeed, 9 July witnessed German breakthroughs on the ground in all sectors on the southern flank of the Kursk Bulge. In the south-east, *Armeeabteilung Kempf* succeeded in widening its wedge on the eastern side of the Donets. But decisive action by 17 VA's *Shturmoviks* saved the situation to Soviet 7th Guards Army. The commander of the 7th Guards Army's 25th Guards Rifle Corps, *General-Mayor* Sayfyulin, sent his gratitude to 17 VA for the successful action by its *Shturmoviks*, which – according to *General-Mayor* Sayfyulin's estimations – had destroyed 47 German tanks. [204]

The operation referred to by the *General-Mayor* was an example of the new and improved Soviet fighter escort methods. 2 VA's 270 IAP had dispatched fourteen Yak-1s to escort eight Il-2s of 5 GShAD's 94 GShAP. The Soviet aircraft were faced with opposition from two formations of German fighters, altogether fifteen aircraft. The Yaks were divided into two groups. While six remained with the Il-2s, the top cover of eight Yak-1s dived down to attack the German fighters and locked these into a combat which prevented them from engaging the *Shturmoviks*. When the combat ended, not a single Soviet aircraft had been lost.

Chapter Six

Exhaustion in the North

Having failed to achieve any decisive breakthrough, *General* Model regrouped his forward forces of 9. *Armee* for another attempt on 9 July. But he nurtured no great hopes. During four days of immense pressure from 9. *Armee*, the troops of Soviet Central Front and the airmen of 16 VA had fought back all of Model's attacks, displaying an incredible stamina. This psychological aspect of the battle is at least as important as the echeloned defence lines which the Soviets had created. A resolution adopted by soldiers of Soviet 15th Motorised Rifle Batallion is indicative of this resolve which made any German advance impossible:

'*Our will to resist becomes stronger day by day. We remain absolutely steadfast. As long as we are alive, the enemy will not pass. We swear before our Motherland that we shall not sway, and if necessary we shall die to protect our Motherland against the blood-soaked enemy. Just as we have destroyed the Hitlerite reptile at Stalingrad, we will destroy it again here near Orel and Kursk. We are prepared to die in the last ditch. The enemy shall not pass, we shall overcome!*' [205]

The airmen of 16 VA were no exception regarding this fighting stamina. In spite of bitter losses – the loss rate was around seven per cent for their fighters and *Shturmoviks*, i.e. on average a pilot was shot down after just 14 combat missions – the relentless pressure exerted by the Soviet airmen posed an increasing problem to the Germans. Also of great concern to *Generalmajor* Deichmann, the commander of 1. *Fliegerdivision*, was the evaluation of the first four days of air combat which showed that on most occasions his Fw 190 fighters had failed to penetrate the Soviet fighter cover to attack the bombers. Between 5 and 8 July, 16 VA's bomber formations – 3 BAK and 221 BAD – had performed 632 combat sorties without losing more than 21 bombers (including 19 Bostons and just two Pe-2s), many of which were due to ground fire. [206]

While Model's forces prepared to launch their next attack at dawn on 9 July, *General-Leytenant* Rudenko dispatched the whole 3 BAK with 110 Pe-2s and 299 ShAD with 62 Il-2s for a concentrated blow against 47. *Panzerkorps*'s rear area near Saborovka. This was a great risk taking, since 16 VA was unable to provide an adequate fighter cover.

The grievous losses sustained during the previous days had reduced 16 VA's fighter strength considerably. For this mission, Rudenko had also brought 234 IAD into action. This was the fighter formation which 16 VA had been assigned two days previously to make up for heavy losses. But

Rudenko had been hesitant to use it. Arriving from 15 VA, 234 IAD constituted largely of inadequately trained novice pilots without any combat experience, who obviously would stand little chance against the veterans of JG 51 and JG 54. The low pressure which had brought rain, low cloud ceiling and fog to the area on 8 July would dominate the weather for the next four days. Thus, most of the pilots of 234 IAD's 233 IAP and 234 IAP which were dispatched at dawn on 9 July, simply lost their orientation. Ten failed to return to their airfields. Eight of these made emergency landings after their aircraft had run out of fuel, but two others remained missing – falling prey to free-hunting Fw 190s.

Most significant, all of the pilots of 234 IAD which returned from that first mission at dawn on 9 July had failed to locate either German fighters or their own *Shturmoviks* which they were supposed to provide with escort. Hence, a formation of 299 ShAD Il-2s was caught unescorted by I./JG 54, which claimed six shot down in a matter of seven minutes. Two of these were chalked up by *Lt.* Günther Scheel, who had claimed an Airacobra half an hour earlier.

It was the sheer luck of the Pe-2 crews that the Fw 190s of 1. *Fliegerdivision* arrived too late to intervene before the bombing, which took place at around 05.00 hours (German time). 241 BAD managed to carry out its task at the cost of no more than a single Pe-2 which was shot down by ground fire. A second Pe-2 which also went down after sustaining a *Flak* hit, belonged to 301 BAD.

However, when the 33 Pe-2s of 301 BAD turned away from the target area for their return flight, Fw 190s from IV./JG 51 appeared. While the escorting 192 IAP lost two La-5s, 207 six Pe-2s went down. The German airmen returned to base to report six Pe-2s, one Il-2 and three "LaGGs" shot down – all of this without loss.

Immediately afterward, *Oblt.* Joachim Brendel led his 1./JG 51 into an attack against 12 other Il-2s from 299 ShAD, escorted by only six Yakovlev fighters. [208] The Fw 190s tore into the *Shturmovik* formation with terrible impact. Brendel blew two Il-2s and one of the escort fighters out of the sky and his fellow pilots shot down three more ground-attack aircraft.

Nevertheless, 16 VA's concentrated bombing was apparently a great success. The subsequent strike by 47. *Panzerkorps* was the weakest attack to hit the Soviet positions since Operation *Zitadelle* had commenced. Although the whole of St.G 1 was airborne to support the attack through intense dive-bombing, the German ground troops failed once again.

The Germans made a last effort at around 18.30 that evening when almost 100 He 111s of KG 4 and KG 53 were sent in to cover the Soviet positions with bombs. But not even such a massive air attack would suffice. The German assault was bogged down. To Model, who had committed fresh new troops almost every day, there could be no doubt that he had lost the battle. This was particularly humiliating in view of the supremacy which the Germans enjoyed in the air. During the first four days, 1. *Fliegerdivision* had been able to carry out a larger number of sorties than its opponent. Friday, 9 July saw, for the first time, 16 VA approach 1. *Fliegerdivision's* number of sorties for direct intervention on the battlefield. 1. *Fliegerdivision* carried out 371 bomber, Stuka and *Zerstörer* sorties, as compared with 16 VA's 327 bomber and *Shturmovik* sorties. But this would prove to be the exception during *Zitadelle*.

The *Luftwaffe* was still superior in aerial reconnaissance; 1. *Fliegerdivision's Aufklärungsgruppen* made 164 individual flights on 9 July. Moreover, the day had demonstrated the growing weakness of 16 VA's plagued fighter units – the number of fighter sorties carried out by 16 VA dropped from 817 on 5 July to merely half that number, 448, on 9 July. The pilots of 16 VA continued to file excessive overclaims – reporting 52 victories for the day. [209] According to German records, 1. *Fliegerdivision's* losses were confined to a mere eight aircraft destroyed and two severely damaged to hostile action on that day. [210]

General Model remained under pressure from the OKH to continue his attacks. He was allowed to rest his weary troops for one day, 10 July, and in the meantime the OKL reinforced 1. *Fliegerdivision* by bringing in elements from *Fliegerkorps* VIII in the south. It is possible that the Soviets received information about this. In any case, the ADD was employed against 1. *Fliegerdivision's* airfields around Orel and at Karachev throughout the night of 9–10 July. These operations cost four Il-4 bombers. [211] The fact that these nocturnal bombings failed to achieve any significant result was proven to the troops of the Central Front, who on 10 July had to endure intensified attacks by German aircraft. A total of 375 Stuka sorties, 220 bomber sorties and 66 *Zerstörer* sorties were flown against artillery positions at Teploye, Molotutshchiki, Ossinova and Yendovishche, as well as concentrations of tanks and other vehicles. As a result of these attacks, which were carried out in spite of adverse weather, eleven tanks, ten other motor vehicles and four artillery batteries were claimed destroyed. [212]

Meanwhile, 1. *Fliegerdivision's* fighters were sent out to hunt down 16 VA's aircraft over their own airfields. Engaging 30 GIAP near Fatezh, in the vicinity of that unit's airfield, 2./JG 54's *Lt.* Günther Scheel reportedly shot down three Airacobras. Two more claims against Soviet fighters on other missions that day brought Scheel's tally for 10 July to five kills.

16 VA struck back shortly before noon, when Rudenko employed another concentrated blow – this time against German troop concentrations in the Kashara region, from where the assault against Olkhovatka had been launched on the previous day. 106 Pe-2s from 3 BAK and 65 Bostons from 221 BAD attacked from medium altitude, and 37 Il-2s from 2 GShAD attacked from altitudes below 915 metres. 6 IAK participated with all available fighters. Apparently caught off-guard, 1. *Fliegerdivision* appeared with only a handful of fighters on this occasion. Among these were Bf 109s of I./JG 52 – the first among *Fliegerkorps* VIII's units to arrive with 1. *Fliegerdivision*. *Uffz.* Günther Josten of 1./JG 52 bagged a Pe-2 and an Il-2, his ninth and tenth victories.

Defying a dense *Flak* curtain, the Soviet aircraft claimed the destruction of 15 tanks, three armoured vehicles, 12 other motor vehicles, two *Flak* positions and two ammunition dumps. [213] Although these figures may be inflated, the air attack was undoubtedly a success. Afterwards, the headquarters of Soviet 2nd Tank Army expressed its gratitude to Rudenko:

A ground crew is prepares an Il-2 for another combat mission.

"*To the commander of 16 VA. In the afternoon of 10 July, the aircraft performed a massed blow against an assembly of armour and infantry in the area to the north of Ponyrey. With admiration, our tankmen were witness to the operations of your falcons, for which we would like to express our deep gratitude. We are convinced that our united fight will speed up the final victory over the enemy. We will remind the enemy of Stalingrad once again.*" [214]

But the accomplishments of the Soviet bombers and *Shturmoviks* stood out in contrast to the meagre performance of the fighters. The *Luftwaffe's* Fw 190s and Bf 109s undoubtedly continued to dominate the skies wherever they appeared. This was testified by a formation of Il-2s in the afternoon of 10 July, when Fw 190s from I./JG 54 attacked and shot down four *Shturmoviks* without sustaining any losses. In repeated skirmishes throughout the day, 1. *Fliegerdivision's* fighter pilots submitted claims for 43 shot down Soviet fighters, while losing only three of their own number.

When the La-5 flown by 92 IAP's *M.Lt.* Fetisov was shot down by a pilot of IV./JG 51 (possibly *Hptm.* Adolf Borchers) on 10 July, it was 92 IAP's 24th combat loss in the past six days. The newly arrived 234 IAD recorded eleven losses on 10 July, five of those belonging to 133 IAP.

Desperate to achieve a breakthrough, the Germans pushed their air units to the limit. Generalmajor Paul Deichmann, commanding 1. Fliegerdivision, ordered his fighter units to employ fighter-bomber missions in support of the ground attacks at Ponyrey and Olkhovatka on 11 July 1943. But even in spite of an unchallenged German air superiority, the Soviet defence positions would not budge. These photographs show Fw 190s of I./JG 54 loaded with bombs for Jabo – fighter-bomber – missions.

This Soviet Douglas A-20 Havoc crash-landed after sustaining severe battle damage. During most missions in the Battle of Kursk, the Soviet Havoc/Boston crews fared better than their US colleagues had done with the same aircraft in the summer of 1942. This was mainly due to the efficiency of the Soviet fighter escort.

Eventually, the accumulated effect of such losses began to wear down the surviving Soviet pilots.

Just when they had completed their task of halting the German offensive – on 10 July, the Soviets reported nothing but reconnaissance activities and weak skirmishing along the entire front – the stamina of the Soviet fighter pilots began to falter. *Polkovnik* Fedor Dementyev, 274 IAD's commander, submitted a sharply critical evaluation of the fighter operations on 10 July:

"*All of our fighters carry out their patrols 10 kilometres behind the front line. They never approach the front line, fearing the anti-aircraft fire, and thus enable the enemy's bombers to remain over the battlefield at will.*"[215]

In a rage, *General-Leytenant* Rudenko vowed to transfer any fighter pilot who showed cowardice, to penal batallions, and even threatened 'the worst cases' with execution. '*It is time to stop dishonouring the Soviet fighter force,*' Rudenko wrote. The highly inflated victory claims submitted by 16 VA's fighters obviously did not impress the air commander. In fact, on 10 July, 1. *Fliegerdivision* lost no more than two He 111s, two Bf 110s and three Fw 190s to hostile action.[216]

Rudenko immediately removed *General-Mayor* Andrey Yumashev from his post as 6 IAK's commander. He was replaced by *General-Mayor* Yevgeniy Yerlykin, who flew in from Leningrad, where he had led 7 IAK PVO with great success since 1941.

Both Rudenko and Yerlykin realised the need of 16 VA's exhausted airmen to get some rest. In spite of renewed German efforts to break through at Ponyrey and Olkhovatka, 11 July saw a considerable reduction of 16 VA's activity. While 1. *Fliegerdivision* continued to carry out massive attacks against the Central Front's artillery positions and concentrations of armour – flying 933 sorties on 11 July – 16 VA sent only 218 fighters, 80 *Shturmoviks* and three bombers into the air on that day.

Needless to say, the *Luftwaffe* was in almost total control of the skies. This is reflected not least in the fact that only three of 1. *Fliegerdivision's* aircraft were shot down on 11 July. In one of these, IV./JG 51 lost its *Gruppenkommandeur*, 94-victory ace *Major* Rudolf Resch. In return, IV./JG 51 recorded nine victories on the same day, and in 2./JG 54, *Lt.* Günther Scheel recorded another successful day by adding three victories to his account.

But by that time, the exhausted and quite demoralised men of 9. *Armee* were unable to match the Soviet troops who were spurred by their defensive victory. Not even by throwing in his last reserve, the 10. *Panzergrenadier Division*, was Model able to accomplish any success. The Soviet ground troops counter-attacked and took back the high ground around Olkhovatka.

The fighters of 1. *Fliegerdivision* – even reinforced by Bf 109s from *Fliegerkorps* VIII – almost drove their opponent away from the contested skies; on 12 July, 16 VA performed less than 100 sorties. This was the result mainly of the effectivness of the Fw 190-equipped *Jagdgruppen*.

Between 5 and 12 July, 16 VA recorded 391 aircraft lost in combat – 262 fighters, 90 *Shturmoviks*, and 39 bombers.[217] When damaged aircraft which were written off are included, the total loss figure reaches 439 aircraft.[218]

The inequality in the air war is clearly displayed by the fact that 1. *Fliegerdivision* reported 57 aircraft destroyed and 34 receiving severe or medium damage due to hostile action or unknown causes between 5 and 11 July. Indeed, there were cases where the Germans deliberately filed combat losses as "accidents", but during the same period, the units of 1. *Fliegerdivision* recorded no more than 26 aircraft destroyed or damaged in accidents. The sum of all these destroyed or damaged aircraft to all causes does not even amount to one quarter of the 517 German aircraft reported shot down by 16 VA between 5 and 12 July 1943.[219]

This is in stark contrast with the Soviet era historiography, according to which 16 VA gained and held air supremacy from 7 July onward.[220]

However, although 1. *Fliegerdivision* emerged as the victor in the air battle, the decisive ground battle had been irrevocably won by the Soviets, and 16 VA's contribution to this achievement should not be underestimated. *General Armii* Rokossovskiy, the Central Front's C.O., reported to the Stavka:

"*The troops of the Central Front, which stood as a deadly wall against the enemy, displaying Soviet steadfastness and tenacity, have halted his attack in eight days of constant and bitter combat. The first stage of the battle is over.*"

The Battle of Kursk now approached its final phase. In the south, both sides prepared for a bitter fight over a small village by the name of Prokhorovka. Meanwhile, in the north, the Soviets moved ahead for a counter-strike which would annihilate the German Orel Bulge.

A formation of Pe-2s over the battle zone.

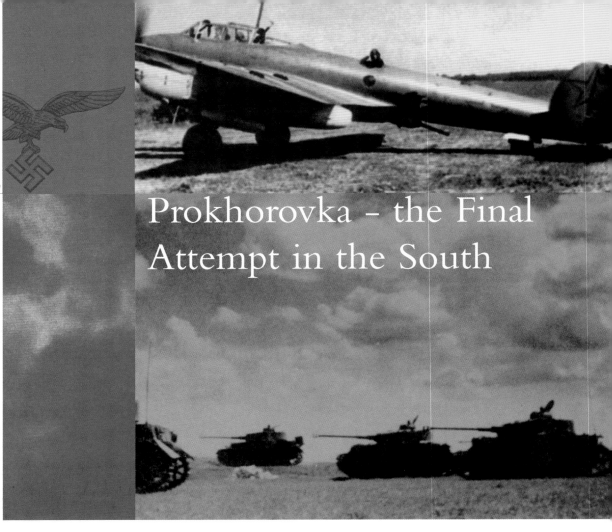

Chapter Seven

Prokhorovka – the Final Attempt in the South

In deteriorating weather, 4. *Panzerarmee's* 48. *Panzerkorps* resumed its offensive at Verkhopenye at 03.30 hours on 10 July. The first attack was disturbed by the ADD, which sent out 174 bomber crews against German troop concentrations. [221] '*Just before dawn,*' recorded the '*Grossdeutschland*' Division, '*there was some slight Soviet air activity, including bombing and strafing attacks, mainly against the leading attack forces and on the road.*' But *Fliegerkorps* VIII also intervened; as *Grossdeutschland* reported: '*The Luftwaffe supported the advance of the German troops with very effective repeated sorties.*' [222]

General von Mellenthin, Chief of Staff of 48. *Panzerkorps*, recorded with satisfaction: '*Supported by the splendid efforts of the Luftwaffe, Grossdeutschland made a highly successful advance.*' [223]

Further to the east, the *Waffen-SS* '*Totenkopf*' Division succeeded in crossing the Psyol River just where it turned from the northeast to the northwest before it ran towards Oboyan.

Soviet fighters intervening against the *Luftwaffe* operations apparently met with only little success, although 270 IAP returned from one engagement with Ju 88s escorted by Bf 109s to report several victories. The mission had been led by the ace *Kpt.* Sergey Luganskiy, who claimed one Ju 88 while *St.Lt.* Nikolay Shutt was credited with the destruction of two Ju 88s and *M.Lt.* Gurkov claimed one of the Bf 109 escort fighters – all without loss. [224] No corresponding German bomber losses can be found in *Luftwaffe* records, but II./JG 3's *Lt.* Hans Reiser was reported shot down by Soviet fighters during an escort mission for He 111s. The operation carried out by II./KG 55 had to be aborted, reportedly due to adverse weather conditions. [225]

Meanwhile, Pe-2s from 1 BAK, led by *Polkovnik* Ivan Polbin, were dispatched to attack the German air base at Varvarovka. *M.Lt.* Ivan Kozhedub, who was part of the fighter escort, wrote:

"*Early in the morning of 10 July I was, for the first time, tasked to lead a group of fighter pilots on an escort mission for Petlyakovs. The mission was to attack an enemy airfield in the Belgorod area where the Junkers were stationed. When we approached the target area, we saw dark thunderclouds that were building to the south, some of them reaching down to the ground: A thunderstorm was under way. Our bombers had to go down to 400-500 metres, and this alerted the enemy. Suddenly a fierce AAA fire set in from all sides. Tracer bullets climbed up against us, and the sky, which was black with clouds, was lit up by flashes. By that time we*

reached the target and the Pe-2s dropped their bombs all at once. The air base belo[w] was covered by smoke from exploding bombs. A few Junkers tried to take off, but ou[r] bombers and fighters attacked them and destroyed them all. Next our fighters strafe[d] the AAA positions and silenced them. None of our aircraft was shot down, but man[y] had been damaged by ground fire. My own La-5 had received a considerable numbe[r] of 'extra holes.''

However, we did not encounter any enemy fighters. The enemy fighters ha[d] probably considered the weather conditions too adverse for a take-off. The news abou[t] how the Petlyakovs of Polbin's Korpus had shot down Junkers taking off soon sprea[d] among the troops in the front line." [226]

Thunderstorms and rain soon grounded most aircraft on both sides, an[d] only in short spells of fairly good weather were any aircraft able to take t[o] the skies. The subsequent combats confirmed that the Soviets had improve[d] their performance considerably. Throughout 10 July, *Fliegerkorps* VIII fighters submitted no more than nine victory claims, but in return eight o[f] its aircraft were put out of commission – including three total losses. Agai[n] the Stukas suffered the heaviest toll, with six Ju 87s being put out o[f] commission.

The most important event on 10 July 1943 took place far from th[e] Eastern Front. In the Mediterranean, the Western Allies landed on the Italia[n] island of Sicily. Hitler had long feared that his Italian ally would pull out, an[d] the new dramatic development of the war in the South compelled him t[o] consider sending the II. SS *Panzerkorps* from the Eastern Front to Italy. It wa[s] only the 48. *Panzerkorps's* successful advance on 10 July which at leas[t] delayed this decision. *Generalfeldmarschall* Erich von Manstein, commande[r] of *Heeresgruppe Süd*, knew that he was running out of time, and decided t[o] direct all his forces towards the north-east – where he hoped to be able t[o] achieve a decisive breakthrough. This would lead his troops to the vicinit[y] of a small town called Prokhorovka. Meanwhile, his opponent, *Genera[l]* Vatutin, ordered the Voronezh Front to "… encircle and destroy the mai[n] German grouping penetrating Oboyan and Prokhorovka."

In preparation for the forthcoming Battle of Prokhorovka, the Soviet[s] pulled some of their most worn-down air units out of combat. One of thes[e] was 27 IAP, which in a matter of only five days had lost eleven Yak-1s an[d] eight pilots. [227] In fact, the whole 205 IAD – including 27 IAP, 438 IAP an[d] 508 IAP – was shifted to the rear for rest and recuperation. Its Yak fighter[s] were handed over to 737 IAP and 256 IAD. The latter arrived from the rear to replace 205 IAD.

256 IAD mustered 96 fighters. These included 53 Yak-7Bs of the latest series and 43 of the new Yak-9s – the latter equipping 91 IAP and parts of 32 IAP. The *Diviziya's* commander, *Polkovnik* Nikolay Gerasimov, was a veteran fighter pilot who had seen combat in five wars: the Spanish Civil War (for which he had been appointed a Hero of The Soviet Union), at Khalkhin-Gol, against Poland in 1939, in the Winter War against Finland in 1939/40 and against Germany since 1941. In all, Gerasimov had flown more than 500 combat missions and was credited with 14 individual and 10 shared victories.

11 July 1943: Southern Flank

At dawn on 11 July, the forces of *Heeresgruppe Süd* were ready to advance towards Prokhorovka with II. SS *Panzerkorps* and 48. *Panzerkorps* from the south-west and *Armeeabteilung Kempf* from the south. But they were aware of the reinforced Soviet defence positions that lay ahead. Although the forecast promised somewhat improved weather, the meteorological conditions still did not allow any large-scale air support. At 06.00 hours 48. *Panzerkorps* reported: '*The 11.* Panzer Division *waits for the weather to clear up. Its commander considers frontal attack against the hill position, saturated with tanks and anti-tank guns, too risky without air support.*' [228]

Still, II. SS *Panzerkorps* opened its attack early in the morning. Its troops were immediately beset by repeated counter-attacks from Soviet tanks operating in small groups. Air assistance was called in, and from around 06.30 hours, Ju 87s were able to make hourly attacks against enemy defence positions. But the Red Army put up tenacious resistance. Only after repeated Stuka attacks and artillery shelling was the SS '*Leibstandarte*' able to break through at around 09.00 hours. However, shortly afterward, its troops were mistakenly attacked by Stukas – as described by one SS man:

"We called in Stuka assistance, which was still possible to do at this time. But once again things went wrong! Some bombs hit [*Sturmbannführer* Joachim] Peiper's III. *Panzergrenadierbatallion* and elements of [*Obersturmbannführer*] Rudolf von Ribbentrop's 6. *Panzerkompanie* of 1. SS *Panzerregiment*/LSSAH, which was held in reserve on this day. In spite of the fact that an air liaison officer from the *Luftwaffe* was stationed with his armoured radio vehicle next to the batallion's staff vehicle, our Stukas again hit our own positions. Our comrades were very upset about this." [229]

On '*Leibstandarte's*' left flank, the '*Totenkopf*' Division received powerful air support as it hurled itself towards the seam between Soviet 95th Guards Rifle and 9th Guards Airborne divisions – as captured by a Soviet account:

"It was an overcast day. A fresh breeze disturbed the boundless sea of ripened grain between Prokhorovka, Prelestnoye, and Pravorot. Up to a

The official photograph captions states that this pilot and observer of a Ju 88 look down at the cameraman through the glazed nose of their aircraft just prior to take-off. However, considering the fact that Luftwaffe airmen were generally very superstitious of being photographed prior to a combat mission, it may be assumed that the photograph was either arranged or taken during routine instrument check.

Ivan Polbin commanded 1 BAK during the Battle of Kursk. Born in 1905, Polbin was one of the VVS bomber arm's most able tacticians. He served as a combat pilot during the Battle of Khalkhin-Gol against the Japanese in the 1930s, and against Finland during the Winter War in 1939-1940. He flew an SB bomber at the outbreak of the war with Germany in 1941, and in 1942, shifted to the new Pe-2. Polbin developed the dive-bombing methods for this aircraft. In 1942, he led 150 SBAP with great success during the Battle of Stalingrad, and was appointed a Hero of the Soviet Union on 23 November 1942. In April 1943, Polbin was made commander of the first Bomber Corps, 1 BAK – which in February 1944, was elevated into the 2nd Guards Bomber Corps. Although a corps commander, eventually with the rank of a General-Mayor, Polbin continued to fly combat missions. He was killed in action on 11 February 1945. On 6 April 1945, Polbin was posthumously appointed to a Double Hero of the Soviet Union – an honour which was bestowed upon only 104 Soviet citizens – including 65 airmen - during the course of the war.

A Pe-2 bomber just ahead of its take-off for a new combat mission. Owing to inadequately organised fighter escort, Polkovnik Ivan Polbin's 1 BAK sustained heavy losses in combat with German fighters on the first day of Operation Zitadelle, losing 18 Pe-2s in the process. However, this flaw was corrected the next day. Operating in tight formations provided with a shield of escort fighters, 1 BAK carried out its operations with only a minimum of losses during the remainder of the Battle of Kursk. Between 6 and 10 July, only a single loss was recorded by this unit.

battalion of infantry, supported by forty tanks and self-propelled guns, among them heavy Tigers and Panthers, and by hundreds of Ju 87 and Ju 88 aircraft, attacked…" [230]

On this day, the Soviet air commanders decided to save their *Shturmoviks* and bombers for the planned counter-attack, and instead confined their efforts in the air to sending large numbers of fighters with the task of warding off the *Luftwaffe* attacks. This resulted in renewed and intense air fighting.

The first aerial combat of the day took place only shortly before 10.00 hours. The *Kommandeur* of III./JG 52, *Hptm.* Günther Rall, had taken off at 09.20 hours together with his wingman, *Uffz.* Karl-Heinz Meltzer, for a free-hunting mission over the armoured spearheads of II. SS *Panzerkorps.* [231] In the vicinity of Nagolnoye they attacked a formation of La-5s and shot down one each. Shortly afterwards, *Oblt.* Paul Stolte's 6./JG 3 clashed with a formation of Il-2s escorted by La-5s and Yak-1s in the same area. While *Oblt.* Stolte claimed to have shot down four Soviet aircraft (three of which were confirmed as his 28th to 30th victories), a young *Gefreiter* from 6./JG 3 failed to return from that engagement.

The most dramatic air combat on 11 July took place further south-east, where *Armeeabteilung Kempf's* III. *Panzerkorps,* supported by III./St.G 77's Stukas, attacked towards the north from its bridgehead in the eastern side of the Donets. This drive threatened the southern flank of the Soviet forces which prepared for the counter-attack at Prokhorovka. Soviet fighters were sent to relieve the defending troops of the 69th Army in this sector from the pressure from the air. Eight Yak-1s and Yak-7Bs of 183 IAP were dispatched from 5 VA and intercepted a formation of nine Ju 87s. The German fighter escort, comprising six Bf 109s, manoeuvred towards the Soviet aircraft, but in doing so they lost contact with the Ju 87s in the clouds. This left the Ju 87s alone against a group of Yakovlevs. 9./St.G 77 was severest hit. In a matter of minutes, five Ju 87s had been shot down – four of these from 9. *Staffel.* Included among the casualties was 9./St.G 77's *Staffelkapitän, Hptm.* Rudolf Blumenthal. [232] 183 IAP claimed to have knocked down all nine Ju 87s, plus two Bf 109s, against only one loss in this engagement. The latter was the Yakovlev flown by *Serzh.* A. N. Agdantsev; he was credited with the almost unsurpassable feat of first shooting down three German aircraft in this combat, and then – when he had run out of ammunition – destroying a fourth through a *taran* from which he survived. The young Soviet pilot (who celebrated his 20th birthday one week later) was rewarded with the Order of the Red Banner.

Another success was achieved by pilots of 586 IAP who shot down two Ju 88 D-1s of 2.(F)/22 – one of which was piloted by the unit's *Staffelkapitän, Hptm.* Toni Kock. [233]

But the Soviet airmen were still in a position of numerical inferiority. *Generalmajor* Seidemann placed heavy demands on his heavily exerted airmen. Over one thousand sorties were flown, including 447 by Stukas, 197 by bombers and 157 by *Schlacht* aircraft. Against this scale of operations, 2 VA and 17 VA were able only to perform 595 sorties. Thus, in most places the sky was still dominated by the *Luftwaffe,* with dire consequences to the Soviet ground troops.

After a 'softening up' attack by fifty Ju 87s in a concentrated formation, the '*Leibstandarte*' Division stormed the strategic Hill 252.2 on the road to

Prokhorovka at 13.00 hours. He 111s of KG 27 meanwhile bombed Soviet troop concentrations north of the town. The German bombers were met by intense *Flak* and fighter opposition and two He 111s were lost. [234] In return pilots of JG 3 *Udet* claimed four La-5s – of which two were chalked up by *Oblt.* Emil Bitsch and one was recorded as *Gruppenkommandeur Major* Wolfgang Ewald's 73rd victory. The *Generalquartiermeister* loss records only list one Bf 109 lost by *Fliegerkorps* VIII on 11 July, but the Air Liaison officer at AOK 2 recorded that four Bf 109s were shot down. [235] That would bring *Fliegerkorps* VIII's total combat losses on 11 July to sixteen aircraft totally destroyed, against claims for 23 shot down Soviet aircraft.

But the formidable air support enabled all three corps of *Heeresgruppe Süd* to make good advance through the network of Soviet defence positions. '*Leibstandarte*' of II. SS *Panzerkorps* managed to capture Hill 252.2. Further to the west, all Soviet efforts to crush the bridgehead across the Psyol River which had been established by '*Totenkopf*' on the previous day, were blown to pieces by *Luftwaffe* attacks. The '*Totenkopf*' troops even managed to expand their bridgehead. Thus the II. SS *Panzerkorps* had not only occupied good positions for the attack against Prokhorovka – they had also managed to take control of the jumping-off positions that had been selected for Vatutin's planned counter-attack. The Soviets were forced to hastily renew their preparations for the offensive.

The Germans knew that they had a strategic breakthrough within reach. From Hill 252.2, the *Waffen*-SS had a good view of the town of Prokhorovka, only slightly more than one and a half kilometres below the eastern slopes of the hill. Historians David M. Glantz and Jonathan M House describe the situation as it looked in the evening of 11 July: 'The seizure of Prokhorovka by Hausser's armoured armada was also timed to coincide with the 48th *Panzerkorps's* capture of the Psyol River crossing south of Oboyan. Once these critical river crossings and Prokhorovka were in German hands, the two *Panzerkorps,* with the III *Panzerkorps* not far behind, would complete their victorious drive on Oboyan and Kursk.' [236]

The situation looked even more promising, from the German point of view, because of the good advance made by Kempf's forces on 11 July. Its 6 *Panzer Division,* with the Tigers of 503. *Panzer Abteilung* in the vanguard pushed forward thirteen kilometres northwards to seize Kazache, just twenty-four kilometres south of Prokhorovka.

12 July 1943: Southern Flank

The air battle on 12 July 1943 is quite complex and contradictory, very like the famous tank battle at Prokhorovka which was fought simultaneously on the ground.

During the night of 11/12 July, the ADD was absent from the skies in the Belgorod-Prokhorovka sector. This was because all of its units were occupied in 'softening-up' raids in preparation for the Soviet counter-offensive which was about to start on the northern flank of the Kursk Bulge the next day. [237] Still, that night saw some of the greatest air activity over the southern flank of the Kursk Bulge. 12 July would be the day when *Generalfeldmarschall* von Manstein launched what he hoped would be the death blow against the Red Army forces which were preventing the final strategic breakthrough towards Oboyan and Kursk. During the preceding night, *Fliegerkorps* VIII sent out 61 aircraft to prepare the offensive. Seven bombers attacked the railway station at Staryy Oskol, where the rail line was

Obersturmbannführer Rudolf von Ribbentrop's tank crew next to their tank. This photograph was taken on 11 July 1943, the day when von Ribbentrop's 6. Panzerkompanie of Division Leibstandarte's 1st SS Panzerregiment was attacked by German Stukas in error. (Photo: Via Mânsson)

A Ju 88 of the Hungarian 4/1. Bombázó század at Kharkov in July 1943. Led by Százados Tihamér Ghyczy, this bomber unit was active in the support of the Battle of Prokhorovka. This particular aircraft was flown by Főhadnagy (Oberleutnant) László Pajtás. The unit crest, a witch, can be clearly seen. Pajtás and his bomber crew earned fame during Operation Zitadelle for shooting down two intercepting Soviet fighters. In fact, Pajtás went on to claim a total of five Soviet aircraft shot down during the war – thus becoming the only Hungarian bomber pilot to reach an "ace status". (Photo: Becze.)

out and fires and explosions could be seen by the German aircrews. Also, *Luftflotte* 4's *Störkampfgruppe* sent out 49 harassment aircraft to strike against Soviet troop encampments and vehicle columns. [238]

Meanwhile, 2 VA and 17 VA dispatched 240 of its night bombers. The U-2 crews of *Polkovnik* Leonid Yuzeyev's 208 NBAD performed 126 sorties throughout the night, dropping bombs over the rear area of II. SS *Panzerkorps* at Malye Mayachki, Bolshiye Mayachki, Pokrovka and Gremuchiy with the purpose of exhausting the *Waffen*-SS units. [239] Meanwhile, night bombers of 17 VA's 262 NBAD conducted 183 sorties against railway stations and roads leading to the front, aimed at disrupting the German supply lines. [240]

This was in preparation for the Voronezh Front's intended major attack against 4. *Panzerarmee*. The previous evening, *General Armii* Vatutin had ordered *General-Leytenant* Pavel Rotmistrov: 'At 10.00 hours on 12 July, you will deliver a counter-strike in the direction of Komsomolets State Farm and Prokhorovka and, in cooperation with 5th Guards Army and 1st Tank Army, destroy the enemy in the Kochetovka, Pokrovka and Gresnoye regions.'

Rotmistrov's 5th Guards Tank Army had been transferred from the Steppe Front, in the rear, to the Voronezh Front. Moving mainly at night – in order to avoid German air attacks – the march of the Tank Army had been a great success. Its 593 tanks, 37 self-propelled guns, thousands of artillery pieces and thousands of support vehicles were brought forward first the 200 kilometres from Ostogozhsk to Staryy Oskol, and then the 64 kilometres to Prokhorovka. In doing so, it had escaped *Luftwaffe* attacks, avoided *Armeeabteilung Kempf*'s attempt to intercept it and prevent it from linking up with Soviet 1st Tank Army, and arrived in good order to join forces with the 5th Guards Army. The 80,000 men of the latter had also performed a march from the Steppe Front, and now prepared to cover the 5th Guards Tank Army's armoured strike against the weakened II. SS *Panzerkorps* on 12 July. By this time, the latter had fewer than 300 tanks and assault guns out of its initial force of nearly 500.

Two Hungarian Ju 88s in flight. (Photo: Becze.

A Junkers Ju 87 G-1, probably of the Versuchskommando für Panzerbekämpfung. Trials with 37 mm Flak guns, one under each wing, were carried out by this test unit in the winter of 1942/1943. During the Battle of Kursk, Hptm. Hans-Ulrich Rudel used one of these aircraft against Soviet armour with great success.

On 2 VA's airfields, hectic activity characterised the night of 11/12 July. Following the bitter losses of the past week, 2 VA's strength had fallen to 472 operational aircraft – 266 fighters, 140 bombers (including U-2 night bombers) and 96 *Shturmoviks*. 17 VA was in no better shape, with just slightly more than 300 operational aircraft. Because of this, careful planning of operations was more imperative than ever.

General-Leytenant Stepan Krasovskiy, 2 VA's commander, ordered 1 BAK and 1 ShAK against II. SS *Panzerkorps*, and 291 ShAD was instructed to support the 1st Tank Army's attack against 48. *Panzerkorps's* western flank. 17 VA was to be concentrated against *Armeeabteilung Kempf*.

Meanwhile, *Fliegerkorps* VIII had also become worn down quite considerably. The *Stukageschwader*, which had taken such punishment during the past week, were unable to operate on anything more than a fairly limited scale. Instead, *Generalmajor* Seidemann demanded an all-out effort by the *Schlachtflieger* of Sch.G 1 and its subordinate unit *Panzerjägerstaffel*/JG 51. *Fliegerkorps* VIII's bombers were tasked to operate in support of *Armeeabteilung Kempf*. One of the keys to German victory at Prokhorovka was *Armeeabteilung Kempf's* push to the north from its positions on the eastern side of the Donets River.

But the weather continued to be adverse. The whole region was covered by thick clouds which hung low. This compelled Krasovskiy to delay 1 BAK's opening attack by four hours. At 03.30 hours (04.30 German time), around seventy Soviet bomber crews who had already climbed into their Petlyakovs, were ordered out of their aircraft just seconds before the planned take-off.

Seidemann was less cautious. As usual, a few Bf 109s were sent out on early dawn fighter sweeps over the front area. Apparently, some VVS fighters also were airborne. II./JG 3's *Fw.* Hans Grünberg returned from one of these early missions with a claim for a La-5, which was recorded as his 50th victory. But in general, the skies were relatively calm during the first hours of the day. Of far greater significance was the mission which was performed by some twelve He 111s at around the same time. These were instructed to attack Soviet ground forces which stood between *Armeeabteilung Kempf* and Prokhorovka. At Rzhavets, six and a half kilometres north of Kazache, which had been taken by 6. *Panzer Division* the previous day, a concentration of tanks and armoured vehicles were spotted, and the Heinkels attacked. Their bombs fell with deadly precision and with devastating consequences to the armour below. But what the Heinkels actually blew to pieces was a German assembly! During the night, 6. *Panzer Division* dispatched elements of *Panzerregiment* 11 and

Panzergrenadierregiment 114 with a captured T-34 in the lead on a daring raid across Soviet-held territory to take the important bridge across the northern Donets at Rzhavets. The Germans managed to fool the Soviets and were able to take hold of the river crossing, but as we have seen, it was not only the Soviets who were taken in by this trick. Unfortunately for the Germans, the SD.Kfz. 305 armoured vehicle which carried the *Luftwaffe* liaison officer assigned to this group had broken down during the march so there was no possibility of informing *Fliegerkorps* VIII of the whereabouts of the advanced group. Among the large number of German casualties from the Heinkel raid were the commanders of 6. *Panzer Division*, *General* Walter von Hünersdorff and *Panzergrenadierregiment* 114, *Major* Konstantin Rogalla von Bieberstein. While the latter was killed, von Hünersdorff survived with injuries – only to fall prey to a Soviet sniper two days later.

By that time, more and more aircraft were taking off from airfields on both sides of the front line. At 18.00 hours, groups of Il-2s from 1 ShAK arrived over Prokhorovka to carry out low-level attacks against II. SS *Panzerkorps*. They met no German fighter opposition and were able to return to base without having suffered any losses.

Half an hour later, several formations of Bf 109s appeared over Prokhorovka. By that time most Soviet aircraft had disappeared from the scene. Only a single La-5 was reportedly shot down by *Ofw.* Alfred Surau of 9./JG 3. The German fighters were followed by reconnaissance aircraft. Guided by visual signs from the these aircraft – such as rocking with their wings, shooting smoke flares or dropping message canisters – II. SS *Panzerkorps* initiated its attack at 06.50 hours. A few minutes later, the bomb-carrying aircraft from both sides appeared.

1 BAK's Pe-2s arrived in a large formation and struck II. SS *Panzerkorps's* rear area. The SS reported: '*Very strong enemy air activity […] at 07.10 hours 34 bombers attacked the northern edge of the Kolkhoz Luchki.*' [241] Although Bf 109s attempted to intercept the Pe-2s, the Soviet fighter escort locked the Messerschmitts into a swirling combat which in the end resulted in no losses to either side.

In spite of the fact that heavy and decisive battles raged on all three sides of the bulge which had been created by 4. *Panzerarmee's* flank, the number of engagements between Soviet and German aircraft was quite low on this historical date. This is particularly remarkable in view of the fact that the VVS, for the first time, surpassed the *Luftwaffe* in the number of aircraft sorties over the southern flank of the Kursk Bulge – on 12 July, 2 VA and 17 VA performed 893 sorties against 654 by *Fliegerkorps* VIII. One of the main reasons for this contradiction is the fact that the declining strength of *Fliegerkorps* VIII's close-support and fighter units compelled Seidemann to concentrate these mainly to one sector, around II. *Panzerkorps's* offensive at Prokhorovka in the north-east. Meanwhile, 48. *Panzerkorps* and *Armeeabteilung Kempf* had to settle with only sporadic intervention from JG 3 and JG 52. This inevitably had a negative effect on the German operations on both these flanks.

Just as 48. *Panzerkorps* prepared to launch its attack across the Psyol River – a drive which was planned in coordination with II. SS *Panzerkorps's* offensive further to the north-east, and aimed at breaking through towards Oboyan, just 19 kilometres farther to the north – it was struck by several groups of rocket-firing *Shturmoviks*. These belonged to 291 ShAD, commanded by the *Shturmovik* veteran and Hero of the Soviet Union *Polkovnik* Andrey Vitruk. The impact of 291 ShAD's attacks can be read in a report submitted by the 'Grossdeutschland' Division: '*Considerable enemy air activity, with bombing and strafing.*' [242] Vitruk's airmen were provided with a formidable fighter escort, but to the despair of the German ground troops, there were hardly any Messerschmitts around to protect them. The 11. *Panzer Division* observed that "… there was some German air activity but more Soviet, including some dive bomber attacks." [243] In any case, until well into the afternoon, no losses as a result of air combat were reported from either side in this sector.

Next, Soviet 1st Tank Army went into action in a powerful thrust against 48. *Panzerkorps's* positions. The chronicle of 1st Tank Army's 10th Tank Corps notes: '*After a strong artillery and aviation preparation, at 08.00 hours [07.00 German time] on 12 July, the corps went over to the offensive.*' [244] This forced 48. *Panzerkorps* to cancel its offensive and instead turn onto the defensive.

Meanwhile, 17 VA sent its *Shturmoviks* and fighters – performing a grand total of 134 sorties throughout the day – to support 69th Army in its struggle to prevent *Armeeabteilung Kempf* from joining forces with II. SS *Panzerkorps*. Following the devastating blow from the Heinkels in the morning, and because of the low cloud ceiling which posed a great obstacle to the bombers which operated at medium altitude, *Fliegerkorps* VIII's bombers did not appear again in the skies on 12 July. This meant that *Armeeabteilung Kempf* also received little support from the air. Throughout the day it would remain locked in bitter fighting with defending Soviet troops which rendered any further German advance impossible.

Thus, the II. SS *Panzerkorps* had to launch its offensive against Prokhorovka without the support of strikes by 48. *Panzerkorps* or *Armeeabteilung Kempf*. Moreover, it was beset by the massive attack by Rotmistrov's 5th Guards Tank Army. Both sides actually launched their ground offensives simultaneously.

General-Leytenant Rotmistrov committed around 430 tanks and self-propelled guns in one large and frightening mass initial attack, and these were followed by another 70 in a second attack wave. But here the Soviets were faced with the concentrated effort of *Fliegerkorps* VIII's close-support units. The sky was filled with Hs 129 and Fw 190 ground-attack machines and Ju 87s. Of terrible disadvantage to the Soviets was the fact that their tanks had to cover over one and a half kilometres of open terrain before they could engage the German tanks. In the meantime, the Soviets were pounded by the heavy guns from the German tanks – which had a much greater range than the Soviet tank guns – and *Fliegerkorps* VIII's *Schlachtflieger*.

In this situation, the German practice of deploying *Luftwaffe* liaison officers with the first-line troops was of crucial importance. Sch.G 1 and *Panzerjägerstaffel/JG* 51 performed 248 sorties. Nearly all of these were flown in direct support of II. SS *Panzerkorps*. Guided via radio from liaison officers on the ground just below, who pinpointed their air attacks, the German airmen were able spread destruction among the Soviet armoured forces on the open fields outside Prokhorovka.

Historians David M. Glantz and Jonathan M. House describe the scene: 'A swirling, deadly, three-hour battle ensued, during which the Soviet tanks suffered appalling losses as they closed within killing range of the German armour to even the odds." [245]

The cannon-equipped Hs 129s exacted a terrible toll on the Soviet tanks as these rode in dense groups across the open terrain. On this day, the *Stukageschwader* St.G 2 and St.G 77 made their weakest numerical contribution since the start of the battle – only 150 sorties during the whole day (as compared with 447 the previous day and 1,071 on 5 July). But the Stukas still struck with great success, and in one case for a very special reason. *Hptm.* Hans-Ulrich Rudel – the *Staffelkapitän* of 1./St.G 2 *Immelmann* who had performed over 1,000 Stuka sorties – had been one of the pioneers of Ju 87s equipped with 37mm Flak guns, one carried under each wing, as part of the trials unit, *Versuchskommando für Panzerbekämpfung*,

Hptm. Hans-Ulrich Rudel, the Staffelkapitän of 1./St.G 2 Immelmann, flew more than 1,000 Stuka sorties and was one of the pioneers of Ju 87s equipped with 37mm guns with the Versuchskommando für Panzerbekämpfung. In the spring of 1943, he had used one of these cannon-equipped Ju 87s with great success against Soviet landing boats in the Kuban. In one day of action, Rudel was also credited with the destruction of 12 Soviet tanks.

during the previous winter. In the spring of 1943, he had used one of these cannon-equipped Ju 87s with great success against Soviet landing boats in a lagoon area of the Kuban in north-western Caucasus. Now he brought the cannon-equipped Ju 87 into use against the Soviet armour. In one day of action, Rudel was credited with the destruction of 12 Soviet tanks. Although the exact date that this took place is not entirely clear, circumstances indicate that it was 12 July (as opposed to the oft-assumed 5 July 1943). Rudel wrote:

"Catching sight of these numbers of tanks, I remembered my plane with its cannon from the *Erprobungskommando*, which I had brought along from the Crimea. With these gigantic offerings of enemy tanks, an attempt would be possible. The Soviet armour formations were provided with strong *Flak* defences, but I figured that if we flew at between 1,200 and 1,800 metres altitude, I would be able to nurse a damaged aircraft to our own territory, unless of course one did not fall like a stone. Loaded with bombs the aircraft of the first *Staffel* flew behind me in my single cannon plane. This is how we tried it!

"In my first attack, four tanks exploded through the fire from my cannons. By the evening, the total had risen to twelve." [246]

Rudel's tank kills have been put into question by both historians and other *Luftwaffe* pilots. This is not the place to deal with Rudel's total claims for the war – 519 tanks – but as far as his tally during Operation *Zitadelle* is concerned, there is little reason for any doubt. Indeed, a 37mm Flak gun fired from an aircraft generally would not suffice to knock out a Soviet tank. However, at Prokhorovka, many Soviet tanks carried metal drums containing reserve fuel on their rear decks, and a hit in one of these drums would have been sufficient to set the whole tank alight.

Indeed, the German airmen inflicted terrible losses on the advancing Soviet tanks. The 31st Tank Brigade of 29th Tank Corps reported: '*We suffer heavy losses in tanks through enemy aircraft and artillery. At 10.30 hours our tanks*

Pzkpfw IVs move forward across the open Steppe in the area of Kursk.

German tanks and infantry advance towards Russian positions in the area of Kursk in July 1943 after a surprise attack by Russian aircraft.

reached the Komsomolets State Farm, but due to continuous air attacks, they were unable to advance further and shifted to the defence.' [247] Included among the casualties inflicted through these air attacks was *Podpolk.* Mitroshenko, the commander of the 36th Tank Brigade, who was seriously injured when *Luftwaffe* aircraft destroyed his Churchill tank. [248]

In his book *Verbrannte Erde*, German writer Paul Carell allegedly quotes *General-Leytenant* Rotmistrov in describing the scene in the air over the Prokhorovka battlefield on 12 July:

'Soviet as well as German airmen tried to help their ground forces to win the battle. The bombers, close-support aircraft and fighters seemed to be permanently suspended in the sky over Prokhorovka. One aerial combat followed another. Soon the whole sky was shrouded by the thick smoke o[f] the burning wrecks.' [249]

This account has influenced several studies of the battle. However, th[e] reality was quite different.

The air over the battlefield at Prokhorovka was completely dominated b[y] the *Luftwaffe*. This may sound surprising, but there are several reasons fo[r] this. The most important is the inadequate communication between Sovie[t] ground and air units. Moreover, during the initial phase of the battle, it wa[s] almost exclusively Soviet tanks that were hit and they burned fiercel[y] creating a thick smokescreen between the forward Soviet columns and th[e] Soviet command posts, and this made it difficult for the Soviet commander[s] get a clear picture of what really took place. Thus, during the most crucial hours, Soviet aviation had not yet been informed of the terrible destruction which was being wrought upon 5th Guards Tank Army by German close-support aircraft.

It also must be kept in mind that whereas *Fliegerkorps* VIII assembled such powerful concentration of forces in the Prokhorovka area, major battles raged all along 4. *Panzerarmee's* bulge. 17 VA was badly needed to support the 9th Army against *Armeeabteilung Kempf* further to the south, and a large number of 2 VA's *Shturmoviks* and fighters were operating in support of 1st Tank Army's offensive against 48. *Panzerkorps* in the west.

Also of great importance was the fact that the VVS did not have the same direct guidance from the ground which *Fliegerkorps* VIII enjoyed. In consequence the Soviet airmen were unable to intervene in support of their armoured forces; when the ground attacks started, it was impossible to ascertain from the air who was friend and who was foe. Thus the Soviet airmen had to abandon the battlefield for the sake of attacking targets which could be positively identified as German – i.e. in the rear area. They also operated more rigidly, according to plans decided several hours in advance, lacking the *Luftwaffe's* flexible ability to revise air operations according to changes on the ground.

Between 09.45 and 10.00 hours, the Il-2s of 1 ShAK arrived to bomb and strafe vehicle columns and artillery positions in the area of Pokrovka, Sukho-Solotino and Ozerovskiy, more than 16 kilometres from the scene of main events. The escorting fighters managed to save the *Shturmoviks* from suffering any losses to German fighters.

But over the main battlefield, not even the Soviet fighters made any large-scale appearance to challenge *Fliegerkorps* VIII's supremacy. As we have seen, by this time, 2 VA's fighter force was down to a strength of 266 aircraft, and most of these had to be used to provide the bombers and *Shturmoviks* with fighter cover – a task which was obviously carried out with great success. In consequence, there were only few Soviet fighters left to carry out defensive fighter operations over their own troops at Prokhorovka. 2 VA dispatched small groups of fighters on patrol missions from around 10.00 hours. But these were mainly from 256 IAD, which had been assigned to the combat area only two days previously. Its pilots were unaccustomed to the geography of the region and encountered great difficulties with the infamous Kursk Magnetic Anomaly. On 11 July, a formation of ten of 256 IAD's Yak-9s had become totally lost, with the result that five of the pilots ran out of fuel and had to perform emergency landings in the countryside. On this day, the adverse weather appears to have prevented many of 256 IAD's pilots from locating the Prokhorovka area at all.

A report from Soviet 31st Tank Brigade remarks: '*Our own air cover was fully absent until 13.00 hours.*' [250] The report of 5th Guards Tank Army confirmed this by establishing that '*…the enemy's aircraft literally hung above our combat formations throughout the entire battle, while our own aircraft, and particularly the fighter aviation, was totally insufficient.*' [251]

Although the German fighter pilots were continually in the air over the battlefield, they reported no Soviet aircraft shot down in this sector during the first seven hours of the battle. The 31st Tank Brigade's report continues: '*After 13.00 hours, our fighter cover began to appear, but only in groups of two to ten aircraft.*' [252]

At 13.45 hours, Lt. Johannes Bunzek of 7./JG 52 claimed a single La-5 over Prokhorovka. Over the battlefield at Prokhorovka, *Fliegerkorps* VIII was mainly challenged by Soviet ground fire. As Hptm. Rudel pointed out, the Soviets had brought forward strong AAA units to the area, and these took a fair number of the *Schlachtflieger*. On 12 July, Sch.G 1 and its subordinate *Panzerjägerstaffel*/JG 51 recorded eleven aircraft put out of commission, of which six Hs 129s were total losses. All of these were due to ground fire. [253]

Most of the few scattered air combats which were fought on 12 July took place when, sporadically, JG 3 and JG 52 sent some small groups of Messerschmitts to 4. *Panzerarmee's* western flank or the air over *Armeeabteilung Kempf's* operational area. This resulted in German claims for twelve Soviet aircraft shot down. One of the fighter pilots which 2 VA lost during these encounters was M.Lt. Leonov from 270 IAP. He baled out over German-controlled territory, after getting shot down possibly by II./JG 3's Oblt. Joachim Kirschner, and was captured. (Interestingly, Leonov managed to escape and after five months managed to reach contact with Soviet troops and returned to his unit!) [254]

In the afternoon 1 BAK went into action again. Once more the Pe-2s were able to escape without loss to German fighters. The SS *Panzerkorps* reported: '*14.10 hours: Enemy aerial bombardment and strafing against main road and the airstrip at the northern part of the Kolkhoz Luchki.*' [255] The German fighters were more successful 90 minutes later, when a *Rotte* of 6./JG 3

comprising Oblt. Ernst-Heinz Löhr and Uffz. Walter Steinhans intercepted a group of Il-2s which attempted to attack troops of *Armeeabteilung Kempf*. In just three minutes, Löhr shot three Il-2s out of the sky, while his wingman shot down a fourth – which was recorded as II./JG 3's 2,000th victory.

While Rotmistrov's tankmen fought desperately, virtually without any air support to at least ward off II. SS *Panzerkorps's* attack, losing hundreds of tanks in the process – the weather continued to deteriorate. Heavy rain fell and thunderstorms rolled through the region, definitely ruling out any Soviet hopes for support from the air on the bloodstained fields at Prokhorovka.

At 16.00, Hptm. Günther Rall and his adjutant in III./JG 52, Oblt. Rudolf Trepte, took off from Ugrim for a free-hunting mission which would lead to the last air combat over Prokhorovka on 12 July. The two Germans spotted a pair of La-5s, and closing in on one of them, Rall misjudged the distance – with the result that he collided with his enemy. Only a combination of luck and high flying skills enabled Rall to nurse his badly damaged Bf 109 back to base. He later recorded: "Shaking my head, I examined the damage to my aircraft. The three propeller blades were bent like empty banana skins. From a position under the cockpit and to the rear wheel, the underside of the fuselage looked like if a gigantic can opener had chewed its way through the aluminium. That must have been the work of the propeller of my unhappy opponent. If it had gone just ten centimetres deeper, it would have torn the fuel tank behind the pilot seat wide open…" [256] Intriguingly, Rall's severely damaged Bf 109 is another example which does not appear in the loss lists of *Generalquartiermeister der Luftwaffe*.

The outcome of the great battle on 12 July is quite contradictory in many ways. In the air, the VVS dominated 4. *Panzerarmee's* two flanks, leaving the *Luftwaffe* in almost total control of the skies above Prokhorovka. Against 19 of *Fliegerkorps* VIII's aircraft put out of commission, its fighter pilots were only able to bring home 16 victories. This appears to be a quite negative exchange, but a closer study reveals that among these German losses only one aircraft was recorded as being shot down by Soviet fighters in the southern flank of the Kursk Bulge on 12 July: a Ju 52 which was intercepted as it flew wounded men from the battlezone, and most of the remainder were victims of ground fire. [257] In return, 14 Soviet fighters were lost (the German fighters claimed seven shot down). But at the same time, the Soviet fighters succeeded in providing their bombers and *Shturmoviks* with an effective cover.

Through their sheer numerical weight, Rotmistrov's fiercely attacking tank forces were able to block II. SS *Panzerkorps's* intended march to Prokhorovka. But Rotmistrov's offensive also failed bitterly. The balance of losses between both sides was strikingly unequal: The Soviet casualties amounted to 5,500 men, and II. SS *Panzerkorps's* were limited to 850. While 300 Soviet tanks were put out of commission, II. SS *Panzerkorps* lost between 60 and 70.

Undoubtedly, without *Fliegerkorps* VIII's contribution – not only through direct and devastating attacks against Soviet tanks in the open terrain to the west of Prokhorovka, but also by keeping the Soviet troop movements under a constant surveillance, informing the German ground troops of each significant move by their opponents – these figures, and perhaps even the whole outcome of the battle, would have been entirely different. It is not to say too little that the *Luftwaffe's* decisive contribution to the famous battle of Prokhorovka has been underestimated in most published accounts.

Meanwhile, on the two flanks where *Fliegerkorps* VIII had hardly been able to intervene – with the most notable exception of the unlucky attack by He 111s against own troops at Rzhavets – the Soviets achieved significant defensive successes. A dejected General Friedrich von Mellenthin, the Chief of Staff of 48. *Panzerkorps*, wrote: '*The situation on the left flank had deteriorated to such a degree that an attack northwards was no longer possible.*' [259]

In the evening of 12 July, *Armeeabteilung Kempf's* forward elements of III. *Panzerkorps* on the right bank of the Donets River – opposite Rzhavets – came under attack from nearly one hundred T-34 and T-70 tanks. Formed as the ad-hoc 'Group Trufanov', these belonged to 5th Guards Mechanised Corps and 2nd Guards Tank Corps, which had been hastily diverted from the Prokhorovka region to meet the threat from the south. After a bitter tank battle, the Germans were pushed back across the Donets in this sector. This quick Soviet action "…temporarily restored Soviet defences along the Northern Donets and, most important, prevented the III. *Panzerkorps* from marching towards Prokhorovka on 12 July." [260]

Chapter Eight

Operation *Kutuzov*

Attack in the North – 12 July 1943

While German 4. *Panzerarmee* launched its attack against Prokhorovka in the south on 12 July, the Soviet offensive, was launched against the northern flank of *Heeresgruppe Mitte's* Orel Bulge in the north. The Western and Bryansk fronts hurled over 300,000 men, supported by 1,000 tanks against the well fortified positions which were held by German 2. *Panzerarmee.*

The offensive was preceded by a night of intensive Soviet air attacks against the German defence positions. U-2, R-5 and R-Z biplane harassment bombers from 1 VA's 213 NBAD and 15 VA's 282 NBAD and 313 NBAD were in action over 2. *Panzerarmee's* rear area throughout the night, dropping their small bomb loads against troop quarters, supply bases and airfields. Meanwhile the ADD carried out a most concentrated operation over the Orel Bulge, performing 360 bombing sorties alone against strongholds in the German defence lines opposed to the Bryansk Front at Novosil on the eastern flank of the Orel Bulge. Another 182 ADD sorties were made against the German 55. *Armeekorps* opposing the Western Front 160 kilometres further to the north-west. These attacks were supplemented by 180 flights by U-2 and R-Z crews from 1 VA's 213 NBAD. Altogether, 210 tons of bombs were dropped against 55. *Armeekorps* alone during this night.

At dawn on 12 July, a massive artillery barrage was opened up against 2. *Panzerarmee's* positions on three sectors in the Orel Bulge – in the north, the north-east and the east. Shortly afterward, Soviet aircraft appeared and subjected the German

positions to an intense aerial bombardment. *Lt.* Ivan Gnezdilov of 18 GIAP describes the opening attack in the Western Front's sector early on 12 July:

"Flying in perfect formations, our bombers appeared above the enemy positions just as the artillery preparation ended. Seventy Petlyakovs and almost one hundred Ilyushins attacked the enemy positions. For a quarter of an hour, the air was filled with the rumble of their aircraft engines. Bomb and rocket projectiles exploded on the ground below. Our *Shturmoviks* and bombers finished off what was left after the artillery fire.

"The whole operation was concluded by a group of Ilyushins which laid a smoke screen over the German advanced positions, effectively blinding the enemy. Meanwhile, our artillery shifted its fire to the enemy's rear area. Under the cover of their fire, and protected in the air above by our aircraft – among them the fighters of 18 GIAP and the *Normandie-Niemen Eskadrilya* – the tanks and infantry of the 11th Guards Army opened the offensive." [261]

To the Germans, it was clear that the long awaited Soviet offensive was about to commence, but they still believed that the Western Front attacks were of a diversionary nature. Hence, when the first aircraft of 1. *Fliegerdivision* took off from the airfields around Orel at dawn, they were almost exclusively sent toward the east.

The German airmen were very tired after six days of extremely heavy air fighting, and had seen just one calm day when they now took off for what they realised would be another great surge in aerial combat. But the fighting spirit among the fliers in 1. *Fliegerdivision* were running high; they had dealt their enemy a crushing defeat and

Shturmovik pilots study a map ahead of a combat mission. The most severe flaw of the VVS at Kursk in July 1943 was the lack of combat experienced airmen. It is estimated that nearly eight in ten Soviet aviators in 15 VA lacked combat experience prior to the great battle.

Preparation in the North

As we have seen, the Soviets were well-prepared to counter Operation Zitadelle with a deep echeloned defence. As part of the larger plan, the Soviets also planned a series of counter-attacks which would follow the successful defensive battle of Kursk. The largest of these attacks was aimed against the German Orel Bulge which was held by Heeresgruppe Mitte's 9. Armee in the south and 2. Panzerarmee in the north. Dubbed Operation Kutuzov – after the famous Russian Field Marshal who fought Napoleon in 1812 – and approved by the Stavka in May 1943, Operation Kutuzov envisaged a pincer attack against the Orel Bulge with the Western Front striking from the north and the Central Front from the south, while the Bryansk Front would attack the eastern nose of the Bulge, with the aim of tying down German troops that eventually would become surrounded.

On 10 July, when General Model's troops of 9. Armee had been conclusively halted on the southern flank of the Orel Bulge, the Stavka ordered Operation Kutuzov to be launched two days later. However, by that time, due to the severe losses which the Central Front had sustained while fighting back Model's attacks, the southern attack could not be immediately implemented. Thus, Operation Kutuzov was hastily modified.

According to the new instructions, the Western Front would still attack at Ulyanovo, south-west of Belev. But these forces – the 11th Guards Army, supported by the 5th Tank Corps – would be divided into two directions: one which struck straight southward in order to block German retreat movements from the Orel Bulge, and one which would march towards the south-east. The latter would co-operate with the Bryansk Front's 61st Army and 20th Tank Corps which would attack north of Mtsensk in a smaller pincer movement aimed at surrounding elements of German 53rd Armeekorps in the Bolkhov sector. The Bryansk Front's most powerful thrust would be carried out by the 3rd and 63rd armies, attacking frontally in the Novosii sector.

On the second day, the Western Front would launch another attack, delivered by the 50th Army on the 11th Guards Army's western flank, and directed towards Zhizdra in the west with the aim of isolating 2. Panzerarmee in the Orel Bulge from Heeresgruppe Mitte's 4. Armee.

At dawn on 12 July, the Western Front's two attack forces could muster a total of over 200,000 troops with 745 tanks and 4,285 artillery pieces and mortars, and the Bryansk Front's three first-line armies had lined up a total of 170,000 troops and 350

tanks and SPGs. Finally, on 15 July, the Central Front would join in through an attack against the contested area in the south.

In one important sense, the roles during Operation Kutuzov would be reversed as compared with Operation Zitadelle. Orel was one of the German main supply bases and cornerstones of their entire Eastern Front defence. Having held positions around this city since the autumn of 1941, the Germans had constructed a deeply echeloned system of fortifications, trenches and minefields which could be well compared with the Soviet system of defence lines in the Kursk Bulge.

Moreover, the OKW was well aware of Soviet preparations for an attack against the northern flank of the Orel Bulge. First of all, the Bulge in itself – extending between 80 and 104 kilometres from the west to the east – quite naturally provoked a Soviet attack, just like the Kursk Bulge naturally provoked a German attack. But Luftwaffe reconnaissance flights and intercepted radio messages also had provided the Germans with a fairly good picture of the Bryansk Front's intentions. This nevertheless proved to be a two-edged sword: while the Germans made preparations to counter the Bryansk Front's attacks on both sides of Mtsensk in the north-east, the Western Front succeeded in concealing much of its build-up in the north.

When General Ivan Bagramyan's 11th Guards Army carried out a series of reconnaissance attacks on 11 July, aimed at establishing the exact positions of the German defence lines, the Germans concluded that this was merely a diversionary attack. To the east of Orel, General Lothar Rendulic's 53. Armeekorps was made ready to meet the attack from Novosil, and to the north of the contested city, the 55. Armeekorps dug in to prepare for the attack against Bolkhov from the east.

General Ivan Bagramyan's attack in the north, supported by General-Mayor Mikhail Gromov's 1 VA, would startle the Germans through its great and unexpected strength.

However, German reinforcements already were underway. On 10 July, the 8. Panzerdivision was instructed to move to Orel. As soon as the Soviet offensive commenced, strong elements of the 9. Armee were also shifted northward to contain the attacks. Manning strong defensive positions, the 160,000 troops of 2. Panzerarmee and 9. Armee's 300,000 men constituted a magnificent defensive force.

---

vere unchallenged masters of the sky over 9. *Armee's* positions in the south f the Orel Bulge. They were absolutely convinced that they would achieve he same against this 'new' enemy in the north.

On the other side of the front line, the VVS commanders were well aware f what a formidable enemy their young aviators would be launched against. One imperative measure was to arm the Soviet fliers with a steadfast esolution to fight. The following account describes the scene as the fighter ilots of 15 VA's 1 GIAK – many of whom had never seen a German aircraft n the air – were prepared for the upcoming battle:

"At 10 minutes past five in the morning of 12 July, the Guards banners vere hoisted at all our airfields. Simultaneously, all commanders, political vorkers, pilots and technicians of 32, 63, 64, 65 and 66 GIAP as well as 160 AP were lined up at each airfield. The ceremony takes place half an hour efore they will take-off in order to enter the deadly battle with the enemy. During these short minutes ahead of the battle they have gathered before he sacred silk of their Guards banners, which have been won in blood. veryone swears before their Guards banners that it is better to perish in ombat than to withdraw from the battle in disgrace!

"The fighters of the 32nd Guards Fighter Regiment are also lined up on heir airfield. The standardbearer, Hero of the Soviet Union [Guards *St.Lt.* /asiliy] Savel'yev and his assistants, pilots Gorshikov and Korchachenko, have nfolded the Guards banner and hold it in front of the men who are lined p. The meeting is opened by Hero of the Soviet Union *Mayor* [Ivan] Kholodov. He reads out the order of the day of the Military Council of the 3ryansk Front: '*Today the great offensive begins. Our task is to win and maintain uperiority in the air, to steadfastly and self-denyingly fight the enemy and thus add lory to our proud banner.*'" [262]

Having sworn to fight to their last drop of blood, the Soviet airmen limbed into their aircraft and took off with the rays of the rising sun on heir necks.

Divided into groups of two, three or four aircraft, 225 ShAD's Il-2s flew vestward to support the 63rd Army's opening attack at Novosil. Fighter scort was provided by the Yak-1s of 832 IAP. This regiment was part of Polkovnik Viktor Litvinov's 315 IAD, which dispatched all of its four

An Il-2 Shturmovik's rear gunner in battle position. In 1941 and 1942, the Il-2 had relied on its strong armour for protection against German fighter attacks. However, with the introduction of 20mm gun pods under the wings of the Bf 109, and in particular when the more heavily armed Fw 190 commenced operations on the Eastern Front, Il-2 losses rose sharply and quickly reached an almost unbearable level. It was in response to this that the Soviets started to modify Il-2 into a twin-seater with a rear gunner.

regiments on the first mission at dawn on 12 July 1943. First to take off in this *Diviziya* were the La-5s of 50 IAP which went out to sweep the skies in the area where the 63rd Army would attack in advance.

At Sakovnino, *Podpolk*, Semyon Orlyakhin led the La-5s of 171 IAP into the sky. They met five Il-2s from one of 3 ShAK's *Shturmovik* regiments and escorted them towards Grachevka, where German artillery positions posed a dangerous threat to the Soviet 63rd Army. High above, 431 IAP's Yak-7Bs

Soviet aviation for Operation Kutuzov on 12 July 1943

With Operation Kutuzov, another two Soviet air armies would join the great battle – 1 VA, operating in support of the Western Front, and 15 VA, operating in support of the Bryansk Front.

On 12 July 1943, General-Mayor Mikhail Gromov's 1 VA could muster a total of 720 aircraft – 500 fighters, 150 Shturmoviks and 70 bombers. These were distributed among the following units:

8 IAK (General-Mayor Fyodor Zherebchenko):
215 IAD (Polkovnik Mikhail Yakushin) with 156 IAP (La-5), 263 IAP and 813 IAP
323 IAD (Polkovnik Pavel Rybakov) with 149 IAP, 269 IAP (Yak fighters) and 484 IAP.
303 IAD (General-Mayor Georgiy Zakharov) with 18 GIAP (Yak-7B), 20 IAP (Yak-9),
168 IAP (Yak fighters), 523 IAP (La-5) and Normandie-Niemen – the French
    volunteer unit, equipped with Yak-7Bs.
309 IAD (Podpolkovnik Iosif Geybo) with 49 IAP (Yak-1), 162 IAP and 272 IAP.
2 ShAK (General-Mayor Vasiliy Stepichev):
231 ShAD (Polkovnik Leonid Chizhikov) with 568 ShAP, 570 ShAP, 873 ShAP and 946
    ShAP, all equipped with Il-2s.
233 ShAD (Polkovnik Vladimir Smirnov) with 62 ShAP, 122 ShAP, 98 ShAP, 312 ShAP
    and 996 ShAP, all equipped with Il-2s.
224 ShAD (Polkovnik Mikhail Kotelnikov) with 513 ShAP, 565 ShAP, 566 ShAP,
    571 ShAP and 996 ShAP.
2 BAK (General Vladimir Ushakov):
223 BAD with 224 BAP and 587 BAP, both equipped with Pe-2s.
285 BAD (Polkovnik Sandalov) with 35 GBAP; equipped with Pe-2s and Tu-2s.
204 BAD (Polkovnik Sergey Andreyev) with 2 BAP, 130 BAP, 179 BAP and 261 BAP
    – all equipped with Pe-2s.
213 NBAD (General-Mayor Vasiliy Molokov) with 15 NBAP, 17 NBAP, 22 GNBAP,
    24 GNBAP, 615 NBAP, 634 NBAP and 644 NBAP.

On 12 July 1943, General-Leytenant Nikolay Naumenko's 15 VA could muster around 1,000 aircraft, distributed among:
1 GIAK (General-Leytenant Yevgeniy Beletskiy):
3 GIAD (Polkovnik Valentin Ukhov) with 32 GIAP (La-5FN), 63 GIAP (La-5FN) and
    160 IAP (La-5FN).
4 GIAD (Polkovnik Vladimir Kitayev) with 64 GIAP, 65 GIAP and 66 GIAP –
    all equipped with Yak-7Bs.
234 IAD (Polkovnik Yevstafiy Tatanashvili) with 133 IAP, 233 IAP and 248 IAP.
315 IAD (Polkovnik Viktor Litvinov) with 50 IAP (La-5), 171 IAP (La-5), 431 IAP
    (Yak-7B) and 832 IAP (Yak-1).
3 ShAK (General-Mayor Mikhail Gorlachenko):
307 ShAD (Polkovnik Aleksandr Kozhemyakin) with 211 ShAP and 893 ShAP –
    both equipped with Il-2s.
308 ShAD (Polkovnik Grigoriy Turykin) with 135 ShAP, 64 ShAP and 948 ShAP –
    all equipped with Il-2s.
225 ShAD (Polkovnik Aleksey Obukhov) with 118 GShAP, 614 ShAP, 810 ShAP and
825 ShAP – all equipped with Il-2s.
11 SAK (General-Mayor Stepan Danilov):
4 IAP, 148 IAP and 293 IAP – all equipped with Yak-9Ts armed with
    37mm OKB-16 guns.
594 ShAP, 658 ShAP and 724 ShAP – all equipped with Il-2s.
284 NBAD (Mayor Grigoriy Pokoyevoy) with 4 NBAP, 387 NBAP, 638 NBAP,
    640 NBAP and 701 NBAP.
313 NBAD (Polkovnik Aleksandr Voyevodin) with 690 NBAP, 707 NBAP, 765 NBAP,
    99 NBAP, 997 NBAP and 998 NBAP.
99 GORAP (Podpolkovnik Nikolay Shchennikov) with Pe-2s.

Ahead of Operation Kutuzov, these Soviet air units were scrupulously prepared for their operations. Photo reconnaissance missions which had been carried out over the Orel Bulge since May 1943 provided the bomber and Shturmovik units with detailed target information. For the command of the air operations, a network of air command posts was created in the vicinity of the front line. Each such command post was manned by

liaison officers of both the aviation and the army. A wide network of radio stations for direct communication between the command posts and unit commanders in the air had also been created.

The prime task of the Soviet air armies in Operation Kutuzov was to provide the ground offensives with close air support. The main targets were artillery positions, defensive strongpoints, troop congestions and headquarters. All Shturmoviks and day bombers in 1 VA and 15 VA were concentrated against those targets; direct attacks against lines of communication or airfields were not a priority. The aim was to deal a swift and completely crippling blow against the Orel Bulge. The Luftwaffe was to be fought mainly in the air – a task which fell upon the shoulders of the fighter units. However, the prime task of 1 VA's and 15 VA's fighters was defensive – to provide the ground troops with cover through area patrols and to escort Shturmoviks and bombers.

In order to secure the implementation of the operations plan and the execution of new tactics and methods, the C-in-C of VVS KA, General-Polkovnik Aleksandr Novikov, arrived to the headquarters of 15 VA in the morning of 12 July.

The operations by VVS KA's air armies over the Orel Bulge was supplemented by the ADD, which directed its entire strength to this sector during the initial stage – five Bomber corps (1 GBAK, 2 GBAK, 3 GBAK, 5 BAK and 7 BAK) and two Divizii, 45 BAD and 113 BAD. The latter formation – commanded by General-Leytenant Fyodor Michugin and constituted of 6 GBAP and 815 BAP, both equipped with Il-4s – was even assigned to operate in daylight in support of the Bryansk Front and in cooperation with 15 VA. The ADD operations in support of Operation Kutuzov were supervised by the ADD's C-in-C, General-Mayor Aleksandr Golovanov.

In pure numerical terms, the three Soviet air armies which operated against the Orel Bulge – 1 VA, 15 VA and 16 VA – appeared to enjoy a more than three-fold numerical superiority against their opponent, Generalmajor Paul Deichmann's 1. Fliegerdivision with approximately 700 aircraft in the Orel Bulge. But a closer examination shows that the balance was more even. First of all, 16 VA made only a very weak appearance in the air during the first days of Operation Kutuzov – and when it finally joined the battle again, 1. Fliegerdivision had been considerably reinforced.

Moreover, many Soviet aircraft were night harassment bombers and could not be used in daytime. The share of night bombers was particularly high in 15 VA, where around one quarter of all aircraft was of this kind. While 1 VA was dominated by fighters, 15 VA had the strongest concentration of Shturmoviks among these two air armies. Slightly more than half of 15 VA's aircraft intended for day operations were fighters, but three fighter regiments were equipped with Yak-9Ts for anti-tank operations with their 37mm guns.

The greatest disadvantage to the VVS was the fact that both 1 VA and 15 VA also were marred by a recent large influx of inadequately trained novice pilots and inexperienced unit commanders. This problem was particularly grave in 15 VA, which had an even larger share of novice pilots than 16 VA. As we have seen previously, when 234 IAD was shifted from 15 VA to 16 VA, the headquarters of the latter pointed out the particularly large number of novice pilots in this Diviziya. Nevertheless, in 15 VA, 234 IAD had been regarded as one of the best fighter formations. On 11 July, 234 IAD was shifted back to 15 VA. These novices stood little chance against the battle-hardened veterans of 1. Fliegerdivision's Jagdgruppen.

A La-5FN fighter at a Soviet first-line airfield.

On 12 July 1943, Stab, II. and IV./JG 54, together with 7./JG 26, were hastily flown south to the Orel area from the Leningrad sector. Seen in this photograph are Fw 190s of 5./JG 54. 'Black 7' was flown by Lt. Emil 'Bully' Lang, a famous track-and-field athlete before the war. Lang served with JG 54 on the Eastern Front from early 1943. Lang would begin his real successes as a fighter pilot during the Battle of the Orel Bulge. By the time he arrived at Orel on 12 July 1943, he had achieved three victories. As early as the next day he would double this total, and by the end of July 1943, his score had reached 12. The next months saw Lang bring home an almost unparalleled row of victories – boosting his total to over 100 in November 1943. When Emil Lang was shot down and killed on the Western Front on 3 September 1944, his tally stood at 173 victories.

oined a formation of Il-4s from 113 BAD which would also attack German rtillery positions at Grachevka as well as Setukha and Berezovets. The latter ormation was escorted by Yak-7Bs from 66 GIAP/1 GIAK.

At 06.00 hours (Russian time), just a few minutes ahead of the ground ttack, a group of Il-2s swept down over the front line at Novosil and laid a hick smoke screen. Covered by smoke, the 63rd Army's first armoured hrust began to move across no-man's-land along a 16 kilometre front. Meanwhile, the *Shturmoviks* and Pe-2s appeared in the air above.

But the Soviets ran into fierce German opposition, both on the ground nd in the air. While the KV tanks drove straight into German mines and a barrage from anti-tank guns, the Soviet airmen were subjected to attacks rom above by Fw 190s of JG 51 *Mölders*.

The Il-4s from 113 BAD were intercepted by 7./JG 51, led by *Oblt.* Karl-Heinz Weber, during their approach flight. Three bombers fell in lames – one due to Weber and two under the guns of *Uffz.* Franz Meindl's Focke-Wulf. One of the escorting Yak-7Bs also was claimed by a third pilot of 7./JG 51.

I./JG 51 met the Il-2s as these buzzed in over German-controlled erritory at low altitude. Six Fw 190s of 2./JG 51 attacked a group of 832 AP Yak-1s led by *Lt.* Shoti Grdzelishvili, which escorted Il-2s from 14 ShAP, and shot down two of the Soviet fighters. Meanwhile Uffz. Klaus Dietrich of the same *Staffel* reportedly knocked down a pair of *Shturmoviks*. Another Il-2 was shot to pieces by 10./JG 51's Fw. Rudolf Wagner.

As the next Soviet formations appeared – 225 ShAD Il-2s escorted by 171 AP's La-5s – more German fighters arrived. *Oblt.* Joachim Brendel reported n encounter with "…20 Il-2s and 15 La-5s." [263] In the subsequent clash, the Germans claimed to have shot down nine Il-2s and three La-5s – among which Brendel bagged three of the former. 171 IAP recorded the loss of one of their own.

The continued air fighting proved to the Soviet airmen that the image of formidable enemy whom they had been made prepared to meet at dawn, definitely was no exaggeration. Most air encounters caught the Soviets in a position of tactical inferiority, and the clashes frequently displayed a highly disciplined German enemy, while the large number of inexperienced Soviet pilots often resulted in Soviet formations becoming scattered, allowing German aces to pick their victims at will. 32 GIAP, which had lost its commanding officer and his deputy while supporting 16 VA on 6 July, lost M.Lt. Nikolay Zhukov and *Lt.* Nikolay Safonov under such circumstances.[264] They were apparently shot down by *Oblt.* Karl-Heinz

Weber and *Uffz.* Heinrich Dittlmann on 7./JG 51's second mission on 12 July. The day's fighting with 15 VA cost 1. *Fliegerdivision's* fighter units a loss of no more than three Fw 190s. One of these, flown by 11./JG 51's *Uffz.* Erwin Grossmann, was rammed by a Yak-7B piloted by *M.Lt.* Nikolay Alekseyev of 64 GIAP, with Grossmann posted as missing and the young Soviet pilot killed.

1. *Fliegerdivision* and 15 VA continued to focus their prime attention on the Novosil sector, where Soviet 63rd Army became locked in a dogged fight with *Generalmajor* Lothar Rendulic's well prepared German 35. *Armeekorps.* On the Bryansk Front's right flank, north of Mtsensk, the 61st Army assaulted German 53. *Armeekorps* with only limited air support from both sides. Fifty-six kilometres further to the north-west, *General-Major* Mikhail Gromov's 1 VA enjoyed an almost unchallenged air superiority. Pe-2s of 2 BAK and *Shturmoviks* of 224 ShAD and 2 ShAK with 231 ShAD and 233 ShAD, pounced on the positions of the German 55. *Armeekorps* meeting almost no opposition from the *Luftwaffe*. Ivan Gnezdilov wrote:

"*During the first day of the offensive, the enemy's air force performed only a weak counter-action. Only ten Junkers managed to break through to our ground troops. But when they spotted our fighters, they jettisoned their bombs and made a hasty escape. It was obvious that they feared our Yaks.*

"*The enemy command's attempt to get a view of the situation by dispatching reconnaissance aircraft was also frustrated. During the first half of the day, a Ju 88 appeared in the Sukhinichi area, heading in the direction of Kaluga. The pilots G.I. Titaryov, and V.I. Shalev, of 168 IAP, were scrambled to intercept this aircraft. In his first attack, Titaryov put the enemy's radio operator out of action. Then he closed in to a distance of only 30 metres before opening fire again, aiming at the cockpit and the fuel tanks. The Junkers burst into flames and descended a little before it blew up violently in mid-air.*

"*A little while later, a He 111 reconnaissance aircraft appeared on the same route. This aircraft was intercepted by the pilots S.G. Struzhkin and A.S. Petrov, who shot it down near the airfield at Vyazovaya. Thus ended the enemy's attempts to send his reconnaissance aircraft to our rear area.*" [265]

Throughout 12 July, 1 VA carried out 868 combat sorties, against which only 74 German flights were recorded. [266] Provided with such a splendid air support, *General* Ivan Bagramyan's 11th Guards Army achieved a major breakthrough on Western Front's sector.

But in the south-east, the Bryansk Front was unable to accomplish much. Its troops were relentlessly attacked by formations of between thirty and fifty German bombers and Stukas. As a measurement of the intense *Luftwaffe*

Fw 190 A-4s of JG 51 in their dispersal at one of the airfields around Orel.

activity, one Stuka pilot in III./St.G 3, *Lt*. Erhard Jähnert, carried out six dive-bomber missions between 06.40 and 19.45 hours. [267]

German reinforcements also were arriving. The 35. *Armeekorps* would receive 2. and 8. *Panzer* divisions from the OKH reserve, and 9. *Armee* on the Orel Bulge's southern flank released the 12., 18. and 20. *Panzer* divisions and sent them to the north to counter Bagramyan's attack. At Siverskaya, to the far north in the Leningrad area, JG 54's *Stabsstaffel* and the *Grünherzgeschwader's* two *Gruppen* which had not yet been dispatched to the south, were place on alert. *Hptm*. Heinrich Jung's II./JG 54 hastily flew its Fw 190s south to Orel. Commanded by 74-victory ace *Hptm*. Erich Rudorffer, IV./JG 54 had just been formed from the old 4./JG 54, but before it was fully equipped it had to be rushed to the Orel area. The last German fighter *Staffel* at Siverskaya, 7./JG 26 – the only remaining element of JG 26 *Schlageter* on the Eastern Front – flew south together with these two *Gruppen* and JG 54's *Stabsstaffel*.

Thus the Leningrad area was completely abandoned by *Luftwaffe* fighters. But in the air over the Orel Bulge, the increased presence of the *Luftwaffe* was painfully felt by the Soviets – particularly in the Bryansk Front's and 15 VA's sector, where 1. *Fliegerdivision* continued to place its main emphasis. Fighters from 15 VA which attempted to intervene against the onslaught from the air were repeatedly assaulted by swarms of Fw 190s which provided the bombers and Stukas with an effective fighter cover. This day's fighting cost 1 GIAK alone a loss of 25 fighter aircraft and 19 pilots. [268]

On 12 July, 1. *Fliegerdivision* flew over 1,000 effective combat sorties – including 345 by fighters, which was the highest number since 5 July. [269] Most of these sorties were carried out in the Bryansk Front's and 15 VA's operational area, where the *Luftwaffe* succeeded in achieving a numerical superiority – similarly to what had been the case during the Operation *Zitadelle* attacks during the previous week. 15 VA performed 737 combat sorties – 406 by fighters, 182 by *Shturmoviks* and 89 by bombers. [270] This resulted in a loss of altogether 45 of 15 VA's aircraft. [271] Including losses sustained by 1 VA and 16 VA, a total of 59 Soviet aircraft were shot down in the Orel combat zone on 12 July 1943.

The large-scale air fighting inevitably resulted in overclaiming. 1. *Fliegerdivision* recorded 87 aerial victories. [272] As had been the rule during

the previous week, the Soviets exaggerated their own successes to an even larger extent. 1 GIAK alone reported 54 German aircraft shot down. [273] *Luftwaffe* statistics show that on 12 July 1943, only ten aircraft of *Luftflotte* 6 were destroyed due to hostile action – including just three fighters. [274]

As a consequence of the German dominance in the air, the *Luftwaffe* bombers and Stukas were able to carry out highly successful operations throughout the day, claiming the destruction of 35 tanks, 50 other motor vehicles and 14 artillery pieces in the process. [275] This, in turn, contributed greatly to the Bryansk Front's difficulties; by the end of Operation *Kutuzov* (see later in this chapter) first day, it had merely been able to overrun the first German defence line.

The situation however was different further to the north-west, where the Western Front's 11th Guards Army, supported by 1 VA, had achieved a penetration of between eight and ten kilometres in the Ulyanovo sector.

13 July 1943 – Air battle in the North

By the end of Operation *Kutuzov's* first day, the Germans had finally realised that the Western Front's attack on the Orel Bulge's northern flank was much more than a diversionary operation. However, the Bryansk Front's attack in the east towards Orel – a vital cornerstone in the German defence on the Eastern Front – still was regarded as the main threat. Thus, *Generalmajor* Deichmann decided, firstly, to concentrate his 1. *Fliegerdivision* against the Bryansk Front in the Novosil sector, east of Orel from dawn on 13 July. The prime task assigned to his air units was to support the counter-attacks which 53. *Armeekorps* initiated in this sector.

15 VA also sent its airmen to support their ground troops, but being dispatched in small formations, the Il-2s became easy prey to the fighters of a considerably reinforced 1. *Fliegerdivision*. As 13 July dawned 1. *Fliegerdivision* had amassed a formidable fighter force to meet the Soviet onslaught in the air: The equivalent of eight *Jagdgruppen* were ready for action over the Orel Bulge – 7./JG 26; *Stab*, I., III., IV. and 15./JG 51; elements of I./JG 52; and *Stab*, I., II. and IV./JG 54.

At around 07.00 hours, the pilots of I./JG 51, IV./JG 51 and I./JG 54 claimed to have shot down 17 Il-2s in the Novosil area. Flying slowly next to the Il-2s in close escort, the Soviet escort fighters failed to achieve much

Two Yak-9s dive to perform an attack.

but instead lost a number of their own to German fighter attacks from above. *Lt.* Horst Ademeit of 6./JG 54 bagged one Il-2 and two escort fighters in three minutes, while his *Staffel*-mate *Fw.* Albin Wolf shot a fourth Soviet fighter out of the sky. Two hours later, another wave of Il-2s arrived, and this time I./JG 51, II./JG 54 and IV./JG 54 reported 12 shot down. When the third wave of *Shturmoviks* was sent in ninety minutes later, Fw 190s from I. and IV./JG 54 were in place and claimed ten more Il-2s shot down. Above all, due to the German fighters, 15 VA's concentrated efforts during the morning of 13 July failed to have any real impact on the German ground troops. All of this was achieved without a single loss to the German fighter units.

Thus effectively covered by 1. *Fliegerdivision's* fighters against the Soviet Air Force, 53. *Armeekorps* was able to carry out a strong counter-attack. Meanwhile the German bombers and Stukas were dispatched in large formations against the Bryansk Front's troops, which were forced to discontinue its attack in the forenoon. 15 VA sent in large numbers of fighters to cover the ground troops of 3rd and 63rd Armies, and more large-scale air fighting developed. Five bombers from III./KG 1 and II./KG 4 were shot down. [276] But the Soviet fighters took a heavy beating from the escorting Fw 190s. Intervening to ward off Soviet fighter attacks against a formation of German bombers, I./JG 54's *Lt.* Günther Scheel reportedly shot down three Yak-9s in just two minutes.

Further to the north-west, in the Ulyanovo sector, the German 55. *Armeekorps* fought desperately to halt *General-Leytenant* Bagramyan's 11th Guards Army — the Western Front's main attack force — at the German second defence line. But supplied with virtually no air support, the Germans stood little chance. *Shturmoviks* of 224 ShAD silenced the German artillery positions, and in this situation the Soviet ground troops were able to outflank their opponent, seize the village of Staritsa, north-west of Ulyanovo, and break through the German second defence line.

The *Luftwaffe's* operations on the Eastern Front had long had the character of that of a 'fire brigade' and responding to the urgent requests from 55. *Armeekorps*, *Generalmajor* Deichmann directed his 1. *Fliegerdivision* towards the north at around noon.

Formations of twenty to thirty Ju 87s, provided with strong fighter escort, appeared and hurled themselves against the Western Front's troops. In his memoirs, *General-Leytenant* Bagramyan wrote: "*Our airmen fought with great courage but were not always able to repel the enemy air attacks. Several Junkers aircraft broke through the fighter shields and the AAA barrages and dropped their bombs on our ground troops.*" [277]

The 50th Army, which operated on the Western Front's right flank, was severely hit and had to discontinue its offensive so as to shift to the defensive. But Bagramyan's 11th Guards Army were actually better off; through its deep penetration, the fighting had reached a densely forested area. *General der Flieger* Friedrich Kless, the Chief of Staff of *Luftflotte* 6, described the situation from the German point of view:

'The advancing Soviet armies had to be delayed long enough to allow the German reserves being shifted by Army Group Centre to arrive in time. This was an especially difficult proposition where wooded areas afforded the Russians excellent opportunities for concealment, which meant that the *Luftwaffe* could do little more than prevent Soviet troop movements — especially those of tank units — on the very few existing highways and roads.

Off the roads it proved nearly impossible to discover, let alone attack, enemy units moving through the woods.' [278]

These difficulties of course, applied to the Soviet airmen too. The Pe-2 crews of 2 BAK and *Shturmovik* fliers of 224 ShAD and 2 ShAK could not afford to offer their ground troops as effective air support as earlier in the day.

Since 1 VA did not have the same problem with too large a number of inadequately trained pilots as 15 VA and 16 VA, the Soviets were able to put up a more effective fight in the air in this sector. 1 VA's undoubtedly finest fighter unit was 303 IAD, which was commanded by *General-Mayor* Georgiy Zakharov, a veteran from the Spanish Civil War and one of the most able VVS unit leaders. Among the regiments under his command was 18 GIAP (formerly 6 IAP), which had been one of the best Soviet fighter units during the first year of the war, and *Mayor* Jean Tulasne's Free French fighter *Eskadrilya Normandie-Niemen*, which consisted of seventeen very experienced French volunteer fighter pilots.

The aviators of 1 VA reported the first encounters on 13 July at around noon. *M.Lt.* Nikolay Pinchuk of 1 VA's 18 GIAP recalls: "The enemy made desperate attempts to halt our armies. He sent large forces of aircraft to the most critical front sectors. The sky began to be filled by bombers and fighters from both sides and relentless air combats commenced." [279]

49 IAP, which had pioneered the La-5 in battle one year previously, lost two La-5s, while *Kpt.* Emir Chalbash was credited with the destruction of one Fw 190. [280] Obviously in the same engagement, *Oblt.* Kurt-Reinhard Fischer and *Uffz.* Anton Held of I./JG 54 and *Uffz.* Robert Sauber of JG 51's *Stabsstaffel* claimed one La-5 each while *Oblt.* Albert Walter, a 37-victory ace of the latter unit was reported shot down by a Soviet fighter and killed — all of which took place in the vicinity of Ulyanovo. [281]

18 GIAP was more successful. At around 12.00 hours, eight Yak-7Bs from this unit, led by *Kpt.* Semyon Sibirin, escorted ten Il-2s of 224 ShAD near Melekhovo in the vicinity of Ulyanovo. The Yak fighters were divided into two groups — *M.Lt.* Dmitriy Lobashov led four aircraft as close escort while Sibirin commanded the other four as top cover, 600-800 metres higher. "Suddenly," *M.Lt.* Nikolay Pinchuk recalled, "we heard the commander's voice in the radio: "*Attention! German fighters below!*" We spotted four Fw 190s which, from low altitude, tried to attack the Ilyushins."

Obviously the Germans aimed to hit the unprotected radiators in the bellies of the heavily armoured Ilyushins. But the Soviet fighter pilots managed to ward off the initial attack. Pinchuk continues his account: "A few minutes later, a 'Focke' appeared at high speed slightly to the right in front of me. I gave full speed and positioned myself behind him. In that moment I got a second German on my tail, and he opened fire. Fortunately, the enemy pilot appeared to be a bad marksman. Immediately afterward, Vladimir Balandin hit him with his first burst and the German aircraft went down. I managed to out-turn another 'Focke', which, after a prolonged turning fight, I sent to his forefathers." [282]

M.Lt. Balandin's victory was recorded at 12.00 hours, followed by Pinchuk's at 12.05. [283] The remaining Focke-Wulfs sought refuge into the clouds. Five minutes later, *Kpt.* Sibirin attacked and claimed a Bf 110 shot

Scramble! Soviet fighter pilots rush to their La-5FN fighters. For Operation Kutuzov, 15 VA had a whole fighter Diviziya, Polkovnik Valentin Ukhov's 3 GIAD, which was equipped with the new La-5FN fighter.

On 13 July 1943, Fw. Peter Bremer of 3./JG 54 was shot down in this Fw 190 and belly-landed on the Soviet side of the front line. The capture of this ace – credited with 40 victories – was indeed a great trophy to the Soviets. Bremer was awarded with the German Cross in Gold in absentia on 31 August 1943. Seen in this photograph, a Soviet soldier examines Bremer's 'White 3'.

down. [284] 2./ZG 1 recorded a Bf 110 G-2 as sustaining 25 per cent damage from a Soviet fighter near Ulyanovo. 2./JG 51 reported *Fw.* Klaus Dietrich (an ace with ten victories) wounded in combat with Soviet fighters, while *Fw.* Michaels's Fw 190 was lost. [285] All these losses occurred without any German victories being submitted – a significant difference as compared with the situation where the opponents belonged to 15 VA or 16 VA.

The Il-2s of 224 ShAD, which were being escorted by 18 GIAP, were able to perform four attacks against their target – a column of German vehicles with artillery – and returned to base without having suffered any own losses.

Other airmen of 1 VA which flew deep into German-occupied territory detected long vehicle columns moving northwards on the roads from Orel. These was the reinforcements which 9. *Armee* had sent to join 55. *Armeekorps* in its defensive fight against Bagramyan's troops. Because of this discovery, the Soviets decided to reinforce Bagramyan's army with the 1st Tank Corps – which would place 55. *Armeekorps* in an even more difficult position. But 1. *Fliegerdivision* could not strike against 1st Tank Corps as it rumbled hurriedly southward to reach the battlefield south of Ulyanovo.

When the German air activity in the east slackened at noon on 13 July, the Bryansk Front resumed its offensive – this time with an exceptionally strong air support. Not only the whole of 15 VA, but also Boston bombers of 16 VA's 221 BAD and the ADD's 113 BAD were dispatched to ensure a breakthrough on the ground in this area. Subject to hellish bombardment from the air, 53. *Armeekorps* was unable to hold out and started to fall back. The Bryansk Front's troops broke through and were able to expand their penetration to a depth of 16 kilometres.

Generalmajor Deichmann had no option but to abandon the support of 55. *Armeekorps* in the north and order his air units back to fight the Bryansk Front and 15 VA in the east. A huge air battle ensued.

The newly arrived II. and IV./JG 54 *Grünherz* pounced on 16 VA's Bostons and claimed five of these shot down – including three by *Uffz.* Reinhold Hoffmann. Fw 190s from both I. and III./JG 51 *Mölders* attacked the 36 twin-engined Il-4 bombers from 113 BAD, which flew at 1,300 metres altitude, and claimed fourteen of these shot down. *Lt* Heinrich

Höfemeier was credited with the destruction of two Il-4s and one of the escorting Yak fighters, and *Uffz.* Franz Meindl of 7./JG 51 reportedly knocked down four of these bombers before he was shot down and wounded. 113 BAD actually lost 12 Il-4s. [286]

During an air battle over the Novosil sector between 15 VA and 1. *Fliegerdivision* which lasted for more than an hour, the German fighters claimed to have shot down around 70 Soviet aircraft – half of them Il-2s – for six aircraft lost. 15 VA was in shambles following this drawn out clash. Included among the many pilot casualties was *Lt.* Aleksey Goncharov, an ace in 171 IAP/315 IAD, who had been credited with at least eight victories. 32 GIAP lost Hero of the Soviet Union, *Kpt.* Aleksandr Moshin, an ace with 19 victories, and *Lt.* Yakov Kramchenkov. [287]

Having contributed decisively to bring the situation in the east to a fragile balance, *Generalmajor* Deichmann's airmen were again sent towards the north in the afternoon to support 55. *Armeekorps*, which was subject to increasing pressure. Here, I./JG 54 pounced on a formation of Il-2s escorted by Yak-9s of 20 IAP. This regiment also belonged to *General-Mayor* Zakharov's 303 IAD, but did not have the same quality as 18 GIAP and *Normandie-Niemen*. 20 IAP was a veteran unit from the early days of the war, but its best pilots had been killed since then. Hence, *General-Mayor* Zakharov assigned 20 IAP with the task of escorting bombers and *Shturmoviks*. In this clash, the Germans claimed to have shot down five Il-2s (two by *Lt.* Günther Scheel – his 4th and 5th victories on that day – and three by *Ofw.* Rudolf Rademacher) and two Yak-9s (by *Ofw.* Kurt Olsen), but lost one of their own pilots. *Fw.* Peter Bremer, who with 40 victories on his account belonged to the top aces in JG 54 *Grünherz*, was forced down on the Soviet side of the front line and was captured.

Thus, a few hours of fierce engagements with the fighters of 1 VA had cost 1. *Fliegerdivision* the loss of three of its most experienced *Jagdflieger*: *Oblt* Albert Walter, *Fw.* Peter Bremer and *Fw.* Klaus Dietrich. But it would not stop there. Four Ju 88s from KG 51 were shot down by 1 VA's fighters. [288] Later that afternoon, ZG 1 was unfortunate enough to encounter the Yak-7B fighters of Zakharov's 303 IAD once again. This time it was the French pilots of *Normandie-Niemen*.

Kpt. Albert Littolff and *Leytenants* Noël Castelain and Albert Durand were tasked to escort a formation of Il-2s. Littolff, who led the formation, had seen action both with the French Air Force during the Battle of France in 1940 and with the RAF in North Africa in 1941, and was credited with 10 victories. Durand had a similar experience and by this date he had logged four aerial victories.

Arriving over the battlefield, the Yak-7Bs and Il-2s came across a formation of reportedly twenty-four Bf 110s. *Major* Joachim Blechschmidt, the *Geschwaderkommodore* of ZG 1, was leading his Bf 110s on a fighter-bomber mission against the advancing Soviet troops. But when he spotted the *Shturmoviks*, Blechschmidt decided to take four *Zerstörer* along with him to intercept these. Like his French opponents in this encounter, Blechschmidt was a veteran – he had performed more than 400 combat missions. But this would be his last. Shot down by Castelain, *Major* Blechschmidt was reportedly captured by the Soviets together with his radio operator, *Uffz.* Hans Wörl.

Meanwhile, on the ground, the battle between Bagramyan's 11th Guards Army – bolstered by the 1st and 5th Tank corps – and the 55. *Armeekorps* finally ended in a Soviet victory. By the evening of 13 July, the Western Front had achieved a breakthrough 16-kilometres deep along a 23-kilometre front. *Polkovnik* S. P. Koroteyev's 70th Tank Brigade had even infiltrated the German lines and now started operating in 2. *Panzerarmee's* rear area.

The result of the air fighting over the Orel Bulge on 13 July was varied. On one hand, 1. *Fliegerdivision* had proved to be an absolutely decisive asset in the German defensive fight. The fact that all Soviet ground forces apart from the 11th Guards Army – which was covered from air attacks by dense forests – had been bogged down after only two days of offensive, owed much to the German air support. Also, 1. *Fliegerdivision* undoubtedly had dealt 15 VA a major defeat during the day's air fighting.

When the day was over, Deichmann made a summary of the results and arrived at an amazing result: 183 Soviet aircraft were reported shot down, including all but around 20 in 15 VA's area of operations. According to Soviet reports, 15 VA actually lost 94 aircraft on 13 July.[289] The *Shturmovik* units had suffered most from the day's air fighting. Fifty Il-2s had been lost – 20 from 3 ShAK and 30 from 225 ShAD. In the latter unit, 783 ShAP had lost nine, 810 ShAP had lost five, and 825 ShAP had lost no fewer than sixteen crews.

15 VA's largely inexperienced fighter units had not only failed to cover the bombers and *Shturmoviks* from devastating German fighter attacks and the troops of the Bryansk Front from powerful air strikes, but they had also

Junkers Ju 87 D dive-bombers, photographed in the moment when they released their bombs during an attack on the Eastern Front. (Photo: Martin Pegg.)

A Yak-9 passes low above a Soviet airfield.

losses. Nine of its Fw 190s were shot down with five pilots killed or missing, and two injured.

The accumulated losses began to take a severe toll on JG 51's combat strength. By this time, fifty of the *Jagdgeschwader's* aircraft had been put out of commission since the major fighting started on 5 July – or nearly 40 per cent of its original strength nine days previously. Forty-one of these were due to hostile action. [293]

It was all too obvious that in spite of its reinforcements 1. *Fliegerdivision* was unable to provide all endangered sectors along the Orel Bulge with air support. Thus the OKL took the decision to shift most of *Fliegerkorps* VIII's anti-tank units, plus further fighter units, to 1. *Fliegerdivision*.

At dusk on 13 July, 15 VA was in shambles. Its badly mauled formations were in no position to perform anything which could be described as a major air support operation on the next day. To both sides, it was clear that the main air fighting on 14 July would take place on the northern flank of the Orel Bulge – where 1 VA guarded the air above Bagramyan's 11th Guards Army.

14 July 1943 – The Bastille Day Honoured in Orel's Skies

During the night of 14 July, the ADD was focused primarily against the Orel Bulge. While 148 sorties were flown against German troop positions, another 111 bombers of the ADD struck hard against Orel's railway junction, considerably delaying the flow of reinforcements from 9. *Armee* in the south of the Bulge to 2. *Panzerarmee* in the north and the east. [294] Hampered by the effect of these air attacks, German 18. *Panzer Division* was unable to hold out and was defeated in a tank battle against the forward elements of Bagramyan's 11th Guards Army on 14 July. Smashing their way past dispersed German forces, Soviet 5th Tank Corps continued towards the south-east with the aim of cutting off the German strongpoint at Bolkhov.

In response to desperate calls for air support from the heavily pressured 53. *Armeekorps* in this sector, *Generalmajor* Deichmann sent his aviation to support the remnants of the German defence forces which had become caught behind enemy lines through the Soviet advance in the north. *Obfhr.* Norbert Hannig of 5./JG 54 later recalled one of those missions:

"On 14 July we were scheduled to fly escort for a *Staffel* of Ju 87s. [...] One group of infantry had lost contact with its rearguard which had been cut off and surrounded by Russian troops and was now holed up in a station along the railway line leading north-eastwards out of Orel towards Tula.

"The infantrymen were about to mount a local counter-attack to rescue their trapped comrades and the Stukas were being dispatched in support. We rendezvoused with the dive-bombers above our landing field. As they were flying at an altitude of only 800 metres, the events on the ground were clearly visible to the naked eye. The rescue party sent up red flares to indicate their position. The Stukas formed into a large circle, a battle formation which allowed every machine to select its own objective and dive on it separately. For this mission they were carrying only their 50-kg underwing bombs. These could be launched singly, which meant that each aircraft was able to carry out several attacks on specific targets such as machine-gun emplacements, trenches, mortar positions – even individual Russian soldiers.

"Circling above the Stukas to give fighter cover, we saw our infantry leap from their armoured half-tracks and storm the station building. Moments later they reappeared, shepherding the rearguard survivors, several of whom were carefully carrying a makeshift stretcher fashioned out of tent halves, presumably a wounded comrade. As there were no enemy fighters about [*Ofw.* Xaver Müller] and I joined in the ground action, strafing the surrounding Russian positions to keep their heads down while our own troops climbed back aboard their carriers. Green flares signalled mission completed as they set off for the front lines only a few kilometres away.

"The Stukas continued to watch over them until they reached the safety of German-held territory. There the leading dive-bomber waggled its wings

sustained grievous losses. Possibly as a result of this humiliating defeat, they submitted very high overclaims. 1 GIAK claimed 68 victories on 13 July 1943. [290] In 315 IAD, 171 IAP alone reported 31 German aircraft shot down – an amazing result for a single regiment. The *Polk* commander, *Podpolk.* Vasiliy Bilkun, sent the following report to the commander of the Political Department of 315 IAD:

"*I report that on 13 July 1943 our regiment performed fighter patrols to cover our armies in the areas of Sonin Lug, Yevtekhovo and Rzhavets. In this sector we encountered the enemy in the air, with the result that the pilots of our regiment shot down 31 enemy aircraft.*" Bilkun mentioned a number of pilots who were reported to have achieved particularly outstanding results – *Kpt.* Gennadiy Trubenko was said to have shot down four German fighters, and *St.Lt.* Stefan Ivlev and *Serzh.* Mikhail Golik were credited with two victories each. Next, it was mentioned that 171 IAP's ace, *Lt.* Aleksey Aleksandrovich Goncharov, had also shot down an enemy aircraft, and the note ended with the remark: '*It cost the Communist his life.*' [291]

Meanwhile the bomber, Stuka and ground-attack units of 1. *Fliegerdivision* reported that they had destroyed 32 tanks, 50 motor vehicles and one artillery piece, and damaged another 25 tanks. [292]

But as we have seen, 1. *Fliegerdivision's* operations were not without complications. There was a marked difference in the opposition encountered by 15 VA and 1 VA. Although most of 1. *Fliegerdivision's* sorties were flown against 15 VA, half of its 20 combat losses on 13 July – a record for one day since Operation *Zitadelle* had commenced – were caused in 1 VA's operational area in the north. JG 51 *Mölders* indeed attained an impressive tally of victories, but *Jagdgeschwader Mölders* also sustained fairly heavy own

A Fw 190 A-3 of the Spanish 15./JG 51. In return for Hitler's assistance during the Spanish Civil War, Spain's dictator Franco contributed a fighter squadron known as the Escuadrilla Azul, 'Blue Squadron', to Hitler's invasion of the Soviet Union in 1941. The 1st Escuadrilla Azul was not particularly successful and was withdrawn from first-line service in early 1942. Escuadrilla Azul No. 2 and No. 3 operated, one succeeding the other, on the Eastern Front in 1942. The 4th Spanish Escuadrilla Azul received combat training by the first 200-victory ace Major Hermann Graf in southern France in the spring of 1943. It arrived at the Eastern Front in June 1943 and received the official designation 15.(Span.)/JG 51. The 4th Spanish Escuadrilla Azul would eventually develop into the most successful of the Escuadrillas Azules.

o thank us for our services, and we turned away for our temporary home near Orel." [295]

But far from all of 1. *Fliegerdivision's* missions on 14 July were as successful as the one *Obflr.* Hannig described. Several of its formations ran into dogged resistance by 1 VA's fighters and took heavy losses. *General* Ivan Bagramyan himself became the witness of one such occasion:

"On 14 July, holding our breath with excitement, we watched an air combat above the settlement of Dudorovskiy, south-west of Bolkhov. Forty Junkers approached our positions, and agitated screams warned of an imminent air attack. Our soldiers darted into cover. Meanwhile we could see six red Yak fighters turn towards the enemy aircraft.

"Six against forty… At high speed, the small aircraft closed in on the enemy bomber formation – which suddenly dispersed. Then we could hear machine gun fire from the sky above. With beating hearts we could see one enemy bomber catch fire and start to descend towards the earth with an eerie howling sound – followed by another and another… By this time, our infantrymen had forgotten the dangers. Everyone looked at the sky and cheered, wild with enthusiasm – '*Hooray!*' for each shot down Junkers. By the time we had seen six Junkers shot down, the Fascist pilots had lost their nerves and jettisoned their bombs over their own troops, leaving the scene in disorder. Our six 'Falcons' continued their patrol mission above our heads." [296]

St.G 1 actually lost four Ju 87s to Soviet fighter interception, and II./St.G 3's *Gruppenkommandeur, Hptm.* Eberhard Jacob, was also shot down and injured. [297] 49 IAP was one of the successful Soviet fighter units, with *St.Lt.* Vasiliy Kolomoyets and *M.Lt.* Ivan Khodun claiming one Ju 87 and one Fw 190 without loss at noon. [298] Other Soviet fighters shot down four of KG 4's He 111s. [299]

Reports from the Western Front on 14 July indicate that the Soviet air defence effectively prevented the *Luftwaffe* from inflicting any serious losses on the Soviet troops. [300] This is confirmed in corresponding German documents, according to which 1. *Fliegerdivision's* airmen claimed no more than 12 tanks destroyed on 14 July – far less than on the previous day. [301]

Meanwhile, covered by Lavochkin and Yakovlev fighters, Il-2s and Pe-2s of 1 VA kept pouncing on German positions and troop columns all day. *Shturmoviks* of 2 ShAK were reported to have carried out a particularly successful attack against a column of 150 vehicles at Zikeyevo near Zhizdra. [302]

Early in the afternoon on 14 July, a group of Il-2s was being escorted by seven Yak-7Bs of *Normandie-Niemen* over the Bolkhov region when four Bf 110s suddenly appeared. Led by *Mayor* Pierre Pouyade, the French fighter pilots immediately attacked the Germans. In a brief encounter, two Bf 110s were shot down – one by Pouyade together with *Lt.* Didier Béguin and one by *Lt.* Marcel Albert – and the two others driven off, without loss to either the Il-2s or the Yak-7Bs. These Bf 110s belonged to ZG 1, which lost five aircraft in combat on this day. In one of these – Bf 110 G-2 'S9+FB' – the *Gruppenkommandeur* of I./ZG 1, *Hptm.* Wilfried Herrmann, and his radio operator, *Ofw.* Albert Wenhold, were killed.

Lt. Ivan Gnezdilov of 1 VA's 18 GIAP recalled: "On 14 July, the pilots of our regiment and the French *Eskadrilya* flew numerous missions to provide *Shturmoviks* with fighter cover. The combat activity was very high on this day. One take-off followed after another, and the Frenchmen hardly found any time to celebrate their national holiday – the Day of the Seizure of the Bastille. But at last, in a small fringe of the nearby woods, the '*Normands*' found some time to hoist the French *Tricolour* and the red Soviet flag, and

Dug-in German tanks and anti-tank guns await the Soviet counter-attack in a typical Russian cornfield.

they swore to intensify their fight to defeat the Fascists and restore the national honour of France." [303]

Throughout 14 July, the airmen of 1. *Fliegerdivision* became entangled in air combat with the fighter pilots of 1 VA – who demonstrated that they were a far more dangerous opponent than which these *Luftwaffe* fliers had previously encountered during the Battle of Kursk. This was also the experience of II./JG 54, which just had arrived from the Leningrad sector. This *Jagdgruppe* had chalked up around forty victories for no loss in June 1943, and in combat against 15 VA on 12-13 July, it added another 32 victories against one own aircraft shot down. Against 1 VA's fighters on 14 July, II./JG 54 claimed five "LaGG-3s" shot down but lost two Fw 190s.

At 15.30 hours (German time), I./JG 54 clashed with a formation of Il-2s from 873 ShAP, escorted by 49 IAP La-5s. In a 20-minute running fight, the Germans claimed two Il-2s (one of them by *Lt.* Günther Scheel) and a La-5. This actually exactly matches the actual Soviet losses in this engagement. [304] Meanwhile 49 IAP's *M.Lt.* Ivan Khodun was credited with the downing of one Fw 190 although this can not be substantiated in German records.

Overall however, 1 VA's fighters managed to provide their bombers and *Shturmoviks* with quite effective cover on 14 July; only five of 1 VA's Il-2s and not a single bomber was lost to German fighter interception on 14 July.

Two pilots of 20 IAP performed a remarkable feat during an escort mission for Il-2s on this day. Led by *St.Lt.* Nikolay Svitchenok, six of the Regiment's Yak-9s were assigned to cover the return flight from the battle zone of six Il-2s. Suddenly the ground control was heard over the radio, addressing the fighters of 20 IAP by their code name:

'*Arkan, Arkan! Attention – Junkers to starboard!*'

After a short while, *St.Lt.* Svitchenok spotted two groups of German aircraft to the right: a formation of twenty-two Ju 88s were approaching the Soviet field positions. A little further in the distance, he could see four Soviet fighters which had, apparently in vain, tried to reach and intercept the bombers, engaged in a whirling dogfight with a group of Fw 190s. Tochkov decided immediately to divide his six Yakovlevs. He ordered *M.Lt.* Zveryov's *Para* to bring the Il-2s back to safety, and *St.Lt.* Mikhail Tochkov's *Para* to

attack the Fw 190s while he brought his wingman, *M.Lt.* Steblyanko, along to intercept the bombers.

Performing a daring head-on assault, Svitchenok blew the leading Ju 88 out of the sky, and Steblyanko shot down its wingman. A third Ju 88 was claimed shot down by Svitchenok before the two Yak-9s ran out of ammunition. However, when they later submitted their reports at base, the intelligence officer would not believe that two fighters in a combat against twenty-two enemy aircraft could have been able to shoot down three and even survive to tell the story. Thus, 20 IAP's report states merely that '*It may be assumed that some Ju 88s were damaged, since both pilots clearly saw pieces of aluminium flying off the aircraft as a result of their fire.*' [305]

However, II./KG 51 reported that three Ju 88s were shot down by Soviet fighters. A fourth Ju 88, from 8./KG 51, also was lost to Soviet fighter interception.

Badly outnumbered, relentlessly attacked by scores of *Shturmoviks* and Pe-2 bombers and constantly complaining over inadequate air support, German 2. *Panzerarmee* was pushed to the south and south-east by *General* Bagramyan's 11th Guards Army – which by this time was supported not only by the 1st and 5th Tank corps, but also by the 11th Army. Having executed a march of 160 kilometres in two days, the troops of this army joined the attack on 14 July and contributed to an almost total breakdown of the German defence south of Ulyanovo. A German account reads: '*The Soviet offensive created panic in the rear area. On their march to reach the battle zone, the [German] reinforcements were met by masses of fleeing, dispersed troops who blocked the roads on their way backwards [...] In one case, a whole division lost its nerves.*' [306]

The gap which had been created in the German lines in the north had soon had expanded to a width of 40 kilometres and a depth of nearly 48 kilometres. Late in the afternoon of 14 July, KG 53 was called upon to carry out a concentrated bombing attack against the advancing Soviet troops in this area. The He 111s took off from Olsufyevo near Bryansk at around 17.30 hours. [307]

Meanwhile, the Spanish Fw 190 pilots of 15./JG 51 arrived over the intended target area in order to clear the sky from Soviet fighters. But this task proved to be more difficult than the Spaniards had anticipated. They ended up in a rugged combat with 18 GIAP, which resulted in two losses on each side. The two La-5 pilots *Lt.* Pilipeyko and *M.Lt.* Borodavko were downed by *Comandante* Mariano Cuadra and *Teniente* Manuel Sanchez Taberno de Prada, but Taberno de Prada was also shot down, as was the Fw 190s piloted by *Alfarez* Eduardo Garcia Amigo. These victories were credited to *Kpt.* Vasiliy Terentyev and *Serzh.* Ivan Stolyarov.[308] Shot down over Soviet-controlled territory, both Spanish pilots were listed as missing, but Taberno de Prada managed to return to German lines after several adventurous days in hiding.

When KG 53's bomber crews finally arrived over the battle zone, there were no German fighters in sight – but several with red stars on their wings…

Oblt. Martin Vollmer of I./KG 53 wrote in his diary:

'*Today was a black, heavy day. One mission – three total losses in our Gruppe, and in addition to that, two force-landings. Both aircraft which flew in the Kette with me were shot down. It was terrible. Loaded with AB 70s, we flew towards the penetration area north of Orel, thinking that this would be an easy mission. But we would soon learn that it would be anything but easy! During our approach flight we were received by a heavy anti-aircraft fire, and my aircraft sustained a hit on the right hand side, close to the engine. Then the Russian fighters arrived! They were ten or twenty, I can't tell exactly, and they attacked us for more than twenty minutes. Nowhere were any of our own fighters to be seen. First my left Kettenhund was shot down – it was Uffz. Riehl's crew. We saw the aircraft explode on the ground below. Only one parachute was spotted. Then the turn came to my right Kettenhund, Fw. Engals's crew. Fortunately, they managed to perform a force-landing. But all in all, it was a disaster. I don't even know how anyone among us managed to survive this onslaught.*'[309]

Apparently, German fighters tried to relieve KG 53, but Soviet fighters managed to prevent the Fw 190s from reaching the He 111s. La-5-equipped 49 IAP seems to have been one of the 1 VA fighter units which participated in the attack against KG 53. The records of this unit shows that at around 18.55 Russian time (17.55 hours German time), *Kapitans* Emir Chalbash and Nikolay Spiridenko teamed up to shoot down one He 111, one Fw 190 and an Fw 189.[310] The latter was probably an aircraft of NAGr 15 in which the observer was reported as wounded in action.[311] Meanwhile II./JG 51 reported two La-5s and a "LaGG-3" shot down in the same area, while sustaining 25 per cent battle damage to one of its

Fw 190s.[312] In total, the operations on 14 July cost KG 53 the loss of seven He 111s.

Normandie-Niemen was in action again that evening, when nine Yak-7Bs – led by the unit's commander *Mayor* Jean Tulasne – escorted a formation of Il-2s. Two Fw 190s appeared and attempted to intercept the *Shturmoviks* but were driven off by Tulasne and *Lt.* Béguin. Immediately afterwards, three more Fw 190s attacked the French fighters and managed to separate *Lt.* Noël Castelain from the formation. However, the experienced French pilot – who had previously served for two months with the RAF – managed to turn the tables and shoot down one of the Focke-Wulfs. This was probably Fw 190 A-5, 'Black 5', of *Stabsstaffel*/JG 51, which was shot down south-east of Ulyanovo. The pilot, *Uffz.* Robert Sauber, was an ace credited with seven victories.

In this desperate situation, 1. *Fliegerdivision* received further reinforcements from *Fliegerkorps* VIII. Of great importance was the arrival of III./JG 52 – the *Luftwaffe*'s most successful *Jagdgruppe* – during the afternoon of 14 July. The logbook of *Hptm.* Günther Rall, III./JG 52's *Gruppenkommandeur*, details take-off from Ugrim in the south at 11.00, landing at Sovyetskiy near Orel at 13.40 hours.[313] Nevertheless, it took until the evening before this crack unit was ready for operations in its new area. *Hptm.* Rall took off for a free-hunting mission at 19.00 hours. He flew southward and came across one of the few Yakovlev fighters which 16 VA had sent out on this day – which he promptly shot down. This was recorded as Rall's 158th victory.

But even Rall's elite unit would soon discover hardships in this new operational sector. Erich Hartmann, who served in Rall's *Gruppe* with the rank of *Leutnant*, later recalled:

"On 14 July, 15 Ju 52s transferred an advanced detachment to our new airfield at Orel. Our *Gruppe* departed from the *Geschwader* and was operationally subordinated to JG 51. At that place we were subjected to heavy air attacks each night. Miraculously, no one was hurt when during one night a heavy bomb went down just between the tents of the *Stab*."[314]

14 July 1943 indeed saw a radical turning point in the air war during the Battle of Kursk, and that was primarily due to the effectiveness of 1 VA. On this day, 1 VA reported more than 100 German aircraft shot down, against around twenty losses of its own. German sources admit at least 38 of

Despite the letter code on the fuselage, normally seen on aircraft operating with the Schlachtflieger, this Fw 190 A-5, 'White K' belonged to 4./JG54. From July 1943 to February 1944, this Staffel operated as fighter-bombers on the Northern Sector of the Eastern Front under the command of IV./JG 54.

A La-5FN returns from a combat mission.

These two Fw 190 A-5s, 'Black 7' and 'Black 5', photographed in the Summer of 1943, both belonged to 5./JG 54 and are seen at a forward airfield in Central Russia.

Bf 109 G-6s, almost certainly of I./JG 52 at a forward landing ground probably situated east of Belgorod in July 1943.

. *Fliegerdivision's* aircraft were put out of commission. Of these, 32 were reported as a result of hostile action or unknown causes, of which 23 were total losses. [315] However, it is entirely possible that 1. *Fliegerdivision's* osses actually were higher. The bomber and *Zerstörer* units suffered devastating losses. ZG 1, which had lost its *Geschwaderkommodore* on the previous day, flew 40 sorties on 14 July, and reported five Bf 110s shot down – a 12.5 per cent loss ratio. The *Kampfgeschwader* flew 210 sorties and had 15 He 111s or Ju 88s shot down – a 7 per cent loss ratio. [316]

Interestingly, although 1. *Fliegerdivision* was reinforced by III./JG 52 n the afternoon of 14 July and *Panzerjagdstaffel/*JG 51 the next day – and n the face of a considerably deteriorating situation on 15 July – the number of combat sorties flown by 1. *Fliegerdivision* dropped from 1,113 on 13 July o just 703 on 15 July. The decline was particularly sharp regarding the bomber units; an average of 212 bomber sorties were flown each day between 10 and 14 July (with 210 being carried out on 14 July), but on 5 July the bomber units of 1. *Fliegerdivision* were able to perform only 36 combat sorties. [317]

5 July 1943 – the Central Front Joins the Offensive

During the night of 15 July, the bulk of the ADD was in action over the Orel Bulge, and the railway junction at Orel was again subject to aerial bombardment. This was the prelude to the Central Front's participation in Operation *Kutuzov*, which commenced early the next day when the 13th, 8th and 70th armies and 2nd Tank Army stormed German 9. *Armee* in the outh of the Orel Bulge.

General-Leytenant Sergey Rudenko's 16 VA, which had enjoyed a badly needed rest for five days, was in full action from first light. The first among 6 VA's aircraft to appear over the battlefield were the Bostons and Pe-2s of 6 ODRAP, which together with fighters from 283 IAD and 286 IAD, arried out reconnaissance over the German lines and rear area, and the Yak- and Airacobra fighters of 6 IAK which were tasked to keep the *Luftwaffe* way from the air above the battlefield. Next followed the Pe-2s of 3 BAK, scorted by other fighters from 6 IAK; Bostons of 221 BAD, escorted by Yak-1s of 282 IAD; and *Shturmoviks* of 2GShAD and 299 ShAD, escorted by 283 IAD and 286 IAD. [318]

Their German opponents became completely overwhelmed by the oncentrated strikes from the air and the ground, and had great difficulties n countering the attacks. 1. *Fliegerdivision* made only a weak appearance in he air over 9. *Armee's* sector. Ahead of the offensive, 16 VA had considerably mproved its structure for command and control in that a dense network of adio stations for direct control of air operations had been established in the irst line. Thus, the sky was effectively cleansed of German aircraft. An effort by *Panzerjagdstaffel/*JG 51 to intervene on the battlefield cost the loss of hree Hs 129s.

Throughout 15 July, 16 VA carried out three massive attacks against German defence positions, tactical reserves and concentrations of troops and armour. Each of these operations involved between 300 and 400 aircraft, which dropped their bombs in a space of between 35 and 50 minutes. Between these large attacks, small groups of *Shturmoviks* exerted a relentless pressure on the German troops. In total, 16 VA performed no less than 1,002 combat sorties on this day, and suffered only minor losses.

The airmen of 1 VA also encountered a conspicuously weaker resistance in the air on 15 July than on the previous day. At dawn, eight 20 IAP Yak-9s, led by *Kpt.* Yakov Udovitskiy, escorted eight Pe-2s of 2 BAK on a bombing mission. During the return flight, the Pe-2 formation became strung out, which complicated the task of the escort fighters. *General-Mayor* Georgiy Zakharov, 303 IAD's commanding officer, wrote: '*The bombers often broke the elementary safety rules by disbanding their tight formations and simply turning for home at full speed as soon as they had completed their assigned attack mission, trying to rely on the speed of the Pe-2.*' [319] However, although eight Fw 190s dived down to attack the Pe-2s in this situation, the Yak-9 pilots managed not only to ward off all their attempts to shoot down any of the Pe-2s, but also claimed two Fw 190s destroyed for no losses of their own. The victories were chalked up by *Kpt.* Udovitskiy and *M.Lt.* Anatoliy Mashkin.

Meanwhile, 15 VA's airmen took advantage of the situation to carry out a number of highly successful operations in support of the Bryansk Front's troops, who still remained bogged down to the east of Orel. Near Podmaslovo, four Il-2 crews of 614 ShAP/225 ShAD attacked 25 German tanks. Dropping a hailstorm of 1,190 PTAB anti-tank bombs from horizontal flight at just 130-150 metres altitude, they reportedly knocked out seven tanks, including four heavy tanks.

The rapidly deteriorating situation caused the OKL to order further units to shift from *Fliegerkorps* VIII to 1. *Fliegerdivision*. But new crises posed new obstacles. *Luftwaffe* reconnaissance crews detected a looming threat in the shape of a major build-up of Soviet troops 160 kilometres further down the Donets, and this forced the OKL to hurriedly dispatch most of *Fliegerkorps* VIII to this sector. Although under mounting pressure, Model's and Deichmann's forces had to wait for the badly needed reinforcements.

Ten days after the commencement of Operation *Zitadelle*, the German plans were in tatters. The Orel Bulge was on the verge of crumbling, with the perspective of a new German disaster of the dimensions of Stalingrad. The turnabout had been extremely rapid. 1. *Fliegerdivision* had been so immensely successful up until 12 July – dealing devastating blows against the Soviet ground troops, and inflicting losses on the VVS which were ten times higher than its own losses. But with the appearance of the considerably more effective 1 VA in the air battle, 1. *Fliegerdivision's* superiority was broken. Meanwhile, to the battle's southern flank, the Germans also were losing the initiative both on the ground and in the air.

Chapter Nine

The End of *Zitadelle*

With von Kluge's and Model's troops in the north on the retreat, and von Manstein's *Heeresgruppe Süd* locked into a costly slogging match no more than 40 kilometres from its initial point of departure, it was obvious even to Adolf Hitler that Operation *Zitadelle* had failed. On 13 July, the two army group commanders were summoned to the *Führer's* headquarters, the *Wolfsschanze* near Rastenburg in East Prussia. They found Hitler to be most worried with the situation in Italy. Although the Eastern Front also was a cause of grave concern to the Nazi dictator, he feared that the whole of Italy might crumble like a house of cards. After the the Allied invasion of Sicily three days previously, alarming reports about unwillingness to fight among the Italians were arriving with increasing frequency. Fearing an Allied landing on the Italian mainland or in the Balkans within a short time, Hitler told his two field marshals that he needed to release *Panzer* units from the Kursk sector and transfer them to Italy. "Because of that, I have to cancel Operation *Zitadelle*," Hitler said.

These were the words of a panic-stricken leader, and not the result of any careful analysis. But the crisis on the Eastern Front made the two field marshals in no better position to judge the situation. Von Kluge, worn out by the setback of his army group, was only too willing to agree to anything which would relieve him of the pressure to continue the unrealistic offensive towards Kursk. Von Manstein, on the other hand, was raging at what he heard. Refusing to acknowledge defeat, he asserted:

"Victory on the southern flank of the Kursk Bulge is within reach. The enemy has committed all of his operative reserves into the battle, and they have been badly depleted. To break off the offensive now would mean to give away victory!"

Von Manstein was so convinced that he would succeed that he had ordered his own operational reserve – 24. *Panzerkorps* – northwards into assembly areas around Kharkov. He even asserted that von Kluge's forces would be able to "…carry on and annihilate the enemy forces south of Kursk"![320]

Hitler's objection that there were signs of a Soviet build-up in the south, at Kharkov and at the Mius, was brushed aside by von Manstein.

All of this made the weakened Hitler even more confused. He agreed that von Kluge should definitely cancell all offensive operations, and also allowed himself to be persuaded by the aggressive von Manstein that the offensive

should be continued in the south. "Finally Hitler once again wanted to achieve everything: Go ahead with 'Zitadelle' and following victory in that operation transfer the forces which thus had been made available to the countries which were under invasion threat – France, Italy and the Balkans."[321]

However, the news from the Eastern Front on 13 July was hardly reassuring to the German commanders.

Adopting the German method of concentrating the main effort of aviation to just one sector, *General-Leytenant* Krasovskiy ordered the bulk of 2 VA to support 'Group Trufanov's' counter-offensive against III. *Panzerkorps* at the Northern Donets on 13 July. Provided with an effective fighter cover according to the new tactics, Il-2s of 1 ShAK and 291 ShAD and Pe-2s of 1 BAK attacked the troops of *Armeeabteilung Kempf* with devastating effect, as noted in the *Armeeabteilung's* war diary for 13 July 1943: 'Superior enemy air activity in the Kazache area led to heavy own losses.'[322]

Fliegerkorps VIII sent 204 fighters into the air, most of which appear to have been directed to *Armeeabteilung Kempf's* combat zone. However apparently in most cases, the Soviet fighters managed to prevent the Messerschmitts from breaking through to the bombers and *Shturmoviks*. 1 BAK recorded five Pe-2s lost on 13 July, of which two occurred in a mid-air collision and three were due to other causes than fighter interception. Owing to an effective fighter cover, 800 ShAP was saved from sustaining any losses to enemy fighter interception between 11 and 13 July. The men of this unit expressed their gratitude in a letter to the fighter pilots of 270 IAP, which was led by the ace *Mayor* Vasiliy Merkushev:

'Comrades in arms! We are very pleased with your actions in supporting and covering the Shturmoviks. Between 11 and 13 July, we have not lost a single aircraft in air combat. This is to your merit, dear friends! We have witnessed how you repelled the enemy's fighters, and have admired your courage. We are particularly grateful to the pilot Lt. V. I. Andriyanov because he escorted the damaged aircraft of St.Lt. Poshivalnikov.'

Throughout 13 July, the German fighters managed to break through to attack Soviet ground-attack aircraft on only two occasions. In the morning, a *Rotte* of 3./JG 52 comprising *Lt.* Franz Schall and *Ofw.* Franz Woidich made a steep diving attack through the Soviet fighter shield and shot down three Il-2s, two of them by Woidich, in an instant. At around 14.00 hours several pilots of II./JG 3 and I./JG 52 managed to shoot down eight Il-2s f which *Ofw.* Woidich again bagged two. But otherwise, the Il-2s and e-2s were able to wreak havoc among III. *Panzerkorps's* forces without eing much troubled by German fighters.

During one of the air combats which were fought over Prokhorovka on hat day, the Spanish pilot José Sánchez-Montes, serving with one of 2 VA's ak-7B equipped regiments, attacked a formation of Ju 87s escorted by f 109s. In the following combat, Montes managed to shoot down one of he Ju 87s before he himself became shot down and injured by one of he escorting Bf 109s. Montes described how he shot down the Ju 87 — vhich was his fourth victory during the Battle of Kursk:

"On our right-hand side flew a squadron from our neighbouring fighter egiment. This group was assigned with the task of preventing the enemy rom breaking through to our positions, but this was not an easy task. n desperation, the enemy dispatched large masses of Junkers 87s, escorted y 'Messers' and 'Fockes'. This time, my group had no chance to avoid ombat with the enemy fighters; we had to amuse ourselves with them in rder to give our other fighters the opportunity to attack the bombers. But the German fighters, painted in mottled grey, disengaged from us and ttacked the other squadron. Apparently, their numerical superiority made ne German pilots assured that they would be able to provide the Junkers vith an effective cover.

"As the enemy fighters disengaged from us, I immediately increased speed and approached the enemy bombers. I positioned myself in the dead angle behind and slightly below one of the dive-bombers. At quite a short distance, I pressed the firing button of my cannon. The impact was terrible. The Junkers immediately lit up like a huge torch, and in the next moment, with a terrible sound, it blew up in mid-air. The whole sky became filled with debris from the disintegrated Fascist aircraft, and I had to bank sharply in order to avoid a collision. I looked behind me, to see if there was an enemy fighter on my tail, and in order to search for my wingman. I could see 'Messers' everywhere, but I soon was calmed to see my wingman.

"By this time, another enemy aircraft descended towards the earth, and the enemy formation had disintegrated. All of the enemy pilots tried to escape the danger zone as quickly as possibly, and none of them seemed to care much about where their jettisoned bmbs came down. In the next moment the sky was empty. I called my wingman via the radio, and we continued our assigned patrol mission."[323]

A comparison with German sources shows that while St.G 2 recorded two Ju 87s shot down, Montes was probably shot down by either *Uffz.* Franz Birnstill or *Uffz.* Gerhard Pankalla of 7./JG 3.

In all, the air units of 2 VA and 17 VA conducted 777 sorties on 13 July, most of which were directed against *Armeeabteilung Kempf.* Owing much to

essonovka airfield, 17 July 1943. Hptm. Johannes Wiese, the Gruppenkommandeur of /JG 52, has just returned from a mission during which he claimed three Il-2s – one of vhich was recorded as his 100th aerial victory. Wiese was one of the most successful ighter pilots during the Battle of Kursk, claiming twelve Soviet aircraft shot down on July 1943 alone. He served with JG 52 from June 1941 and slowly accumulated uccesses in air combat with the VVS until he was appointed the Staffelkapitän of

2./JG 52 in June 1942. From that time on, he became one of the main scorers in JG 52 – boosting his victory total from seven to over one hundred in only little more than one year. When Wiese was injured in a flight accident on 19 June 1944, his tally stood at 133 victories. Back in first-line service as the Geschwaderkommodore of JG 77 in the autumn of 1944, Wiese was shot down and injured on Christmas Eve 1944.

Arseniy Vorozheykin's 14 July

On 14 July 1943, 728 IAP's Kapitan Arseniy Vorozheykin claimed three victories in two missions. 728 IAP was part of 265 IAD, which had been sent to the Kursk combat zone on 9-10 July, and whose pilots encountered great navigational difficulties in the new area. Because of this, a navigational expert was assigned to 728 IAP. Vorozheykin gives a vivid description of the dramatic events on 14 July 1943 in his memoirs:

"Rainshowers had made the morning of 14 July cool. A smell of gun powder hung in the air.

In the command post, a clay hut which was lit up by a small home-made lamp, our flight maps showed the front lines. […] The pilots sat in the grass, which was wet from dew, and listen to the regimental commander [Mayor Vladimir Vasilyaka]. He introduced an instructor, a Kapitan. Our task was to provide the ground troops with air cover.

You have no use of the compass here, the instructor said categorically, boasting with his experience.

The damned Kursk Magnetic Anomaly turns everything upside down. The main thing is that you have points of orientation on the ground. The rail line never betrays you. […]

Everyone must maintain a tight formation in combat, the instructor finished his speech with:

Don't part from each other, and everything will be all right. Then we will be able to teach Fritz a good lesson.

'Maintain a tight formation' might have been a good advice if you flew I-16s or Chaykas [I-153 biplane fighters], which were not fast enough and thus had to stick together in order to defend each other in combat. But regarding our modern aircraft? Was that not an obsolete instruction? […] The Kapitan was a young lad. He had only recently graduated from flight school. Apparently he belonged to the category of people who fear nothing on Earth. These people often became brave fighter pilots, but as experience would prove, many among them were killed within a short time. […]

When the instructor had finished his lecture, my Eskadrilya commander [Starshiy Leytenant Nikolay Khudyakov] turned towards me and whispered so silently that no one but me could hear him:

I don't like our new leader. He is a greenhorn and seems to be unreliable… […]

The Kapitan led our Eskadrilya towards the front along the rail line which runs to Belgorod. About halfway a sidetrack bent off towards Staryy Oskol, and he followed this. This is a mistake, I thought. I radioed him to warn him. He hummed something inaudible. I called him once again. No reply. Assuming that the Kapitan had failed to hear me, I increased speed and placed my aircraft next to his and started to waggle the wings in order to draw his attention. But our leader just maintained his course. That was it! I switched my radio to transmission and called out:

Everyone, follow me!

Only four pilots followed me, the others continued their flight path…

On the approaches to the front we ran into six Messerschmitts, but we did not have to clash with them – our task was to destroy the bomber. […]

Suddenly a Henschel Hs 126 reconnaissance aircraft emerged in front of us, at a lower altitude. It was provided with fighter escort… I ordered [M.Lt. Arkhip Melashenko] to shoot down the Henschel. But just as he was about to do so, the Messerschmitts attacked us frontally. Usually the enemy avoided such frontal attacks, but the task to cover their artillery spotter gave them no choice this time. We would not meet their attack, but instead break off in front of the enemy fighters. […]

Now! All of us banked sharply to the left. The Messerschmitts flashed past like meteors and then started to turn after us. But in a turning fight our aircraft were superior, and soon we were in position behind them. I had one of the Messerschmitts in front of me. The German pilot tried to shake me off his tail, but in vain. When he realised that he could not continue this turning fight, he pulled up sharply. Apparently he had forgotten that he had lost much speed because of the turning manoeuvres, but nevertheless he continued to climb…

My Yak stuck like glue behind the Messerschmitt. I was so close that his round fuselage covered almost my entire gunsight and under each wing I could see the two cannon gondolas…

A burst of fire. Looking like little glittering knives, my tracer bullets disappeared into the slender aircraft. The Messerschmitt shook and shivered, reeled over, then seemed to hesitate for a brief second, and finally plummeted vertically downwards, leaving a thick plume of black smoke behind.

Below me, Melashenko's Para was tangling with two Messerschmitts. Nearby, [Nikolay] Timonov and [Serzhant Aleksandr Vybornov] were circling around with three other enemy aircraft. One of the enemy fighters was released from this furball, turning around its own axis and suddenly bursting into flames. The dome of a parachute unfolded in the sky. […]

Suddenly I caught sight of the escaping Henschel, which initially had been attacked by Melashenko. I wouldn't say that it was flying; it rather crept away, and I caught up with it in no time. One minute later it fell towards the earth like a flaming torch. The four remaining German fighters abandoned the scene by diving steeply."

The group of pilots which had followed the Kapitan who had been assigned to 728 IAP

as a navigational expert, became lost and had to perform emergency landings in the countryside. The pilots returned to their unit the next day, but the Kapitan was never seen again. Vorozheykin was commended by his Polk commander for his initiative to take the correct flight path to the battle zone. At noon on 14 July, Vorozheykin took off for his second combat mission that day:

"By midday, only four aircraft remained out of our Eskadrilya's ten. The Polk commander formed a group composed of two Zvenos. […] Again we followed the rail line. My Zveno flew at 2,000 metres altitude, and the other one was positioned 3,000 metres higher. Having learned from our previous mistakes, we now flew in an echeloned formation. […]

In front of us we could see the ruins of the station at Prokhorovka. Below the drifting smoke we could see relentlessly muzzle flashes on the battlefield. Meanwhile, the overcast had grown thicker. […] What if the bombers would sneak in below the clouds? We couldn't allow that, so we decided to dive into the haze, down closer to the earth. We immediately were met by a furious anti-aircraft fire. One aircraft was hit and disappeared down below, leaving nothing but a pile of smoke behind. Now we were only three – on my right hand side Vybornov, and to the left Timonov.

Suddenly I spotted Junkers planes in front of me – twenty of them! And in the distance I could distinguish another formation. […]

Messerschmitts are attacking, I heard a calm voice warn. […]

There was no chance to avoid the enemy fighters. But we still were closer to the Junkers than they were. […]

Timokha, you take the one to the left! Vybornov, cover us! I cried in the radio, but forgot to mention the enemy fighters.

The Junkers in front of me grew in size. I closed in on it from the astern. The bombers were flying wingtip to wingtip in a close formation. I let the bead of my gunsight wander along the aircraft until it stopped straight on the engine of the ugly Junkers. I opened up with all I had and kept firing until the bomber just broke apart right in front of me. One of its wings whirled away above my head, and I barely was able to avoid running into the pieces of the Junkers.

Vybornov also opened fire at a Junkers. A Messerschmitt came turning in on Timonov. I banked sharply and drove off the Fascist. Meanwhile Vybornov covered 'his' Junkers with bullets. The Ju 87 formation lost some of its compactness. They apparently had no more time to enter a dive, because they just dropped their bombs from their horizontal flight. Kozlovskiy, who apparently had become drawn into a combat somewhere, was unable to help us. The second bomber group started to turn slightly in order to enter the diving attack. […]

Having driven off a Messerschmitt from Timonov's tail, I called him via the radio and ordered him to attack the new group of Junkers. Nikolay immediately obeyed my order. I covered him as he fell down upon the Junkers, wildly firing his guns. One of the aircraft caught fire. But the remainder continued their flight path towards their target.

Enemy fighters came diving down against us. Nikolay departed from the bombers. Three Messerschmitts picked my aircraft, so I had to escape into the clouds. In the next moment, I found myself in a thick, snow white haze. Without losing one second, I turned to the side, relying on my feeling where the second group of Junkers ought to be positioned. And there they were – below my aircraft!

I immediately attacked and opened fire at great distance. One burst of fire, a second. I saw pieces getting torn off from the starboard wing of the Junkers, which started to emit black smoke. Suddenly I realised that my target had become too large. In my excitement, I had failed to notice how close I had come! I pulled the joystick as hard as I could, flashed by just above the row of Junkers planes – and then they were gone! I saw the nose of my aircraft rise, and then it almost hung still in the air as it stalled. In that moment there was a terrible bang and I felt heat and I was covered by something grey and hot. I tried to open the canopy but it had jammed. I tried again. I hammered with my fist against the canopy and pulled it with both hands but it stuck like had it been welded to the aircraft. It became unbearably hot in the cockpit. […] I desperately grabbed the joystick and pushed the gas handle, which I found to be stuck in the extreme forward position. But everything was working – the engine was running and my aircraft obeyed me. […] It turned out that it was not smoke that had filled the cockpit – it was steam! My engine had been damaged, and boiling water had entered the cockpit. This had been going on for two or three minutes, then the liquid in the radiator was gone. […]

Another two minutes passed. There I could see it – the good old Earth! Altitude 1,500 metres. I searched for a point of orientation, and then I saw it – the ruins of the station at Prokhorovka. It was as if a heavy burden had fallen from my shoulders. Not far from here was the airfield of 32 IAP of our Diviziya. I hurried to land!

Then I was among friends again…"

During his last mission on 14 July, Vorozheykin probably encountered III./St.G 2 Immelmann and III./JG 3 Udet. While the former unit recorded one Ju 87 shot down, Uffz. Norbert Geyer of the latter unit was credited with the shooting down of a 'LaGG-3' near Prokhorovka at 12.35 hours. Apparently, other Soviet fighters engaged the Germans, since 9./JG 3's Hptm. Wilhelm Lemke, claimed a La-5 on the same mission.

Quotations from A. S. Vorozheykin, Nad Kurskoy Dugoy, pp. 106–125.

On 14 July 1943, III./JG 3's Gruppenkommandeur, Major Wolfgang Ewald, was shot down north-east of Belgorod. Ewald baled out and was captured by Red Army troops. He was an ace with 78 victories. Ewald's Bf 109 G is seen in the foreground of this photograph.

his support from the air, 'Group Trufanov' managed to halt III. *Panzerkorps's* intended attack towards the north.

Fliegerkorps VIII performed 656 sorties on 13 July. The bomb-carrying aircraft were mainly focused to support 4. *Panzerarmee.* Sixty bombers were employed singly or in *Ketten* in support of 4. *Panzerarmee,* as were 103 aircraft of Sch.G 1 and many of the 239 Stuka sorties. The German airmen claimed 25 tanks and seven ammunition dumps destroyed. [324]

But these air missions apparantly had no decisive influence on the ground operations. Along 4. *Panzerarmee's* front lines, both sides continued to punch at each other throughout 13 July, without any results being achieved. In the morning of 13 July, SS-*Obergruppenführer* Hausser had still nurtured the hope that his SS *Panzerkorps* would be able to force the Soviets out of Prokhorovka. Instead, a Soviet counter-attack pushed back the '*Totenkopf*' Division three kilometres from the positions which it had gained north-west of the contested city.

During the following night, II. SS *Panzerkorps's* positions were futher weakened as the ADD concentrated its prime effort against its rear area in the Prokhorovka sector. The Soviet bomber crews made two, three or four sorties each against mass of German vehicles at Greznoye, Malye Maychkiy and Luchki. Altogether, 418 Soviet bombers were in action against this small sector during the night of 13/14 July. [325]

With Hausser's forces on the Prokhorovka sector in the north if not in shambles, then at least the very much worn down, von Manstein tried to achieve a decision by shifting focus to the 4. *Panzerarmee's* flanks.

Through II. SS *Panzerkorps'* and *Armeeabteilung Kempf's* separate advances towards the north, an 11-kilometre wide and 16-kilometre deep wedge had been created between these forces. The Soviet troops in this narrow wedge – elements of the 69th Army – were, of course, in a most exposed position. II. SS *Panzerkorps'* '*Das Reich*' Division, lined up on Hausser's right flank, managed to restore its strength to over one hundred tanks and SPGs. On the other side of Soviet 69th Army's bulge, III. *Panzerkorps* sent 19. *Panzer Division* across the northern Donets to reinforce 7. *Panzer Divison.* These forces were instructed to launch a pincer operation against the wedge.

Meanwhile, on 4. *Panzerarmee's* left flank, the '*Grossdeutschland*' Division was ordered to discontinue its fruitless efforts to break through towards

Oboyan in the north and instead join forces with 3. *Panzer Division* in an attack on the left flank.

Von Manstein hoped that through these attacks, he would inflict such heavy losses on the Soviets that his forces somehow would be able to achieve a breakthrough of strategic decisiveness. Although desperate in its nature, it was von Manstein's only hope.

The *Luftwaffe* was tasked to make an all-out effort in support of both operations. *Fliegerkorps* VIII actually made a stronger effort on 14 July than in many days, flying as many as 1,452 sorties – 510 by Stukas, 486 by bombers (the largest figure since 8 July), 135 by *Schlacht* aircraft, 83 by reconnaissance crews and 238 by fighter pilots. On the morning of 14 July, the bombers were used as flying artillery in support of '*Grossdeutschland*' and 3. *Panzer Division.* Thus, for instance, the He 111s of I./KG 100 dropped masses of AB 70 bomb containers and SD 50 fragmentation bombs in repeated missions against Soviet 183rd Tank Brigade at Novenkoye, just in front of 3. *Panzer Division's* troops. [326] While I./KG 100 managed to escape the attention of Soviet fighters and was saved from sustaining any losses, KG 27 was met by both fierce ground fire and Soviet fighter interception, which resulted in one He 111 becoming lost and two other sustaining battle damage. *Fliegerkorps* VIII's Stuka units were in action on all sectors and sustained quite severe losses in supporting 48. *Panzerkorps.* Of eight Ju 87s shot down or severely destroyed on 14 July – of which six belonged to St.G 77 – all but one of these losses occurred while supporting 48. *Panzerkorps.* Included among the personnel losses was *Hptm.* Hans Werner, the *Staffelkapitän* of 8./St.G 77.

The Soviet 1st Tank Army managed to prevent the '*Grossdeutschland*' Division and 3. *Panzer Division* from achieving a major breakthrough, but the concentrated attacks on the ground and from the air exacted a severe toll on the army. On 4. *Panzerarmee's* right flank, the '*Das Reich*' Division's attack against the village of Belenikhino was supported by a concentrated Stuka attack which succeeded in breaking up the Soviet resistance. This support mission cost St.G 2 the loss of *Oblt.* Günther Schmid, the *Staffelkapitän* of 5./St.G 2 and holder of the Knight's Cross. Schmid – who was killed when his Ju 87 exploded in mid-air near Vinogradovka – had

Displaying an apparently content expression, the pilot of this II-2 climbs out of his cockpit after a combat mission. During the latter half of July 1943, Soviet aviation took an increasingly firm control of the air space over the southern flank of the Kursk Bulge.

The next day, 15 July, German aerial reconnaissance reports of a worrisome Soviet troop build-up 160 kilometres further to the south on the eastern side of the Donets, forced *Fliegerkorps* VIII to divert the bulk of it sorties to this sector. All of *Fliegerkorps* VIII's *Kampfgruppen* plus two *Stukagruppen* flew south to attack Soviet troop concentrations and railway stations in the Izyum area. From that day onward, the VVS enjoyed an increasingly strong air superiority in the Belgorod combat zone. Several *Fliegerkorps* VIII units – including all *Panzerjäger* units and a substantial part of the *Schlachtflieger* – had to be shifted to 1. *Fliegerdivision* in order to prevent a total disaster in the Orel Bulge.

On 16 July, 2 VA and 17 VA conducted 926 combat sorties while *Fliegerkorps* VIII was unable to perform more than 499. *Fliegerkorps* VIII's remaining close-support units were called in to assist 4. *Panzerarmee*, but in order to avoid heavy losses to Soviet fighters, these missions were flown only early in the morning and in the evening, and provided with strong fighter escort. During the remainder of the day, the Bf 109 fighters performed defensive patrols but they proved to be insufficient to prevent the Soviet aviation from hammering the German ground troops.[329] The Germans had no choice but to begin an orderly withdrawal of 4. *Panzerarmee* and *Armeeabteilung Kempf*. Operation *Zitadelle* had irrevocably failed.

The retreating columns of German troops became the targets for 222 ADD crews which went into action against the Belgorod area on the night of 16/17 July. The next day, Soviet South-western Front and *General-Polkovnik* Fyodor Tolbukhin's Southern Front launched a timely coordinated attack against the German positions at the northern Donets near Izyum, 100 kilometres south of Belgorod, and at the Mius River, another 160 kilometres to the south. This was precisely what Hitler had feared at the conference at the *Führerhauptquartier* four days earlier. The II. SS *Panzerkorps* immediately was ordered to shift southwards to meet this new Soviet onslaught as rapidly as possible. Meanwhile, most of what remained of *Fliegerkorps* VIII again flew south to support the hard-pressed German ground troops at Izyum and Mius.

In the Belgorod-Prokhorovka sector, *Fliegerkorps* VIII performed no more than 138 sorties on 17 July – against 484 by 2 VA. *Fliegerkorps* VIII's fighters recorded six victories – two each by I./JG 52's *Hptm.* Johannes Wiese (who thus attained his 100th victory) and II./JG 3's *Major* Kurt Brändle (his personal 160th and 161st kills). Meanwhile, II./St.G 2 lost three Ju 87s due to hostile action. Between 15 and 18 July, the Soviets carried out 2,209

flown more than 700 dive-bomber missions. Such an experienced flier simply could not be replaced.

The VVS responded to the increased German air activity by boosting its number of combat sorties on 14 July to 1,033. Engaging *Fliegerkorps* VIII in forty-two air combats – often in a position of numerical inferiority – the Soviet airmen claimed to have shot down 67 German aircraft. According to German records, *Fliegerkorps* VIII's actual losses were not quite so heavy; nine aircraft were destroyed and nine sustained medium or severe damage to hostile action.[327]

The Germans apparently reported their successes with greater accuracy on this day, when *Fliegerkorps* VIII claimed 24 Soviet aircraft shot down, with another seven destroyed through ground fire – quite close to the 27 aircraft recorded lost by 2 VA and 17 VA on 14 July.[328]

The bulk of what was obviously a substantial Soviet overclaiming apparently was due to 256 IAD, which reported no fewer than 42 aerial victories for the loss of nine Yak fighters. This *Diviziya* had been brought forward to first-line service only on 9-10 July, and had sustained quite severe losses during its first three days of operations in the battle. "We simply were not acquainted with the enemy's tactics or the geography of the area," explained one of its pilots, Arseniy Vorozheykin, who flew a Yak-7B as a *Kpt.* with 728 IAP/256 IAD. Vorozheykin was credited personally with three victories in two missions on 14 July.

III./JG 3 *Udet* was dealt a particularly severe loss when its *Gruppenkommandeur, Major* Wolfgang Ewald, an ace with 78 victories on his account, was shot down north-east of Belgorod. Ewald baled out and was captured by Red Army troops. The next night, the troops of 4. *Panzerarmee's* 'Das Reich' Division and *Armeeabteilung Kempf's* III. *Panzerkorps* met on 4. *Panzerarmee's* right flank, thus eliminating the wedge between the two German armies. But this would prove to be von Manstein's last tactical success in Operation *Zitadelle*.

German Bomb Container AB 70

Abwurfbehälter 70 – the German AB 70 bomb container – was used to drop SD 2B fragmentation bombs or flares. Each AB 70 could contain twenty-three SD 2Bs or three flares.

Equipped with a time fuse, a small internal explosion charge went off at a predetermined time after the AB 70 was released, bursting the container open and releasing its load.

The Soviet counter-attacks in the south – at Donets and at Mius – put an increasingly severe pressure on Fliegerkorps VIII, which had to divert many units to this area. On 18 July, KG 3 alone lost six Ju 88s during operations in this sector. With one of them, the Geschwaderkommodore, Oberstleutnant Walter Lehwess-Litzmann barely managed to

survive. This photograph shows a Ju 88 of II./KG 3. During the first fortnight after Operation Zitadelle commenced, this Kampfgruppe lost 12 Ju 88s, with another five sustaining various degrees of damage above 10 per cent.

orties in daylight over the southern flank of the Kursk Bulge, as compared with 1,422 sorties by *Fliegerkorps* VIII. Among these were 1,277 Soviet and 372 German fighter sorties. At night, the figures were even more unequal during the same period – 1,298 Soviet sorties versus 241 German. The ADD alone performed 450 sorties in the same area on the night of 17/18 July, bombing the railway junction of Barvenkovo, the railway station at Ilovayskaya, and the German air base at Stalino.

On 18 July, the Steppe Front and 5 VA joined the Voronezh Front and 2 VA in a counter-offensive to clear the area which the Germans had seized north of Belgorod during Operation *Zitadelle*. With the greatest crisis further south, *Luftflotte* 4 was hardly able to act at all to counter this pressure. On 19 July, *Fliegerkorps* VIII performed 92 sorties – 28 by fighters and 64 by reconnaissance aircraft. The next day, 7./St.G 77 was completely wiped out during a Soviet air attack against the airfield at Kramatorskaya, whereby ten Ju 87s were knocked out. Also on that day, 4./St.G 77 had three Ju 87s put out of commission through Soviet fighter interception. [330]

It took the Voronezh Front and the Steppe Front no more than five days of comparatively undramatic advance past devastated villages and burned down crops – littered with the hulks of burned-out military vehicles – to recapture all the territory which had been lost to the Germans during

Operation *Zitadelle*. The air above was completely dominated by Soviet aviation, on a scale similar to peace time. On 23 July, the day when the Soviet troops triumphantly put their boots on the ground from where 4. *Panzerarmee* had launched its offensive on the fateful 5 July 1943, the fighters of *Fliegerkorps* VIII made exactly four sorties in that area.

Meanwhile, new disasters struck Germany. On the night of 25 July, RAF Bomber Command managed to blind the German radar defences by dropping millions of aluminum strips. This was the beginning of a week of heavy attacks against the city of Hamburg which would claim over 30,000 lives and shatter the morale of the German population. On 25 July came the news that the king of Italy had dismissed Mussolini and even had the former dictator arrested. In panic, Hitler ordered the II. SS *Panzerkorps* to be transferred to Italy. But before this order could be implemented, new crises on the Eastern Front forced the Germans to change their plans once again, to the effect that ultimately only the SS 'Leibstandarte' Division reach Italy.

The Voronezh Front and the Steppe Front paused briefly to the north of Belgorod. On 3 August, they launched their attack against Belgorod. Two days later the city was in Soviet hands again. This was merely the beginning of a relentless Soviet offensive.

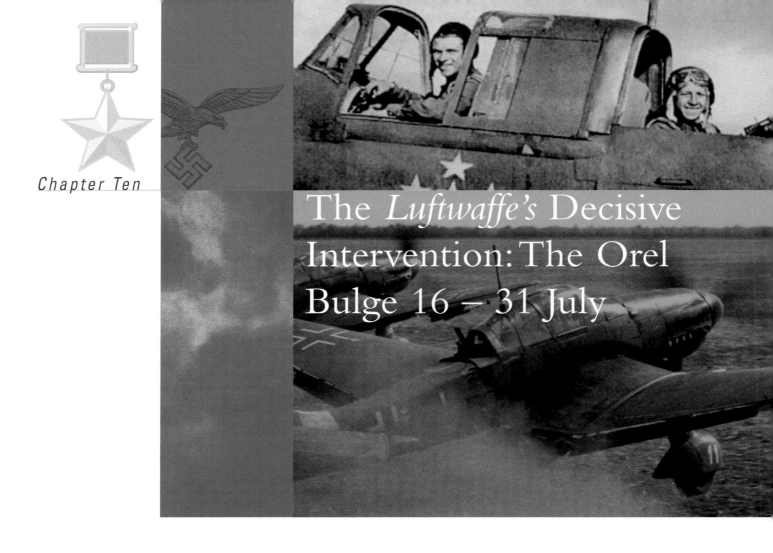

Chapter Ten

The *Luftwaffe's* Decisive Intervention: The Orel Bulge 16 – 31 July

Late on 15 July 1943, the fate of the German 2. *Panzerarmee* and 9. *Armee* in the Orel Bulge, under pressure from three directions, was hanging in the balance. *Generaloberst* Walter Model, who commanded both German armies, knew that his only hope rested with support from above. Once again, the *Luftwaffe* was called upon to save the German situation. The OKL released considerable reinforcements for 1. *Fliegerdivision* which also had taken a considerable beating. *Hptm.* Günther Rall's crack III./JG 52 and *Panzerjägerstaffel*/JG 51 had arrived on the 14th, while late on the 15th and early on the 16th, the remaining three Hs 129 *Staffeln* of *Hptm.* Bruno Meyer's *Panzerjagdkommando*/Sch.G 1 arrived to join *Panzerjägerstaffel*/JG 51, as well as I. and III./St.G 2 (the latter including Ju 87 Gs led by *Hptm.* Hans-Ulrich Rudel), and I./Sch.G 1 with Fw 190 ground-attack aircraft. 1. *Fliegerdivision's* depleted bomber force was reinforced through the arrival of II./KG 27 and II./KG 53.

With these forces, a massive counter-offensive in the air was launched. It started with the bombers, which were assigned the task of striking the Soviet supply lines in the rear. The prime targets in this new air operation were the railheads around Sukhinihi and rail facilities and rail traffic in the Kaluga and Kozelsk areas. The fighter pilots of 1 VA had taught the He 111 and Ju 88 crews of KG 1, KG 4 and KG 53 that it would be impossible to strike against these targets in daylight, so the attacks had to be carried out at night. The offensive commenced during the night of 15/16 July, when 155 German bombers were in action against the Soviet Western Front's rear area. Seventy-five bombers – most of them from KG 53 – attacked Sukhinichi; twenty-four raided the railway station at Kozelsk, while others went 'train-hunting' along the rail lines. [331]

However, at the same time, the ADD dispatched 222 bomber crews against similar targets on the German side of the front line, attacking Mokhovaya railway station, 32 kilometres to the east of Orel, and troop concentrations in the Bolkhov sector. [332]

As the sun rose, the Stukas, *Schlacht* aircraft and bombers of 1. *Fliegerdivision* took off from their airfields in large numbers. In the north of the Bulge, *General* Ivan Bagramyan's powerful forces marched victoriously towards the south, approaching the Bryansk-Orel highway and the rail line at Khotynets. If this could be reached, 2. *Panzerarmee* and 9. *Armee* would become surrounded in a repetition of the battle at Stalingrad.

By this time, all that remained to defend the vital lifeline were the weak and dispersed German ground forces which had already been utterly defeated in battle by Bagramyan's men. It would be a great test of the *Luftwaffe's* ability to intervene against the ground.

Due to the reinforcements, 1. *Fliegerdivision* was able to perform no fewer than 1,595 combat sorties on 16 July – more than twice the number of the previous day, and the highest level of activity since 7 July. The Stukas flew 732 sorties – an all-time high since the beginning of Operation *Zitadelle* – and the *Schlacht* aircraft made 103 individual flights. But since the fighting in the northern sector of the Bulge took place in deep forests, the task of even locating targets on the ground was extremely difficult. In spite of impressive activity, 1. *Fliegerdivision* claimed to have destroyed no more than 19 tanks and 70 lorries, and damaged another 25 tanks. A strategically important bridge was also blown to pieces. [333]

In the detailed history of the Hs 129, historian Martin Pegg described the situation: '4. and 8./Sch.G 1, 4./Sch.G 2 and *Pz.Jä.St.*/JG 51 were ordered to transfer immediately to Orel West in order to engage enemy tanks which had broken through. [...] In view of the serious situation, *Luftflotte* 6 '...chased everything that had wings into the air', but anti-tank operations along this sector of the front proved difficult, extremely wasteful and met with little success. Georg Dornemann, the *Staffelkapitän* of 4./SchG 1, remembered this as a period of particularly heavy losses and *Luftwaffe* records confirm the loss or serious damage of up to four Hs 129s a day during this period. In total, the Hs 129 anti-tank *Staffeln* lost some 30% of valuable aircraft and pilots to air and ground defences in the 11 days between 14 and 25 July without having the opportunity to carry out the tasks for which they had been intended and specially trained. It seems the battle-tried and tested policies were ignored and, with a complete disregard for the specialised role of the *Panzerjäger Staffeln* which operated best in areas of weak enemy air activity against tanks which had penetrated the front lines and were moving across open ground, the Hs 129s were ordered into the air on fruitless attacks against near-invisible tanks sheltering in forested areas or to carry out virtual suicidal missions of reconnaissance and orientation in an area where enemy aircraft were becoming more and more dangerous.' [334]

Hptm. Bruno Meyer, the commander of *Panzerjagdkommando*/Sch.G 1, recalled that over the Orel Bulge, his unit '...was opposed by Russian fighters belonging to an elite unit, who were brave daredevils, well trained and excellent fliers with a sure flair for German weaknesses." Equipped with Yak fighters, the pilots of this unit "attacked in a superior manner with short bursts of fire from all guns at short distances, directing their fire mainly at the lead aircraft of the German [formation], eight of which were shot down in a week.'[335]

Meanwhile, 1. *Fliegerdivision's* fighters performed 369 sorties – which was the largest number since the first day of Operation *Zitadelle*. In bitter air fighting, 40 victories were reported against 16 own aircraft shot down. Both sides sustained heavy personnel losses. One of them was I./JG 54's *Lt.* Günther Scheel, who had attained 71 air kills on only 70 missions. The loss report reads:

"Lt. *Scheel took off at 07.07 hours together with 3. Staffel of I./JG 54 in order to provide a Stuka formation with fighter escort in the vicinity of Orel. After completion of this mission,* Lt. *Scheel shot down 2 Yak-9s during a subsequent fighter sweep. During the second combat, his 71st in total, his left wing hit the enemy aircraft. The wing broke off at the fuselage, which caused the aircraft to immediately start descending from an altitude of 800 metres. In 50 metres altitude the aircraft caught fire and exploded on impact in* Planquadrat *64356, at 08.06 hours. Point of impact: about 15 kilometres northeast of Bolkhov."*[336]

On the other side of the hill, *General-Major* Georgiy Zakharov's crack 303 IAD also was dealt a heavy blow on this 16 July. At 12.45 hours, III./St.G 3 took off for its fourth dive-bomber mission of the day.[337] Near Krasnikovo, south-west of Bolkhov, its Ju 87s ran into eight Yak-7Bs of 18 GIAP and eight of the *Normandie-Niemen Eskadrilya*. Before the escorting Fw 190s had time to intervene, 8 GIAP's *Kpt.* Semyon Sibirin and *Serzh.* Ivan Stolyarov, and the French pilot *Mayor* Pierre Pouyade had claimed one Ju 87 each shot down. III./St.G 3 recorded two Ju 87s shot down.[338] But in the next moment, Fw 190s and Bf 109s intervened with devastating effect, costing the loss of four Yak-7Bs. Thus died the French veterans *Kpt.* Albert Littolff, *Lt.* Noël Castelain and *M.Lt.* Adrien Bernavon, and 18 GIAP's 11-victory ace *Serzh.* Ivan Stolyarov. Due to disorder in the corresponding documents,

it has been difficult to establish exactly which German pilots were responsible for this, but it seems plausible to assume that the Soviet fighters reported shot down by III./JG 52's *Lt.* Erich Hartmann, I./JG 54's *Oblt.* Hans Götz and IV./JG 54's *Oblt.* Herbert Aloé in the early afternoon of 16 July are identical with some of these Yak-7Bs.

However, not even 1. *Fliegerdivision's* massive effort would suffice to put a break on the Soviet assaults. In the south of the Orel Bulge, 16 VA carried out three major air attacks against German strongpoints around the villages of Kunach and Kudeyarovo. Each of these was preceded by fighter sweeps which took control of the air above the target area. The first operation was made between 12.00 and 13.00 hours (Russian time), with 155 bombers and 101 *Shturmoviks* escorted by 154 fighters. This met no opposition from German fighters. The second attack took place three hours later, involving 140 bombers and 123 *Shturmoviks*, escorted by 181 fighters. A group of Fw 190s from I./JG 51 tried to intervene, but it cost them one of their own for no gain.[339] The third attack was delivered between 19.00 and 20.00 hours by 146 bombers and 126 *Shturmoviks*, escorted by 188 fighters. Only on this occasion did they encounter any serious resistance in the air. Adhering to desperate calls from 9. *Armee, Generalmajor* Deichmann had dispatched Fw 190s and Bf 109s of III./JG 51, III./JG 52 and II./JG 54 to the area, but they failed to shoot down more than an Il-2 and a Pe-2 out of the massive attack force, and this brought virtually no relief to the tormented German ground troops.

In intervals between these three major strikes, 16 VA sent smaller groups of bombers and *Shturmoviks* to subject the German troops to an unremitting pressure. In total the air units of 16 VA performed 1,713 combat sorties on this day alone.[340] According to the Central Front's battle analysis, 16 VA's concentrated attacks on 16 July decided the outcome of the whole ground battle and allowed Soviet troops to achieve a major breakthrough.[341]

The situation was similar to the north-east, where the Bryansk Front struggled to reach Orel. With 1. *Fliegerdivision* mainly concentrated against the Western Front further to the north-west, the aircraft of 15 VA was able to

The BK 3.7 Flak cannon of a Junkers Ju 87 G-1 is loaded with a clip of 37mm anti-tank rounds.

Ju 87 D-5s of the so-called Alarmverband (alert unit) of III./St.G 2 race into the air. The Alarmverband consisted of aircraft and crews drawn from all Staffeln of III./St.G 2. This Stukagruppe was commanded by Hptm. Hans-Ulrich Rudel after

Hptm. Walter Krauss was killed in an ADD bombing raid against the airfield Orel-East on the night of 17 July. The first Ju 87s of the version D-5, featuring extended outer wing panels, were delivered to St.G 2 in July 1943.

operate almost freely to support the Bryansk Front. Throughout the day, the German defenders in this sector were subject to intense air attacks. These were mainly carried out by Il-2s which dropped out from the clouds in small groups, but on one occasion, 99 Il-2s escorted by 54 fighters performed a concentrated attack against German armour near Zhelyabug. Observation posts belonging to Soviet 63rd Army reported that four German tanks were destroyed and 28 damaged as a result of the attack. [342]

The reports from 810 ShAP/225 ShAD describe a most successful day. During one mission on 16 July, 23 Il-2s led by *Kpt.* Chernyavskiy attacked armour with 2,700 PTAB anti-tank bombs in the area of Podmaslovo, Fyodorovka and Filatovo, and claimed to have destroyed no fewer than 17 tanks. [343] During a subsequent mission early in the afternoon, nineteen crews of the same unit managed to successfully ward off interception attempts by Fw 190s – apparently from II./JG 54. The Soviet report reads:

"*On 16 July 1943, at 13.03 hours, 19 crews – the first group commanded by St.Lt. Rogatchyov and the second group by Kpt. Chernyavskiy – attacked tanks in the area of Podmaslovo, Prilep, Filatovka and Mokhovaya. 10 tanks were destroyed and 3 Fw-190s were shot down by Serzh. Marchkov, St.Lt. Solyanikov and St.Lt. Kozlovskim.*" [344]

However, similar to the problems encountered by the *Luftwaffe*, 15 VA's intense activity was not sufficient to break the tenacious German resistance in this sector. The troops of the Bryansk Front encountered a deeply echeloned system of defence lines which the Germans had constructed over the past eighteen months. The 2. *Panzerarmee's* 53. *Armeekorps*, which was assigned to defend this sector, had also received significant reinforcements – 2. and 8. *Panzer* divisions from 9. *Armee*, the 653. *schwere Panzerjäger-Abteilung* (equipped with 65-ton *Ferdinand* anti-tank SPGs) and the 36th Infantry Division from the Army Group reserve.

Although of some consolation to the increasingly worried Model, it was clear that unless the Western Front in the north was halted, the defence in the east would be in vain.

The desperate situation on the battlefield in the north compelled Deichmann to assign most of his bombers to purely tactical missions during the following night. One hundred and fifty bomber sorties were flown against the rear area of Bagramyan's troops in the Ulyanovo area. Fifty-two other bombers were sent out against rail targets and reported five trains and one locomotive destroyed. In all, 1. *Fliegerdivision's* bomber units carried out

a record 206 sorties on the night of 16/17 July – of which 88 were made by III./KG 4 alone. [345]

But this was superceded by the ADD, which made more than 400 individual bomber flights against the Orel Bulge on the night of 17 July. One hundred and ten of these subjected German troops at Bolkhov to a concentrated attack, around fifty others bombed supply routes from Orel to Bolkhov, while others flew against the railway station at Mokhovaya, the railway junction at Orel, and the airfields at Orel. [346] At the airfield of Orel-East, 1. *Fliegerdivision's* Stuka units were dealt bloody losses. Several airmen were killed by the Soviet bombs. One of these was *Hptm.* Walter Krauss, the *Gruppenkommandeur* of III./St.G 2 *Immelmann*, which just had arrived from *Fliegerkorps* VIII in the south.

For 17 July, Deichmann demanded the most from his units. 1. *Fliegerdivision's* operations on this day were characterised by two features. First of all its air units were primarily concentrated against the critical northern and southern sectors of the Orel Bulge, at the cost of air support of the eastern sector (where the German ground troops still managed fairly well without air support). Secondly, the fighters made a massive effort to take control of the air. On this day, 1. *Fliegerdivision's Jagdgruppen* made 469 individual flights – a higher number than any other previous day after 5 July 1943.

Thus, the air in the Bryansk Front's combat zone remained dominated by Soviet aircraft – to the dismay of the soldiers of 53. *Armeekorps*. 15 VA's chronicle describes the scene on 63rd Army's sector on this day: "*Our aircraft carried out massed strikes. Shturmoviks attacked Hill 269,5, the western surburbs of Arkhangelsk, and congestions of armour and infantry in the area of Podmaslovo and Tsarevka. As a result of these air operations, the enemy removed up to 30 damaged tanks from the latter sector.*" [347] All day, not a single *Shturmovik* or bomber from 15 VA was shot down by German fighters. There were only few encounters between the *Luftwaffe* and aircraft of 15 VA on 17 July. During one of these, however, a whole *Zveno* of Yak-1s from 65 GIAP was shot down by Fw 190s. Among the four pilots, who all were killed, were *St.Lt.* Gavril Guskov, a 15-victory ace, and *M.Lt.* Antonina Lebedeva, who had been among the first batch of female fighter pilots to see action over Stalingrad the previous autumn. In this context, an account by *Hptm.* Bruno Meyer of *Panzerjagdkommando*/Sch.G 1 is quite interesting. This describes an incident during the Battle of the Orel Bulge in July 1943, although the exact date is not clear: Meyer's Hs 129 was shot down by a Yak fighter, but as Meyer was about to bale out, his jettisoned canopy hit the pursuing fighter, which crashed. Meyer succeeded in making an emergency landing close to the point where the Yak fighter had crashed. He examined the wreckage and found that "…the dead pilot turned out to be a woman, without rank insignia, identification or parachute."[348]

But this blow to 65 GIAP would be the exception of the day in the eastern sector. The situation was entirely different in the northern and southern sectors of the Orel Bulge, where huge air battles raged from dawn to dusk. Early in the morning, 1 VA dispatched 34 Pe-2s from 204 BAD to attack the railway station at Belyye Berega, some 16 kilometres to the west of Bryansk. Fighter escort was afforded by 303 IAD with 18 Yak-7Bs of 18 GIAP, led by the regimental commander *Mayor* Anatoliy Golubov, and ten Yak-7Bs of *Normandie-Niemen*, led by *Mayor* Jean Tulasne. These warded off some weak German fighter attacks, and not a single Soviet aircraft was lost.

The Soviet report states that the Pe-2s carried out a highly successful dive-bombing of the railway station, for which 1 VA's C-in-C, *General-Mayor* Mikhail Gromov, later sent his personal congratulations. 18 GIAP's *Lt.* Ivan Gnezdilov gave the following eye-witness account in his memoirs: "The Petlyakovs performed a masterly bombing. Through direct bomb hits, railway cars loaded with ammunition and fuel exploded. The entire station rapidly became enveloped with flames. Two whole sets of trains were completely destroyed."[349]

However, a formation of 2 BAK Pe-2s fared worse during a mission to the west of Orel. These bombers had to run the gauntlet of numerous groups of Fw 190s and Bf 109s – from I./JG 51, III./JG 51, IV./JG 51, III./JG 52 and I./ZG 1, who claimed to have shot down 10 Pe-2s for no loss.

In the south of the Bulge, the skies over the battlefield where the Central Front was pushing 9. *Armee* backwards were filled with aircraft from both sides. According to reports from the Central Front, the *Luftwaffe* repeatedly tried to intervene on the battlefield by sending in waves of aircraft, but many of these attacks had to be abandoned because of interception by Soviet fighters. Throughout the day, 1 GIAD and 6 IAK dispatched fighters in groups of between four and thirty to cover their own troops from German air attacks. The markedly improved performance of 16 VA's fighters as compared with the situation during the defensive battle was largely due to the adoption of new fighter tactics and a better organised ground control. At the end of the day, it was noticed that following relentless Soviet fighter attacks, the German bombers started to operate at higher altitudes, which reduced the effectiveness of their bombings.

Meanwhile, 16 VA's *Shturmoviks* and bombers continued to strike hard against the German troops – obviously without 1. *Fliegerdivision's* fighters

A Soviet female combat pilot. Hundreds of Soviet woman served as first-line combat pilots during World War II. While many operated with all-woman air units, others served in dominantly male air regiments.

The remnants of a shot down Il-2 twin-seater is inspected by German airmen. The Il-2 twin-seater was often erroneously referred to by the Germans as 'Il-5', 'Il-7' or even 'Il-4' – the latter being the new designation of the twin-engined DB-3F bomber.

Kapitan Semyon Sibirin, one of the aces of 18 GIAP, and the French fighter pilot, Kapitan Albert Littolff, of Normandie-Niemen in the summer of 1943. Littolff served with three air forces - the French Armée de l'Air during the Battle of France in 1940, the RAF in North Africa in 1941, and the VVS in 1943. By the time he arrived in the USSR, Littolff was credited with 10 victories. Littolff was killed in air combat on 16 July 1943 – possibly shot down by III./JG 52's Lt. Erich Hartmann, who attained his 37th and 38th victories on this day. Sibirin survived the war with a tally of 16 individual and one shared victory, but was killed in a flight accident in 1949. (Viktor Kulikov Photo Archive)

being able to do much to prevent this. Again, 16 VA's aircraft were brought together in massive formations. Three major air attacks were carried out, each involving 350 aircraft or more. On the first occasion, at 06.00 hours in the morning (Russian time), III./JG 51 tried to counter the attack and claimed three Il-2s and a Soviet fighter shot down. The next major attack took place five hours later, and this time the Soviet aircraft were met by I./JG 51, III./JG 51, I./JG 54 and I./ZG 1, which reportedly shot down six Il-2s and four escort fighters. When the third major air operation was launched at noon, IV./JG 51 was in place to shoot down two of 221 BAD's Bostons. But of course none of this could take the edge off the massive Soviet air strikes. *Polkovnik* Devyatov, the Chief of Staff of the Central Front's 3rd Tank Corps, submitted the following report on the air support which his tank force received:

"On 17 July 1943 the bombers and Shturmoviks of 16 VA carried out five concentrated attacks in support of the 2nd Tank Army's 3rd Tank Corps. These air attacks were directed against congestions of enemy troops in the areas of Arkhangelsk, Ozerki, Vesyolyy, Berezhok, Ochki, and Sokolniki. The ground troops are full of praise for the excellent accomplishments of the aviation. The fighter pilots particularly distinguished themselves by clearing the skies from enemy aircraft, thus providing the 3rd Tank Corps with a considerable relief." [350]

Even though 1. *Fliegerdivision* carried out hundreds of sorties to support 9. *Armee* against the Central Front and 16 VA in the south, the mission to counter the threat from Bagramyan's troops and 1 VA in the north was given the highest priority, and it was in this sector that the hardest air fighting took place.

About one hour after combats with 1 VA's Pe-2s, a cluster of aces from 2. and 6./JG 54 – including *Lt.* Horst Ademeit, *Ofw.* Otto Kittel, *Ofw.* Heinrich 'Bazi' Sterr and *Fw.* Albin Wolf – clashed with La-5s and Yak fighters of 1 VA north-west of Bolkhov, claiming eight shot down. Nevertheless, they were not able to prevent the La-5s from shooting down 2./St.G 2's *Staffelkapitän,* Knight's Cross holder, *Oblt.* Egbert Jaekel. Hans-Ulrich Rudel described this event in his memoirs:

"Not many words are spoken in our *Gruppe* during these days, only what is most important is said. The severity of the struggle is weighing heavy on all of us. It is the same situation in all other units. During a morning attack … against Soviet artillery positions, the *Staffeln* of the I. *Gruppe* fly next to my *Gruppe,* among them the Second *Staffel* commanded by *Oberleutnant* Jaekel. He has developed into a great aviator and has become famous for a certain habit. Whenever he spots any fighters, he attacks them, even though they are superior in both speed and armament. […]

"On this morning he and his *Staffel* attacked an artillery battery next to the one which we attacked. During our return flight – we were just crossing our own forward line below – someone cried out: 'Fighters!' I saw them at great distance, and they obviously had no intention of attacking. But Jaekel turned towards them and soon he had engaged them in a turning fight. He managed to shoot down one, but even Jentsch, his faithful radio operator, seemed to be looking forward and not towards the rear! In the next moment, a La-5 was in position behind him. I saw how their aircraft reeled over at two hundred metres altitude, and then plummet downwards and crash in flames…" [351]

Shortly afterwards, the elite 18 GIAP was in the air again, on its second mission of the day – as described here by *Lt.* Ivan Gnezdilov:

"At 09.00 hours, *Mayor* Anatoliy Golubov led three six-plane formations of fighters – led by *Eskadrilya* commander [*Kpt.* Semyon] Sibirin, [*Kpt.* Ivan

Zamorin and [*Kpt.* Nikolay] Semyonov respectively – into the air. Our mission was to provide our ground troops of the 11th Guards Army with air cover. As we approached the assigned patrol area, our regimental commander received a call from the ground control:

'*Yastreb* One', '*Utes*' calling! Enemy bombers in square grid 16, approaching your positions. Attack them and prevent their bombing!

'*Utes*', I confirm. I am heading for square grid 16.

"It did not take long before we spotted a column of enemy bombers. There were five groups with eight to ten Junkers and Heinkels in each. They were covered by 12 Focke-Wulfs. *Mayor* Golubev pressed the transmission button and called out his instructions:

"Semyonov and Sibirin, attack the bombers! Zamorin, engage the Fockes!

"With Golubev in the lead, two six-groups of Yaks made a daring frontal attack against the bombers, with blazing guns. The Germans panicked and turned to all sides to avoid a collision. Two of them were hit by Semyonov's and Sibirin's fire, and both descended to the ground, where they exploded.

"Our guardsmen continued to harass the Junkers, who hurriedly jettisoned their bombs and made a quick escape – but not before Vladimir Zapaskin and Dmitry Lobashev had shot down two more of their number.

"180-degree turn! Golubev ordered.

"Performing a rapid turn, our fighter formation attacked the Heinkel bombers. *Mayor* Golubev approached to within short distance of a Heinkel. Behind him, [*M.Lt.* Konstantin] Pilipeyko was also closing in. Both opened fire simultaneously, blowing the enemy bomber to pieces.

"Meanwhile the six-plane group which was led by Zamorin attacked the Focke-Wulfs from above. Being divided into two groups of six in each, these became entangled in a descending turning combat. Taking advantage of the Yak's superior manoeuvrability, Zamorin, [*Lt.* Ivan] Sobolev, [*M.Lt.* Nikolay] Zamkovskiy and [*M.Lt.* P.] Osipenko shot down four Fockes. The remainder chose to disengage.

"Thus, despite the foe's three-fold numerical superiority, our guardsmen managed to shoot down nine enemy aircraft and return to base without having suffered any losses." [352]

The files in the Russian Central Military Archive (TsAMO) show that, in fact, 13 German aircraft – eight Fw 190s, two He 111s, two Ju 88s and a Ju 87 – were claimed shot down by 18 GIAP between 09.30 and 09.45 hours in the Krasnikovo-Yagodnaya-Ulyanovo area. [353] Bearing in mind that a large share of the corresponding German records have been lost, it is difficult to identify positively this event in German sources. No He 111s were reported lost on 17 July, but II./KG 51 and III./St.G 1 each recorded two aircraft shot down in air combat. It may be assumed that *Obstlt.* Horst-Wilhelm Hossfeld, a General Staff officer who had been sent to the Eastern Front to serve as *Staffelführer* in 2./Sch.G 1, piloted one of the Fw 190s which was claimed by 18 GIAP. Hossbach was reported missing after his Fw 190 F-8, coded 'M', was shot down by Soviet fighters. However, that nine Fw 190s should have been shot down appears to be a major exaggeration. In any case, it may be concluded that 18 GIAP achieved yet another great defensive victory on that mission.

I./KG 53 fared a little better during a mission in the afternoon, as *Oblt.* Martin Vollmer's diary relates: "*One daylight mission – in clouds, with the result that the formation got dispersed. We were subjected to individual attacks by enemy fighters, who picked our aircraft at will. But each time we managed to seek cover in the clouds – although at the price of terrible icing*" [354] I./KG 53 escaped with just one He 111 damaged as a result of fighter interception, and a crew member injured.

But the day was not over. Although 1. *Fliegerdivision's* fighters failed to shoot down more than six of 1 VA's *Shturmoviks* on this day, they undoubtedly achieved some notable success against the Soviet fighters. In the afternoon, *Mayor* Jean Tulasne led nine *Normandie-Niemen* Yak-7Bs to escort a group of Il-2s against Znamenskaya, 19 kilometres north-west of Orel, when the Soviet aircraft were suddenly pounced upon by sixteen

rhard Jähnert (left, facing the camera) and Oblt. Helmut Müller of III./StG 3. Jähnert tarted his pilot career in 1938 with Fliegergruppe 30, which later was redesignated /Sch.G 162, then II./St.G 2. He flew numerous Stuka missions during the invasion of oland and France, in North Africa and against Malta. In January 1942, II./St.G 2 was redesignated III./StG 3, and this unit was transferred to the Eastern Front in May 1943. Jähnert survived the war with over 700 combat missions recorded in his logbook, and was awarded with the Knight's Cross.

German fighters. The Frenchmen managed to save the Il-2s from sustaining any losses, but it cost them dearly. When the pilots returned to base, three pilots were missing – *Lt*. Didier Béguin, *Lt*. Firmin Vermeil and the unit commander, *Mayor* Tulasne. Fortunately, Béguin survived and later returned to his unit, but the loss of Tulasne was another hard blow for the French volunteers. It appears as though these losses were due to a concerted attack by the Fw 190s from I./JG 54 and IV./JG 54, resulting in claims for two Soviet fighters – one of them by Walter Nowotny's old wingman, *Uffz*. Karl Schnörrer. It also is possible that III./JG 52's *Hptm*. Günther Rall intervened in the combat; he scored his 160th victory – against a "LaGG-3" – at 17.08 hours during a free-hunting mission west of Bolkhov between 16.45 and 17.20 hours. [355]

In total, 1. *Fliegerdivision* carried out 1,693 combat sorties on 17 July, thus surpassing the previous day's number. Again, the results reported by its ground-attack and bomber units were quite meagre: 24 tanks and 31 lorries were claimed destroyed.

Instead, the German fighters submitted an impressive record: over 90 victories, including JG 54's 5,000th in total. Of great significance, however, is the fact that the *Jagdflieger*, in spite of these impressive claims, failed to accomplish their main mission – to prevent Soviet air attacks against German ground targets.

According to the loss returns to the *Generalquartiermeister der Luftwaffe*, 1. *Fliegerdivision's* own combat losses on 17 July were limited to 12 aircraft destroyed and four damaged – which would indicate that the Fw 190s and Bf 109s at least succeeded in providing their own bombers and ground-attack aircraft with reliable protection. [356]

Included among 1. *Fliegerdivision's* losses on 17 July were three Knight's Cross holders – all from the *Stukageschwader*: Krauss and Jaekel from St.G 2, and I./St.G 1's *Hptm*. Friedrich Lorenz, who was lost when his Ju 87 D-3 was shot down by anti-aircraft fire near Strelnikovo.

By this time, many units on both sides had become badly worn down. Only nine pilots remained on *Normandie-Niemen's* roster out of 17 from five days earlier. Six had been killed in action and two were in hospital. On 18 July Soviet fighters shot down and killed *Lt*. Alfons Mittelmeier in 9./JG 51's last serviceable Fw 190. The situation was even worse for IV./JG 51 which lost all its Fw 190s in a fortnight and then had to re-equip with Messerschmitt Bf 109 G-6s, simply because there were too few Fw 190s available to replace the losses.

The notion that the *Luftwaffe* succeeded in halting the Western Front's advance on 17 July – which appears in many publications – is, at best, an error involving the date. This was actually achieved, but only two days later. On 17 July, Bagramyan launched another tank corps, the 25th, into battle, thus increasing the menace against the rear of the German troops which defended Bolkhov.

1. *Fliegerdivision* performed slightly more than 1,100 combat sorties on 18 July – including 449 by Stukas, 237 bomber sorties, 17 by *Panzerjäger* and 40 by other *Schlacht* aircraft. The German report on their operations read: *"Attacks were carried out against armour, trucks, artillery positions, rocket launchers and troop concentrations south-east of Ulyanovo, to the east of Bolkhov and to the west of Novosil. Shot down in the air: 25 enemy aircraft. [Other] results: 15 tanks,*

18 trucks, 16 other vehicles, 5 artillery pieces and 9 rocket launchers destroyed. 4 tanks probably destroyed, 7 damaged, 5 artillery pieces and 3 anti-aircraft batteries put out of commission. 4 machine gun positions taken out, 4 large explosions probably fuel or ammunition dumps; further explosions with thick smoke observed. Bomb hits in artillery positions and vehicle columns. Heavy personnel losses inflicted [on the enemy]. 670,000 kg bombs dropped." [357]

The famous air operation when the *Luftwaffe* alone halted the Western Front's attack against the Orel – Bryansk communication route took place on 19 July, when Soviet armoured forces emerged from the forested area further north and entered the open terrain just north of Khotynets.

Late on 18 July, having advanced 64 kilometres in six days, the 1st Tank Corps's forward elements had reached a position just eight to eleven kilometres north of Khotynets. But these were spotted by German air reconnaissance, and before the march to sever the lifeline of two entire German armies could commence the next morning, scores of low-flying German aircraft appeared. There was nowhere the Soviet troops could take cover, and the result was a terrible carnage. *Oblt*. Georg Dornemann of 4./SchG 1 described the scene as it looked from the air:

"Shortly after crossing the front line, we discovered in the first rays of the sun, the parked tanks with their crews still asleep near them. After my first armour-piercing rounds struck the tanks and the first of them had been turned into a blazing wreck, the tank crews sprang to life. But I and each of my pilots quickly fired off the rest of our ammunition and were soon heading back to our airfield, flying now in brighter sunlight and already bracketed by some light flak.

"In this attack, our cannon fire proved devastating. Fifty or more Russian tanks littered the ground, burnt out or incapacitated. My own score was three. None of our aircraft was lost in this attack, though my own aircraft was slightly damaged by small arms fire in the port wing immediately outboard of the engine nacelle." [358]

Polkovnik S. P. Koroteyev's 70th Tank Brigade nevertheless had managed to infiltrate the German lines and was operating in a guerilla fashioned nature to sever the vital rail line. A small group of tanks from this brigade was spotted by four Hs 129 pilots – as historian Martin Pegg describes:

"A *Schwarm* of Hs 129s from 4./Sch.G 2 was alerted that five T-34s had again appeared at a point on the railway line where they had stopped a goods train and their crews were busy destroying the tracks with demolition charges. The *Schwarm* immediately engaged the tanks and knocked them out, but suffered a major loss in the process. *Major* Matuschek, the *Staffelkapitän* had expended almost all his ammunition on a tank without causing any apparent damage. In a final and determined assault which he pressed home to point-blank range, he fired off his remaining ammunition but misjudged the moment he should have pulled up and flew full tilt into his intended victim. As his comrades watched in horror, both aircraft and tank disappeared in a single massive explosion." [359]

But this was merely the beginning of the 70th Tank Brigade's suffering. By coincidence, a Yak-9 fighter pilot contributed to revealing the brigade's hiding place behind the German lines. Shot down by this Yak-9, the commanding officer of *Panzerjagdkommando/Sch.G 1*, *Hptm*. Bruno Meyer crash-landed his Hs 129 on the edge of a marsh. "To his astonishment

The crew of an Ilyushin Il-2 Shturmovik smiles at the photographer just ahead of another combat sortie. The four red stars beneath the cockpit mark shot down German aircraft. The introduction of a rear gun in the previously single-seat Il-2 greatly improved the Shturmovik's vulnerability to German fighter attacks.

'Brown 8' of 3./JG 51 Mölders at Orel in July 1943. Fw. Werner Prinz was shot down in aerial combat while flying this aircraft on 21 July 1943. However, he escaped with only injuries and later returned to service, where he went on to amass a total of 15 victories before he was killed in action in June 1944.

wrote Martin Pegg, "Meyer discovered that he had come down in front of a force of some 80 Soviet tanks of all types which had broken through the front line unobserved into German-held territory. They had been so skillfully camouflaged with straw that from the air they were indistinguishable from ordinary haystacks." [360]

The radio in Meyer's damaged aircraft proved to be working, so the German pilot was able to report what he had seen to his unit. At that time, *Major* Georg Dörffel, the Oak Leaves holder who commanded I./Sch.G 1, was airborne in the vicinity in the lead of a large formation of Fw 190s loaded with 250 kg bombs intended for another target. Picking up Meyer's radio call, Dörffel immediately decided to divert his formation against this new target. Other close-support units of 1. *Fliegerdivision* soon swarmed to the area. The Soviet tankmen were allowed no respite. One *Luftwaffe* formation was succeeded by another. The logbook of III./St.G 3's *Lt.* Erhard Jähnert shows no fewer than six missions on 19 July. [361]

Over three days, 1. *Fliegerdivision* was in relentless action against the 1st Tank Corps and 70th Tank Brigade. *Ofw.* Hans Krohn, radio operator in the 37 mm cannon-equipped Ju 87 flown by 1./St.G 2's *Staffelkapitän, Oblt.* Heinz Junclaussen, recalls:

"Our 'cannon planes' took a terrible toll on the Russian armour. We attacked at very low altitude – I often feared that we were going to hit a ground obstacle with our landing gear – and my pilot opened fire at the tanks from a distance of only 50 metres. That gave us very little margin to pull up and get away before the tank exploded, so immediately after the cannons were fired I always prepared myself for a very rash manoeuvre. At the same time, in that moment I had to be very watchful because in this area the Russian fighters were very active and they sure were most serious adversaries!

"Most of our attacks against tanks were made against the side of the tanks, because in that way the tanks offered the largest targets. I know that some pilots attacked from behind because that was where the armour was weakest, but that also meant that the target was so small that it was difficult to hit. By this time the Russian tank crews appeared to be well aware of the potency of our 'cannon planes'. Whenever we appeared, the tanks would start wild evasive manoeuvres, turning in all directions. Occasionally we could see tank crews jump out of the hatches and abandon their tanks when we dived to attack them. I can understand them, for our attacks must have been very fearsome!" [362]

These concentrated *Luftwaffe* attacks succeeded in completely removing the immediate threat against the crucial rail line and highway which connected 2. *Panzerarmee* and 9. *Armee* in the Orel Bulge with the rear. Historian Cajus Bekker wrote: "At this moment the *Luftwaffe* struck. With Stukas, which took off from Karachev, situated close to the penetration area; with bombers, fighters and *Panzerjäger*. [...]

"The result was an inevitable success. Destructive air strikes forced the Soviets to retreat. Throughout the day the Stukas of *Obstlt.* Dr. Kupfer and the *Panzerschlachtflieger* of *Hptm.* Meyer pursued the Soviet tanks as these withdrew towards the north.

"During the following days, the Soviet penetration area was cleared by ground troops. Thus the preconditions were created for the evacuation of the Orel Bulge into the so-called Hagen Line, which followed shortly afterward.

"In a wire which *Generaloberst* Model sent to express his gratitude, he stated that for the first time it had been possible to halt an enemy tank offensive through air attacks alone. Here, at Karachev between 19 and 21 July 1943, the *Luftwaffe's* intervention was absolutely decisive to prevent a second, even more disastrous Stalingrad." [363]

Finally able to catch the Soviet troops in open terrain, the airmen of 1. *Fliegerdivision* claimed to have put 135 Soviet tanks out of commission on 19 July alone. Of this number, 66 were reported as completely destroyed.

The large Soviet official work on the Battle of Kursk, Grigoriy A. Koltunov's and Boris Solovyev's 400-page *Kurskaya bitva* (published in 1970), concedes the important role played by the *Luftwaffe* to 11th Guards Army's failure to cut off the Orel Bulge: "The troops of the 11th Guards Army, and particularly the armoured forces, were exposed to extremely heavy air attacks. During the course of the offensive operations, a considerable amount of our tanks were lost. On 20 July, the 1st Tank Corps had only 33 tanks remaining." [364]

German Night Fighters over Orel

Night fighting long remained the weakest spot of the Luftwaffe on the Eastern Front. This is hardly surprising, since the new German night fighter force was primarily needed to defend the German homeland against RAF Bomber Command's increasingly effective attacks.

However, already in June 1941, a Night Fighter Command from NJG 5 commanded by Oblt. Alois Lechner had operated on the Eastern Front. Stationed at Libau, they were directed by radar. But their first operational period was not too successful. Only two Soviet aircraft were shot down – both by Lechner on 18 August 1941. Thus the unit was soon ordered back to Germany.

In late 1941, the DBA – the forerunner of Soviet ADD Long-Range aviation – shifted its operations to mainly night time. Meanwhile, the first light night bombers – U-2s, R-5s and R-Zs – went into action. This increased the requests for German night fighters, but the commencement of British 'area bombing' – which started in March 1942 with the old town of Lübeck, almost completely wiped out in a single night – prevented the transfer of new Nachtjagd units to the East. Instead, individual German fighter pilots took advantage of the bright nights in the summer of 1942 to perform sporadic night fighter missions in the East. Thus, on the night of 7/8 June 1942, III./JG 54's Oblt. Günther Fink and Lt. Hans-Joachim Heyer claimed to have shot down five R-5s. This success was repeated four night laters when III./JG 54 was accounted for the destruction of five Soviet night bombers. The most famous event during III./JG 54's brief night fighter activity took place on the night of 22/23 June 1942, when Lt. Erwin Leykauf of JG 54 blew six R-5s out of the sky with his Bf 109 F.[1] Three nights later, 662 NBAP lost two U-2s to Leykauf's Gruppenkommandeur, Hptm. Reinhard Seiler.

But Soviet nocturnal bombing steadily grew more successful. In July 1942, ADD bombers made an attempt at Hitler's life as he visited Poltava, and they also made repeated attempts to kill Generalfeldmarschall Wolfram Freiherr von Richthofen in his headquarters. Von Richthofen described some of those raids as "…very dreadful".[2] Worse was to follow in the summer of 1942, when the ADD carried out a number of very destructive raids against German air bases.[3] Meanwhile, German soldiers could testify to the effectivity of the VVS light night bomber regiments, whose single-engined biplanes deprived the Landser of their badly needed sleep.

The Germans reacted this by forming their own light night bomber units – Behelfskampfstaffeln, later designated Störkampfstaffeln – and increasing their efforts to improve their night fighter capacities. General der Flieger Josef Kammhuber, the commander of the German Night Fighter Arm, assigned the night fighter expert Major Wolfgang Falck with the task of re-organising the night fighter force in the East. After a long inspection tour, Falck suggested that volunteer crews from various Kampfgeschwader, Zerstörergeschwader and even Luftwaffe reconnaissance units should be shifted to night fighter operations and equipped with bombers armed with machine guns and 20 mm cannons and gunsights in the nose[4]

Kammhuber accepted the idea, and five Nachtjagdschwärme were formed on the Eastern Front. Uffz. Arnold Döring of 9./KG 55 reportedly claimed three TB-3 shot down with his He 111 in the Stalingrad area. But such feats remained an exception. Since these highly improvised German night fighter operations were conducted by pilots who were not trained for the task and guided in the darkness by nothing but searchlight illuminatings, overall results were disappointing.[5] Knight's Cross holder Ofw. Waldemar Teige, one of the most experienced fliers in KG 53, was lost on one of those night fighter missions.

During the Soviet winter offensive, the 2. Nachtjagdschwarm on the southern combat zone had to be committed to difficult ground-attack missions and was almost completely obliterated. The remaining crews and aircraft were incorporated with the train-hunting bomber Staffeln in January 1943. In February 1943, the three Nachtjagdschwärme on the southern and central combat zone mustered altogether no more than six He 111s, one Ju 88 C-6 and a Bf 110. In April 1943 this force was bolstered to reach a number of 28 available night fighters. Between April and June 1943 the German night fighters claimed slightly more than thirty Soviet bombers shot down in the Orel/Bryansk area. The most successful pilots were Hptm. Wolfgang Schneeweis of Nachtjagdschwarm/Luftflotte 6 who claimed 17 victories. On the southern combat zone, Ofw. Walter Engel of Nachtjagdschwarm/Luftflotte 4 claimed 11 victories. However, this was a mere pinprick and far from sufficient to have any significant effect on the increasingly effective Soviet night bombings, as we have seen in chapter 2. During the ADD's large-scale nocturnal air offensive in June 1943 against the rail line which linked Orel with the hinterland, the Nachtjagdschwarm of Luftflotte 6 had no more than three operational aircraft.

The threat which Soviet night bombers posed against the German supply system in the Orel area caused so much concern that Reichsmarschall Hermann Göring, the Luftwaffe's C-in-C, in June 1943 approved the transfer of a regular night fighter unit from Germany to the Orel area. IV./NJG 5, which previously had been

The crew of a Soviet Pe-8 four-engined heavy bomber of the ADD. Originally designed TB-7, the four-engined Petlyakov bomber was comparable to the American four-engined heavy bombers. It was equipped with four M-82 engines, rated at 1,400 horse power at take-off. Its bomb load was 6,000 kg.

responsible for the air defence of East Prussia and thus already had fought Soviet night bombers, was selected. On 26 June 1943, this unit was transferred to Luftflotte 6. Equipped with Ju 88 C-6, Do 217 J and Do 217 N night fighters, IV./NJG 5 was comprised of very experienced night fighter crews. The Gruppenkommandeur, Knight's Cross holder Hptm. Heinrich Prinz zu Sayn Wittgenstein, was regarded as one of the Luftwaffe's top night fighter aces. By this time, he had two personal Ju 88 C-6 – 'C9 + AE' and 'C9 + DE'.

Further reflecting the gravity of the situation, General Kammhuber despatched five radars mounted on a railway train to control IV./NJG 5's operations in the East.

The Luftwaffe's first aerial victory in the Kursk-Orel area on 5 July 1943 was attained by a pilot of IV./NJG 5 when a Li-2 was shot down sixteen minutes after midnight. But by this time, the radar equipment was not in place, so IV./NJG 5's operations were aided only with simple searchlight illumination. Hardly surprising, Wittgenstein's night fighters failed to reach contact with Soviet bombers more often than not during the following nights. The meagre accomplishment by IV./NJG 5 on the night of 12 July caused an outrage by Generaloberst Ritter von Greim. Although the ADD had flown nearly 550 sorties over the Orel Bulge, supplemented by 180 flights by U-2 and R-Z crews from 1 VA's 213 NBAD, the German night fighters managed to shoot down only a single Soviet bomber – an Il-4 through Wittgenstein. But with the radar sets still not available, the skies over the Orel Bulge were completely dominated by hundreds of ADD bombers during the first nights of Operation Kutuzov. On the night of 13/14 July they hit Orel's railway junction to the effect that reinforcements from the 9th Armee to the 2nd Armee became badly delayed.

IV./NJG 5 did not achieve any notable success over the Orel Bulge until on the night of 14/15 July, when the ADD hit the railway junction at Orel hard again. This time Hptm. Wittgenstein and Hptm. Alois Lechner claimed the destruction of three Soviet bombers – one of them, through the German Gruppenkommandeur, a four-engined Pe-8, 746 AP's 'Blue 12' with pilot Modestov; seven crew members were killed. [6]

On the night of 16/17 July, IV./NJG 5 flew thirteen sorties. [7] Five R-5s were claimed, including four by Oblt. Robert Landau. This was a quite remarkable feat; the slowly flying U-2s of the Soviet light night bomber regiments were a particularly difficult target because these aircraft flew slower than the stalling speed of the German night fighter planes. But again nothing was accomplished against the ADD, which wrought havoc on German troop positions, supply routes and airfields in the Orel Bulge. At Orel-East airfield, Hptm. Walter Krauss, the Gruppenkommandeur of III./StG 2, was one of the victims of an ADD bombing raid. IV./NJG 5 also sustained its first loss in this new theatre on 16 July when a Do 217 J-1 piloted by Fw. Heimann made a crash-landing.

The situation changed dramatically when radar guidance became available from the following day and onward. Finally, the so-called Himmelbett system was made operational at Orel. In each Himmelbett sector, a controller on the ground directed a single German night fighter crew towards enemy aircraft which were detected by a Würzburg-Riese radar station, called Roter Riese ('Red Gigant'). A second Würzburg-Riese radar set, called Grüner Riese ('Green Gigant') located the German night fighter. The Würzburg-Riese transmitter had a range of about 40 miles, and the air situation was plotted on a light table in the control station.

The first "Himmelbett night" – on 17/18 July – was an immediate success: IV./NJG 5 flew fourteen sorties and was credited with the destruction of eight Soviet bombers. Five new victories were logged on the night of 18/19 July. One of these was a B-25 Mitchell of the ADD's 4 GAD. Hptm. Wittgenstein chalked up two victories on the night of the 19th, followed by four more the next night. The latter however was balanced by a severe loss: Oblt. Landau crashed his Ju 88 C-6 at Bryansk and was killed. [8] But by now, IV./NJG 5 started to take control of the air over the Orel Bulge at night – chiefly due to radar guidance.

The night of 20/21 July became decisive. That night, the ADD sent 400 bombers against various targets in the Orel Bulge. [9] Wittgenstein and sixteen of his crews were airborne and waiting for them. As if Fate played a grim joke, the earphones of the German night fighters were filled with music – "…the harmonious and graceful Eine kleine Nachtmusik, evening serenade in G major". [10] Herbert Kümmritz, who with the rank of a Feldwebel served as Wittgenstein's radio operator, recalled this night:

"Clear and pure, drowned only by brief ground control orders which were, however, increasing in intensity […] the melodies from a nearby forces station inundate the consciousness of the crew directed at the battle. Irritated by the almost painful contrast between the harmonious and ethereal and the brutal and earthly, the pilot asks: 'Can't you switch the music off?' To which I, obviously more deeply influenced by the music reply almost joyfully: 'No, Herr Hauptmann, the forces station is sitting on top of our R/T frequence.'" [11]

To the tune of Mozart's peaceful music, the German night fighters took a bloody toll on the Soviet night bomber crews. 746 AP's Podpolkovnik Sergey Ushakov describes how the four-engined Pe-8 'Red 14', flown by his mate Kapitan Vladimir Ponomarenko, was shot down that night:

"When we approached the target area, there were neither searchlight beams, nor any anti-aircraft artillery fire. What could it mean? The navigator submitted his instructions and then he could be heard calling out: 'Bombs gone!'

Ponomarenko's aircraft jerked violently as it was released from its heavy cargo – one FAB-2000 and two FAB-1000s. Just as the third bomb was dropped, something struck the aircraft from the right. Vladimir involuntarily turned his head: Had the first shot really been a direct hit?

In that moment, the searchlights were switched on and the anti-aircraft artillery opened a fierce barrage. By virtue, Ponomarenko pushed the large aircraft into a left roll which brought it out of the dangerous area. Ponomarenko called the right waist gunner and asked him to report if there was any damage, but he receieved no answer. The gunner was either killed or injured.

"Comrade commander, engine No. 3 is on fire!' the top turret gunner reported. The flight engineer was heard: 'Engine No. 3 switched off. Fire extinguisher in action!'

Vladimir started to side-slip on the left wing, attempting to put out the flames through the air current. But neither this, nor the fire extinguisher had any result. Smoke started to enter the cabin, and it was obvious that the flames would reach the fuel tanks. Ponomarenko realised that he now had to think of the crew's safety so he called out:

'Bale out! Bale out immediately!'

The flames were already reaching his fur boots when he switched on the auto pilot. Suddenly the whole aircraft shuddered and shook violently – probably when the burning engine broke off and fell away…" [12]

Ponomarenko and six other crewmembers managed to parachute into Soviet-controlled territory, but five other men from the giant bomber were reported as missing. 45 AD lost two more four-engined Pe-8s that night – 'Red 15' with the crew of Kpt. Ugryumov from 746 AP, and 'Blue 14' of Kpt. Vikharev from 890 AP. [13]

All of these fell prey to Wittgenstein, who also destroyed three of 4 GAD's Mitchell bombers and an Il-4.

One of Wittgenstein's pilots, Fw. Kuntze, shot down a four-engined TB-3 of 7 GAP. This set a rather unusual feat in motion. Noticing the white parachutes of the baled out crew, and realising that the airmen would come down in hostile territory, the pilot of another of the obsolescent TB-3s, Lt. Vladimir Bezbokov, landed his aircraft in a corn field in order to pick up his comrades. Quite incredibly, Bezbokov managed not only to perform a landing in the darkness and locate the landed comrades, but he also managed to take off with the other crew on board and fly back to safety at the base. For this accomplishment, Bezbokov was awarded with the Order of the Red Banner.

In total, the German night fighters shot down twelve Soviet bombers on the night of 20/21 July 1943. It was clear that with the Himmelbett system in action, Wittgenstein's experienced night fighters had no problem covering the relatively limited area against Soviet night bombers. With the great menace from the radar guided German night fighters, it was evident to the Soviet commanders that there was no alternative to discontinuing the ADD's major operations over the Orel Bulge. The last nights showed that while performing evasive manoeuvres in order to evade the attacking night fighters, a large number of the bomber crews were unable to concentrate on their target. [14]

Thus, IV./NJG 5 contributed quite decisively to the successful German evacuation of the Orel Bulge in that delays caused by ADD bombings were prevented at the most critical stage. In total, IV./NJG 5 was credited with 49 victories during July 1943 – against only two own losses. [15] On 31 August 1943, Wittgenstein was awarded with the Oak leaves to his Knight's Cross.

1. Bergström and Mikhailov, Black Cross/Red Star: Air War Over the Eastern Front. Vol. 2, Resurgence, January – June 1942, pp. 189-190.
2. Bergström, Dikov and Antipov, Black Cross/Red Star: The Air War Over the Eastern Front. Vol. 3, Everything for Stalingrad, p. 31.
3. Ibid., p. 116.
4. Falck, Wolfgang Falck: The Happy Falcon, p. 127.
5. Interview with Adolf Galland.
6. Mir Aviatsii, 2/1997.
7. Fliegerverbindungsoffizier beim AOK 2: Luftwaffenübersicht 17.7. 1943. NARA, T-312.
8. Flugzeugunfälle und Verluste bei den (fliegenden) Verbänden (täglich), ob.d.L.Gen-Qu. Gen. 6. Abt. Bundesarchiv/Militärarchiv RL 2 III/1191.
9. Skripko, Po tselyam blizhnim i dal'nim, p. 306.
10. Roell, Laurels for Prinz Wittgenstein, p. 104.
11. Ibid., p. 105.
12. Ushakov, V interesakh vsekh frontov, pp. 139 – 140.
13. Mir Aviatsii, 2/1997.
14. TsAMO, f. 20505, op. 1, d. 4.
15. Flugzeugunfälle und Verluste bei den (fliegenden) Verbänden (täglich), ob.d.L.Gen-Qu. Gen. 6. Abt. Bundesarchiv/Militärarchiv RL 2 III/1191.

The dorsal gun turret of a Soviet Pe-8 bomber. The Pe-8's armament consisted of a twin 7.62mm ShKAS machine-gun in the spherical nose turret, a 20mm ShVAK automatic cannon in a rotating rear turret, one hand-operated 12.7mm Berezin machine-gun in the rear of each inboard engine nacelle under the wing trailing edge, and a 20mm cannon in the dorsal turret.

Russian tanks and infantry advance in a counter-offensive on the Voronezh Front moving southward towards Belgorod.

While the Western Front failed to the west of Orel, the situation for the Bryansk Front to the east of that city improved dramatically.

The *Stavka* had decided, on 13 July, to reinforce the Bryansk Front with *General-Leytenant* Pavel Rybalko's 3rd Guards Tank Army. Mustering 700 tanks and SPGs and 37,000 troops, it was hoped that this force would bring about a decision in the battle for Orel. According to the original plan, Rybalko's army would attack from the north and west to envelop Orel in conjunction with the Central Front's assault from the south. But by the time the tank army reached the battle zone, the new situation compelled the Stavka to alter its objective in the last minute. In view of the Central Front's fairly limited territorial gains in the south and the tenacious German resistance to the east of Orel, the 3rd Guards Tank Army was ordered to supplement the Bryansk Front's general assault by striking in a south-western direction towards Stanovoy Kolodez and Kromy in the 3rd Army's sector between Novosil and Mtsensk.

General-Leytenant Nikolay Naumenko's 15 VA was tasked to make an all-out effort to support the new offensive. First of all, its fighters were constantly patrolling the 3rd Guards Tank Army's assembly area. Early on 19 July, five La-5 pilots of 171 IAP intercepted a formation of Ju 87s which approached this sector, claimed two of them shot down for no losses, and forced the remainder to jettison their bombs and turn away. St.G 1 reported four Ju 87s lost – including one due to a ramming conducted by a Soviet fighter. [365]

But this was just the beginning. At 09.30 hours (Russian time) on the morning of 19 July, 200 fighters from 15 VA filled the sky above the tankmen's heads south of Mtsensk. The Soviet fighters struck down on the few German aircraft which were airborne in the area, shot down an Fw 190 and drew off the remainder. Next, 120 *Shturmoviks* and more than 100 Soviet bombers appeared and subjected the German positions to a concentrated bombardment. Ten minutes later, the 3rd Tank Army's 12th and 15th Tank corps initiated their attack, almost straight from the march. By now, 15 VA's command and control system had become considerably improved, as Grigoriy Chechelnitskiy describes in the chronicle on 15 VA:

"The offensive was supported by *Shturmoviks*, bombers and fighters. The armoured columns were assigned with air liaison officers who were in radio contact with the fighters and *Shturmoviks*. Thus, they could call in air support to suppress enemy strongpoints, to hold down the enemy, to pave the way for the tanks, to intercept Junkers aircraft and engage enemy fighters." [366]

In relentless action to support the 3rd Guards Tank Army throughout 19 July, 15 VA's 225 ShAD claimed to have destroyed 35 tanks, 130 motor vehicles, and one river ferry at Platonovo. Three hundred and sixty-seven *Luftwaffe* fighters failed to shoot down more than five of 15 VA's Il-2s and not a single bomber on this day.

Historians David M. Glantz and Jonathan M. House emphasise the importance of 15 VA's air support, which in combination with a heavy artillery barrage "…allowed the tank corps to cross the Oleshen River and to advance twelve kilometres." [368]

Meanwhile, in the southern part of the Orel Bulge, 16 VA carried out 1,222 combat sorties in support of the Central Front's troops, which managed to break through the German defence lines south of Kromy. [369] In this area, the Soviets completely dominated the air.

1. *Fliegerdivision's* units continued to be rushed from one sector to another like a fire brigade. It was impossible to meet the requests from all front sectors. After the most critical situation at Khotynets, to the west of Orel, had been temporarily saved through the commitment of most of the Stukas and *Schlacht* aircraft, the bulk of 1. *Fliegerdivision* was directed towards the east to meet the new threat from the 3rd Guards Tank Army. Although 9. *Armee* in the south desperately kept pressing for air support, Deichmann's decision to focus primarily on the eastern sector was probably the most rational thing to do. *Oblt.* Martin Vollmer of I./KG 53 describes the events of the evening of 19 July:

"*One evening mission was flown against the penetration area to the east of Orel. I can't help admiring Ivan. Wherever you fly, they have installed lots of AAA guns. Today the AAA fire was enormous. When I flew my my 40th mission today, I received a hit in the cockpit. Fortunately I carried my sun glasses, and apart from a shattered glas canopy there was no further damage.*" [370]

Under threat of being surrounded by the 3rd Guards Tank Army's offensive, the German troops in the Mtsensk sector were ordered to fall back. This compelled the *Stavka* to redirect the 3rd Guards Tank Army again. Early on 20 July, its armoured spearheads were turned towards the north-west, against the Mtsensk-Orel highway, the main German retreat route from Mtsensk. The German retreat column was subject to intense Soviet air attacks. 1. *Fliegerdivision* sent all available fighters to ward off these attacks and fierce air fighting ensued. By diving down on formations of Il-2s with fighters tied to close escort assignment, the *Jagdflieger* once again managed to give good account of themselves. By the end of the day, 1. *Fliegerdivision* reported that 29 Soviet aircraft had been shot down in air combat and another 25 by *Flak*. One of the Soviet pilots who got shot down in these aerial engagements was 32 GIAP's *Mayor* Aleksandr Fyodorov, an ace with 12 victories. With his Yak-1 set burning, Fyodorov baled out at just 75 metres altitude, and was badly hurt by the impact on the ground. He would never again be fit for combat service. [371] On 24 August 1943, Fyodorov was appointed a Hero of the Soviet Union.

However, in spite of impressive victory records, the German fighters failed to save their withdrawing ground troops from sustaining bloody losses from air attacks. In fact, in a by now classic pattern, at a high cost to themselves, the Soviet escort fighters managed to tie the German fighters into combat, allowing the *Shturmoviks* and bombers to carry out their missions without sustaining a single loss to fighter interception. The Il-2s of 225 ShAD and 3 ShAK claimed to have destroyed around 30 tanks and 100 motor vehicles on the road from Mtsensk to Orel on this 20 July.

Without underestimating the pressure from the air which the German front line troops were subjected to, it should, however, be emphasised that of far greater importance was the fact that the threat against the German rear area had been removed. The reinforced *Luftwaffe* fighter strength in the Orel Bulge had one clear strategic effect, and that was to discourage the Soviets from continuing their air attacks against the retreat routes to the rear. Moreover, the highly successful German air attacks against the Soviet forces at Karachev coincided in time with a series of nocturnal air battles in which *Luftwaffe* night fightgers under command of *Hptm.* Heinrich *Prinz* zu Sayn Wittgenstein succeeded in bringing a halt to the massive ADD bombings of the lines of communication between Orel and Bryansk.

And just as 1. *Fliegerdivision's* fighters proved unable to put an end to Soviet air attacks in daytime, 15 VA's fighters failed to provide their own ground troops with an effective air cover. *Luftwaffe* bombers, Stukas and *Schlacht* aircraft struck down on the Bryansk Front's advancing troops. As a result of these air attacks, Soviet 3rd Army – which operated on the 3rd Tank Army's northern flank - was unable to cross the Oka river to the west of Mtsensk.

Realising that the German armies were about to slip out of the trap, the *Stavka* issued another instruction to Rybalko to redirect his 3rd Tank Army in the morning of 21 July. This time the armour would veer to the south-west, aiming at Stanovoy Kolodez, with the purpose of cutting off German 35. *Armeekorps* in the area to the east of Orel.

But on this day, Rybalko's forces, which became dispersed and worn down through these repeated shifts of attack direction, were confronted with *Luftwaffe* attacks on a scale they had never encountered. Relieved of the need to save the Bryansk-Orel line at Khotynets, 1. *Fliegerdivision* was now fully concentrated its support for 35. *Armeekorps*. More than 1,500 sorties were flown. Thirty-eight tanks, 85 trucks, eight tank transporters and ten pontoon bridges were reportedly destroyed. [372]

According to German records, 13 of 1. *Fliegerdivision's* aircraft were shot down on 21 July – seven of those in air combat – while 16 Soviet aircraft were claimed. [373] 2./JG 51's *Ofw.* Josef Jennewein – the 1939 world ski champion in the Alpine Combination – was credited with five victories in less than five minutes.

During another engagement that day, III./JG 52 lost one Bf 109 in combat with Soviet fighters to the east of Orel, without any victories

submitted. Interestingly, according to a Soviet account, *M.Lt.* Druzhkin of 66 GIAP forced a Bf 109 to crash-land behind Soviet lines near Mtsensk. Seeing the German pilot jump out of his bellied aircraft and starting to run towards a nearby wood, Druzhkin reportedly landed his own fighter nearby, ran after the Bf 109 pilot and captured him, eventually handing the unhappy German over to troops of the 235th Rifle Division. [374]

It is plausible to assume that this story may be the origin of a story which circulated among *Luftwaffe* veterans after the war, and which eventually made its way into the German edition of Raymond F. Toliver's and Trevor J. Constable's book on German fighter aces: "It has been said that on one occasion the Soviet Lieutenant Vladimir D. Lavrimkov [sic] (30 victories) shot down an Me 109, which force-landed in a meadow. Next, the Soviet Lieutenant is supposed to have landed next to the Me 109 and run to the ditch where he strangled the German pilot, and after that he took off and flew away." [375] No Soviet records have been found which can confirm this incident. To the contrary – Russian veterans who flew with Vladimir Lavrinenkov (who died in 1988), such as Arkadiy Kovachevich – emphatically deny that Lavrinenkov was ever involved such an incident).

The operations on 21 July cost III./St.G 2 *Immelmann* the loss of yet another of its precious veterans, the *Staffelkapitän* of 9. *Staffel*, *Oblt.* Willi Hörner. *Hptm.* Hans-Ulrich Rudel, who succeeded *Hptm.* Krauss as the unit's *Gruppenkommandeur*, wrote:

"The string of bad luck had no end here in Orel. The *Staffelkapitän* of my 9th *Staffel* flew with his radio operator, *Oberleutnant* Hörner; he was a holder of the Knight's Cross and was among the most experienced fliers in our *Gruppe*. Having sustained hits from ground fire in the area northeast of Orel, he descended in a steep angle and crash landed in no-man's land. His aircraft stopped just short of a gully. At first I thought that he had consciously performed a forced landing, but the touchdown seemed to be quite hard. I flew past the point of impact several times but was unable to see any motion at all. Gadermann went to the front line, and with the assistance from the Army he made it to the aircraft. There was nothing to be done about the crew…" [376]

Demand was placed on every pilot and soldier on the ground. The entry for 21 July in the diary of I./KG 53's *Oblt.* Martin Vollmer reads:

"It started in the middle of the night – we were awoken at 02.00 hours – and then it was relentless action. Today we were in the air altogether more than eight hours, spread over five missions, and we dropped 176 *Zentner* [19,400 lbs.] of bombs. Actually, that is a pretty good day's result for a

Hs 129s just off on another sortie in search of Russian tanks.

single aircraft. During our first and last missions, in the twilight, we encountered anti-aircraft fire. But apart from that, we operated fairly easily today, only little resistance. But eight hours as a *Kettenhund* is more than enough." [377]

The logbook of 8./JG 51's *Lt.* Günther Schack shows three combat missions in the afternoon of 21 July: The first was flown to the east of Orel between 13.20 and 14.25 hours and resulted in no combat. The next mission, between 16.45 and 17.55 hours, led to combat with three "LaGG-3s" and three La-5s without either side sustaining any losses. At 19.15 hours, Schack took off again in his Fw 190 'Red 9', and this time he became involved in combat with La-5s north-east of Zhizdra, and shot down one for his 56th victory. [378]

Lt. Erhard Jähnert, who flew with III./St.G 3, told the author of his very vivid memories of 22 July 1943 – a day when 1. *Fliegerdivision* performed 1,386 combat sorties, mainly in the area to the east of Orel:

"On 22 July, we took off for our first mission at 06.30 hours. We still felt the exertion of two difficult missions against Russian tanks in the afternoon of the previous day, and we were all exhausted. We bombed enemy troops in a village northeast of Orel and landed at 07.15 hours. Two hours later we took off for our next mission – an attack against Russian tanks. I was so tired that I feared I was going to fall asleep in the air. After the attack, I did not climb to the assigned flight altitude. Why? Because I thought that if I flew low, I would have been so concentrated that I would not fall asleep. But this almost cost me my life. At a speed of nearly 300 km/h, the landing gear of my aircraft touched the ground. Only luck saved me from crashing. I was all shook up when I landed shortly before ten o'clock. There were two hours of rest, then we were sent into the air again, bombs hung beneath our Ju 87s, to attack Russian tanks. Again I was so close to falling asleep during the flight that I decided to strain myself with a low-level flight during the return

flight. This time my landing gear touched the ground twice before I finally reaced our new airfield at Orel North!

"When we landed, the midday sun had created an incredible heat on the airfield. I looked at the faces of all the other men. Everyone was just a dead tired as me. I reported to *Major* Hamester the *Gruppenkommandeur* When I had submitted my report, I gave voice to a very special request 'Herr Major, I request that the *Luftflotte* allows us some rest during the afternoon!' Hamester was an old hand in the *Stuka* aviation and already wore the Knight's Cross. Without uttering a word, he just turned around and walked away. But obviously my request was granted. There were no more missions that day!"

By that time, III./St.G 3 had carried out 69 dive-bombing missions in the eighteen days since 5 July 1943 – and Jähnert had participated on 57 of those. [379]

The air fighting intensified and inflicted losses during the last days of July Eleven of 1. *Fliegerdivision's* aircraft were shot down on 22 July. [380] Meanwhile 14 Soviet aircraft were claimed shot down. [381] Included among the personnel losses was *Fw.* Rudolf Gerecke of IV./JG 54. This victor in 27 aerial combats was killed in combat with four Yak fighters of 16 VA.

Soviet fighters dealt harshly with JG 51 on 23 July. I./JG 51 reported four victories against three own aircraft shot down. III./JG 51 fared even worse. In the afternoon, it clashed with 66 GIAP at 1,800 metres altitude near Mokhovaya. *Oblt.* Hermann Lücke managed to shoot down one Yak 7B. This proved to be piloted by *Lt.* Petr Vostrukhin, the leading ace of 66 GIAP, credited with 28 victories. Vostrukhin, who had celebrated his 22nd birthday only eight days previously, never got out of his descending Yak fighter. But this cost III./JG 51 dearly – three of its Fw 190s were shot down. In total, 19 of 1. *Fliegerdivision's* aircraft were shot down on 23 July. [382] In return, 18 aerial victories were reported. [383] The next day the

Introduced just in time, the Hs 129 fitted with the MK 103 was able to take part in the German offensive at Kursk. Here, armourers are busy servicing the cannon and loading ammunition. This aircraft belonged to 10.(Pz)/SG 9.

gures were nine German and eight Soviet ircraft shot down – all according to German ources. III./JG 51 lost two Fw 190s against wo victories submitted. On the Soviet side, 3 GIAP's *Lt.* Petr Ratnikov – an ace with leven personal and four shared victories on is account – was lost when he rammed an w 189 piloted by *Uffz.* Fritz Haase of NAGr 5. Three days later, another of the great aces who fought the epic air battle over Orel was ost – *Ofw.* Josef Jennewein (the correct date f his loss was 27 July, although other, rroneous dates, appear in various ublications.) Jennewein had just shot down n Il-2 – recorded as his 86th victory – when is own Fw 190 was hit by bullets. Jennewein eclared over the radio: "I am hit in the ngine, am flying towards the sun!" That was he last his comrades heard of him. The next ay, another great ace from I./JG 51, *Oblt.* oachim Brendel, was shot down in his w 190 'White 1' and wounded. Finally on 0 July, *Lt.* Otto Tange, a 68-victory ace in the *tabsstaffel*/JG 51, was shot down and killed.

But all of this was of limited importance in iew of the battle on the ground, which was urning for the better from the German point of iew. Owing much to the *Luftwaffe's* intense ction against their ground troops, the Soviets ad lost the important momentum with which hey planned to achieve their goal of urrounding and annihilating the German roops at Orel.

On the night of 22 July, 9. *Armee* began an rderly withdrawal from the sector south-east f Orel. The elements of Soviet 48th Army vhich attempted to pursue the retreating German troops in this sector were severely ampered by air attacks which were carried ut by formations of 15 to 30 bombers, Stukas nd *Schlacht* aircraft. *General der Flieger* riedrich Kless, the Chief of Staff of *Luftflotte* , wrote:

An Hs 129 makes a low-level approach to a target, while another takes up position at a higher level to observe the results of the attack.

"*As the ground troops withdrew from phase line phase line, our flying formations and Flak units continued to provide support, hough the retirement went off without many of the critical moments that had been o numerous throughout July. Luftflotte 6 concerned itself primarily with the following issions: delaying enemy pressure in direct pursuit; combating occasional incipient ncircling attempts by the pursuing Soviet armies; preventing the VVS from nterfering with the movements of our withdrawing columns; and delaying the forward novement of Russian air assets to occupy our evacuated airfields.*

"*Enemy flanking pressure from the area north-east of Karachev remained weak nd required no substantial countermeasures by* Luftflotte 6. *The chief missions were own directly over the main route of the retreat along the Bryansk-Orel highway. Later we concentrated against Soviet attempts to effect an encirclement during pursuit outh of that highway and south of Navlya. During this period, Generalfeldmarschall von Greim [the commander of Luftflotte 6] directed his ttention to the withdrawal of our flying formations behind the Desna River in an rderly fashion and to the preparations for a possible defensive battle along the river ine. All measures necessary to these tasks were carried out without friction and vithout Russian interference.*

"*The ability of Soviet aerial formations to interfere with the withdrawing troops – ven in the critical traffic center at Bryansk – was minimal, and Russian aircraft had irtually no effect to the west of the Desna.*" [384]

On 24 July, the first elements of the 'Grossdeutschland' Division arrived in he Karachev-Khotynets area, where they established a strong barrier against Bagramyan's depleted tank forces. In the east, the Bryansk Front's 3rd Army inally managed to cross the Oka river to the west of Mtsensk on 25 July, ut waves of attacking German aircraft blocked any further advance by the rmy. Meanwhile, the 3rd Guards Tank Army was transferred to the Central Front in order to support the 48th Army, which encountered great ifficulties in pursuing the withdrawing 9. *Armee*. But by the time Rybalko's ankmen were in place for this new offensive, the incessant shiftings

from one sector to another had finally worn down the army to a level where was no longer able to accomplish its mission. The Soviet analysis does not fail to confirm the role played by the *Luftwaffe* in creating this situation:

"The frequent regroupment of the Tank army's corps from one sector to another with the purpose of achieving new breakthroughs was in fact necessary for several reasons: a deeply echeloned German defence system; the enemy's persistant resistance; his frequently launched powerful counter-attacks, which received strong support from heavy tanks and large forces of bomber aircraft; a terrain which complicated operations of large armoured forces." [385]

On 28 July, the German Army High Command ordered Operation 'Herbstreise' to commence – the evacuation of the Orel Bulge. While the German first-line divisions were slowly evacuated, other forces streamed into the Orel Bulge to fill in the gaps which had been created by Bagramyan's forces to the west of Orel. In total, seventeen divisions – including ten *Panzer* or motorised divisions – arrived to bolster 2. *Panzerarmee*, which nearly doubled in size.

In his biography of Model, Walter Görlitz wrote: "As in the case with 'Büffel' [the evacuation of the Rzhev Bulge in the spring of 1943], Operation 'Herbstreise' was a very successful example of Model's leadership." [386] Two whole armies, 20,000 injured soldiers and 53,000 tons of supplies were evacuated – mainly along the critical life line from Orel to Bryansk which had been kept open chiefly due to the *Luftwaffe's* operations.

When the evacuation of the Orel Bulge was completed in early August 1943, the Battle of Kursk was over. Ultimately, it had seen two major defensive victories – one Soviet and one German. In both cases, aviation had played a crucial role.

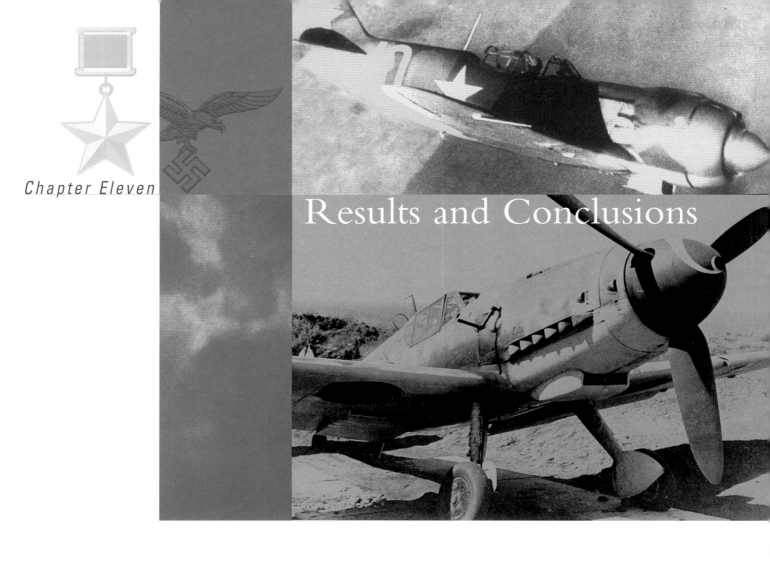

Chapter Eleven

Results and Conclusions

The battle at Kursk, Orel and Belgorod in July 1943 resulted in two defensive successes of major importance: At first, the Soviet defenders managed to prevent a strategic German breakthrough and thwart Operation *Zitadelle*. Next, the Germans were able to prevent the Red Army from surrounding and annihilating 2. *Panzerarmee* and 9. *Armee* in the Orel Bulge. In both these stages of the battle, aviation played a most important role.

When the battle commenced on 5 July 1943, both attackers and defenders were well prepared for the fight. The long German delay in launching the offensive provided the Soviets with much time to make meticulous counterpreparations. Rarely has a defender been in such a good position to act in advance precisely against the intention of an attacker. However, owing to a lack of experience at medium command level, the Soviet plans could not be adapted to the rapidly changing realities of combat during the first stages. This, in combination with the prevailing vast gap of experience between most German airmen and many VVS fliers, was the prime reason for the atrocious losses sustained by the Soviet airmen during the first days of the battle. The importance of experienced airmen is also evident from a comparison between 15 VA – whose strength had been built up rapidly through the influx of inadequately trained fliers – and 1 VA with its composition of more experienced airmen.

Another important reason for the very high Soviet losses in fighter aircraft during the Battle of Kursk was the Soviet close escort tactic, according to which VVS fighters had to fly slowly close to the Il-2s or bombers which they were tasked to escort. This was a tactic which had caused the German *Jagdgeschwader* and *Zerstörer* units appalling losses during the Battle of Britain in 1940. At a quite early stage, *Reichsmarschall* Hermann Göring, the *Luftwaffe's* C-in-C, arrived at the conclusion that 'extended fighter escort' – the sending out of fighters ahead of the bombers to clear the skies of enemy fighters – was far more effective. However, on the Eastern Front, in spite of the blood-letting among young VVS fighter pilots which these close escort missions led to, the Soviet commanders would never abandon the close escort tactic. In view of the appalling losses sustained by the Soviet bomber aviation when it flew unescorted missions against the German invaders in the summer of 1941, this stubborn attitude may actually be quite easy to understand. Moreover, as we have seen, it is a fact that Soviet fighter pilots

were often quite successful in saving their escorted bombers from sustaining heavy losses at the hands of intercepting Bf 109s or Fw 190s.

At Kursk in July 1943, the Soviet plans were more elaborate and left less to coincidence than did the German plans. The Soviet air army commanders provided their units with detailed operationl instructions which included not only the objective of the mission, but also the exact number of participating aircraft, flight altitude, instructions regarding formation flight, flight route and times for the undertaking of these air missions. Everything was prepared down to the closest detail. On the German side, aviation was provided with more general tasks ahead of the great battle. Once the battle commenced more detailed instructions were sent from *Fliegerdivision* or *Fliegerkorps* level to the various *Geschwader*, but the exact planning of how the missions were to be undertaken was made at *Geschwader*, or *Gruppe*-level.

This difference can be quite easily explained. When Germany invaded the Soviet Union in June 1941, the *Luftwaffe* had gained immense operational experience in the Spanish Civil War, and from almost two years of fighting since the invasion of Poland in September 1939. Soviet aviation had also experienced several wars – against the Japanese in the late 1930s, in the Spanish Civil War and against Finland in the Winter War of 1939-1940. However, in contrast to the *Luftwaffe*, where Göring in fact encouraged new ideas (although a popular, but largely unfounded, myth asserts the opposite), the Soviets were hobbled by the conservatism and suspicion against all new ideas which characterised Joseph Stalin's paranoid dictatorship. From 1937 and well into 1941, Stalin carried out a ruthless 'political cleansing' of the Red Army – which was originally the creation of his arch enemy, Leon Trotsky – whereby the bulk of the military intelligentsia in the Soviet Union were executed.

Stalin's political campaign against the Red Army started when the Red Army's C-in-C, *Marshal* Mikhail Tukhachevskiy, was arrested in May 1937. Under Tukhachevskiy's command, the Red Army, and particularly military aviation, rose to a high point in world ranking during the early 1930s. By 1935, the Soviet Union had the largest and most modern bomber force in the world. Meanwhile, the Soviet aviation industry created some of the best fighter aircraft, such as the I-16. But this would not save the brilliant Red Army commander, who was executed in June 1937.

That set a whole wave of purges in motion, and already by the autumn of 1938, it had deprived the Red Army of between one quarter and half of all its officers, three of five *Marshals*, thirteen of fifteen army commanders, fifty-seven of eighty-five corps commanders and 110 of 195 brigade commanders. Aviation was no exception in this regard in fact to the contrary. In the political campaign against Leon Trotsky, Arkadiy Rosengoltz, one of the first commanders of the Soviet Air Force, had been removed from his command as early as in 1924.

A total of 772 Soviet airmen took part on the Republican side in the Spanish Civil War between 1936 and 1939. Several of the most successful Soviet pilots in the first years of the war with Germany drew their first blood in the skies over Spain. The most successful, *Polkovnik* Vladimir Bobrov, claimed 13 individual and four shared victories in Spain and went on to claim a further 30 individual and 20 shared victories in the war with Germany. *Mayor* Mikhail Fedoseyev, who was one of the top scoring fighter aces in the VVS when he was killed in combat in the spring of 1942, achieved seven victories in Spain.

During the Spanish Civil War, the Soviet pilots discovered the advantages of the German *Schwarm* – 'finger-four' – fighter formation and the value of the enemy's radio-controlled ground-attack sorties. Back in Soviet Union, the High Command completely disregarded this valuable experience. An atmosphere of distrust, particularly against new thinkers met the returning Spaniards', a large number of whom actually became victims of the political purges'. Soviet fighter pilot *Polkovnik* Yevgeniy Stepanov provides some details:

"In 1939 and 1940, a number of Soviet pilots who had fought in Spain were framed and arrested, usually without being charged formally and without any kind of investigation – Feliks Arzhenukhin, [Yevgeniy] Ptukhin, [Petr] Pumpur, Emil Shakht, Pavel Proskurin and others. Most of these were executed by firing squad. Yakov Smushkevich, who had been awarded the Gold Star as a Hero of the Soviet Union on 21 June 1937, and a second Gold Star on 17 November 1939, rose to deputy commander of the Air Force, only to be arrested for treason shortly afterwards. He spent almost two years in an NKVD (*Narodnyy Komisariat Vnutrennikh Del,* or Secret Police) prison. As the invading Germans approached Moscow in October 1941, he was executed on the assumption that he might be freed by the Germans. Pavel Rychagov, a 15-victory ace of the Spanish conflict, delivered a critical speech on the state of the Air Force at the end of December 1940. He was arrested early the next year and eventually executed."[387]

Between 1937 and 1939, repressive actions were carried out against 5,616 Soviet airmen. [388] A so-called 'dual command system', with political commissars supervising all unit commanders was implemented in 1937. This prevented pilots from using their initiative at field-level.

In view of this background, it can be understood that the VVS had to catch up. Under severe pressure from the invading German armed forces, the Soviet leadership was forced to progressively back down from its conservatism and repressive control. Major modernisations of the methods used by the VVS were implemented in 1942, and in the autumn of that year the 'dual command system' was finally abolished. However, the damage which had been done prevaled for yet some time to come – not least in the minds of terrorised Soviet citizens, who had learned to suppress critical thoughts and new ideas which a political commander might regard as "challenging".

It was only at the Battle of Kursk in July 1943 – more than two years after the German invasion – that Stalin and the rulers in the Kremlin finally let go of the brakes which previously had held back the Red Army and its aviation from fully adopting the modern methods which were used by the *Luftwaffe*. It is self-evident that the lack of previous experience in implementing such new methods led to several errors being made on the Soviet side. That, in fact, also characterised the air war during the Battle of Kursk in July 1943.

The command and control of air operations from the ground is quite illustrative of this fact. Since the beginning of the war, the *Luftwaffe* had a corps of air liaison officers – by July 1943 comprised of men who were most experienced in ground-support operations. In this field, the Soviets had to learn from the beginning, at all levels. Thus, when Operation *Zitadelle*

In front of their Yak fighter, a group of Soviet fighter pilots listen attentively as one of their comrades describes how he shot down a German aircraft. in spite of very heavy losses, fighting spirits remained high among the Soviet airmen throughout the Battle of Kursk. One reason for this may have been the optimistic success reports which the Soviet fighter pilots made. Through July 1943, 2 VA's 5 IAK was credited with 484 aerial victories against own losses of 117 fighters.

A Soviet La-5FN. After the Battle of Kursk, the Soviet Air Force began to reach a level where the quality of its equipment ultimately became on par with the best of the Luftwaffe.

commenced, the Soviet air liaison officers were inexperienced, often inadequately trained for their task, sometimes deployed in the wrong areas, and on occasion even equipped with radio equipment which did not function as it should.

However, the battle at Kursk also showed a Soviet ability to rapidly adopt to new situations and improve methods even by the day – all of this in a way which, to a certain level, managed to counter-balance the negative effect of lack of experience and inadequately trained men. Examples of this were the new echeloned fighter combat tactics, which considerably improved the effectivity of Soviet fighter operations, and the employment of *Shturmoviks* in mass formations – first introduced by 16 VA's *General-Leytenant* Rudenko on the second day of the battle. The air battle at Kursk also saw, for the first time, really effective Soviet fighter escort of VVS bombers, which reduced bomber losses to neglible levels.

Without doubt, the *Wehrmacht* and the Red Army clashed with the best of what they had at Kursk in July 1943, and this is true not least in the case of aviation. The Battle of Kursk saw the first mass use of true anti-tank aviation in history. The cannon-equipped Hs 129s of the *Panzerjagdkommando* under the command of *Hptm.* Bruno Meyer – supplemented by cannon-equipped Ju 87 G Stukas as envisaged by *Hptm.* Hans-Ulrich Rudel – displayed a devastating effectiveness in action against Soviet tank formations both at Belgorod and at Orel. The fact that aircraft – with these *Panzerjäger* playing the lead role – managed to halt a whole Soviet offensive, at Khotynets, and thus save two whole armies from being surrounded, is unique in military history. On the Soviet side, the PTAB cumulative anti-tank bomb was brought into action for the first time at Kursk. This was probably an even more effective anti-tank weapon than the cannon employed by the German *Panzerjäger*. Had the Soviet airmen been better trained, and had they enjoyed the same wealth of experience as their German counterparts (*Hptm.* Rudel logged his 1,200th combat mission on 25 July 1943, which can be compared with the fact that among the 237 ShAP *Shturmovik* pilots which took off at dawn on 5 July 1943, all but two were out on their first combat mission ever), the PTAB bombs would probably have dealt an even more heavy blow against German armour at Kursk.

The fighters which clashed in the air over the battlefield in the Kursk and Orel bulges were of the highest standard on both sides. As we have seen, the most common Soviet fighters employed at Kursk – the Yak-1, Yak-7B and Yak-9, and the La-5 – were inferior to the two German fighters in action in this area by this time, the Focke-Wulf Fw 190 A and the Messerschmitt Bf 109 G. However, the best fighter on both sides was probably the new Soviet La-5FN which had been introduced shortly prior to *Zitadelle*.

The air war over Kursk marked the beginning of the end of the *Luftwaffe's* superiority in the air on the Eastern Front. Indicative of the improved quality of the Soviet fighter aviation were the mounting losses among the *Luftwaffe's* Ju 87-equipped units. The *Stukageschwader* of *Fliegerkorps* VIII sustained numerous losses almost each day during *Zitadelle* – eight Ju 87s

were shot down on 8 July, six on 9 July, six again on the 10th, seven on th 11th and eight on the 14th.

St.G 77 alone recorded 24 Ju 87s shot down and destroyed between 5 an 31 July 1943, with another 30 sustaining battle damage. [389] This amounts t around half the unit's serviceable aircraft at the time Operation *Zitadell* commenced. These figures can also be compared with the whole period o July-December 1942, when St.G 77 recorded 23 total losses due to hostil action. St.G 2 *Immelmann* lost 30 Ju 87s shot down and destroyed betwee 5 and 31 July 1943. [390]

The Battle of Kursk cost the Stuka arm the loss of eight of its mos outstanding pilots, all holders of the Knight's Cross:

Hptm. Kurt-Albert Pape, the *Staffelkapitän* of 3./St.G 1, on 7 July 1943
Hptm. Karl Fitzner of 5./St.G 77 on 8 July 1943
Hptm. Bernhard Wutka, the *Staffelkapitän* of 8./St.G 2, on 8 July 1943
Oblt. Günther Schmid, the *Staffelkapitän* of 5./St.G 2, on 14 July 1943
Major Walter Krauss, the *Gruppenkommandeur* of III./St.G 2, on 17 July 194.
Hptm. Egbert Jaekel, the *Staffelkapitän* of 2./St.G 2, on 17 July 1943
Hptm. Konrad Lorenz, the *Staffelkapitän* of 1./St.G 1, on 17 July 1943
Oblt. Willi Hörner, the *Staffelkapitän* of 7./St.G 2, on 21 July 1943

All of this reflects the increasing efficiency of the VVS fighter arm. Thre months later, the *Stukageschwader* were transformed into *Schlachtgeschwade* and most Ju 87s were phased out and exchanged for Fw 190s which a stoo greater chance against Soviet fighters.

Nevertheless, in pure fighter combat, the German advantage of having fa more experienced pilots still tipped the scale decisively during the Battle o Kursk. The relation between victories and combat losses in th *Jagdgeschwader* active during the Battle of Kursk were as follows for th period 1-31 July 1943:

JG 3 – over 400 victories against 44 Bf 109s put out of commissio due to hostile action in the air (including 28 total losses). (Figures onl for elements of JG 3 in *Fliegerkorps* VIII.)
JG 52 – over 300 victories against 43 Bf 109s put out of commissio due to hostile action in the air (including 29 total losses). (Figures onl for elements of JG 52 in *Fliegerkorps* VIII.)
JG 51 – 800 victories against 77 Fw 190s put out of commissio due to hostile action in the air (including 50 total losses). (Figures onl for elements of JG 51 in *Luftflotte* 6.)
JG 54 – 450 victories against 34 Fw 190s put out of commissio due to hostile action in the air (including 24 total losses). (Figures onl for elements of JG 54 on the Eastern Front.)

Even though it may be assumed that between one third and one quarte of these German victory claims were optimistic exaggerations, the statistic confirm a considerable German superiority in aerial combat.

Oberstleutnant Karl-Gottfried Nordmann –
seated with two members of his ground
crew – led JG 51 'Mölders' during the
Battle of Kursk. Under Nordmann's
command, JG 51 attained its 5,000th victory
during Operation 'Carmen' on 2 June 1943,
and reached No. 5,500 on 10 July 1943 and
No. 6,000 on the 27th of that month. While
claiming these 1,500 victories from 2 June
to 29 July 1943, JG 51 recorded 55 of its
own aircraft destroyed and 31 damaged
(with damage degrees of 10 % or more) as
a result of hostile action or due to
unknown causes on operations. This is
indicative of the qualitative superiority still
enjoyed by the German fighters on the
Eastern Front at this stage of the war.

Four prominent pilots of 32 GIAP walk in
front of a row of the unit's Yakovlev
fighters. From left to right: Kapitan
Aleksandr Moshin, Andrey Baklan, Ivan
Kholodov and Kapitan Sergey Dolgushin.
All four were highly acclaimed fighter
aces. This photograph was taken prior to
the Battle of Kursk in July. Moshin was
killed in air combat on 13 July 1943, having
attained a total of 19 victories.

Figures for aircraft losses during the Battle of Kursk have been subject to much dispute. It is not uncommon to find that accounts which focus on the ground war relate to the highly exaggerated Soviet figures on German aircraft losses – ranging from 'over one thousand German aircraft lost' to 3,700 German aircraft losses during the Battle. [391] Other accounts are based on German wartime figures which exaggerate Soviet losses and give figures for German aircraft losses which are lower than the reality. One frequently related source asserts that 1. *Fliegerdivision* alone claimed 1,733 victories for the loss of 64 aircraft from 5 July 1943 to mid-August 1943. The origin of the latter figure can not be established, but an examination of the loss returns to *Generalquartiermeister der Luftwaffe* shows that 1. *Fliegerdivision's* actual losses were considerably higher. [392]

The immediate daily battle reports submitted by the *Fliegerverbindungsoffizier* of 2. *Armee* is often quoted in more scholarly accounts. [393] But these figures were preliminary and do not include all losses. A comparison between Soviet claims, the figures from daily battle reports submitted by the *Fliegerverbindungsoffizier* of 2. *Armee* and the more reliable loss returns to *Generalquartiermeister der Luftwaffe* for the first four days of the battle draw an interesting picture:

Date	Fliegerkorps VIII aircraft losses			Luftflotte 6 aircraft losses			Total German aircraft losses		
	Soviet claims*	According to Flivo 2. Armee	According to Generalquartiermeister der Luftwaffe**	Soviet claims***	According to Flivo 2. Armee	According to Generalquartiermeister der Luftwaffe*	Soviet claims	According to Flivo 2. Armee	According to Generalquartiermeister der Luftwaffe*
5 July	154	19	27	106	7	18	260	26	45
6 July	105	7	11	113	7	11	218	14	22
7 July	122	10	11	96	3	8	218	13	19
8 July	106	5	9	76	2	2	182	7	11
Totals	**487**	**41**	**58**	**391**	**19**	**39**	**878**	**60**	**97**

* Only claims made by 2 VA.
** Only total losses due to hostile action in the air included.
*** Only claims made by 16 VA. [394]

Bf 109 G-6, W. Nr 15999, of I./JG 52 at Anapa in 1943. The machine carries the double chevron of the Gruppenkommandeur and may have been flown by Hptm. Helmut Bennemann or Hptm. Johannes Wiese of I./JG 52.

The corresponding figures for Soviet aircraft losses during the same period break down as follows:

Date	Soviet aircraft losses in the southern sector of the Kursk Bulge				Soviet aircraft losses in the southern sector of the Kursk Bulge (16 VA)		Actual losses sustained by 2 VA, 17 VA and 16 VA* German claims of Soviet aircraft shot down in the southern sector of the Kursk Bulge	
	Actual losses by 2 VA	Actual losses by 17 VA*	Total number of Soviet aircraft losses in the southern sector of the Kursk Bulge*	German claims of Soviet aircraft shot down in the southern sector of the Kursk Bulge	Actual losses by 16 VA	German claims of Soviet aircraft shot down in the northern sector of the Kursk Bulge		
5 July	78	80	158	260	100	165	258	425
6 July	45	45	90	74	91	130	181	204
7 July	37	50	87	96	43	81	168	177
8 July	41	10	51	43	49	73	100	116
Totals	**201**	**185**	**386**	**473**	**283**	**449**	**707**	**922**

* Estimations due to incomplete figures for 17 VA.

For the whole period 5-31 July 1943, the files of the *Generalquartiermeister der Luftwaffe* give a total of 681 *Fliegerkorps* VIII and *Luftflotte* 6 aircraft reported as put out of commission due to hostile action or unknown reasons on operations – 335 from *Fliegerkorps* VIII and 346 from *Luftflotte* 6. Of this total, 420 were completely destroyed or written off (192 from *Fliegerkorps* VIII and 229 from *Luftflotte* 6).

In return, during the same period, these formations reported 2,197 Soviet aircraft shot down (night victories not included) – 670 by *Fliegerkorps* VIII and 1,527 by *Luftflotte* 6. Interestingly, while *Fliegerkorps* VIII reported two Soviet aircraft shot down for each own aircraft which was put out of commission due to hostile action or unknown reasons on operations, the situation in *Luftflotte* 6 was twice as good from the German point of view. This is probably mainly attributable to the higher amount of overclaims whih were submitted by JG 51 and JG 54, rather than any significant difference in the qualities of the *Luftwaffe* units at *Fliegerkorps* VIII and 1. *Fliegerdivision*.

To return to the Soviet side, Soviet archive records show that 2 VA claimed to have shot down 811 enemy aircraft during the most intense phase of the battle – between 5-18 July 1943. These were spread across the various *Diviziyas* as follows:

4 IAK – 175 victories
5 IAK – 451 victories
1 ShAK – 121 victories
291 ShAD – 48 victories
1 BAK – 16 victories

However, the Soviets were aware that a substantial amount of these claims were optimistic exaggerations. The same document comments on these figures: '*Most probably the reports of 811 shot down enemy aircraft is exaggerated, since this is based on the pilots' own reports, which have not been verified by the commanders of the units or larger formations.*' [395]

The same source specifies 2 VA's aircraft losses during the same period as follows:

Aircraft type	Aircraft losses on operations		Reported missing on operations due to unknown causes	Recovered damaged on friendly territory	Aircraft irrevocably lost
	In aerial combat	To AAA fire			
Fighters	26	8	254	117	171
Shturmoviks	11	20	215	76	170
Bombers	4	3	46	22	31
Totals	41	31	515	215	372

For the whole month of July 1943, Soviet archive documents specify the statistics for 2 VA's operations as follows: [396]

Formation	Aircraft losses on operations				Enemy aircraft reported shot down
	In aerial combat	To AAA fire	Irrevocably missing on operations	Total sum of losses	
4 IAK	12	4	45	61	184
5 IAK	59	18	40	117	484
10 IAK	3	-	-	3	10
1 ShAK	44	35	20	99	196
291 ShAD	35	41	34	110	80
1 BAK	12	9	15	36	19
208 NBAD	-	-	3	3	-
454 BAP	2	1	1	4	6
Totals	167	108	158	433	979

Although the statistics for 17 VA are not as detailed as those regarding 2 VA, the following statistics for 17 VA for the period 1-31 July 1943 apply: [397]

Formation	Aircraft type	Aircraft losses on operations				Total sum of losses
		In aerial combat	To AAA fire	Irrevocably missing on operations	Destroyed on the ground through enemy action	
1 SAK	Fighters	6	-	-	-	6
	Shturmoviks	6	7	11	-	24
3 SAK	Fighters	12	6	3	2	23
	Shturmoviks	2	18	16	2	38
9 SAK	Fighters	10	3	15	-	28
	Shturmoviks	25	26	55	-	106
244 BAD	Bombers	3	8	6	-	17
262 NBAD	Bombers	-	-	2	-	2
Totals		64	68	108	4	244

In conclusion, all of this shows that according to the respective side's own loss statistics, the air war on the southern flank of the Kursk Bulge resulted in 677 Soviet and around 220 German aircraft losses.

On the northern flank of the Kursk Bulge, 16 VA was reported to have carried out 8,393 combat sorties during the defensive stage of the battle – between 5 and 12 July 1943. Of this total, 4,050 sorties were carried out by fighters, 1,181 by Shturmoviks, 984 by day bombers and 2,178 by night bombers. In the course of these operations, 16 VA claimed to have shot down 517 enemy aircraft. Own losses were 439 aircraft. [398]

In conclusion, the air war on the northern flank of the Kursk Bulge between 5-11 July 1943 – before Operation Kutuzov commenced – resulted in around 430 Soviet and 57 German aircraft losses.

During the offensive stage – from 13 July to 15 August 1943 – the air units of 16 VA performed more than 22,000 combat sorties and reported around 400 German aircraft shot down. [399] As far as Soviet losses are concerned, the offensive in the Orel area cost all participating Soviet air

formations a total loss of 1,104 aircraft between 12 July and 18 August 1943. [400]

One interesting feature of the air war during the Battle of Kursk was the 'internationalisation' of the campaign. Spanish pilots fought on both sides during the battle. Flying a Yak-7B with 2 VA, José Sánchez-Montes became the most successful Spanish fighter pilot in the Kursk battle by achieving four aerial victories before he was shot down and wounded on 13 July 1943. On the Axis side, his fellow countryman *Teniente* (*Oblt.*) Lorenzo Lucas Fernandez became 15./JG 51's – *Escuadrilla Azul* – top scorer by bringing home three victories in July 1943. In total, the Spaniards of 15./JG 51 performed 392 combat sorties – with a total of 583 flight hours – through July 1943, claiming eleven victories against three own combat losses. The French fighter pilots of the *Normandie-Niemen Eskadrilya* meanwhile claimed 22 victories against nine own losses in July 1943. The records of the Hungarian air units have proved very difficult to locate. Meticulous research by historian Csaba Becze indicates that the fighter squadron 5/1. *Vadasz század* performed 138 combat sorties and was credited with five confirmed and five unconfirmed victories in July 1943. The results for fighter squadron 5/2. *Vadasz század* are even more difficult to establish; it filed at least four claims in July 1943. [401]

Indeed, if merely loss statistics are analysed, the Soviets got the worst of the Kursk battle. The situation was similar in the ground war. According to historians Anders Frankson and Niklas Zetterling, the Soviets sustained 177,000 casualties and lost between 1,600 and 1,900 tanks during Operation *Zitadelle*, while the German loss figures were 56,000 casualties and 280 tanks irrevocably lost. [402]

However, of far greater importance than these figures was the impact of the strategic victory achieved by the Soviets. Günther Rall, one of the most outstanding German fighter aces and the *Gruppenkommandeur* of III./JG 52, asserts that the Battle of Kursk was the real turning point in the air war on the Eastern Front: "The Russians are absolutely correct when they state that the Battle of Kursk decided the outcome of the war", Rall recorded. "From then on and onward, the Russian Air Force would only grow better and better while the *Luftwaffe* went into decline. After Kursk, we all asked ourselves how we would get out of this mess." [403]

Another German fighter pilot who took part in the Kursk Battle – or at least in the Battle of the Orel Bulge – was *Obfhr.* Norbert Hannig of 5./JG 54. In his memoirs he commented on the mood after the defeat in July 1943: "A new expression was coined mocking the official communiqués which spoke reassuringly of straightening the lines and advancing to prepared defensive positions: 'Forward, comrades! We've got to pull back!'" [404]

To the VVS, the Battle of Kursk meant a decisive turning point, as *General-Leytenant* Stepan Krasovskiy, who commanded 2 VA, pointed out: "The Battle of Kursk saw the Soviet air forces successfully accomplish extremely complex tasks, starting with the fight for the domination of the air, and finishing in the participation of the pursuit of the retreating and defeated enemy armies and the battle against his operational reserves. The Battle of Kursk signified a most important milestone in the development of the application of operational and tactical forms and methods of the Soviet military aviation." [405]

By defeating the German offensive plan at Kursk, Soviet soldiers and airmen not only forced the Germans onto the defensive and compelled Hitler to abandon his plan to attack Leningrad; the initiative on the Eastern Front firmly passed to the Soviets. The Germans would spend the rest of the war reacting to the Red Army's moves. Instead of providing the Germans and those who fought on Germany's side with encouragement – which had been one of the prime intentions of Operation *Zitadelle* – the Battle of Kursk gave the Allied side in general, and the Soviets in particular, a great moral boost.

Generaloberst Heinz Guderian, the Inspector-General of the German *Panzer* troops, wrote:

"With the failure of '*Zitadelle*' we had suffered a decisive defeat. The armoured formations, reformed and re-equipped with so much effort, had lost heavily in both men and in equipment and would now be unemployable for a long time to come. It was problematical whether they could be rehabilitated in time to defend the Eastern Front... [...] Needless to say the Russians exploited their victory to the full. There were to be no more periods of quiet on the Eastern Front. From now on, the enemy was in undisputed possession of the initiative."

Hs 129s begin their decent for a low level attack on Russian armour.

Unit	Airfield	Commander	Aircraft type	Number of aircraft available*
III./KG 1	Orel-West	Hptm. Werner Kanther	Ju 88	25
Stab/KG 4		OTL Werner Klosinski	He 111	2
II./KG 4	Seshchinskaya	Major Reinhard Graubner	He 111	39
III./KG 4	Karachev	Major Kurt Neumann	He 111	42
Stab/KG 51	Bryansk	Major Hanns Heise	Ju 88	2
II./KG 51	Bryansk	Major Herbert Voss	Ju 88	44
III./KG 51	Bryansk	Hptm. Wilhelm Rath	Ju 88	21
Stab/KG 53	Olsufyevo	OTL Fritz Pockrandt	He 111	6
I./KG 53	Olsufyevo	Major Karl Rauer	He 111	35
III./KG 53	Olsufyevo	Major Emil Allmendinger	He 111	28
Stab/St.G 1	Orel-North	OTL Gustav Pressler	Ju 87, Bf 110	10
I./St.G 1	Orel-East	Hptm. Helmut Krebs	Ju 87	32
II./St.G 1	Orel-East	Hptm. Frank Neubert	Ju 87	42
III./St.G 1	Orel-East	Hptm. Friedrich Lang	Ju 87	43
III./St.G 3	Konevka	Major Bernhard Hamester	Ju 87	39
Stab/ZG 1		OTL Joachim Blechschmidt	Bf 110	4
I./ZG 1	Ledna-East	Hptm. Wilfried Hermann	Bf 110	37
Panzerjägerstaffel/ZG 1	Ledna-East		Bf 110	14
Stab/JG 51		OTL Karl-Gottfried Nordmann	--	
Stabsstaffel/JG 51	Orel	Oblt. Diethelm von Eichel-Streiber	Fw 190	16
I./JG 51	Orel	Major Erich Leie	Fw 190	40
III./JG 51	Orel	Hptm. Fritz Losigkeit	Fw 190	36
IV./JG 51	Orel	Major Rudolf Resch	Fw 190	38
15.(Span)/JG 51	Orel	Comandante Mariano Cuadra Medina	Fw 190	18
I./JG 54	Orel	Hptm. Reinhard Seiler	Fw 190	38
Stab/NAGr 4 (AOK 9)		Major Toni Vinek	Bf 109	3
1./NAGr. 4			Bf 109	15
2./NAGr. 4			Bf 109	13
3./NAGr. 4			Bf 110	8
NAGr 10 (AOK 2)		Oblt. Werner Stein	--	
1./NAGr. 10 — 3.(H)/21	Stanovka		Hs 126	9
2./NAGr. 10 — 2.(H)/31			Fw 189	9
Stab/NAGr 15 (Pz.AOK 2)	Kuznetsy	Major Hubert Correns	--	--
1.(H)/11	Oserskaya		Fw 189	10
11.(H)/12	Kuznetsy		Fw 189	8
Total number of aircraft				**726**

* Figures for 1 July 1943.

Units directly subordinated to Luftflotte 6 (Generaloberst Robert Ritter von Greim), available for operations in the Orel combat zone on 5 July 1943

Unit	Airfield	Commander	Aircraft type	Number of aircraft available*
IV./NJG 5	Seshchinskaya, Bryansk, Roslavl	Hptm. Heinrich Prinz zu Sayn Wittgenstein	Ju 88, Bf 110 and Do 217	42
FAGr 2		Major Oskar Otolsky		
2. Nachtaufklärungsstaffel (F)	Orel-West and Orsha-South		Ju 88, He 111, Do 217	11
4.(F)/11			Ju 88	10
4.(F)/14	Smolensk-North		Ju 88	14
1.(F)/100	Orel-West, Orsha-South		Ju 88, Ju 86, Ar 240	16
4.(F)/121	Seshchinskaya		Ju 88	11
Störkampfgruppen Luftflotte 6				30 (total for all
Störkampfstaffeln as below)				
1./Störkampfgruppe Luftflotte 6			Ar 66, He 46	
2./ Störkampfgruppe Luftflotte 6			Go 145	
3./Störkampfgruppe Luftflotte 6			Ar 66, Fw 58	
Stab/TG 3		OTL Fritz Schröder	-- --	
I./TG 3		Hptm. Hans-Hermann Ellerbrock	Ju 52	52
II./TG 3		Major Otto Baumann	Ju 52	52
Stab/TG 4		OTL Richard Kupschus	Ju 52	--
II./TG 4		Major Ludwig Beckmann	Ju 52	52
Transportstaffel Luftflotte 6			Ju 52	11
Verbindungskommando (S) 5			He 111, Do 17, Hs 126,	
			DFS 230	n.d.
Flugbereitschaft Luftflotte 6			Fi 156	n.d.
San.Flugbereitschaft 4			Fi 156, Ju 52	n.d.
Total number of aircraft				**301****

* Figures for 1 July 1943.
** Excluding Verbindungskommando (S) 5, Flugbereitschaft Luftflotte 6, and San.Flugbereitschaft 4.

Fliegerkorps VIII (Generalmajor Hans Seidemann) [German units]

Unit	Airfield	Commander	Aircraft type	Number of aircraft available*
Stab/KG 3		OTL Walter Lehwess-Litzmann	Ju 88	1
I./KG 3	Stalino and Poltava	Major Joachim Jödicke	Ju 88	34
II./KG 3	Poltava	Major Jürgen de Lalande	Ju 88	37
Stab/KG 27		OTL Hans-Henning Freiherr von Beust	He 111	2
I./KG 27		Hptm. Joachim Petzold	He 111	21
II./KG 27		Major Karl-August Petersen	He 111	34
III./KG 27	Kharkov-Voychenko	Hptm. Karl Mayer	He 111	34
14.(Eis.)/KG 27			He 111	10
Stab/KG 55	Kharkov-Rogan and Stalino	OTL Ernst Kühl	He 111	4
II./KG 55	Kharkov-Rogan and Stalino	Major Heinz Höfer	He 111	32
III./KG 55	Kharkov-Rogan and Stalino	Major Willi Antrup	He 111	46
14.(Eis.)/KG 55	Poltava	Oblt. Mathias Bermadinger	He 111	n.d.
I./KG 100	Poltava	Hptm. Hans-Georg Bätcher	He 111	38
Stab/St.G 2	Krestovoy	Major Ernst Kupfer	Ju 87	3
I./St.G 2	Kharkov-East	Hptm. Bruno Dilley	Ju 87	37
II./St.G 2	Kharkov-North	Hptm. Hans-Karl Stepp	Ju 87	36
III./St.G 2	Kharkov-North	Hptm. Walter Krauss	Ju 87	35
Panzerjägerstaffel/St.G 2	Kharkov-East	Oblt. Helmut Schübe	Ju 87	11
Stab/St.G 77	Tolokonnoye	Major Helmut Bruck	Ju 87	3
I./St.G 77	Tolokonnoye	Hptm. Karl Henze	Ju 87	40
II./St.G 77	Tolokonnoye	Hptm. Helmut Leicht	Ju 87	41
III./St.G 77	Kharkov-West	Major Georg Jakob	Ju 87	36
Stab/Sch.G 1	Bessonovka	Major Alfred Druschel	Fw 190	4
I./Sch.G 1	Bessonovka	Hptm. Georg Dörffel	Fw 190	52
II./Sch.G 1 (5. – 7. Staffeln)	Bessonovka	Hptm. Frank Neubert	Fw 190 (7. Staffel = Hs 123)	49 (inc. 16 Hs 123)
Pz.Jagd-Kdo/Sch.G 1 (Führer der Panzerjäger)	Zaporozhye (to Varvarovka on 8 July 1943)	Hptm. Bruno Meyer	Hs 129	4
4.(Pz)/Sch.G 1	Zaporozhye (to Varvarovka on 8 July 1943)	Oblt. Georg Dornemann	Hs 129	17
8.(Pz)/Sch.G 1	Zaporozhye (to Varvarovka on 8 July 1943)	Hptm. Rudolf-Heinz Ruffer	Hs 129	16
4.(Pz)/Sch.G 2	Zaporozhye (to Varvarovka on 8 July 1943)	Major Matuschek	Hs 129	17
8.(Pz)/Sch.G 2	Zaporozhye (to Varvarovka on 8 July 1943)	Oblt. Franz Oswald	Hs 129	10
Panzerjägerstaffel/JG 51	Zaporozhye (to Varvarovka on 8 July 1943)	Oblt. Hans Jentsch	Hs 129	15
Stab/JG 52	Bessonovka	OTL Dietrich Hrabak	Bf 109	4
I./JG 52	Bessonovka	Hptm. Johannes Wiese	Bf 109	34
II./JG 52	Kharkov-Rogan	Hptm. Gerhard Barkhorn	Bf 109	31
III./JG 52	Ugrim	Hptm. Günther Rall	Bf 109	42
II./JG 3	Kharkov-Rogan and Ugrim	Hptm. Kurt Brändle	Bf 109	33
III./JG 3	Bessonovka	Major Wolfgang Ewald	Bf 109	40
NAGr 6	Veterinar	Hptm. Heribert Rinke		
1./NAGr 6 - 1.(H)/21			Fw 189	10
2./NAGr 16			Fw 189	10
1./NAGr 2 — 4.(H)/10	Kharkov		Bf 109	13
5.(H)/32			Hs 126	9
2.(H)/33			Bf 110	8
Transportstaffel Fl.K. VIII			Ju 52	13
Flugbereitschaft Fl.K. VIII			Fi 156	n.d.
San.Flugbereitschaft 3			Fi 156 and Ju 52	n.d.
Total number of aircraft				**966***

* Figures for 1 July 1943.

*** Excluding 14.(Eis.)/KG 55, Flugbereitschaft Fl.K. VIII, and San.Flugbereitschaft 3.

Units directly subordinated to Luftflotte 4 (General der Flieger Otto Dessloch), available for operations in the Belgorod combat zone on 5 July 1943

Unit	Airfield	Commander	Aircraft type	Number of aircraft available*
FAGr 4				
		Major Hans-Dietrich Klette	--	--
1. Nachtaufklärungsstaffel (F)	Zaporozhye-South		Do 217 and He 111	12
2.(F)/22	Stalino		Ju 88	12
2.(F)/100			Ju 88	13
2.(F)/11	Kharkov		Ju 88	10
3.(F)/121			Ju 88	2
Wekusta 76	Zaporozhye		Ju 88	7
Störkampfgruppe Luftflotte 4			60 (total for all	
Störkampfstaffeln below)				
1./ Störkampfgruppe Luftflotte 4	Kharkov-North		He 46, Do 17, Hs 126	
2./ Störkampfgruppe Luftflotte 4	Kharkov-North		Ar 66, Fw 189, Ju W 34	
3./ Störkampfgruppe Luftflotte 4	Kharkov-North		Go 145	
4./ Störkampfgruppe Luftflotte 4	Kharkov-North		Ar 66, Fw 58, Ju 87	
5./ Störkampfgruppe Luftflotte 4	Kharkov-North		He 46, Hs 126, Ar 66	
6./ Störkampfgruppe Luftflotte 4	Kharkov-North		Go 145	
Total number of aircraft				**116**

* Figures for 1 July 1943.

Hungarian units subordinated to Fliegerkorps VIII

Unit	Airfield	Commander	Aircraft type	Number of aircraft available*
1. távolfelderítö osztály		Örnagy Gyula Tímár		
1/1. távolfelderítö század	Kharkov-Osnova	Százados Adorján Mersich	Ju 88	
3/1. közelfelderítö század	Kharkov-Grobly	Százados Imre Telbisz	Fw 189	12
4/1. bombázó század	Kharkov-Southeast	Százados Tihamér Ghyczy	Ju 88	
5/I. vadasz osztály	Kharkov-South	Örnagy Aladár Heppes	Bf 109	
5/1. vadasz század	Kharkov-Voychenko	Százados György Ujszászy	Bf 109	
5/2. vadasz század	Kharkov-Voychenko	Százados Gyula Horváth	Bf 109	
Total number of Hungarian aircraft: 30 bombers, 30 fighters, 12 ground-attack aircraft, and 18 reconnaissance aircraft.				

* Figures for 1 July 1943.

16 VA (General-Leytenant Sergey Rudenko): Headquarters Ukolovo

Highest formation	Subordinate Diviziyas	Airfields	Regiments	Aircraft type	Commander
6 IAK General-Mayor Andrey Yumashev HQ: Yarishche	273 IAD Polkovnik Ivan Fyodorov	Limovoye, Novoselki, Yarishche	157 IAP	Yak-1, Yak-7B, Yak-9)	Mayor Viktor Volkov
			163 IAP	(Yak-7B, Yak-9)	Podpolk. Pavel Pologov
			347 IAP	(Yak-9)	Kpt. Pavel Dankevich
	279 IAD Polkovnik Fyodor Dementyev	Mokhozoye, Kolpny	92 IAP	(La-5)	Mayor Boris Solomatin
			486 IAP	(La-5)	Mayor Pelipets
1 GIAD Stalingradskiy Polkovnik Aleksandr Utin HQ: Rzhava		Rzhava, Fatesh	30 GIAP	(Airacobra)	Mayor Ivan Khlusovich
			53 GIAP	(Yak-1)	Mayor Ivan Motornyy
			54 GIAP	(Yak-1)	Podpolk. Yevgeniy Melnikov
			55 GIAP	(Yak-1)	Mayor Vasiliy Shishkin
			67 GIAP	(Airacobra)	Podpolk. Aleksey Panov
3 BAK General-Mayor Afanasiy Karavatskiy HQ: Yelets	241 BAD Polkovnik Ivan Kurilenko	Chernovo-Pyatnitskaya	24 BAP	(Pe-2)	
			128 BAP	(Pe-2)	Podpolk. Mikhail Voronkov
			779 BAP	(Pe-2)	Podpolk. Afanasiy Khramchenkov
	301 BAD Polkovnik Fedor Fedorenko	Voronets	34 BAP	(Pe-2)	
			54 BAP	(Pe-2)	Podpolk. Mikhail Krivtsov
			96 GBAP	(Pe-2)	Aleksandr Yakobson
6 SAK General-Mayor Ivan Antoshkin HQ: Khmelnets	221 BAD Polkovnik Sergey Buzylev	Pelets, Zadonsk	8 GBAP	(A-20B)	Podpolk. G.S. Kucherkov
			57 BAP	(Boston III)	Mayor Bebchik
			745 BAP	(Boston III)	
	282 IAD Polkovnik Yuriy Berkal	Kunach	127 IAP	(Yak-1)	
			517 IAP	(Yak-1)	
			774 IAP	(Yak-1)	
283 IAD Polkovnik Sergey Denisov HQ: Mokva		Mokva	56 GIAP	(Yak-1)	Mayor Stepan Chirva
			176 IAP	(Yak-1)	Mayor Georgiy Makarov
			519 IAP	(Yak-7)	Mayor Kirill Murga
			563 IAP	(Yak-1)	
286 IAD Polkovnik Ivan Ivanov HQ: Zybino		Zybino	165 IAP	(La-5)	
			721 IAP	(La-5)	
			739 IAP	(La-5)	
			896 IAP	(Yak-1)	
299 ShAD Polkovnik Ivan Krupskiy HQ: Kr. Zariya St.		Kr. Zariya St.	41 ShAP	(Il-2)	
			217 ShAP	(Il-2)	
			218 ShAP	(Il-2)	Mayor Nikolay Lysenko
			431 ShAP	(Il-2)	Mayor Gavrilov
			874 ShAP	(Il-2)	Mayor M.G. Volkov
2 GShAD Polkovnik Georgiy Komarov HQ: Ryshkovo		Ryshkovo, Shchigry	58 GShAP	(Il-2)	Mayor Yevgeniy Koval
			59 GShAP	(Il-2)	Mayor Maksim Sklyarov
			78 GShAP	(Il-2)	Mayor Aleksandr Nakonechnikov
			79 GShAP	(Il-2)	Mayor I.D. Borodin
271 NBAD Polkovnik Konstantin Rasskazov HQ: Kazanka		Kazanka	44 GNBAP	(U-2)	
			45 GNBAP	(U-2)	
			970 NBAP	(U-2)	Mayor Nikolay Pushkaryov
			372 NBAP		Podpolk. Nikolay Chernenko
			714 NBAP		Mayor Fyodor Sushko
Regiments directly subordinate to 16 VA Headquarters			16 ORAP	(Boston III, Pe-2)	Mayor D. S. Sherstyuk
			98 GORAP		Mayor Semyon Berman
			11 UTAP		Polkovnik M.M. Kuzmin

6 VA Aircraft strength on 4 July 1943

	Serviceable	Not serviceable	Total strength
Fighters	455	71	526
Shturmoviks	241	28	269
Day bombers	260	14	274
Night bombers	74	2	76
Reconnaissance	4	2	6
Totals	**1034**	**117**	**1151**

2 VA (General-Leytenant Stepan Krasovskiy): Headquarters Spartak

Highest formation	Subordinate Diviziyas	Airfields	Regiments	Aircraft type	Commander
4 IAK **General-Mayor Ivan** **Podgornyy** **HQ: Vasilyev Dol**	294 IAD Polkovnik Vladimir Sukhoryabov	Pestunovo	183 IAP 427 IAP	(Yak-1) (Yak-1)	Mayor Andrey Oboznenko Mayor Anton Yakimenko
	302 IAD Polkovnik Boris Litvinov	Shirokiy Gul	193 IAP 240 IAP 297 IAP	(La-5) (La-5) (La-5)	G.M. Pyatakov Mayor Sergey Podorozhnyy
5 IAK **General-Mayor Dmitriy** **Galunov** **HQ: B. Psinka**	205 IAD Polkovnik Yuriy Nemtsevich	Sukho-Solotino, Kochetovka	27 IAP 438 IAP 508 IAP	(Yak-1) (Yak-1) (Yak-7B)	Mayor Vladimir Bobrov Podpolk. Yakov Utkin Podpolk. Sergey Zaychenko
8 GIAD **General-Mayor Dmitriy** **Galunov** **HQ: Trubezh/Oboyan**		Trubezh, Oboyan, Ivniya	620 IAP 40 GIAP 41 GIAP 88 GIAP	 (La-5) (La-5) (La-5)	 Mayor Moisey Tokarev Mayor Pavel Chupikov Mayor Stefan Rymsha
	1 GBAD Polkovnik Fyodor Dobysh	Ilyinka	80 GBAP 81 GBAP 82 GBAP	(Pe-2) (Pe-2) (Pe-2)	 Podpolk. Vladimir Gavrilov
1 BAK **Polkovnik Ivan Polbin** **HQ: Illovskoye**	293 BAD Polkovnik Guriy Gribakin	Trostanka, Ostrogozhsk	780 BAP 804 BAP 854 BAP 23 GBAP	(Pe-2) (Pe-2) (Pe-2) (Pe-2)	 Mayor A.M. Semyonov Mayor A.A. Novikov
	266 ShAD Polkovnik Fyodor Rodyakin	Dubkiy, Valuyki, Urazovo	66 ShAP 673 ShAP 735 ShAP	(Il-2) (Il-2) (Il-2)	Mayor V. Lavrinenko Podpolk. Aleksandr Matikov Mayor Semyon Bolodin
	292 ShAD Mayor Filipp Agaltsov	Kulma, Novyy Oskol	667 ShAP 800 ShAP 820 ShAP	(Il-2) (Il-2) (Il-2)	Mayor Grigoriy Shuteyev Mayor Anatoliy Mitrofanov Mayor I.N. Afanasyev
1 ShAK **General-Leytenant** **Vasiliy Ryazanov** **HQ: Berovkiy**	203 IAD General-Mayor Konstantin Baranchuk	Ostapovka	247 IAP 270 IAP 516 IAP	(Yak-1) (Yak-1) (Yak-1)	Podpolk. Yakov Kutikhin Mayor Vasiliy Merkushev
291 ShAD **Polkovnik Andrey Vitruk** **HQ: Shumakovo**		Shumakovo	243 ShAP 245 ShAP 313 ShAP 617 ShAP 737 IAP 954 ShAP	(Il-2) (Il-2) (Il-2) (Il-2) (Il-2)	Mayor Aleksandr Nakonechnikov Mayor I.D. Borodin Mayor Dmitriy Lomovtsev Polkovnik Nikolay Varchuk
208 NBAD **Polkovnik Leonid.** **Yuzeyev** **HQ: Kalinovka** **Regiments directly** **subordinate to 2VA** **Headquarters**		Kalinovka	646 NBAP 715 NBAP 887 NBAP 60 OKAE	 (Il-2)	Podpolk. Aleksandr Letuchiy Podpolk. I.I. Zamyatin

2 VA Aircraft strength on 4 July 1943

	Serviceable	Not serviceable	Total strength
Fighters	389	85	474
Shturmoviks	276	23	299
Day bombers	172	18	190
Night bombers	34	15	49
Reconnaissance	10	8	18
Totals	**881**	**149**	**1030**

17 VA (General-Leytenant Vladimir Sudets): Headquarters Rovenki

Highest formation	Subordinate Diviziyas	Airfields	Regiments	Aircraft type	Commander
1 SAK **General-Mayor Vladimir Shevchenko** **HQ: Rybintsevo**	288 IAD Polkovnik Boris Smirnov		659 IAP 866 IAP	(Yak-7B) (Yak-7B)	 Mayor Pyotr Ivanov
	5 GShAD Podpolk. Leonid Kolomeytsev	Novo-Pskov	93 GShAP 94 GShAP 95 GShAP	(Il-2) (Il-2) (Il-2)	
3 SAK **General-Mayor Vladimir Aladinski** **HQ: Novsosinovka**	207 IAD Polkovnik Aleksandr Osadchiy	Novsosinovka, Aleksandrovka	737 IAP 814 IAP 867 IAP 5 GIAP	(Yak-7B) (Yak-1) (Yak-1) (La-5)	Mayor Nikolay Varchuk Mayor Mikhail Kuznetsov Mayor Semyon Indyk Mayor Vasiliy Zaytsev
	290 ShAD Polkovnik Pavel Mironenko		299 ShAP 625 ShAP 775 ShAP	(Il-2) (Il-2) (Il-2)	Mayor Stepan Ananin Mayor Nikolay Zubanev
	305 ShAD Polkovnik Nikolay Mikhyevichev	Pokrovskoye, Lantratovka, Budyonnovka, Olshany, Nizhn. Duvanka	175 ShAP 237 ShAP 955 ShAP	(Il-2) (Il-2) (Il-2)	
9 SAK **General-Mayor Oleg Tolstikov** **HQ: Pokrovskoye**	306 ShAD Polkovnik Aleksandr Miklashevskiy	Budyonnovka	672 ShAP 951 ShAP 995 ShAP	(Il-2) (Il-2) (Il-2)	
	295 IAD Polkovnik Nikifor Balanov	Olshana	31 IAP 116 IAP 164 IAP	(La-5) (La-5) (La-5)	 Mayor Aleksey Melentyov
244 BAD **General-Mayor Vasiliy Klevtsov** **HQ: Belolutsk**		Belolutsk	260 BAP 449 BAP 861 BAP	(Boston) (Boston) (Boston)	 Mayor M.I. Malov Podpolk. N.A. Nikiforov
262 NBAD **Polkovnik Gennadiy Belitskiy** **HQ: Zapadnoye**		Zapadnoye, Vasilyevka	370 NBAP 97 GNBAP	(U-2) (U-2)	Podpolk. Vasilyevskiy Mayor A.B. Styazhkov
Regiments directly subordinate to 17 VA Headquarters			26 ORAP 39 ORAP Podpolk. Aleksey Fyodorov		

17 VA Aircraft strength on 4 July 1943

	Serviceable	Not serviceable	Total strength
Fighters	163	43	206
Shturmoviks	239	27	266
Day bombers	76	2	78
Night bombers	60	1	61
Reconnaissance	--	--	--
Totals	**538**	**73**	**611**

Luftflotte 4

Ju 88 D-1	W.Nr. 430710	G+LK	2.(F)/11	PQ 71/817
Pilot	Lt Schulz, Hans	missing		
Observer	Lt Wiebe, Wolfgang	missing		
Radio operator	Gefr Krebs, Alfred	missing		
Gunner	Gefr Cordes, Martin	missing		

Cause unknown. Damage 100 %.

Bf 110 G-3	W.Nr. 4913	NAGr 6	PQ 61573

Shot down by fighter. Damage 20 %.

Bf 109 G-4	W.Nr. 19732	1./NAGr. 2	Kharkov North Airfield

Technical failure. Damage 50 %.

Hs 126	W.Nr. 4261	5.(H)/32	PQ 67791
Pilot	Fw Zukrowski, Franz		
Observer	Oblt Delp, Heinz KIA		

Shot down by fighter. Damage 100 %.

Ju 88 A-14	W.Nr. 144348	4./KG 3	PQ 6179
Pilot	Fw Zimmermann, Norbert		
Observer	Uffz Liebert, August	KIA	

Hit by AAA. Damage 10 %.

Ju 88 A-4	W.Nr. 888834	4./KG 3	Poltava Airfield

Landing accident. Damage 30 %.

Ju 88 A-4	W.Nr. 144125	5./KG 3	PQ 6119

Engine damage. Damage 100 %.

He 111 H		2./KG 27	Krasnaya-Dorvov

Radio operator Uffz Drisler, Hermann wounded
Damaged by fighter. Damage 20 %.

He 111 H-6	W.Nr. 7738	2./KG 27	Yakovnevo

Damaged by fighter.

He 111 H-6	W.Nr. 4918	3./KG 27	Krasnaya-Dorvov

Shot down by fighter. Damage 20 %.

He 111 H		5./KG 27	Belgorod

Radio operator Ogefr Dittrich, Rudolf wounded
Wounded by fire from fighter.

He 111 H-16	W.Nr. 8159	III./KG 27	Belgorod
Pilot	Oblt Löwe, Johannes	KIA	
Pilot	Lt Rudel, Dankwart	KIA	
Observer	Fw Lang, Walter KIA		
Radio operator	Uffz Sarter, Fritz	KIA	
Flight engineer	Uffz Hirschmann, Emil		

Shot down by AAA. Damage 100 %.

He 111 H-16	W.Nr. 160705	III./KG 27	Kharkov-Voychenko Airfield
Pilot	Oblt Bartel, Klaus	wounded	
Pilot	Lt Wendt, Horst	wounded	
Radio operator	Uffz Thom, Eduard	wounded	

Exploded during landing. Damage 100 %.

He 111 H-16	W.Nr. 8321	6./KG 55	PQ 6156

Shot down by fighter. Damage 20 %.

He 111 H-16	W.Nr. 8468	6./KG 55	Kharkov
Observer	Uffz Müller, Walter	wounded	
Radio operator	Uffz Winkler, Heinz	wounded	
Flight engineer	Uffz Müller, Ludwig	KIA	
Gunner	Gefr Scharmacher, Gerhard	wounded	

Force-landed after getting hit by fighter. Damage 100 %.

He 111 H-16	W.Nr. 161000	G1+KP	6./KG 55	PQ 6132
Pilot	Lt Lachmann, Georg	missing		
Radio operator	Uffz Schmidt, Kurt	wounded		
Flight engineer	Obgfr Maas, Willi	wounded		

Shot down by fighter. Damage 100 %.

He 111 H-6	W.Nr. 7100	1./KG 100	Dimitriyevka
Gunner	Gefr Ebert, Richard	KIA	

Hit by fighters and Flak. Damage 45 %.

He 111 H-16	W.Nr. 8521	6N+IH	1./KG 100	East of Sumy
Pilot	Fw Kaiser, Heinz	wounded		
Observer	Obgfr Schkowski, Bruno	missing		
Radio operator	Uffz Hechtbauer, Anton	missing		
Gunner	Uffz Lethmate, Bernhard	missing		
Gunner	Obgfr Koewara, Karl	missing		

Shot down by fighters and Flak. Damage 100 %.

He 111 H-16	W.Nr. 160260	3./KG 100	Varvarovka
Pilot	Bollmann		

Hit by fighters and Flak. Damage 45 %.

Bf 109 G-4	W.Nr. 15177	II./JG 3	Kharkov

Shot down by friendly Flak. Damage 40 %.

Bf 109 G-4	W.Nr. 19965	white 11	4./JG 3	Kharkov-Rogan Airfield
Pilot	Uffz Liebmann, Helmut	wounded		

Hit by fire from Yak-1 during take-off. Damage 40 %.

Bf 109 G-4	W.Nr. 19976	black 7	5./JG 3	Volchansk
Pilot	Ofw Schütte, Josef	wounded		

Air combat. Damage 100 %.

Bf 109 G-4	W.Nr. 19323	yellow 5	6./JG 3	Belgorod
Pilot	Lt Schmidt, Friedrich Wilhelm	wounded		

Air combat.

Bf 109 G-4	W.Nr. 19302	yellow 4	6./JG 3	Belgorod
Pilot	Gefr Schilling, Hans	wounded		

Air combat. Damage 15 %.

Bf 109 G-4	W.Nr. 19220	<+I	Stab III./JG 3	PQ 6111
Pilot	Hptm Eggers, Leo	KIA		

Air combat with fighter. Pilot baled out but parachute failed to open completely.
Damage 100 %.

Bf 109 G-4	W.Nr. 14941	7./JG 3	PQ 5126
Pilot	Oblt Schleef, Hans		

Force-landed following air combat. 100 %.

Bf 109 G-4	W.Nr. 16172	7./JG 3	PQ 6138

Engine failure. Damage 20 %.

Bf 109 G-4	W.Nr. 19307	black 2	8./JG 3	PQ 613
Pilot	Uffz Lüdtke, Heinz	PoW		

Shot down by ground fire. Pilot later died of wounds. Damage 100 %.

Bf 109 G-4	W.Nr. 19969	8./JG 3	PQ 6138

Technical failure. Damage 30 %.

Bf 109 G-4	W.Nr. 14856	yellow 14	9./JG 3	Airfield Orlovka
Pilot	Uffz Kreul, Erich			

Technical failure. Damage 20 %.

Bf 109 G-4	W.Nr. 14883	9./JG 3	PQ 61182
Pilot	Fw Zibler, Emil missing		

Belly-landed in hostile territory following air combat. Damage 100 %.

Bf 109 G-6	W.Nr. 20030	I./JG 52	Airfield Bessonovka

Overturned during landing. Damage 80 %.

Bf 109 G-6 | W.Nr. 20004 | white 5 | 1./JG 52 | Tomarovka
Pilot | Ofw Maddalena, Basilio | KIA
Shot down in air combat with Pe-2. Pilot of Italian Air Force. Damage 100 %.

Bf 109 G-6 | W.Nr. 15577 | black 6 | 2./JG 52 | Belgorod
Pilot | Uffz Baumgart, Hans | missing
Air combat with 10 Il-2s. Damage 100 %.

Bf 109 G-6 | W.Nr. 20055 | | 2./JG 52
Hit by AAA. Damage 40 %.

Bf 109 G-6 | W.Nr. 20031 | yellow 7 | 3./JG 52 | Belgorod
Pilot | Uffz Hess, Edgar | KIA
Shot down in air combat. Damage 100 %.

Bf 109 G-6 | W.Nr. 20062 | white 9 | 6./JG 52 | Airfield Ugrim
Pilot | Oblt Krupinski, Walter | wounded
Overturned during landing following battle damage in air combat with fighters. Damage 80 %.

Bf 109 G-4 | W.Nr. 19709 | III./JG 52 | | Northeast of Belgorod
Pilot | Fw Schumacher, Karl | wounded
Shot down in air combat. Damage 100 %.

Bf 109 G-4 | W.Nr. 19534 | black 12 | 8./JG 52 | Ugrim
Pilot | Uffz Lotzmann, Manfred | KIA
Shot down in air combat. Damage 100 %.

Bf 109 G-4 | W.Nr. 19709 | | 8./JG 52 | Ugrim
Pilot | Uffz Leschkowitz, Martin | KIA
Cause unknown. Damage 100 %.

Bf 109 G-4 | W.Nr. 19754 | black 8 | 8./JG 52 | Belgorod
Pilot | Fw Hauswirth, Wilhelm | KIA
Shot down by Flak over hostile territory. Damage 100 %.

Bf 109 G-4 | W.Nr. 175819 | | 9./JG 52 | Zaporozhye-East Airfield
Crashed during landing. Damage 60 %.

Bf 109 G-4 | W.Nr. 19300 | yellow 3 | 9./JG 52 | Ugrim
Pilot | Fw Knehs, Walter | missing
Shot down in air combat. Damage 100 %.

Ju 87 D-3 | W.Nr. 131385 | | 1./St.G 2 | PQ 6116
Pilot | Oblt Götzfried, Franz | wounded
Radio operator | Uffz Reinler, Friedrich | wounded
Hit by Flak. Damage 70 %.

Ju 87 D-3 | W.Nr. 110300 | | 4./St.G 2 | Kharkov-North Airfield
Hit by AAA. Damage 35 %.

Ju 87 D-3 | W.Nr. 110049 | | 6./St.G 2 | PQ 61531
Hit by AAA. Damage 35 %.

Ju 87 D-3 | W.Nr. 100440 | III./St.G 2 | PQ 6119
Shot down by AAA. Damage 100 %.

Ju 87 D-5 | W.Nr. 130528 | | III./St.G 2 | PQ 67192
Shot down by AAA. Damage 100 %.

Ju 87 D-3 | W.Nr. 110341 | T6+AT | 9./St.G 2 | PQ 6116
Pilot | Uffz Merk, Karl | KIA
Radio operator | Uffz Schwarz, Jakob | KIA
Shot down by Flak. Damage 100 %.

Fw 190 A-5 | W.Nr. 155959 | | I./Sch.G 1 | PQ 153
Crashed landed due to technical failure. Damage 35 %.

Fw 190 A-5 | W.Nr. 155964 | Code +E | Stab/Sch.G 1 | Belgorod
Pilot | Fw Anders, Alfred | missing
Shot down in air combat. Damage 100 %.

Fw 190 F-3 | W.Nr. 670046 | | 1./Sch.G 1 | Varvarovka Airfield
Crashed on airfield. Damage 15 %.

Fw 190 A-5 | W.Nr. 155961 | | 2./Sch.G 1 | PQ 6158
Pilot | Oblt Zielke, Ernst | wounded
Overturned during landing. Damage 90 %.

Fw 190 A-5 | W.Nr. 155971 | | 2./Sch.G 1 | PQ 6133
Shot down by ground fire. Damage 100 %.

Fw 190 A-5 | W.Nr. 155969 | | 5./Sch.G 1 | Varvarovka
Crashed during landing. Damage 65 %.

Fw 190 F-3 | W.Nr. 670073 | | 5./Sch.G 1 | Varvarovka
Hit by AAA. Damage 40 %.

Fw 190 F-3 | W.Nr. 670038 | | 6./Sch.G 1 | Varvarovka
Hit by AAA. Damage 15 %.

Hs 123 B-1 | W.Nr. 0848 | | 7./Sch.G 1 | Varvarovka
Force-landed after getting hit by Flak fire. Damage 15 %.

Hs 123 B-1 | W.Nr. 2330 | | 7./Sch.G 1 | Varvarovka Airfield
Pilot | Lt Pingel, Konrad | wounded
Landing accident. Damage 40 %.

Luftflotte 6

He 111 H-11 | W.Nr. 110079 | | 7./KG 55 | PQ 5183
Shot down by fighters and Flak. Damage 35 %.

Fw 190 A-5 | W.Nr. 151141 | Stab/Sch.G 1 | PQ 51537
Belly-landed after running out of fuel. Damage 20 %.

Bf 109 F-2 | W.Nr. 8121 | white 18 | Stab/NAGr 4 | Pankovo Airfield
Pilot | Fw Schatzinger, Wilhelm | wounded
Crashed immediately after take-off. Damage 90 %.

Bf 109 G-4 | W.Nr. 19601 | black 2 | 2./NAGr 4 | North of Aleksandrovka
Pilot | Lt von Paczensky, Ferdinand | wounded
Shot down by fighter. Pilot baled out. Damage 100 %.

Fi 156 C-5 | W.Nr. 5021 | L8+JK | 2./NAGr 4 | Novo Trotskoye
Pilot | Fw Roth, Georg | wounded
Technical failure. Damage 50 %.

Bf 109 G-4 | W.Nr. 14779 | white 1 | NAGr 15
Pilot | Lt Jungke, Manfred | missing
Cause unknown. Damage 100 %.

Bf 110 G-2 | W.Nr. 6298 | | Stab/ZG 1 | Ledna-Ost Airfield
Crash landed due to technical failure. Damage 30 %.

Bf 110 G-2 | W.Nr. 6129 | | I./ZG 1 | Kagino
Belly-landed following engine failure. Damage 80 %.

Bf 110 D-3 | W.Nr. 4329 | | 3./ZG 1 | Ledna-East Airfield
Crash landing. Damage 20 %.

Ju 87 D-3 | W.Nr. 131138 | | Stab/St.G 1 | Ivanovka
Pilot | Oblt Goldbruch, Kurt | wounded
Force-landed after getting hit by Flak. Damage 80 %.

Ju 87 D-3 | W.Nr. 2729 | | 1./St.G 1 | Orel-West Airfield
Collided with Ju 87 D-3, W.Nr. 100011, during landing. Damage 60 %.

Ju 87 D-3	W.Nr. 100011	1./St.G 1	Orel-West Airfield

Collided with Ju 87 D-3, W.Nr. 2729, during landing. Damage 60 %.

Ju 87 D-3	W.Nr. 1314066 G+HR	4./St.G 1	Samodurovka
Pilot	Uffz Fischer, Heinz	missing	
Schüler	Uffz Rethorn, Heinz	missing	

Hit by Flak. Damage 100 %.

Ju 87 D-3	W.Nr. 100029 6G+QS	5./St.G 1	West of Verkhtagino
Pilot	Uffz Stolzenburg, Heinz	KIA	
Radio operator	Uffz Erdmann, Wilhelm	KIA	

Engine failure. Damage 100 %.

Ju 87 D-3	W.Nr. 131118 J9+DH	7./St.G 1	PQ 63534
Pilot	Uffz Heil, Heinz	missing	
Radio operator	Obgfr Schramm, Gerhard	missing	

Hit by Flak. Damage 100 %.

Ju 87 D-3	W.Nr. 2817	8./St.G 1	Orel-North Airfield
Pilot	Uffz Knepper, Kurt	KIA	
Radio operator	Obgfr Kiefer, Alfons	wounded	

Crashed following engine failure. Damage 80 %.

Ju 87 D-1	W.Nr. 2340	9./St.G 1	PQ 63543
Pilot	Oblt Rohde, Hermann	wounded	
Schüler	Fw Hupas, Adolf	wounded	

Hit by Flak. Damage 90 %.

Ju 87 D-3	W.Nr. 2627	9./St.G 1	South of Kosakovo

Force-landed. Damage 30 %.

Ju 88 A-4	W.Nr. 886745	II./KG 51	Karachev Airfield

Belly-landed after getting hit by Flak. Damage 30 %.

Ju 88 A-4	W.Nr. 888836	III./KG 51	Orel-West Airfield
Pilot	Lt Stephany, Adolf	wounded	

Crash-landed after getting hit by Flak. Damage 70 %.

Ju 88 A-14	W.Nr. 144659 V4+AS	8./KG 1	
Pilot	Oblt Michael, Hermann	KIA	
Observer	Fw Hurler, Max	KIA	
Radio operator	Fw Güller, Günther	KIA	
Gunner	Uffz Achenbach, Heinz	missing	

Mid-air explosion. Damage 100 %.

Ju 88 A-4 W.Nr. 888802		8./KG 1	Orel-West Airfield
Pilot	Lt Albert, Willi	wounded	

Belly-landed after getting hit by Flak. Damage 60 %.

He 111 H-16	W.Nr. 160563	4./KG 4	PQ 63544

Hit by AAA. Damage 40 %.

He 111 H		9./KG 4	Sabovka
Radio operator	Uffz Sonntag, Paul	KIA	

Wounded by fire from Soviet fighter.

He 111 H		I./KG 53	PQ 63548
Pilot	Lt Braukmeier, Otto	wounded	
Observer	Uffz Müller, Kurt	wounded	
Radio operator	Uffz Henke, Günther	wounded	

Wounded by fire from Soviet fighter.

He 111 H-16	W.Nr. 160516	III./KG 53	PQ 53273

Shot down by fighter. Damage 90 %.

He 111 H-16	W.Nr. 160533	8./KG 53	PQ 63572
Pilot	Uffz Mayer, Eugen	wounded	
Observer	Uffz Beuche, Herbert	missing	
Radio operator	Fw Riek, Willi	missing	
Gunner	Uffz Linssen, Herbert	missing	
Gunner	Uffz Klaus, Hans	missing	

Shot down by fighter. Damage 100 %.

Fw 190 A-4	W.Nr. 147132	1./JG 54	Panikovo Airfield

Crash landing. Damage 20 %.

Fw 190 A-4	W.Nr. 145752 yellow 8	3./JG 54	South of Malo-Arkhangelsk
Pilot	Lt Zürn, Helmut	missing	

Air combat with fighter. Pilot baled out. Damage 100 %.

Fw 190 A-5	W.Nr. 151301 yellow 12	3./JG 54	Karachev Airfield
Pilot	Uffz Raukes, Egon	KIA	

Crashed following air combat. Damage 100 %.

Fw 190 A-5	W.Nr. 157248	1./JG 51	Sloboda

Hit by AAA. Damage 20 %.

Fw 190 A-4	W.Nr. 147124	2./JG 51	PQ 63371

Technical failure. Damage 15 %.

Fw 190 A-5	W.Nr. 157210	2./JG 51	Sloboda

Hit by ground fire. Damage 30 %.

Fw 190 A-4	W.Nr. 142426 brown 7	3./JG 51	North of Malo-Arkhangelsk
Pilot	Uffz Schmitz, Hermann	KIA	

Crashed following Air combat. Pilot baled out over hostile territory. Damage 100 %.

Fw 190 A-5	W.Nr. 157353	7./JG 51	Slovitskiy

Hostile fire. Damage 80 %.

Fw 190 A-5	W.Nr. 157282 black 4	8./JG 51	South of Orel
Pilot	Fw Bracke, Walter	wounded	

Force-landed following air combat with LaGG-3. Damage 100 %.

Fw 190 A-5	W.Nr. 157284	8./JG 51	PQ 63359

Hostile fire. Damage 15 %.

Fw 190 A-5	W.Nr. 157275	10./JG 51	PQ 63392

Hostile fire. Damage 100 %.

Fw 190 A-5	W.Nr. 410030	11./JG 51	PQ 63332

Hostile fire. Damage 100 %.

Luftwaffe standard for the classification of damage

Below 10%:	Minor damage that can be repaired by the aircraft's ground crew.
10%-24%:	Medium damage that can be repaired through small repair works at the unit.
25%-39%:	Damage that requires a major overhaul at the unit.
40%-44%:	Damage to that requires whole replacements of landing gears or other systems, such as hydraulic systems.
45%-59%:	Severely damaged aircraft where large parts of the aircraft needed to be replaced.
60%-80%:	Write-off category. Certain parts could be used as spare parts for other aircraft.
81%-99%:	Totally destroyed, crashed on German-controlled area.
100%:	Totally lost, crashed or disappeared over enemy-controlled area or over sea.

The basic tactical unit of the *Luftwaffe* normally was the *Geschwader*. Each *Geschwader* was identified by a number and had a prefix according to its branch of service:

Jagdgeschwader (JG) = fighter.
Nachtjagdgeschwader (NJG) = night fighter.
Zerstörergeschwader (ZG) = heavy fighter.
Schlachtgeschwader (Sch.G., later SG) = ground-attack.
Sturzkampfgeschwader (St.G.) = dive-bomber.
Schnellkampfgeschwader (SKG) = high-speed bomber.
Kampfgeschwader (KG) = bomber.
Kampfgeschwader zu besonderen Verwendung (KG.z.b.V.) = transport (later *Transportgeschwader*, TG).
Lehrgeschwader (LG) = operational training unit (originally formed for the purpose of training unit leaders).

Several *Geschwader* were given traditional or honorary titles, such as ZG 26 *Horst Wessel* (a Nazi streetfighter 'Hero' of the 1930s).

Each *Geschwader* normally comprised three or four *Gruppen*, numbered with Roman characters:

III./JG 52 = third *Gruppe* of *Jagdgeschwader* 52.

The *Gruppe* comprised three (occasionally four) *Staffeln*, numbered with Arabic numerals:

9./JG 52 = ninth *Staffel* of *Jagdgeschwader* 52.

The exception was the Reconnaissance Wing (*Aufklärungsgruppe*), which was simply abbreviated due to its strategical (*Fernaufklärungsgruppe*) or tactical (*Heeresaufklärungsgruppe*) role. Such as: 4.(F)/122 = 4th *Staffel* of *Fernaufklärungsgruppe* 121 or 1.(H)/32 = 1st *Staffel* of *Heeresaufklärungsgruppe* 32. A particular Reconnaissance Wing was *Aufklärungsgruppe Oberbefehlshaber der Luftwaffe* (AufklObdL), which was directly subordinate to the commander of the German Air Force, *Reichsmarschall* Hermann Göring.

The fighter-*Staffel* was made up of three tactical formations, the so-called *Schwarm*.
Each *Schwarm* was made up of two basic tactical formations, the so-called *Rotte*, two aircraft.
The bomber and dive-bomber-*Staffel* was made up of four tactical formations, the so-called *Kette*, three aircraft.
Thus, the intended outfit of a *Staffel* normally was twelve aircraft.

Apart from the three *Staffeln*, the *Gruppenstab* (Staff) also had a *Stabsschwarm*.
Apart from the three or four *Gruppen*, the *Geschwaderstab* also had a *Stabsstaffel*.

The normal structure of a *Geschwader* was the following:

Stabsstaffel of the Geschwader

I. *Gruppe*:
Stabsschwarm
1. *Staffel*
2. *Staffel*
3. *Staffel*

II. *Gruppe*:
Stabsschwarm
4. *Staffel*
5. *Staffel*
6. *Staffel*

III. *Gruppe*:
Stabsschwarm
7. *Staffel*
8. *Staffel*
9. *Staffel*

IV. *Gruppe*:
Stabsschwarm
10. *Staffel*
11. *Staffel*
12. *Staffel*)

The commander of a *Geschwader* was the *Geschwaderkommodore* or *Kommodore*, which was not a rank in itself. His rank would be *Major*, *Oberstleutnant* or *Oberst*.
The commander of a *Gruppe* was the *Gruppenkommandeur* or *Kommandeur*. His rank would be *Major* or *Hauptmann*.
The commander of a *Staffel* was the *Staffelkapitän*. His rank would be *Hauptmann*, *Oberleutnant* or *Leutnant*.

Several *Geschwader* were organised into a *Fliegerkorps* (Air Corps, numbered with Roman numerals), or a *Fliegerdivision* (Air Division, numbered with Arabic numerals) or a *Fliegerführer*.
The largest tactical organisation within the German Air Force of World War II was the *Luftflotte* or *Luftwaffenkommando*, which normally comprised two *Fliegerkorps* or *Fliegerdivisionen* or *Fliegerführer*. The *Luftflotte* roughly corresponds to a numbered U.S. Army Air Force.

Organisation

In 1943, the Soviet air forces were organizationally divided between:

VVS KA (the Air Forces of Red Army). Commander: *General-Polkovnik* Aleksandr Novikov.

ADD (the Long-Range Aviation). Commander: *General-Mayor* Aleksandr Golovanov.

IA PVO (Fighter Aviation of Home Air Defense). Commander: *General-Mayor* Aleksandr Osipenko.

VVS VMF (the Naval Air Forces). Commander: *General-Leytenant* Semyon Zhavoronkov.

GVF (Civil Aviation). Chief of the Main Directorate of the GVF: *General-Leytenant* Fyodor Astakhov.

Air Armies

Since May 1942, the main higher formation of the VVS was the air army – *Vozdushnaya Armiya,* VA.

The Supreme High Command (RVGK) Reserve Aviation

The main form of the Supreme High Command (RVGK) Reserve aviation was the aviation corps and independent aviation divisions of the RVGK. From 10 September 1942, the RVGK's aviation corps – each comprised of two or three aviation divisions and between 120 and 270 aircraft - were formed. These were composite – *Smeshannyy Aviatsionnyy Korpus,* SAK – and thus comprised of various types of aviation.

IA PVO (Fighter Aviation of the Home Air Defense)

The fighter aviation corps, divisions, and regiments of the Home Air Defence were subordinated to the independent Troops of the Home Air Defence, *Voyska PVO Strany.* The *Voyska Strany* was composed of anti-aircraft artillery, searchlight units, the Troops of the VNOS (Aerial Observation, Information, and Communication) and the fighter aviation – the IA PVO.

VVS VMF (the Naval Air Forces)

The Soviet Navy had an independent air arm. The four Soviet fleets and a number of flotillas were assigned their own air forces.

GVF (Civil Aviation)

The Soviet Civil Aviation was operatively subordinated to the Peoples' Commissariat of the Defence from the outbreak of the war in June 1941. While a part of the GVF carried out civil transport flights in the rear areas, another part was mobilised for combat service. As early as July 1941, six special aviation groups of the GVF were formed on the basis of the territorial detachments of the GVF, and the personnel of these groups were conscripted into the Red Army. The main tasks of these groups were divided between transportation of military supplies and evacuation of injured soldiers, supplying partisan detachments in the enemy's rear area, and liaison flights. By the autumn of 1942, fifteen different GVF units had been brought into first-line service, all subordinated to the military councils of the fronts and armies.

From 26 April 1942, the Chief Administration of the GVF was subordinated to the C-in-C of VVS KA, while the Chief of the Main Directorate of the GVF was appointed Deputy C-in-C of VVS KA.

5.2. Tactical Formations

The basic tactical unit of the Soviet aviation was the regiment, the *Polk.* The nominal strength of a Polk normally was two nine-aircraft squadrons (*Eskadrilya*) plus a staff *Zveno* (flight) of three to four aircraft. With an increasing number of aircraft arriving from production lines, many regiments were expanded to include three *Eskadrilyas* from mid-1942.

Each *Polk* consisted of a number of *Zveno* – normally three aircraft each, piloted by the *Zveno* leader and his two wingmen.

The fighter aviation's three-aircraft *Zveno* formation was successively replaced by the four-aircraft *Zveno* from mid-1942. The fighter aviation's new four-aircraft *Zveno* was divided into two *Para* (Pair), each consisting of two aircraft – piloted by the *Para* leader and his wingman.

Generally, between two and five *Polks* formed a *Diviziya,* with all *Polks* subordinated to a certain *Diviziya* operating in a certain territorial sector.

There were also independent reconnaissance *Eskadrilyas.*

The largest Soviet aviation unit was the *Korpus* (aviation corps). The *Korpus* were the basis of the PVO and the Supreme High Command (RVGK) Reserve Aviation. Each Reserve Aviation *Korpus* was comprised of two or three aviation divisions with altogether between 120 and 270 aircraft.

Each *Korpus, Diviziya* and *Polk* had a unique number – like the *Korpus* 6 SAK, the *Diviziya* 282 IAD and the *Polk* 127 IAP. This is similar to the number system of *Wings, Groups* and *Squadrons* in the RAF or the USAAF. The *Eskadrilyas* which were subordinated to a *Polk* did not have a unique number. This is similar to the number system of *Staffeln* in the *Luftwaffe.*

Particularly distinguished Soviet military units were awarded with the honorary title *Gvardeyskiy* (Guards) units. Such a unit received a special Guards banner at a Guards Award ceremony, each of the soldiers serving in such a unit were awarded with the Guards Emblem, and its officers' ranks were prefixed "Guards" (Guards *Kapitan* etc). The unit also was renumbered into a new Guards unit, according to the order in which it had been appointed a Guards unit. Thus, for instance, after the Battle of Kursk, 775 ShAP became 110 GShAP, and 207 IAD became 11 GIAD.

The Iron Cross awards of the Wehrmacht in 1941

Das Eiserne Kreuz 2. Klasse.
The Iron Cross of Second Grade.

Das Eiserne Kreuz 1. Klasse.
The Iron Cross of First Grade.

Das Ritterkreuz des Eisernen Kreuzes.
The Knight's Cross of the Iron Cross. About 7,500 awards during World War II, including about 1,730 to servicemen of the *Luftwaffe*.

Das Ritterkreuz des Eisernen Kreuzes mit Eichenlaub.
The Knight's Cross with Oak Leaves. A total of 860 awards during World War II, including 192 to servicemen of the *Luftwaffe*.

Das Ritterkreuz des Eisernen Kreuzes mit dem Eichenlaub mit Schwertern.
The Knight's Cross with Oak Leaves and Swords. A total of 154 awards during World War II, including 41 to servicemen of the *Luftwaffe*.

Das Ritterkreuz des Eisernen Kreuzes mit dem Eichenlaub mit Schwertern und Brillanten.
The Knight's Cross with Oak Leaves, Swords and Diamonds. A total of 27 awards during World War II, including 12 to servicemen of the *Luftwaffe*.

Das Grosskreuz des Eisernes Kreuzes.
The Great Cross. Only awarded once, to *Reichsmarschall* Hermann Göring, the C-in-C of the *Luftwaffe*.

Each of the above orders could be awarded to the same individual only once.

During Operation *Barbarossa*, eight German fighter pilots and three dive-bomber pilots and one bomber aviator on the Eastern Front were awarded with the Knight's Cross with Oak Leaves, three fighter pilots were awarded with the 'Swords' and one fighter pilot – *Oberstleutnant* Werner Mölders – with the 'Diamonds'.

The highest military awards and recognitions of the Soviet Union in 1941

Orden Krasnoy Zvezdy. The Red Star Order. More than 2,860,000 awards during the wars against Germany and Japan from 1941 to 1945.

Orden Krasnogo Znameni. The Red Banner Order. More than 580,000 awards during the war.

Orden Lenina. The Lenin Order. More than 41,000 awards during the war.

Geroy Sovetskogo Soyuza. Hero of the Soviet Union. More than 11,000 men and women – 2,420 in the VVS – were appointed Heroes of the Soviet Union during the war. Of these, 104 – including 65 serving in the VVS – were appointed twice, and three – including two serving in the VVS – were appointed triple Heroes of the Soviet Union.

The appointment as a Hero of the Soviet Union was the highest recognition for courage or remarkable feats. It was no military 'award'; it was an honorary title. The men and women who were appointed Heroes of the Soviet Union were simultaneously awarded with the Lenin Order and the Golden Star Medal. The Golden Star Medal was the token of a special distinction, not an award in itself. In the few cases where individuals were appointed Heroes of the Soviet Union a second or a third time, they also were awarded with a second and a third Golden Star Medal, respectively.

Each of the above orders could be awarded to the same individual several times.

Chapter Notes

CHAPTER 1

1. Glantz and House, *The Battle of Kursk*, p. 27.
2. *Flugzeugunfälle und Verluste bei den (fliegenden) Verbänden (täglich), ob.d.L. Gen-Qu. Gen. 6. Abt.* Bundesarchiv/Militärarchiv RL 2 III/1191.
3. *Flugzeugunfälle und Verluste bei den (fliegenden) Verbänden (täglich), ob.d.L. Gen-Qu. Gen. 6. Abt.* Bundesarchiv/Militärarchiv RL 2 III/1191.
4. Plocher, *The German Air Force Versus Russia, 1943*, p. 57.

CHAPTER 2

5. Brütting, *Das waren die deutschen Kampffliegerasse 1939 – 1945*, p. 189.
6. Ibid., p. 244.
7. Skripko, *Po tselyam blizhnim i dal'nim*, p. 262.
8. Schwabedissen, *The Russian Air Force in the Eyes of German Commanders*, p. 233.
9. Skripko, p. 262.
10. *Kriegstagebuch des Oberkommandos der Wehrmacht*, 14. April 1943. *Kriegstagebuch des Oberkommandos der Wehrmacht*, vol. V, p. 328.
11. TsAMO, f. 35, op. 283235, d. 94, l. 4; Bochkaryov and Parygin. *Godyy v ognennom nebe*, p. 136.
12. *Kriegstagebuch des Oberkommandos der Wehrmacht*, 4. Mai 1943. *Kriegstagebuch des Oberkommandos der Wehrmacht*, vol. V, p. 425.
13. *Kriegstagebuch des Oberkommandos der Wehrmacht*, 5. Mai 1943. *Kriegstagebuch des Oberkommandos der Wehrmacht*, vol. V, p. 431.
14. *Flugzeugunfälle und Verluste bei den (fliegenden) Verbänden (täglich), ob.d.L. Gen-Qu. Gen. 6. Abt.* Bundesarchiv/Militärarchiv RL 2 III/1191.
15. Schwabedissen, p. 240.
16. *Flivo A.O.K. 2, Einsatzübersicht Luftw.Kdo. Ost am 7.5.43.* NARA, T-312.
17. *Luftwaffen Ic beim A.O.K. 2, Br.B.Nr. 1121/43 geh. 22.5.43.* NARA, T-312.
18. Bundesarchiv/Militärarchiv, RL 10/514.
19. *Luftwaffen Ic beim A.O.K. 2, Br.B.Nr. 1121/43 geh. 2.6.43.* NARA, T-312.
20. *Flugzeugunfälle und Verluste bei den (fliegenden) Verbänden (täglich), ob.d.L. Gen-Qu. Gen. 6. Abt.* Bundesarchiv/Militärarchiv RL 2 III/1191.
21. *Kriegstagebuch des Oberkommandos der Wehrmacht*, 3. Juni 1943. *Kriegstagebuch des Oberkommandos der Wehrmacht*, vol. V, p. 585.
22. Schwabedissen, p. 240.
23. TsAMO, f. 302, op. 20672, d. 23, l. 5.
24. *Flugzeugunfälle und Verluste bei den (fliegenden) Verbänden (täglich), ob.d.L. Gen-Qu. Gen. 6. Abt.* Bundesarchiv/Militärarchiv RL 2 III/1191.
25. Bundesarchiv/Militärarchiv, RL 10/514.
26. *Luftwaffen Ic beim A.O.K. 2, Br.B.Nr. 1121/43 geh. 10.6.43.* NARA, T-312.
27. Bundesarchiv/Militärarchiv, RL 10/131.
28. *Flugzeugunfälle und Verluste bei den (fliegenden) Verbänden (täglich), ob.d.L. Gen-Qu. Gen. 6. Abt.* Bundesarchiv/Militärarchiv RL 2 III/1191.
29. TsAMO, f. 35, op. 283235, d. 94, l. 4; Bochkaryov and Parygin. *Godyy v ognennom nebe*, p. 138.
30. Quoted in *Kursk: The German View*, p. 207.
31. *Bericht über der Einsatz der Luftflotte 6 während 'Zitadelle' und in der Schlacht im Orelbogen,* Karlsruhe Document Collection, USAF, G/VI/5a, quoted in Newton, *Kursk: The German View*, pp. 159-160.

CHAPTER 3

32. *Gefechtsbericht* Hans Grünberg, 5.7.1943. Prien and Stemmer, *II./JG 3*, p. 189.
33. Rolf Engelke, logbook.
34. Lehwess-Litzmann, *Absturz ins Leben*, p. 204.
35. Erich Hartmann, logbook.
36. TsAMO, f. 241 ShAP, op. 1, d. 9, l. 184.
37. Punka, *Messer*, pp. 32-33.
38. Khazanov and Gorbach, *Aviatsiya v bitve nad Orlovsko-Kurskoy dugoy*, p. 106.
39. TsAMO, f. 12 GIAD, op.1, d. 10.
40. *Kursk: The German View*, pp. 186-187.
41. *The Battle for Kursk 1943: The Soviet General Staff Study*, p. 269.
42. *The Battle for Kursk 1943: The Soviet General Staff Study*, p. 249.
43. Interview with Hansgeorg Bätcher.
44. Spaeter, Helmuth, *The History of Panzerkorps Grossdeutschland*, Vol. II, J. J. Fedorowicz, Winnipeg 1995, p. 116.
45. Hermann Wolf, logbook.
46. TsAMO, f. 40 GIAP.
47. *Flugzeugunfälle und Verluste bei den (fliegenden) Verbänden (täglich), ob.d.L. Gen-Qu. Gen. 6. Abt.* Bundesarchiv/Militärarchiv RL 2 III/1191.

48. Bundesarchiv/Militärarchiv, RL 10/131.
49. *Flugzeugunfälle und Verluste bei den (fliegenden) Verbänden (täglich), ob.d.L. Gen-Qu. Gen. 6. Abt.* Bundesarchiv/Militärarchiv RL 2 III/1191.
50. TsAMO, f. 12 GIAD, op.1, d. 10.
51. Interview with Nikolay Gapeyonok.
52. TsAMO, f. 302, op. 205617, d. 5, l. 5-7.
53. Prien and Stemmer, *Messerschmitt Bf 109 im Einsatz bei der III./Jagdgeschwader 3*, p. 211.
54. Dietrich Hrabak, logbook.
55. Barbas, *Die Geschichte der I. Gruppe des Jagdgeschwaders 52*, p. 209.
56. Via Niklas Zetterling.
57. Interview with Hans Krohn.
58. Via Niklas Zetterling.
59. TsAMO, f. 302, op. 4196, d. 29, l. 386-387; Khazanov and Gorbach, p. 113.
60. Kozhedub, *Vernost Otchiznye*, p. 207.
61. Lehwess-Litzmann, *Absturz ins Leben*, p. 204.
62. *The Battle for Kursk 1943: The Soviet General Staff Study*, pp. 250-251.
63. *Gefechtsbericht Hptm. Josef Haiböck, 1. Staffel JG 52. 5.7. 1943.* Bundesarchiv/Militärarchiv, RL 10/437.
64. *Gefechtsbericht Hptm. Johannes Wiese, I. Gruppe JG 52. 5.7. 1943.* Bundesarchiv/Militärarchiv, RL 10/437.
65. *Gefechtsbericht Ofw. Walter Jahnke, I. Gruppe JG 52. 5.7. 1943.* Bundesarchiv/Militärarchiv, RL 10/437.
66. Interview with Walter Krupinski.
67. Interview with Erich Hartmann.
68. Becze, *Elfelejtett Hosök*, p. 99.
69. *The Battle for Kursk 1943: The Soviet General Staff Study*, p. 245.
70. *Oblt.* Martin Vollmer, logbook.
71. Martin Vollmer, personal diary. Via Peter Vollmer.
72. Bundesarchiv/Militärarchiv, RL 7/521.
73. Interview with Gerhard Baeker.
74. Jähnert, logbook.
75. Martin Vollmer, logbook.
76. Bundesarchiv/Militärarchiv, RL 10/423.
77. *Flugzeugunfälle und Verluste bei den (fliegenden) Verbänden (täglich), ob.d.L. Gen-Qu. Gen. 6. Abt.* Bundesarchiv/Militärarchiv RL 2 III/1191.
78. Khazanov and Gorbach, p. 50.
79. Bundesarchiv/Militärarchiv, RL 10/529.
80. *The Battle for Kursk 1943: The Soviet General Staff Study*, p. 257.
81. Interview with Erhard Jähnert.
82. Erhard Jähnert, logbook.
83. *The Battle for Kursk 1943: The Soviet General Staff Study*, Ed. David M. Glantz and Harold S. Orenstein, p. 257.
84. TsAMO, f. 347 IAP, op. 239656, d. 1, l. 36.
85. Joachim Brendel, logbook.
86. Franz Eisenach, logbook.
87. *Bericht über der Einsatz der Luftflotte 6 während 'Zitadelle' und in der Schlacht im Orelbogen,* Karlsruhe Document Collection, USAF, G/VI/5a, quoted in Newton, *Kursk: The German View*, p. 164.
88. TsAMO, f. 347 IAP, op. 239656, d. 1, l. 36.
89. Erhard Jähnert, logbook.
90. Quoted in Glantz and House, *The Battle for Kursk*, p. 88.
91. Martin Vollmer, personal diary. Via Peter Vollmer.
92. Khazanov and Gorbach, p. 54.
93. Frankson and Zetterling, *Slaget om Kursk*, p. 168.
94. *Fliegerverbindungsoffizier beim AOK 2, Auszugsweise Luftwaffenübersicht.* NARA, T-312/1253.
95. Rudenko, *Kryliya Pobedyy*, p. 163.
96. TsAMO, f. 16 VA, op. 6476, d. 169.
97. TsAMO, f. 16 VA, op. 6476, d. 169.
98. Bundesarchiv/Militärarchiv, RL 7/521.
99. *Flugzeugunfälle und Verluste bei den (fliegenden) Verbänden (täglich), ob.d.L. Gen-Qu. Gen. 6. Abt.* Bundesarchiv/Militärarchiv RL 2 III/1191.

CHAPTER 4

100. Skripko, p. 295.
101. Rudenko, p. 164.
102. Koltunov and Solovyev, *Kurskaya bitva*, p. 193.
103. Kazhanov and Gorbach, p. 59.
104. *Bericht über der Einsatz der Luftflotte 6 während 'Zitadelle' und in der Schlacht im Orelbogen,* Karlsruhe Document Collection, USAF, G/VI/5a, quoted in Newton, *Kursk: The German View*, p. 165.
105. TsAMO, f. 16 VA, op. 6476, d. 169.
106. Joachim Brendel, logbook.

107. Rudenko, p. 166.
108. *Flugzeugunfälle und Verluste bei den (fliegenden) Verbänden (täglich), ob.d.L. Gen-Qu. Gen. 6. Abt.* Bundesarchiv/Militärarchiv RL 2 III/1191.
109. TsAMO, f. 368, op. 19813, d. 26, l. 14.
110. TsAMO, f. 32 GIAP.
111. TsAMO, f. 1 GIAD, op. 673880, d. 42, l. 18/42.
112. *JG 54 Archiv Günther Rosipal.*
113. Martin Vollmer, personal diary. Via Peter Vollmer.
114. *The Battle for Kursk 1943: The Soviet General Staff Study*, p. 204.
115. TsAMO, f. 16 VA, op. 6476, d. 169.
116. Bundesarchiv/Militärarchiv, RL 7/521.
117. Skripko, p. 295.
118. *Shturmovik Il-2* by Vladimir Perov and Oleg Rastrenin, special issue of *Aviatsiya i Kosmonavtika*, 5-6/2001, p. 81.
119. Martin Vollmer, personal diary. Via Peter Vollmer.
120. *The Battle for Kursk 1943: The Soviet General Staff Study*, p. 259.
121. *Bericht über der Einsatz der Luftflotte 6 während 'Zitadelle' und in der Schlacht im Orelbogen,* Karlsruhe Document Collection, USAF, G/VI/5a, quoted in *Kursk: The German View*, p. 165.
122. TsAMO, f. 16 VA.
123. *Flugzeugunfälle und Verluste bei den (fliegenden) Verbänden (täglich), ob.d.L. Gen-Qu. Gen. 6. Abt.* Bundesarchiv/Militärarchiv RL 2 III/1191.
124. Obermaier, *Die Ritterkreuzträger der Luftwaffe 1939-1945: Band II, Stuka- und Schlachtflieger*, p. 171.
125. TsAMO, f. 30 GvIAP.
126. *Shturmovik Il-2* by Vladimir Perov, Oleg Rastrenin, special issue of *Aviatsiya i Kosmonavtika*, 5-6/2001, p. 81.
127. Joachim Brendel, logbook.
128. Bundesarchiv/Militärarchiv, RL 10/423.
129. *Bericht über der Einsatz der Luftflotte 6 während 'Zitadelle' und in der Schlacht im Orelbogen,* Karlsruhe Document Collection, USAF, G/VI/5a, quoted in *Kursk: The German View*, pp. 165-166.
130. TsAMO, f. 16 VA, op. 6476, d. 169.
131. Rudenko, p. 169.
132. *Bericht über der Einsatz der Luftflotte 6 während 'Zitadelle' und in der Schlacht im Orelbogen,* Karlsruhe Document Collection, USAF, G/VI/5a, quoted in *Kursk: The German View*, pp. 165.
133. Martin Vollmer, personal diary. Via Peter Vollmer.
134. TsAMO, f. 16 VA, op. 6476, d. 169.
135. *Fliegerverbindungsoffizier beim AOK 2, Auszugsweise Luftwaffenübersicht.* NARA, T-312/1253.
136. Frankson and Zetterling, p. 180.
137. Joachim Brendel, logbook.
138. *Fliegerverbindungsoffizier beim AOK 2, Auszugsweise Luftwaffenübersicht.* NARA, T-312/1253.
139. Martin Vollmer, personal diary. Via Peter Vollmer.
140. Franz Eisenach, logbook.
141. *JG 54 Archiv Günther Roispal.*
142. *Flugzeugunfälle und Verluste bei den (fliegenden) Verbänden (täglich), ob.d.L. Gen-Qu. Gen. 6. Abt.* Bundesarchiv/Militärarchiv RL 2 III/1191.
143. TsAMO, f. 16 VA, op. 6476, d. 169.
144. Martin Vollmer, personal diary. Via Peter Vollmer.
145. Quoted in Glantz and House, p. 118.
146. TsAMO, f. 16 VA, op. 6476, d. 169.
147. *Flugzeugunfälle und Verluste bei den (fliegenden) Verbänden (täglich), ob.d.L. Gen-Qu. Gen. 6. Abt.* Bundesarchiv/Militärarchiv RL 2 III/1191.
148. TsAMO, f. 16 VA, op. 6476, d. 169.
149. *Bericht über der Einsatz der Luftflotte 6 während 'Zitadelle' und in der Schlacht im Orelbogen,* Karlsruhe Document Collection, USAF, G/VI/5a, quoted in *Kursk: The German View*, pp. 165-166.
150. Glantz and House, p. 121.

CHAPTER 5
151. *Luftwaffen Ic beim A.O.K. 2, Br.B.Nr. 1121/43 geh. 6.7.43.* NARA, T-312.
152. Khazanov and Gorbach, p. 149. See also TsAMO, f. 8GIAP, op. 1, d. 7, l. 145; and TsAMO, f. 33, op. 793756, d. 11, ll. 420-422.
153. *Flugzeugunfälle und Verluste bei den (fliegenden) Verbänden (täglich), ob.d.L. Gen-Qu. Gen. 6. Abt.* Bundesarchiv/Militärarchiv RL 2 III/1191.
154. *Fliegerverbindungsoffizier beim AOK 2: Luftwaffenübersicht 6.7. 1943.* NARA, T-312.
155. *The Battle for Kursk 1943: The Soviet General Staff Study*, p. 213.
156. von Mellenthin, *Panzer Battles*, p. 220.
157. Ibid.
158. *Fliegerverbindungsoffizier beim AOK 2: Luftwaffenübersicht 6.7. 1943.* NARA, T-312.
159. Pegg, *Hs 129 Panzerjäger*, p. 145.

160. Ibid., p. 146.
161. Dietrich Hrabak, logbook.
162. Khazanov and Gorbach, p. 134.
163. *Fliegerverbindungsoffizier beim AOK 2: Luftwaffenübersicht 6.7. 1943.* NARA, T-312.
164. *Kriegstagebuch Nr. 2, Armeeoberkommando 8 (A.Abt.Kempf).* Bundesarchiv/Militärarchiv.
165. *The Battle for Kursk 1943: The Soviet General Staff Study*, p. 213.
166. Krasovskiy, S. *Zhizn' v aviatsii*, p. 207.
167. Spaeter, *The History of Panzerkorps Grossdeutschland*, vol. II, p. 123.
168. TsAMO, f. 40 GIAP.
169. TsAMO, f. 12 GIAD, op. 1, d. 10.
170. *Flugzeugunfälle und Verluste bei den (fliegenden) Verbänden (täglich), ob.d.L. Gen-Qu. Gen. 6. Abt.* Bundesarchiv/Militärarchiv RL 2 III/1191.
171. Glantz and House, p. 127.
172. TsAMO, f. 370, op. 46569, d. 4, l. 38.
173. TsAMO, f. 5 GIAP.
174. Glantz and House, p. 127.
175. Khazanov and Gorbach, p. 135.
176. TsAMO, f. 12 GIAD, op. 1, d. 10.
177. *Flugzeugunfälle und Verluste bei den (fliegenden) Verbänden (täglich), ob.d.L. Gen-Qu. Gen. 6. Abt.* Bundesarchiv/Militärarchiv RL 2 III/1191.
178. Via Nikita Yegorov.
179. TsAMO, f. 306 ShAD, op. 1, d. 14, l. 22.
180. Yevstigneyev, *Krylataya gvardiya*, pp. 97-99.
181. TsAMO, f. 40 GIAP.
182. Pegg, p. 149.
183. Ibid.
184. Günther Rall, logbook.
185. *Flugzeugunfälle und Verluste bei den (fliegenden) Verbänden (täglich), ob.d.L. Gen-Qu. Gen. 6. Abt.* Bundesarchiv/Militärarchiv RL 2 III/1191.
186. Plocher, p. 96.
187. Pegg, p. 149.
188. Glantz and House, p. 135.
189. Glantz and House, p. 134.
190. *Flugzeugunfälle und Verluste bei den (fliegenden) Verbänden (täglich), ob.d.L. Gen-Qu. Gen. 6. Abt.* Bundesarchiv/Militärarchiv RL 2 III/1191.
191. *The Battle for Kursk 1943: The Soviet General Staff Study*, p. 265.
192. Interview with Günther Rall.
193. Interview with Edmund Rossmann.
194. Glantz and House, p. 143.
195. Günther Rall, logbook.
196. Rolf Engelke, logbook.
197. *Flugzeugunfälle und Verluste bei den (fliegenden) Verbänden (täglich), ob.d.L. Gen-Qu. Gen. 6. Abt.* Bundesarchiv/Militärarchiv RL 2 III/1191.
198. Rolf Engelke, logbook.
199. Kozhedub, pp. 207-208.
200. Kozhedub, personal notes - victory list.
201. *Flugzeugunfälle und Verluste bei den (fliegenden) Verbänden (täglich), ob.d.L. Gen-Qu. Gen. 6. Abt.* Bundesarchiv/Militärarchiv RL 2 III/1191.
202. Rall, *Mein Flugbuch*, p. 166.
203. TsAMO, f. 129 GIAP.
204. TsAMO, f. 370, op. 46569, d. 4, l. 40.

CHAPTER 6
205. Quoted in Koltunov and Solovyev, p. 130.
206. TsAMO, f. 16 VA, op. 6476, d. 169.
207. TsAMO, f. 6 IAK, op. 1, d. 6, l. 10.
208. Joachim Brendel, logbook.
209. *Prussakov, 16-ya Vozdushnaya*, p. 98.
210. *Flugzeugunfälle und Verluste bei den (fliegenden) Verbänden (täglich), ob.d.L. Gen-Qu. Gen. 6. Abt.* Bundesarchiv/Militärarchiv RL 2 III/1191.
211. Skripko, p. 297.
212. *Anlage zum KTB Gen.Kdo. XXIII Armeekorps, Abt. Ia, Schriftwechsel und Allgemeines (Luftlagen) Gen.Kdo. XXIII. Armeekorps, Flivo op., Korpsgefechtsstand 11.7.1943.* NARA, T-314/689.
213. Khazanov and Gorbach, p. 86.
214. Prussakov, p. 99.
215. Khazanov and Gorbach, p. 87.
216. *Flugzeugunfälle und Verluste bei den (fliegenden) Verbänden (täglich), ob.d.L. Gen-Qu. Gen. 6. Abt.* Bundesarchiv/Militärarchiv RL 2 III/1191.
217. TsAMO, f. 368, op. 6476, d. 54, ll. 9-10. Quoted in Khazanov and Gorbach, p. 91.
218. Khazanov and Gorbach, p. 92.
219. Prussakov, p. 100.
220. Ibid.; *The Battle for Kursk 1943: The Soviet General Staff Study*, p. 260.

CHAPTER 7

221. Skripko, p. 297.
222. Report from Division *Grossdeutschland*. Via Niklas Zetterling.
223. von Mellenthin, p. 226.
224. TsAMO, f. 12 GIAD, op.1, d. 10.
225. Rolf Engelke, logbook.
226. Kozhedub, pp. 208–210.
227. TsAMO, f. 129 GIAP.
228. Via Niklas Zetterling.
229. Account by Willi Rogmann. Via Walter Schüle/Martin Månsson.
230. Samchuk and Skachko, *Atakuiyet desantniki,* p. 27. Quoted in Glantz and House, p. 173.
231. Günther Rall, logbook.
232. *Flugzeugunfälle und Verluste bei den (fliegenden) Verbänden (täglich), ob.d.L. Gen-Qu. Gen. 6. Abt.* Bundesarchiv/Militärarchiv RL 2 III/1191.
233. TsAMO, f. 586 IAP, op. 196818, d. 11.
234. *Flugzeugunfälle und Verluste bei den (fliegenden) Verbänden (täglich), ob.d.L. Gen-Qu. Gen. 6. Abt.* Bundesarchiv/Militärarchiv RL 2 III/1191.
235. *Fliegerverbindungsoffizier beim AOK 2: Luftwaffenübersicht 11. 7. 1943.* NARA, T-312.
236. Glantz and House, p. 135.
237. Skripko, p. 301.
238. *Fliegerverbindungsoffizier beim AOK 2: Luftwaffenübersicht 12. 7. 1943.* NARA, T-312.
239. TsAMO, f. 302, op. 20671, d. 4.
240. TsAMO, f. 370, op. 40360, d. 2.
241. Stadler, *Die Offensive gegen Kursk 1943; II. SS-Panzerkorps als Stosskeil im Grosskampf,* p. 102.
242. Via Niklas Zetterling.
243. Via Niklas Zetterling.
244. Kravchenko and Burkov, *Desiyatyy tankovyy Dneprovskiy,* p. 92.
245. Glantz and House, p. 185.
246. Rudel, *Trotzdem,* p. 83.
247. TsAMO, f. 332, op. 4948, d. 70, l. 146; Khazanov and Gorbach, p. 165.
248. Khazanov and Gorbach, p. 165.
249. Carell, *Verbrannte Erde,* p. 68.
250. TsAMO, f. 332, op. 4948, d. 70, l. 146; Khazanov and Gorbach, p. 165.
251. TsAMO, f. 332, op. 4948, d. 1, l. 10; Khazanov and Gorbach, p. 165.
252. TsAMO, f. 332, op. 4948, d. 70, l. 146; Khazanov and Gorbach, p. 165.
253. *Flugzeugunfälle und Verluste bei den (fliegenden) Verbänden (täglich), ob.d.L. Gen-Qu. Gen. 6. Abt.* Bundesarchiv/Militärarchiv RL 2 III/1191.
254. TsAMO, f. 12 GIAD, op.1, d. 10.
255. Stadler, p. 102.
256. Rall, *Mein Flugbuch,* p. 169.
257. *Flugzeugunfälle und Verluste bei den (fliegenden) Verbänden (täglich), ob.d.L. Gen-Qu. Gen. 6. Abt.* Bundesarchiv/Militärarchiv RL 2 III/1191.
258. Frankson and Zetterling, p. 217.
259. von Mellenthin, p. 228.
260. Glantz and House, p. 204.

CHAPTER 8

261. Gnezdilov, *Na vysotakh muzhestva,* p. 102.
262. Koltunov and Solovyev, p. 204.
263. Joachim Brendel, logbook.
264. TsAMO, f. 32 GIAP.
265. Gnezdilov, p. 103.
266. TsAMO, f. 208, op. 2511, d. 2340, l. 132.
267. Erhard Jähnert, logbook.
268. TsAMO, f. 1 GvIAK, op. 517117, d. 1, l. 11.
269. *Luftwaffen Ic beim A.O.K. 2, Br.B.Nr. 1121/43 geh. 12.7.43.* NARA, T-312.
270. TsAMO, f. 420, op. 11057, d. 371, l. 77.
271. Koltunov and Solovyev, p. 213.
272. *Luftwaffen Ic beim A.O.K. 2, Br.B.Nr. 1121/43 geh. 12.7.43.* NARA, T-312.
273. TsAMO, f. 1 GvIAK, op. 517117, d. 1, l. 12.
274. *Flugzeugunfälle und Verluste bei den (fliegenden) Verbänden (täglich), ob.d.L. Gen-Qu. Gen. 6. Abt.* Bundesarchiv/Militärarchiv RL 2 III/1191.
275. *Luftwaffen Ic beim A.O.K. 2, Br.B.Nr. 1121/43 geh. 12.7.43.* NARA, T-312.
276. Bundesarchiv/Militärarchiv, RL 10/529.
277. Bagramyan, *Tak shli myy k pobede,* p. 211.
278. *Bericht über der Einsatz der Luftflotte 6 während 'Zitadelle' und in der Schlacht im Orelbogen,* Karlsruhe Document Collection, USAF, G/VI/5a, quoted in Newton, *Kursk: The German View,* p. 169.
279. Pinchuk, *V vozdukhe – 'Yaki',* p. 48.
280. TsAMO, f. 1 VA, op. 3308, d. 19.

281. *Flugzeugunfälle und Verluste bei den (fliegenden) Verbänden (täglich), ob.d.L. Gen-Qu. Gen. 6. Abt.* Bundesarchiv/Militärarchiv RL 2 III/1191.
282. Pinchuk, p. 49.
283. TsAMO, f. 18 GIAP.
284. TsAMO, f. 18 GIAP.
285. *Flugzeugunfälle und Verluste bei den (fliegenden) Verbänden (täglich), ob.d.L. Gen-Qu. Gen. 6. Abt.* Bundesarchiv/Militärarchiv RL 2 III/1191.
286. Via Nikita Yegorov.
287. TsAMO, f. 32 GIAP.
288. *Flugzeugunfälle und Verluste bei den (fliegenden) Verbänden (täglich), ob.d.L. Gen-Qu. Gen. 6. Abt.* Bundesarchiv/Militärarchiv RL 2 III/1191.
289. Via Nikita Yegorov.
290. TsAMO, f. 1 GvIAK, op. 517117, d. 1, ll. 11-12.
291. Chechelnitskiy, *Lyotchiki na voyne,* pp. 80-82.
292. *Luftwaffen Ic beim A.O.K. 2, Flivo – AOK 2 A.H.Qu. 13.7. 1943. Auszugsweise Luftwaffenübersicht.* NARA, T-312.
293. *Flugzeugunfälle und Verluste bei den (fliegenden) Verbänden (täglich), ob.d.L. Gen-Qu. Gen. 6. Abt.* Bundesarchiv/Militärarchiv RL 2 III/1191.
294. Skripko, p.302.
295. Hannig, *Luftwaffe Fighter Ace,* pp. 84–85.
296. Bagramyan, p. 226.
297. *Flugzeugunfälle und Verluste bei den (fliegenden) Verbänden (täglich), ob.d.L. Gen-Qu. Gen. 6. Abt.* Bundesarchiv/Militärarchiv RL 2 III/1191.
298. TsAMO, f. 1 VA, op. 3308, d. 19.
299. Bundesarchiv/Militärarchiv, RL 10/488.
300. Koltunov and Solovyev, p. 219.
301. *Luftwaffen Ic beim A.O.K. 2, Flivo – AOK 2 A.H.Qu. 14.7. 1943. Auszugsweise Luftwaffenübersicht.* NARA, T-312.
302. TsAMO, f. 290, op. 19011, d. 4.
303. Gnezdilov, p. 103.
304. TsAMO, f. 1 VA, op. 3308, d. 19.
305. Zakharov, *Ya – istrebitel, Voyenizdat,* p. 191.
306. Görlitz, *Model,* pp. 151 and 153.
307. *Oblt.* Martin Vollmer, logbook.
308. TsAMO, f. 18 GIAP.
309. Martin Vollmer, personal diary. Via Peter Vollmer.
310. TsAMO, f. 1 VA, op. 3308, d. 19.
311. *Flugzeugunfälle und Verluste bei den (fliegenden) Verbänden (täglich), ob.d.L. Gen-Qu. Gen. 6. Abt.* Bundesarchiv/Militärarchiv RL 2 III/1191.
312. *Flugzeugunfälle und Verluste bei den (fliegenden) Verbänden (täglich), ob.d.L. Gen-Qu. Gen. 6. Abt.* Bundesarchiv/Militärarchiv RL 2 III/1191.
313. Günther Rall, logbook.
314. Interview with Erich Hartmann.
315. *Flugzeugunfälle und Verluste bei den (fliegenden) Verbänden (täglich), ob.d.L. Gen-Qu. Gen. 6. Abt.* Bundesarchiv/Militärarchiv RL 2 III/1191.
316. *Luftwaffen Ic beim A.O.K. 2, Flivo – AOK 2 A.H.Qu. 14.7. 1943. Auszugsweise Luftwaffenübersicht.* NARA, T-312.
317. Bundesarchiv/Militärarchiv, RL 7/521.
318. Prussakov, pp. 107–108.
319. Zakharov, p. 192.

CHAPTER 9

320. Carell, p. 79.
321. Carell, p. 76.
322. *Kriegstagebuch Nr. 2 Armeeoberkommando 8 (A.Abt. Kempf) vom 1. Juli 1943 bis 31. Dezember 1943.* Bundesarchiv/Militärarchiv.
323. Meroño, *Aviadores Españoles en la Gran Guerra Patria,* pp. 213-214.
324. *Fliegerverbindungsoffizier beim AOK 2: Luftwaffenübersicht 13.7. 1943.* NARA, T-312.
325. Skripko, p. 302.
326. Hansgeorg Bätcher, logbook.
327. *Flugzeugunfälle und Verluste bei den (fliegenden) Verbänden (täglich), ob.d.L. Gen-Qu. Gen. 6. Abt.* Bundesarchiv/Militärarchiv RL 2 III/1191.
328. Khazanov and Gorbach, p. 170.
329. *Fliegerverbindungsoffizier beim AOK 2: Luftwaffenübersicht 16.7. 1943.* NARA, T-312.
330. *Flugzeugunfälle und Verluste bei den (fliegenden) Verbänden (täglich), ob.d.L. Gen-Qu. Gen. 6. Abt.* Bundesarchiv/Militärarchiv RL 2 III/1191.

CHAPTER 10

331. *Fliegerverbindungsoffizier beim AOK 2: Luftwaffenübersicht 6.7. 1943.* NARA, T-312.
332. Skripko p. 304.
333. *Anlage zum KTB Gen.Kdo. XXIII. Armeekorps, Abt. Ia, Schriftwechsel und Allgemeines (Luftlagen) Gen.Kdo. XXIII. Armeekorps, Flivo op., Korpsgefechtsstand 17.7.43, Luftlage.* NARA, T-314/689.
334. Pegg, *Hs 129 Panzerjäger!,* p. 150.

335. Schwabedissen, *The Russian Air Force in the Eyes of German Commanders*, p. 201.
336. *JG 54 Archiv Günther Rosipal.*
337. Erhard Jähnert, logbook.
338. *Flugzeugunfälle und Verluste bei den (fliegenden) Verbänden (täglich), ob.d.L. Gen-Qu. Gen. 6. Abt.* Bundesarchiv/Militärarchiv RL 2 III/1191.
339. *Flugzeugunfälle und Verluste bei den (fliegenden) Verbänden (täglich), ob.d.L. Gen-Qu. Gen. 6. Abt.* Bundesarchiv/Militärarchiv RL 2 III/1191.
340. Prussakov, p. 108.
341. TsAMO, f. 368, op. 6512, l. 37, d. 7.
342. Timokhovich, *Sovyetskaya aviatsiya v bitve pod Kurskom*, p. 91.
343. TsAMO, f. 225 ShAD, op. 126712, d. 1, l. 55-57.
344. TsAMO, f. 225 ShAD, op. 25002, d. 5, l. 209.
345. Bundesarchiv/Militärarchiv, RL 10/488.
346. Skripko p. 304.
347. Chechelnitskiy, p. 91.
348. Schwabedissen, p. 201.
349. Gnezdilov, p. 107.
350. TsAMO, f. 368, op. 6776, d. 101, l. 5-6.
351. Rudel, p. 88.
352. Gnezdilov, p. 109.
353. TsAMO, f. 18 GIAP.
354. Martin Vollmer, personal diary. Via Peter Vollmer.
355. Günther Rall, logbook.
356. *Flugzeugunfälle und Verluste bei den (fliegenden) Verbänden (täglich), ob.d.L. Gen-Qu. Gen. 6. Abt.* Bundesarchiv/Militärarchiv RL 2 III/1191.
357. *Anlage zum KTB Gen.Kdo. XXIII Armeekorps, Abt. Ia, Schriftwechsel und Allgemeines (Luftlagen) Gen.Kdo. XXIII. Armeekorps, Flivo op., Korpsgefechtsstand 18.7.1943.* NARA, T-314/689.
358. Pegg, p. 151.
359. Ibid., p. 152.
360. Ibid.
361. Erhard Jähnert, logbook.
362. Interview with Hans Krohn.
363. Bekker, *Angriffshöhe 4000*, pp. 389-390.
364. Koltunov and Solovyev, p. 228.
365. *Flugzeugunfälle und Verluste bei den (fliegenden) Verbänden (täglich), ob.d.L. Gen-Qu. Gen. 6. Abt.* Bundesarchiv/Militärarchiv RL 2 III/1191.
366. Chechelnitskiy, p. 93.
367. TsAMO, f. 225 ShAD, op. 25002, d. 5, l. 228.
368. Glantz and House, p. 236.
369. Prussakov, p. 112.
370. Martin Vollmer, personal diary. Via Peter Vollmer.
371. TsAMO, f. 33, op. 793756, d. 50, ll. 66-67.
372. *Fliegerverbindungsoffizier beim AOK 2: Luftwaffenübersicht 21.7. 1943.* NARA, T-312.
373. *Flugzeugunfälle und Verluste bei den (fliegenden) Verbänden (täglich), ob.d.L. Gen-Qu. Gen. 6. Abt.* Bundesarchiv/Militärarchiv RL 2 III/1191.
374. Timokhovich, p. 93.
375. Toliver and Constable, *Das waren die deutschen Jagdfliegerasse 1939-1945*, p. 415.
376. Rudel, p. 88.
377. Martin Vollmer, personal diary. Via Peter Vollmer.
378. Günther Schack, logbook.
379. Erhard Jähnert, logbook.
380. *Flugzeugunfälle und Verluste bei den (fliegenden) Verbänden (täglich), ob.d.L. Gen-Qu. Gen. 6. Abt.* Bundesarchiv/Militärarchiv RL 2 III/1191.
381. *Fliegerverbindungsoffizier beim AOK 2: Luftwaffenübersicht 22.7. 1943.* NARA, T-312.
382. *Flugzeugunfälle und Verluste bei den (fliegenden) Verbänden (täglich), ob.d.L. Gen-Qu. Gen. 6. Abt.* Bundesarchiv/Militärarchiv RL 2 III/1191.
383. Bundesarchiv/Militärarchiv, RL 7/521.
384. *Bericht über der Einsatz der Luftflotte 6 während 'Zitadelle' und in der Schlacht im Orelbogen*, Karlsruhe Document Collection, USAF, G/VI/5a, quoted in *Kursk: The German View*, pp. 172-173.
385. Koltunov and Solovyev, p. 228.
386. Görlitz, p. 155.

CHAPTER 11

387. *The History Net*, July 1997.
388. Andersson, *Soviet Aircraft and Aviation 1917 – 1941*, p. 25.
389. *Flugzeugunfälle und Verluste bei den (fliegenden) Verbänden (täglich), ob.d.L. Gen-Qu. Gen. 6. Abt.* Bundesarchiv/Militärarchiv RL 2 III/1191.
390. *Flugzeugunfälle und Verluste bei den (fliegenden) Verbänden (täglich), ob.d.L. Gen-Qu. Gen. 6. Abt.* Bundesarchiv/Militärarchiv RL 2 III/1191.
391. Zjukov, *Minnen och reflexioner*, p. 182.
392. *Flugzeugunfälle und Verluste bei den (fliegenden) Verbänden (täglich), ob.d.L. Gen-Qu. Gen. 6. Abt.* Bundesarchiv/Militärarchiv RL 2 III/1191.
393. *Fliegerverbindungsoffizier beim AOK 2, Auszugsweise Luftwaffenübersicht.* NARA, T-312/1253.
394. TsAMO, f. 16 VA, op. 6476, d. 169.
395. Report by *Polkovnik* M.N. Kostin, Senior officer of the General Staff attached to the Voronezh Front, on the defensive operations of the Voronezh Front between 4 and 23 July 1943. TsAMO, f. 203, op. 2843, d. 515a, l. 1.57.
396. TsAMO, f. 302, op. 4196, d. 27.
397. TsAMO, f. 370, op. 6518, d. 87, l. 65. Quoted in Khazanov and Gorbach, p. 189.
398. Khazanov and Gorbach, p. 92.
399. TsAMO, f. 368, op. 6476, d. 102, ll. 6, 41.
400. Krivosheyev, *Grif sekretnosti snyat: Poteri Vooruzhyonnykh Sil SSSR v voynakh, boyevykh deystviyakh i voyennykh konfliktakh.*
401. Via Csaba Becze.
402. Frankson and Zetterling, pp. 220-221.
403. Interview with Günther Rall.
404. Hannig, p. 85.
405. Koltunov and Solovyev, p. 365.

Sources and Bibliography

ARCHIVES

108 Rava-Russkiy GShAP Museum and Archive
146 GvIAP/PVO Private Museum
Bundesarchiv-Militärarchiv, Freiburg
Imperial War Museum, London
Jagdgeschwader 52 Traditionsgemeinschaft & Luftwaffen Museum, Singen
Krigsarkivet, Stockholm
Luftfahrtmuseum Hannover-Laatzen
Monino Air Force Museum, Moscow
National Archive, Kew
National Archives and Records Administration, Washington, D.C.
Rosvoyentsentr, Moscow
Russian Aviation Research Trust
Russian Central Military Archive TsAMO, Podolsk
Russian State Military Archive RGVA, Moscow
Suchgruppe 45 "Günther Rosipal," Salzwedel
WASt Deutsche Dienststelle, Berlin

UNPUBLISHED SOURCES

Abschussmeldungen JG 52. Via Alfons Altmeier.
Antipov Vlad, *Patriots or Red Kamikaze?* 1999.
Bätcher, *Major* Hansgeorg, Logbook.
Brendel, *Hptm.* Joachim, Logbook.
Eisenach, *Major* Franz, Logbook.
Engelke, *Ofw.* Rolf, Logbook.
Grubich, *Kapitan* Viktor, Logbook.
Hrabak, **Oberst** Dietrich, Logbook.
Jähnert, Hptm. Erhard, Logbook.
JG 52 *Archiv.* Courtesy of Alfons Altmeier.
JG 54 'Grünherz' *Archiv. Courtesy of Günther Rosipal.*
Kampfgeschwader 1, Hindenburg': Geschwadergeschichte in Kurzfassung. Av
Oberst a.D. Gerhard Baeker.
*Kratkaya istoricheskaya spravka boyevogo puti 108 Gvardeyskogo Shturmovogo
Aviatsionnogo.*
Rava-Russkogo Ordena Suvorova Polka. [History of 108 Rava-Russkiy
GShAP.] Sovet veteranov 108 Gv.ShAP, 1992.
Via Aleksandr Pavlichenko.
Kurayev, *Starshina* Vasiliy, Logbook.
Luftwaffe aircraft loss list. Courtesy of Matti Salonen.
Rall, *Generalleutnant* Günther, Logbook.
Rossmann, *Lt.* Edmund, Logbook.
Schack, *Hptm.* Günther, *Leistungsbuch.*
Schack, *Hptm.* Günther, Logbook.
Traditionsgeschichte der I./Jagdgeschwader 52. Via Alfons Altmeier.
Traditionsgeschichte III. Jagdgeschwader 52. Via Alfons Altmeier.
Vollmer, *Hptm.* Martin, Logbook.
Wolf, *Lt.* Hermann, Logbook.

BOOKS

*17-ya Vozdushnaya Armiya v boyakh ot Stalingrada do Veny. Moscow:
Voyenizdat, 1977.*
*Abramov, A.S. Dvyenadtsat' taranov. Sverdlovsk: Sredne-Ural'skoe knizhnoe
izdatel'stvo,1970.*
Aders, G. Die Geschichte der deutschen Nachtjagd 1917-1945. Stuttgart:
Motorbuch Verlag,1977.
Andersson, L. Soviet Aircraft and Aviation 1917 – 1941.
London: Putnam, 1994.
Anfinogenov, A.Z. Mgnoveniye – vechnost.
Moscow: Moskovskiy rabochniy, 1994.
Bagramyan, I. Kh. Tak shli myy k pobede. Moscow: Voyenizdat, 1977.
Balke, U. *Kampfgeschwader 100 "Wiking." Stuttgart:* Motorbuch Verlag, 1981.
Barbas, B. *Die Geschichte der I. Gruppe des Jagdgeschwaders 52.
Traditionsgemeinschaft JG 52, 2006.*
The Battle for Kursk 1943: The Soviet General Staff Study, Ed. and
translated by D.M. Glantz and H.S. Orenstein. London:
Frank Cass, 2002.
Bayevskiy, G.A. S aviatsiyey cherez XX vek. Moscow: Delta-NB, 2001.
Becze, C. Elefeljetett Hosök. Puedlo Kiadó, 2007.
Bekker, C. *The Luftwaffe War Diaries.* New York: Ballantine Books, 1969.

– Angriffshöhe 4000. Oldenburg: Gerhard Stalling Verlag, 1964.
Bergström C., and A. Mikhailov. *Black Cross/Red Star: Air War Over the
Eastern Front.* Vol. 2, *Resurgence, January – June 1942.* Pacifia: Pacifica
Military History, 2001.
Bergström, C., with M. Pegg. *Jagdwaffe: The War in Russia November 1942 –
December 1943.* Ian Allan Publishing Ltd. 2004.
Bergström C., A. Dikov, and V. Antipov. *Black Cross/Red Star: The Air War
Over the Eastern Front.* Vol. 3, *Everything for Stalingrad.* Hamilton: Eagle
Editions, 2006.
Bergström, C. *Andra världskriget.* Stockholm: Hjalmarson & Högberg, 2007.
– Stalingrad: The Air Battle. Surrey: Midland, 2007.
Bernád, D. *Rumanian Air Force: The Prime Decade, 1938 – 1947.* Carrollton:
Squadron/Signal Publications, 1999.
– Henschel Hs 129 in Action. Carrollton: Squadron/Signal Publications,
2001.
– Rumanian Aces of World War 2. Oxford: Osprey Publishing, 2003.
Beskorovaynyy, A.I. *Geroi ryadom.* Moscow: DOSAAF, 1979.
Bessmerten podvig ikh vysokiy. Tula: Priokskoe knizhnoe izdatel'stvo, 1983.
Bochkaryov, P.P., and N.I. Parygin. *Godyy v ognennom nebe: Aviatsiya dalnego
deystviya v Velikoy Otechestvennoy voyne 1941 – 1945.*
Moscow: Voyenizdat, 1991.
Bodrikhin, N. *Stalinskiye Sokoly.* Moscow: NPP Delta, 1997.
– Sovyetskiye Asy. Moscow: ZAO KFK "TAMP," 1998.
Bogatyryov, S.V., R.I. Larintsev, and A.V. Ovcharenko Morskaya voyna na
Baltike. Spravochnik-khronika. Part I. Poteri flota protivnika na
Baltiyskom more v 1941-1943, *Arkhangelsk, 1997.*
Bogdanov, N.G. V nebe Gvardeyskiy Gatchinskiy. Leningrad: Lenizdat, 1980.
Boykov, P. M. *Na glavnykh napravleniyakh.* Moscow: Voyenizdat, 1984.
Brütting, G. *Das waren die deutschen Kampffliegerasse 1939 – 1945.* Stuttgart:
Motorbuch Verlag, 1975.
– Das waren die deutschen Stuka-Asse 1939 – 1945. 3rd ed. Stuttgart:
Motorbuch Verlag, 1979.
Buchner, H. *Stormbird: Flying Through Fire as a Luftwaffe Ground Attack Pilot
and Me 262 Ace.* Aldershot: Hikoki Publications, 2000.
Caldwell, D. *The JG 26 War Diary,* Vol. 2, 1943 – 1945. London:
Grub Street, 1998.
Carell, P. *Verbrannte Erde: Schlacht zwischen Wolga und Weichsel.* Berlin:
Ullstein Verlag, 1966.
Chechelnitskiy, G.A. *Lyotchiki na voyne.* Moscow: Voyenizdat, 1974.
Davtyan, S.M. *Pyataya Vozdushnaya.* Moscow: Voyenizdat, 1990.
Denisov, K.D. *Pod nami — Chernoye more.* Moscow:
Voyennoye izdatel'stvo, 1989.
Dierich, W. *Kampfgeschwader 51 "Edelweiss."* Stuttgart:
Motorbuch Verlag, 1975.
– Kampfgeschwader 55 "Greif." Stuttgart: Motorbuch Verlag, 1975.
Die Wehrmachtberichte 1939 – 1945, vol. II: *1. Januar 1942 bis 31. Dezember
1943.* Köln: Gesellschaft für Literatur und Bildung, 1989.
Dolgov, I.A. *Zolotye Zvezdy Kalinintsev.* 2nd ed. Moskovskiy rabochiy,
Moscow 1983.
Drabkin, A. *Ya dralsya istrebitelye: Prinyavshiye pervyy udar 1941 – 1942.*
Moscow: Yauza, 2006.
Ehrengardt, C.-J. *Normandie-Niémen.* Editions Heimdal, 1989.
Erickson, J. *The Road to Berlin,* London: Cassell, 2004.
Falaleyev, F.Ya. *V stroyu krylatykh: Iz vozpomikakiy.*
Izhevsk: Udmyrtiya, 1978.
Falck, W. *Wolfgang Falck: The Happy Falcon.* Hamilton: Eagle Editions, 2002.
Fast, N. *Das Jagdgeschwader 52.* Bergisch Gladbach: Bensberger Buch-
Verlag, 1988 - 1992.
Frankson, A., and N. Zetterling. *Slaget om Kursk.* Stockholm:
Norstedts förlag, 2002.
Fyodorov, A.G. *V nebe Petlaykovy.* Moscow: DOSAAF, 1976.
– Zvyozdy nemerknushchey slavy. 3rd ed. Simferopol: Tavriya, 1984.
– V nebe – pikirovshchiki. Moscow: DOSAAF, 1986.
Geroi ognennykh let. 3rd ed. Yaroslavl: Verkhne-Volzhskoye knizhnoye
izdatel'stvo, 1985.
Geroi Sovetskogo Soyuza. Moscow: Voyenizdat, 1987.
Geroi Sovetskogo Soyuza Mogilyovchane. Minsk: Polyma, 1965.
Geust, C.-F., K. Keskinen, and K. Stenman. *Soviet Air Force in World War
Two: Red Stars.* Kangsala: Ar-Kustannus Oy, 1993.
Glantz, D.M., and J.M. House. *The Battle for Kursk.* Lawrence: University
Press of Kansas, 1999.
Gnezdilov, F. S. *Na vysotakh muzhestva.* Minsk: Belarus, 1987.

Golovanov, A.Ye. *Dalnyaya bombardirovochnaya*. O.O.O. Delta NB, Moscow 2004.

Golubev, V. F. *Kryl'ya krepnut v boyu*. 2nd ed. Leningrad: Lenizdat, 1984.

Gordon, Ye., and D. Khazanov. *Soviet Combat Aircraft of the Second World War. Volume One: Single-Engined Fighters*. Earl Shilton: Midland Publishing Ltd., 1998.
    – *Soviet Combat Aircraft of the Second World War. Volume Two: Twin-Engined Fighters, Attack Aircraft and Bombers*. Earl Shilton: Midland Publishing Ltd., 1999.

Görlitz, W. *Model*. Munich: Universitas Verlag, 1989.

Grechko, S.N. *Resheniya prinimalis' na zemle*. Moscow: Voyenizdat, 1984.

Grichenko, I. T., and N. M. Golovin. *Podvig*. 3rd ed. Kharkov: Prapor, 1983.

Groehler, O. *Geschichte des Luftkriegs*. Berlin (GDR): Militärverlag, 1981.

Gundelach, K. *Kamfgeschwader "General Wever" 4*. Stuttgart: Motorbuch Verlag, 1978.

Halder, F. *Kriegstagebuch*. Edited by Hans-Arnold Jacobsen. Stuttgart: W. Kohlhammer Verlag, 1964.

Hannig, N. *Luftwaffe Fighter Ace*. Ed. and translated by J. Weal. London: Grub Street, 2004.

Hardesty, V. *Red Phoenix: The Rise of the Soviet Air Power 1941 – 1945*. Washington, D.C.: Smithsonian Institution Press, 1982.

Haupt, W. *Army Group Center: The Wehrmacht in Russia 1941 – 1945*. Atglen: Schiffer, 1997.
    – *Army Group North: The Wehrmacht in Russia 1941 – 1945*. Atglen: Schiffer, 1997.

Hooton, E.R. *Eagle in Flames: The Fall of the Luftwaffe*. London: Arms and Armous Press, 1999.

Il'in, N. *V boyakh za chistoye nebo*. Moscow: Izdatelstvo "Patriot", 2002.

Istoriya Velikoy Otechestvennoy voyny Sovetskogo Soyuza 1941 – 1945. Moscow: Voyenizdat, 1960.

Jacobsen, H.-A., and J. Rohwer. *Entscheidungsschlachten des zweiten Weltkrieges*. Munich: Bernard & Graefe Verlag, 1960.

Kalinin, V.V., and D.G. Makarenko. *Geroi podvigov na Khar'kovshchine*. Kharkov: Prapor, 1970.

Kaufov, Kh. Kh. *Oryol umirayet v polyote*. Nalchik: Elbrus, 1970.

Khazanov, D.B. and V.G. Gorbach. *Aviatsiya v bitve nad Orlovsko-Kurskoy dugoi*. Moscow, 2004.

Kozhedub, I.N. *Vernost Otchiznye*. Moscow: Detskaya Literatura, 1969.

Khrushchev, N. *Khrushchev Remembers*. London: Sphere Books, 1971.

Kiehl, H. *Kampfgeschwader "Legion Condor" 53*. Stuttgart: Motorbuch Verlag, 1996.

Kislitsyn, A. S. *Oveyannyye slavoy*. Chelyabinsk: Yuzhno-Ural'skoe knizhnoe izdatel'stvo, 1965.

Klink, E. *Das Gesetz des Handelns: Die Operation "Zitadelle" 1943*. Stuttgart: Deutsche Verlags-Anstalt, 1966.

Kolomets, M., and M. Svirin. *Kurskaya duga*. Moscow: Eks-Print, 1998.

Koltunov, G. A. and B. G. Solovyev, *Kurskaya bitva*. Moscow: Voyenizdat, 1970.

Korolyov, V.O. *Gvardeytsy Pervoy Shturmovoy*. Moscow: Voyenizdat, 1980.

Kozhevnikov, A.L. *Startuyet muzhestvo*. Moscow: Voyenizdat, 1975.

Kozhevnikov, M.N. *Komandovaniye i shtab VVS Sovetskoy Armii v Velikoy Otyechestvyennoy Voyny 1941 - 1945*. Moscow: Nauka, 1977.

Krasovskiy, S.A. *Zhizn' v aviatsii*. Moscow: Voyenizdat, 1968.

Kravchenko, I.M. and V.V. Burkov. *Desiyatyy tankovyy Dneprovskiy*. Moscow: Voyenizdat, 1986.

Krepak, B.A., and L.A. Krushinskaya. *V poyedinkakh na vsyote*. Minsk: Belarus, 1989.

Kriegstagebuch des Oberkommandos der Wehrmacht 1939 – 1945. Edited by Percy E. Schramm. Munich: Bernard & Graefe Verlag, 1982.

Krivosheyev, G. *Grif sekretnosti snyat: Poteri Vooruzhyonnykh Sil SSSR v voynakh, boyevykh deystviyakh i voyennykh konfliktakh*. Moscow: Voyenizdat, 1993.

Kursk: The German View. Ed. by S.H. Newton. Cambridge, MA: Da Capo Press, 2002.

Kuzovkin, A. I., and A. T. Belyayev. *Orlinoye plemya Kolomentsev*. Moscow: DOSAAF, 1985.

Lehmann, R. *The Leibstandarte*, vol. III. Winnipeg: J.J. Fedorowicz, 1990.

Lehwess-Litzmann, W. *Absturz ins Leben*. Querfurt: Dingsda-Verlag, 1994.

Liddell-Hart, B. H. *The Other Side of the Hill*. Vol. III, *Through German Eyes*. 1st ed. London: Cassell and Company Ltd., London, 1948.

Lyudi geroicheskoy professii. Moscow: DOSAAF, 1976.

Lyudin bessmertnogo podviga. Moscow: Voyennaya Literatura, 1992.

von Manstein, E. *Verlorene Siege*. Bonn: Athenäum Verlag, 1955.

Maslennikov, Yu. I. *Taktika v boyevykh primerakh*. Moscow: Voyenizdat, 1985.

von Mellenthin, F. W. *Panzer Battles*. Norman: University of Oklahoma Press, 1956.

Meroño, F. *Aviadores Españoles en la Gran Guerra Patria*, Moscow: Progress Press, 1985.

Michulec, R. *Stalinowskie sokoly*. Gdynia: AJ Press, 1995.

Moskalenko, K. S. *Na Yugo-Zapadnom napravlenii*. Vol. I. Moscow: Voyenizdat, 1979.

Murray, W. *Luftwaffe: Strategy for Defeat 1933 – 45*. London: Grafton Books, 1985.

Nashi Zemlyaki—Geroi Sovyetskogo Soyuza. 3rd ed. Cheboksary: Chuvashskoye knizhnoye izdatel'stvo, 1980.

Nauroth, H. *Stukageschwader 2 Immelmann*. Preussisch Oldendorf: Verlag K. W. Schütz, 1988.

Obermaier, E. *Die Ritterkreuzträger der Luftwaffe: Band 1--Jagdflieger 1939 - 1945*. Mainz: Verlag Dieter Hoffmann, 1966 and 1989.
    – *Die Ritterkreuzträger der Luftwaffe 1939 – 1945: Band II—Stuka/ und Schlachtflieger*. Mainz: Verlag Dieter Hoffmann, 1976.

Osipov, G.A. *V nebe bombardirovshchiki*. Shchelkovo: Biblioteka zhurnala Shchelkovo, 2003.

Pavlov, G. R. *Odnopolchane*. Moscow: DOSAAF, 1985.
    – *Kryl'ya muzhestva*. Kazan: Tatarskoye knizhnoye izdatel'stvo, 1988.

Pegg, M. *Hs 129 Panzerjäger*. Burgess Hill: Classic Publications, 1997.

Perov, V., and O. Rastrenin. *Shturmovik Il-2*. Special Issue of *Aviatsiya I Kosmonavtika,* May – June 2001.

Pinchuk, N. G. *V vozdukhe – "Yaki"*. Minsk: Belarusyy, 1977.

Plocher, H. *The German Air Force Versus Russia, 1943*. USAF Historical Division, Air University. New York: Arno Press, 1966.

Polak, T., and C. Shores. *Stalin's Falcons: The Aces of the Red Star: A Tribute to the Notable Fighter Pilots of the Soviet Air Forces, 1918 – 1953*. London: Grub Street, 1999.

Polyam, P.M. *Moy Voyna,* Irkutsk, 1998.

Polynin, F.P. *Boyevyye marshruty*. 2nd ed. Moscow: Voyenizdat, 1981.

Prien, J., and G. Stemmer. *Messerschmitt Bf 109 im Einsatz bei der III./Jagdgeschwader 3*. Eutin: Struve-Druck, n.d.
    – *Messerschmitt Bf 109 im Einsatz bei der II./Jagdgeschwader 3*. Eutin: Struve-Druck, n.d.

Prussakov, G. K. *16-ya vozdushnaya: Voyenno-istoricheskiy ocherk o boyevom puti 16-y vozdushnoy armii 1942 – 1945*. Moscow: Voyenizdat, 1973.
    – *Doletim do Odera*. Moscow: Voyenizdat, 1985.

Pstygo, I. I. *Na boyevom kurse*. Moscow: Voenizdat, 1989.

Punka, G. *Hungarian Air Force*. Carrollton: Squadron/Signal Publications, 1994.
    – *Messer: The Messerschmitt 109 in the Royal Hungarian "Honvéd" Air Force"*. Budapest: OMIKK, 1995.

Pustovalov, B.M. *Tè trista rassvetov*. Moscow: Voyenizdat, 1990.

Rall, G. *mein Flugbuch: Erinnerungen 1938 – 2004*. Moosburg: Neunundzwanzigsechs Verlag, 2004.

Roell, W.P. *Laurels for Prinz Wittgenstein*. Keston: Independent Books, 1994.

Rudel, H.-U. *Trotzdem*. Göttingen: Verlag K. W. Schütz, 1970.

Rudel, H.-U. *Stuka Pilot*. Costa Mesa: Noontide Press, 1990.

Rudenko, S.I. *Kryl'ya Pobedy*. Moscow: Mezhdunarodnyye otnosheniya, 1985.

Rumyantsev, N.M. *Lyudi legendarnogo podviga*. Saratov: Privolzhskoye knizhnoye izdatel'stvo, 1968.

Russkiy arkhiv: Velikaya Otechestvennaya: Kurskaya bitva. Dokumenty i materialy 27 marta – 23 avgusta 1943 g. T 15 (4-). Moscow: TERRA, 1997.

Samchuk, I. A. and P. G. Skachko. *Atakuiyet desantniki*. Moscow: Voyenizdat, 1975.

Schreier, H. *JG 52: Das erfolgreichste Jagdgeschwader des II. Weltkrieges*. Berg am See: Kurt Vowinckel Verlag, n.d.

Schwabedissen, W. *The Russian Air Force in the Eyes of German Commanders*. USAF Historical Division, Air University. New York: Arno Press, 1960.

Seidl, H. *Stalin's Eagles: An Illustrated Study of the Soviet Aces of World War II and Korea*. Atglen: Schiffer, 1998.

Semyonov, A.F. *Na vzlyote*. Moscow: Voyenizdat, 1969.

Shevchuk, V.M. *Komandir atakuyet pervym*. Moscow: Voyenizdat, 1980.

Shirer, W. *Det tredje rikets uppgång och fall.* Stockholm: Forum, 1989.

Shmelyov, A.N. *Nebo dobroye i zloye.* Moscow: DOSAAF, 1979.

Skripko, N.S. *Po tselyam blizhnim i dal'nim.* Moscow: Voyenizdat, 1981.

Skulski, P., J. Bargiel, and G. Cisek. *Asy frontu wschodniego.* Wroclaw: Ace Publication, 1994.

Sovetskiye VVS v Velikoy Otechestvennoy voyne 1941 – 1945. Moscow: Voyenizdat, 1968.

Spaeter, H. *The History of Panzerkorps Grossdeutschland,* vol. II. Winnipeg: J. J. Fedorowicz, 1995.

Stadler, S. *Die Offensive gegen Kursk 1943; II. SS-Panzerkorps als Stosskeil im Grosskampf.* Osnabrück: Munin Verlag GmbH, 1980.

Stepanenko, I. N. *Plamennoye nebo.* Kiev: Politizdat Ukrainy, 1983.

Sto Stalinskikh sokolov v boyakh za rodinu. Moscow: Voyenizdat, 1949.

The Soviet Air Force in World War Two. New York: Doubleday & Co., 1973.

Timokhovich, I.V. *Sovyetskaya aviatsiya v bitve pod Kurskom.* Moscow: Voyenizdat, 1959.

Toliver, R.F., and T.J. Constable. *Das waren die deutschen Jagdfliegerasse 1939 –1945.* Stuttgart: Motorbuch Verlag, 1973.

Uchebnik boytsa i mladshego komandira podrazdeleniy mestnoy PVO. Moscow: Upravleniye protivovozdushnoy oborony RKKA, Voyenizdat, 1939.

Ushakov, S. F. *V interesakh vsekh frontov.* Moscow: Voyenizdat, 1982.

Vajda, F., and P. Dancey. *German Aircraft Industry and Production 1933 – 1945.* Shrewsbury: Airlife, 1998.

Vasco, J. *The Sting of the Luftwaffe: Schnellkampfgeschwader 210 and Zerstörergeschwader 1 "Wespengeschwader" in World War II.* Atglen: Schiffer, 2001.

Velikaya Otechestvennaya voyna. Tsyfry i fakty. Moscow: Prosveshcheniye, 1995.

Vershinin, K.A. *Chetvyortaya vozdushnaya.* Moscow: Voyenizdat, 1975.

V nebe frontovom. Moscow: Molodaya Gvardia, 1971.

Vo imya Rodiny. Moscow: Politizdat, 1982.

Vorozheykin, A. S. *Nad Kurskoy Dugoy.* Moscow: Voyenizdat, 1962.

V sozvezdii slavy. 2nd ed. Volgograd: Nizhne-Volzhskoye knizhnoye izdatel'stvo, 1976.

Waiss, W. *Chronik Kampfgeschwader Nr. 27 Boelcke, Band IV.* Aachen: Helios Verlag, 2005.

Die Wehrmachtsberichte 1939-1945. Band 2 – 1. Januar 1942 bis 31. Dezember 1943, Köln: Gesellschaft für Literatur und Bildung, 1989.

Yevstigneyev, K.A. *Krylataya gvardiy.a* Moscow: Voyenizdat, 1982.

Zakharov, G. N. *Ya – istrebitel.* Moscow: Voyenizdat, 1985.

Zjukov, G. *Minnen och reflexioner.* Moscow: Progress, 1988.

PERIODICALS

52er Nachrichtenblatt (Traditionsgemeinschaft JG 52).

Der Adler.

Air Combat.

Airfoil.

AviaMaster.

Aviatsiya i Kosmonavtika.

Aviatsiya i Vremya.

Fly Past.

Jägerblatt.

Jet und Prop.

Krasnaya Zvezda.

Luftwaffe Verband Journal.

Militaria.

Mir Aviatsii.

Pravda.

Revi.

Voyenno-Istoricheskiy Zhurnal.

VVS i PVO.

PHOTO CREDITS

Adler, Aleksey V. Andreev, Vlad Antipov, *Oberst* Gerhard Baeker, Bernd Barbas, *Oberstleutnant* Hansgeorg Bätcher, Csaba Becze, Dénes Bernád, *Major* Hans-Ekkehard Bob, Jan Bobek, *Oberleutnant* Johannes Broschwitz, Eddie Creek, Andrey Dikov, Chris Dunning, Artem Drabkin, Robert Forsyth, *Generalleutnant* Adolf Galland, *Hauptmann* Alfred Grislawski, Jürgen Grislawski, *Kapitan* Viktor Alekseyevich Grubich, *Major* Klaus Häberlen, Damian Hallor, Peter Hallor, Bert Hartmann, *Oberfeldwebel* Karl-Heinz Höfer, Ivanova Maya Ivanovna, Dmitriy Karlenko, Peter Kassak, *General-Leytenant* Arkadiy Fyodorovich Kovachevich, Krigsarkivet/Stockholm, Viktor Kulikov, *Starshina* Vasiliy Vasilyevich Kurayev, *Oberleutnant* Erwin Leykauf, Martin Månsson, George Mellinger, Andrey Mikhailov, Eric Mombeek, Horst Mutterlose, *Leutnant* Hermann Neuhoff, *Polkovnik* Aleksandr Aleksandrovich Pavlichenko, *General* Günther Rall, Rune Rautio, Günther Rosipal, *Leutnant* Edmund Rossmann, Yuriy Rybin, Pär Salomonson, *Signal, General* Johannes Steinhoff, Peter Taghon, *Traditionsgemeinschaft JG 52, Generalleutnant* Hannes Trautloft, John Vasco, Peter Vollmer, Manfred Wägenbaur, Walter Waiss and director Lyudmila P. Zapryagayeva.

On 28 July 1943, Fw. Hinz of 4.(Pz)/Sch.G 1 was shot down by Russian flak and killed. Here the remains of his Hs 129 B-2 W.Nr. 140519 lie at the top of a Russian scrap heap.

Oblt. Max Stotz of JG 54 discussing his 'Black 5' with technical personnel in the foreground. Like 'Black 5, 'Black 7' retained its inboard undercarriage doors with both aircraft having outboard wing armament.